The Curse

The Curse

A Cultural History of Menstruation

Janice Delaney
Mary Jane Lupton
Emily Toth

REVISED EDITION
With New Afterwords by
Mary Jane Lupton and Janice Delaney

UNIVERSITY OF ILLINOIS PRESS
Urbana and Chicago

Illini Books edition, 1988

P   5   4   3   2

This book is printed on acid-free paper.

Grateful acknowledgment is given the following for permission to quote from copyrighted material:

Debbie Lempke, "The Bloods," from *The Berkeley Music Collective Songbook.* Copyright © 1974 by Debbie Lempke.

Lines from "She Shall Be Called Woman" are reprinted from *Collected Poems (1930–1973)* by May Sarton with the permission of W.W. Norton & Company, Inc., copyright © 1974 by May Sarton.

Nadine MacDonald, "On Menstruating in the Middle of a Lecture on the Fall of the Roman Empire," copyright © 1971 by Thomas E. Sanders. Reprinted from *Currents: Concerns and Composition* (Glencoe Press).

Ellen Bass, "Tampons," reprinted from *For Earthly Survival*, ed. Felecia Rice (Santa Cruz, Calif.: Moving Parts Press, 1980).

Penelope Scambly Schott, "When you phoned from California to tell me it had started," reprinted from *I'm on My Way Running*, ed. Lyn Reese, Jean Wildinson, and Phyllis Sheon Koppelman (New York: Avon Books, 1983).

Portions of this book appeared in somewhat different form in *Rough Times* magazine, the *Women's Almanac*, and *MS.*

Library of Congress Cataloging-in-Publication Data

Delaney, Janice.
  The curse.

  Bibliography:
  Includes index.
  1. Menstruation—Public opinion. 2. Menstruation—Miscellanea. I. Lupton, Mary Jane. II. Toth, Emily. III. Title.
QP263.D45   1988   306'.4   87-5943
ISBN 0-252-01452-9 (alk. paper)

Contents

Acknowledgments

Many generous people have contributed their information and insights to one or both editions of *The Curse*. We would like to thank the following individuals for their special help: Chandra Agrawal, Margaret Anderson, Kenneth Baldwin, Sarah Begus, Arthur Delaney, Mary Claire Delaney, Sue Delaney, Dorothy Ginsberg Fitzgibbons, John Fitzgibbons, Sandra Harding, Genet Heiligh, Nancy Henley, Carol Ann Hohman, John D. Hohman, Ruth R. Hohman, Marion Kelly, Susan Koppelman, Alan D. Latta, Vickie Leonard, Ellen Lupton, Julia Lupton, Mona Lyons, Richard A. Macksey, Mary Brown Parlee, Ken Reinhard, Sally Rynne, May Sarton, Havi Shafer, James G. Sites, Dena Taylor, Bruce Toth, Nan Tyler, Aimee Wiest, J. J. Wilson, and Jane Yates.

Our special gratitude goes to our editors: Carole Appel (University of Illinois Press—present edition) and Marian Skedgell (Dutton—original edition), and to our agents, Elaine Markson and Geri Thoma. We are also grateful to the readers for the present edition, Sharon Golub and Paula Treichler, for their invaluable suggestions.

We particularly thank Emily Toth for her many suggestions and for the information she contributed to our work on this edition. We would also like to thank the staffs of *Women: A Journal of Liberation* and *Women's Express* for material and for support.

This new edition was assisted by a research grant from The Morgan State University Board for Research and the Press, and the draft copy was typed by Kathy Leitzell of the English Department of The Pennsylvania State University.

M. J. L. and J. D.

Preface

It is eleven years since *The Curse* opened the closed door on the tabooed subject, menstruation. *The Curse* told women that menstruation was nothing to be ashamed of; that menstruation need not interfere with their lives as mothers, workers, athletes; that menstrual pain was real, but often complicated by socially conditioned disgust; that napkins and tampons were inadequate to staunch the flow but that manufacturers were constantly trying to improve their effectiveness; that literature was silent on the subject because writers, mostly male, did not consider menstruation an essential forming experience in the human condition; and that anthropologists' study of human societies on this planet revealed the condition of women to be a direct result of their peoples' perception of their mysterious, fearsome, monthly flow of blood.

Eleven years later, many attitudes toward menstruation have changed—but so too has the context in which menstruation is experienced and perceived. The first edition of this book still expected the passage of the Equal Rights Amendment. The first edition was written during the reign of the Shah of Iran. The most important revolution happening during the writing of the 1976 *Curse* was the revolution in sexual behavior: herpes and AIDS had yet to appear. And middle-class American women in 1976 were just beginning to make the traditionally male corporate climb. Their biological clocks were still ticking.

In short, the 1976 *Curse* was written at the beginning of the 1970s wave of feminism in the United States, and the past eleven years have seen that wave crest and break upon the shores of Reaganism and reality. At the same time, the "new openness" about menstruation that we chroni-

cled, the occasional TV sit-com mention, or the taboo-breaking art of
Judy Chicago and her sister artists, became less of an exotic curiosity and
more of a home truth with the eruption of toxic shock syndrome upon
national consciousness and the realization that it was linked to the use of
tampons.

What we believe we began with the publication of *The Curse* was a
decade of education, of ourselves and of all women and men who think
seriously about "the woman question" and the devastation wrought on
the human spirit by the suppression of women's rights in the name of
biology. Our tone in the first edition was almost flippant. Flippancy was
the tool we used to shock women out of their embarrassment into an
acceptance of this natural process and an understanding of how negative
attitudes about menstruation led to the devaluation of women, by themselves and others. Flippancy, however, could not lead women through the
recognition that the makers of tampons did not know that their products
could be harmful or that the "raging hormonal imbalance" indictment
was still around, potentially to be enshrined in law.

Our continual efforts to keep the message of *The Curse* in a context
of rational and thoughtful discussion, even as the "menstrual climate"
kept changing, began with the postpublication promotion of the first edition on TV and radio, and in over- and underground presses. At that time
we found that interviewers were often hostile to us and to our book. For
example, when Janice Delaney appeared on "A. M. New York" with
Stanley Siegel in 1976, he introduced the medical doctor appearing with
her as "the real doctor" while making light of her own Ph.D. When Janice
kept trying to talk about the contents of the book, as requested by the
show's producers, Siegel kept badgering her about whether having sex
with a menstruating woman would cause his bones to melt or his skin to
shrivel. "Why don't you try it, Stanley?" she finally asked. Stanley cut to
a commercial.

Emily Toth found herself on a talk show in Winnipeg with a male
host who called her a man-hater and wanted to know why she hadn't
given equal time to men in *The Curse*. What did he want equal time for,
we wonder? Wet dreams? Later a born-again Christian called the show to
complain that Emily was defiling the institution of marriage.

Mary Jane Lupton spoke at a meeting of a mid-Atlantic psychiatric
association where at least six of the (male) psychiatrists present acknowledged that they did not consider menstruation when treating their female
patients for fluctuations of mood and behavior. During her talk Mary Jane
deliberately mentioned that she was menstruating and said that accounted

for her easy flow of words and casual manner. No one laughed. And afterwards, many of the participants expressed shock that she had so revealed herself. "Why, my own wife doesn't tell me when she is menstruating," said one.

Such ridiculous encounters were, fortunately, only part of the educational process begun by publication of *The Curse*. Affirmative and welcome responses were far more useful in articulating the meaning of menstruation as a determinant of woman's place in society. For example, Mary Jane's ten years as an editor of *Women: A Journal of Liberation*, during which she and her daughters contributed many articles on menstruation, gave her the kind of support, encouragement, and feedback uncommon in the wider world of print and image. Publication of the journal's issue on aging and menopause was the culminating event of her years there, for its frank and sympathetic approach to the ultimate taboo against women.

All three of us spoke at meetings, conventions, and special conferences on menstruation. Janice found that giving the keynote address at a 1980 conference on Women and Wellness at Northwestern University, sponsored by the Illinois Humanities Council, turned out to be educational for all. The event coincided with the first discoveries about toxic shock syndrome and the recall of Rely tampons. The participants asked questions about the morality of the manufacturers' actions and the future of research and development in sanitary products in light of these discoveries. The women were angry and felt betrayed. Janice took pains not to place blame, assuring the conferees that she had spoken with the manufacturers and that they were trying hard to work with the medical profession and concerned consumers to find the cause of this disease before another woman could die.

Today Janice would not be so glib, nor so trusting. Since 1979 millions of lines of print have put the alleged truth to the public about TSS and its connection with menstruating women, and the barrage continues.

Even more intense has been the media attention focused upon the question of women's mental capacity during the premenstruum. We welcome all these efforts at breaking the silence about menstrual taboos and showing men and women how their bodies define them. But they do create a sort of postfeminist backlash.

For *how* menstruation is talked about can still affect how it is perceived. If tampons are linked to a disease that can kill, does this mean that menstruation can kill? And if medicine and law say that premenstrual syndrome can cause profound personality changes, does this mean that a premenstrual woman can kill and get away with it?

These were some of the things that excited us when the University
of Illinois Press asked us a few years ago if they could reprint the 1976
edition of *The Curse*, so that this "classic" could get back into bookstores
and libraries again. In this book you will find the original text of the first
edition with addenda where necessary to correct, amplify, or supplement
the original material. We had a harder time researching and writing this
edition of *The Curse* than writing the original because of the explosion
of materials since 1976. Then we could chronicle nearly all of the references to menstruation in, say, contemporary mainstream fiction and
bring to a wide audience for the first time some of the more unusual
feminist artistic expressions of menstruation. We could cite all of the
significant medical and psychoanalytic research from the nineteenth century forward, so little was there to work with. We certainly had no popular
reference work on menstruation and culture casually to consult when
stuck for an anecdote: *The Curse* was the first of those.

But in the last three years of research we have found hundreds of
new articles and full-length books on menstruation, from sociologists,
anthropologists, physicians, psychologists, and laypersons. Some books tell
us how to identify and treat our PMS; others share the results of medical
research with its practitioners. Most of them, we are gratified to report,
refer to *The Curse* in text or footnote, as a comprehensive treatment of
menstruation for the general reader.

The most valuable works to us were the collections of essays published
by conferees on menstruation research or by practitioners who brought
together the year's most important data in a book. *The Menstrual Cycle*,
edited by Alice Dan, Effie A. Graham and Carol P. Beecher (vol. 1) and
Pauline Komnenich (vol. 2) was an outgrowth of the first and second
Interdisciplinary Menstrual Cycle Research Conferences (Emily Toth represented the work of *The Curse* at the first).

In her introduction to the first volume, Alice Dan says that *The Curse*
created the context in which such an historic conference could take place
but notes that *The Curse* fails "to provide an adequate history of the
efforts to apply science to women's experience."[1] Because that was not
our intention nor our field (we all hold Ph.D.'s in literature), we are grateful
that so many others are working in multi-disciplinary research, and that
their findings are beginning to have some practical effect. Penny Budoff,
M.D., has published two popular books on women's reproductive biology
and has seen her experiments on herself with antiprostaglandin medicine
lead to significant over-the-counter relief for dysmenorrhea.[2] Sharon Golub's *Lifting the Curse of Menstruation* is another collection of essays by

experts in the field of menstrual research whose work we cite here.[3] We welcomed two books published around the time of our first edition, Paula Weideger's *Menstruation and Menopause* and Penelope Shuttle and Peter Redgrove's *The Wise Wound: Eve's Curse and Everywoman* for their own thoughtful explanations of menstrual culture.[4]

Throughout this book you will find references to the other groundbreaking work in progress by the women and men—but mostly women—who are making the menstrual taboo obsolete. They are beginning to tell us how women's reproductive systems really work and how seriously we must continue to take Freud's "anatomy is destiny" indictment today.

The Curse

Introduction

In the beginning, the menstrual process inspired fear and wonder in human beings. Both men and women saw at once that woman's blood set woman apart from man in a mysterious, magical way. This blood flowed but did not bring death or disability; it came and went with a regularity that no human act could change. Only an even greater mystery, the creation of human life, could alter its pattern.

To reduce the threat of destruction by the unseen forces that directed woman's bleedings, early man at first made the womb a goddess. Worship and appeasement of the Great Mother and her bleeding fertility would ensure his temporary safety. Later, when farming began to replace hunting and gathering in the primitive economy, relative stability permitted man to use more direct ways to isolate the menstruating woman. So he made her taboo. The very word may originate in a Polynesian word for menstruation: *tupua*. In early agrarian societies, on the premise that menstruation empowered a woman to cause economic disaster, she was excluded from social and sexual intercourse for the duration of the menses; menarcheal girls underwent a pubertal seclusion that might last a few days, a few months, or a few years.

In our own culture, specifically twentieth-century America, women continue to suffer the taboos of centuries. Law, medicine, religion, and psychology have isolated and devalued the menstruating woman. Women who experience debilitating mental or physical pain at menstruation (despite the easy availability of The Pill and other such remedies) are made the prototype for all; and in the face of statistics to the contrary, women are still considered unreliable workers and unstable human beings at that time of the month. Thus, menstruation is a factor in the control of women by men not only in ancient and primitive societies, where knowledge of physiology is rudimentary at best, but also in our post-industrial world. Women are physically and emotionally handicapped by menstruation, goes the argument, and therefore cannot and may not compete with men.

Even literature has been silent on menstruation, probably because most "literature" has been written by men. To write about menstruation in myth, poetry, fiction, drama, and folktale is to write an essay about disguise and displacement, as the taboos of prehistory find continued expression in modern European and American culture.

To be sure, things are changing. There's a new freedom in the air, on the television screen, in the courts. Women writers and artists are bringing menstruation itself out of the water closet and using it as an emblem of celebration, not shame. We can thank the new feminism for helping us see that our concerns are of equal worth in the marketplace of ideas. And we believe that by approaching the subject "woman" through the most elementary and obvious aspect of womanhood, we will give our sisters a new respect for what has been, for most, a friendly monthly nuisance.

PART ONE

The Tabooed Woman

Chapter 1

Women in the Closet:
Taboos of Exclusion

Greater than his fear of death, dishonor, or dismemberment has been primitive man's respect for menstrual blood. The measures he has taken to avoid this mysterious substance have affected his mealtimes, his bedtimes, and his hunting season; and primitive woman, unable to separate herself from her blood, knew that upon her tabooed state depended the safety of the entire society.

Taboos exist to protect human beings from danger. Franz Steiner says that taboo deals with "the sociology of danger itself" because it is concerned with both the protection of dangerous individuals from themselves and the protection of society from them.[1] In many societies, the menstruating woman is believed to emit a *mana*, or threatening supernatural power. The taboos of menstruation are practices that help others to avoid her and her dangerous influence and that enable her to get through the menstrual period without succumbing to her own deadly power.

Menstrual taboos are among the most inviolate in many societies. How did woman come to merit this dubious privilege? Fear of blood, says Freud, who states furthermore that the blood phobia may also "serve aesthetic and hygienic purposes."[2] Thus, it was probably in the interests of cleanliness that a New Guinea Mae Enga tribesman known to the anthropologist M. J. Meggitt divorced his wife because she had slept on his blanket while menstruating and, still feeling not quite safe from her evil influence, later killed her with an ax.[3] Theodor Reik agrees with Freud's idea that the origin of menstrual taboos lies in the ambivalent attitude toward women in the most "advanced" cultures. He believes that the taboos are both a recollection and a denial of an earlier stage in society when women, like animals in heat, gave off a sexual signal at menstruation. Thus, he says, "the psychological quintessence at the root of the dread of menstruating women is ... the unconscious attraction they exert on men and the power of the opposite feeling restraining them."[4] In the same vein, another anthropologist writes of the dualism implicit in woman's social position: "From one aspect the woman who may not be approached is inviolable, holy; from another aspect she is polluted, unclean. She is what the Romans called *sacra,* sacred and accursed."[5] Mary Chadwick, who in 1932 wrote the first full-length psychological study of menstruation, puts a similar idea more directly, referring to the "discomfort of guilt arising from instinctual wishes."[6]

Still other observers have reached into prehistory to seek a different etiology of these taboos. Bruno Bettelheim and others suggest that childbearing and menstruation were once a source of envy to men, who imposed the taboos in an attempt to equalize the sexes.[7] Elizabeth Gould Davis, who theorizes that matriarchies were the world's first political systems, sees the female-blood taboo as a vestige of the time when the ruling women used the taboo to make men respect and fear women. She cites the crime of matricide, the most serious even in patriarchal civilizations, as evidence in support of her theory. The tales of danger to men from women's blood, she says, "were tales told by primordial matriarchs to scare little boys into obedience and respect for women."[8]

There is as yet no direct evidence in anthropological literature that menstrual taboos originated with one or the other sex. A 1961 cross-cultural study of menstrual taboos found no relation between the extensiveness of such taboos and the importance of women's subsistence work or status in any particular society.[9] We believe, from the available evidence, that the taboos as taboos were probably enforced by men, who connected this mysterious phenomenon with the cycles of the moon, the seasons, the rhythm of the tides, the disappearance of the sun in nightly darkness and who feared such cosmic power in the apparent control of a member of their own species.

Each primitive society has tended to make the threat of menstrual pollution as concrete as possible. Therefore, to the Maori of New Zealand, the dreaded *kahukahu* contained in the menses is the personification of the germs of a human being and is capable of inflicting the most extreme harm on men.[10] The Mae Enga believe that contact with menstrual blood or a menstruating woman will "sicken a man and cause persistent vomiting, 'kill' his blood so that it turns black, corrupt his vital juices so that his skin darkens and hangs in folds as his flesh wastes, permanently dull his

wits, and eventually lead to a slow decline and death."[11] The Tinne Indians
of the Yukon Territory believe that menstrual blood contains the essence
of femaleness; thus, menstruating women must avoid all contact with men,
especially young men, lest they threaten their virility.[12]

To be sure, the magical nature of menstrual blood has some helpful
aspects. Menstrual blood has been known to cure leprosy, warts, birth-
marks, gout, goiter, hemorrhoids, epilepsy, worms, and headache. It was
effective as a love charm, could ward off river demons and other evil
spirits, and was occasionally fit to be an honorific offering to a god. The
first napkin worn by a virgin was to be saved for use as a cure for the
plague. But for most people, menstrual blood remained as the Roman
Pliny described it in his *Natural History*:

> Contact with it turns new wine sour, crops touched by it become
> barren, grafts die, seed in gardens are dried up, the fruit of trees falls
> off, the edge of steel and the gleam of ivory are dulled, hives of bees
> die, even bronze and iron are at once seized by rust, and a horrible
> smell fills the air; to taste it drives dogs mad and infects their bites
> with an incurable poison . . . . Even that very tiny creature the ant is
> said to be sensitive to it and throws away grains of corn that taste of
> it and does not touch them again.[13]

Equivalent beliefs persist to this day. No woman was employed in
the opium industry in Saigon in the nineteenth century because it was
believed that the opium would turn and become bitter if a menstruating
woman was near.[14] Women in the 1920s widely believed that a permanent
wave would not take if they were menstruating. Musicians are likely to
blame broken violin and harp strings on their wives' menstruation. And
most of us still consider it unlucky to walk under ladders, a superstition
derived from the primitive world, where people would not pass under
bridges, clotheslines, trees, or the like if a menstruating woman was about,
lest some of the blood or its mana fall on their heads.

In many primitive societies, the menstruating woman was excluded
from the most ordinary life of her tribe for four or five days every month.
Unable to plant, harvest, cook, associate with her husband, or wander
freely around the village, the woman went instead to the menstrual hut,
a cramped dwelling of leaves and bark, set at some distance from the
village. There a menstruating woman might, depending upon her culture,
be required to undergo purifying practices or simply enjoy the solitude.
In the latter sense, some anthropologists have seen the huts as an expression of a culture's need to establish privacy. But perhaps a better perspective on menstrual seclusion is given by Margaret Mead. She reports

that the mountain Arapesh of New Guinea have a remarkable freedom from menstrual pain, "possibly because the extreme discomfort of sitting on a thin piece of bark on the damp, cold ground in a leaky leaf-hut on the side of a mountain, rubbing one's body with stinging nettles, obscures any awareness."[15]

The ethnologist A. E. Crawley explains the hut phenomenon and the periodic segregation of the sexes in terms of the primitive belief in the evil eye. Comparing such people to ostriches, who bury their heads in the sand to avoid an aggressor, he notes that to the primitive mind, the sight of a dangerous thing is the same as being seen by it.[16] If the dangerous menstruating woman is removed to a place where she can neither see nor be seen by the tribe, they will be assured of freedom from her mana as long as she is so secluded.

Such an extraordinary collection of taboos, taken with deadly seriousness by most of the world, throughout most of history, tells us a great deal about our psychosexual selves. Because the societies combed by the social scientists have been ruled by men, the mana of a menstruating woman was generally believed to be most dangerous to men; and on the conscious level, the taboos seem to aim more for the protection of men than of women. Now, women and men get together in two basic ways: through sex and through food. In both instances, woman provides a service to man that he cannot do without. Thus, the dangers to men (and because we are generally talking of patriarchies, the dangers to the whole society) from menstruating women must be mitigated by means of the strictest possible taboos regarding food and sex.

It should be noted that food taboos are not restricted to menstruating women. Food taboos were useful in preserving a society's totemic animals, in preserving the plants and animals most important to the economy of the group, or in teaching the society how to govern itself; perhaps, because food was undoubtedly the first form of property, the first human laws were these food restrictions, imposed and maintained by the tribal authorities. Although such food taboos continue today in some contemporary religions, the taboos associated with the handling of food by menstruating women have generally ceased to be observed in industrialized countries. But this is a relatively recent development. In most primitive societies, and some advanced ones as well, we find menstruating women tabooed from influencing the hunting, growing, preserving, cooking, serving, and enjoyment of food.

The cycle of food taboos begins with the hunt. Eskimo believe that contact with a menstruating woman can lead to bad luck in hunting; the contamination takes the form of an invisible vapor which attaches itself to the hunter so that he is more visible to game and therefore unable to catch it.[17] Among the Habbe of the western Sudan, a man whose wife is menstruating does not undertake any hunting.[18] Bukka women may not go into the sea to bathe for fear of spoiling the fishing.[19] The Sekani Indians of British Columbia gave menstruating women only dried meat or fish to eat because eating fresh game would spoil the hunter's luck.[20] Hays writes that the Melanesian Ifaluk Islanders have a "free and cheerful sex life ... uncorrupted by any missionary teaching"[21] but nevertheless observe menstrual taboos to the extent that during the fishing season the men must live in the canoe house and abstain from women. Today's hunting lodge, that no-woman's land of whiskey and Winchesters, echoes these primitive taboos.

Besides being dangerous to hunters and the hunt, menstruating women were considered capable of contaminating growing plants. This must have presented a worrisome contradiction to early peoples. The first objects of worship on this planet were probably women, in whom the principle of fertility was most clearly evident; the feasts of the Corn Goddess in ancient Europe indicate the inseparable linking of women and agriculture. Women were responsible for the cultivation of the fields; men went after the game. And women played key roles in the fertility rites of Demeter and Dionysus, in myth and in actuality. Women's success in agricultural labors was probably attributed to their obvious fecundity and was thought to be, like the power of childbearing, inherent in their sex.

But the power to create suggests the power to destroy. If woman could make things grow, she could also make them wither on the vine. Menstrual blood, the outward sign of her duality, could be her weapon to annihilate the society she was responsible for preserving. Thus, menstruating women of the Australian Arunta tribe are not permitted to gather the irriakura bulbs, a staple of their diet, lest the bulbs fail. In Malekula, one of the New Hebrides islands, neither a menstruous woman nor her husband may enter a garden where young plants are growing. A woman of the Toradja people of central Celebes must avoid tobacco fields if her skirts are stained with menstrual blood, lest she blight the crop (but the same stained garment will keep the pigs out of a rice field).[22] Even in this century peasants in Italy, Spain, Germany, and Holland believed that flowers and fruit trees withered from contact with a menstruating woman. And Jewish women have traditionally been forbidden to plant during their periods.

Menstruating women are supposed to have an especially baneful effect on food when it is halfway between one state and another. Peoples in southeastern Europe, for example, will not permit them to salt or pickle because of the belief that the preserving will not take. This belief must have been brought to America early, for we have heard that it persists among some Kentucky coal mining families. The presence of a menstruating woman will prevent a French housewife from achieving a successful mayonnaise and will have an equally bad influence on cider being fermented, sugar being refined, and bacon being cured.[23] The peasants of Eastern Europe know that a menstruating woman must not bake bread or churn butter.

In an attempt to give scientific support to these beliefs, Bela Schick (1920) and David Macht (1924) separately observed, they said, the detrimental effect of menstruation on plant life. In one of Schick's experiments, a servant girl was given a bouquet of roses during her period; by the next day, the plants had faded. Schick coined the term *menotoxins* to describe noxious plant-destroying substances exuded through the skin of menstruating women. He added that menotoxins prevent dough from rising and beer from fermenting.

Macht discovered, he said, that menstrual blood had the power to inhibit the growth of plants. Moreover, it was not only the blood itself that had this power; as with Schick's servant girl, the menotoxic action could also be exercised through saliva, urine, perspiration, milk, tears, and even the air breathed by the menstruating woman.[24] However, two other researchers, attempting in 1934 to duplicate Macht's experiments, could not do so. In their results, nonmenstruating women had higher "toxic" scores than the menstruators did, suggesting, if anything, that women are less foul during their periods.[25]

In 1950, Olive Watkins Smith and George Van S. Smith studied what they called *menotoxin,* a substance in menstrual blood that could cause death within a day if injected into an immature rat. However, Smith and Smith said that the substance was simply an "atypical globulin." It was toxic to immature rats only and had no effect on human beings or, apparently, on flowers.[26]

Even without the benefits of "scientific" research, the Carib of British Guiana have long known that a man who eats food prepared by a menstruating woman will never be well,[27] the Kharwar of India keep menstruating women out of the kitchen altogether,[28] and Ugandans damn the expense and destroy the family cooking pots during the housewife's menstrual period.[29] Iatmul are less rigid; in that tribe, a menstruating woman will not cook for her husband "unless she is out of temper with him and wishes to do him some mild harm."[30] The most ordinary of condiments, salt, comes under special prohibition for menstruating women in many societies. Sir James Frazer notes that in Central Agoniland a woman may cook for her husband while she is menstruating; but if she adds salt to his food, she will give him a disease called Tsempo.[31] In many preliterate societies, salt is connected with sexual intercourse and must be avoided when continence is necessary. Because there is no greater deterrent to sexual intercourse than menstruation, salt and sex must be avoided together.

A menstruating woman does not cease being a danger to food once it reaches the table. Theodor Reik recalls a incident that occurred when he was five and visiting his grandparents in Austria. His grandfather said, *"Mach den Tische rein!"* ("clean the table") to his grandmother. She left because she was *niddah* ("menstruating"), a term that comes from the verb *nadah* ("to expel").[32] In general, moreover, women and men observe some ritual separation at meals, whether they be peoples who fear the mana of the menstrual blood, peasants who assume that the wife serves the husband but does not sit herself, or ladies who withdraw while the men enjoy brandy and cigars. Crawley suggests that the origin of taboos against men and women eating together is "a form of egoistic sensitiveness with regard to the most important vital function" and can also be seen as a source of reinforcing sexual identity. Eating together is more usually seen, however, as a source of contamination to the male because food is commonly believed to acquire the properties of the person eating or serving it. Thus, the contact of food "with the person or influence of the female, transmits to the male the properties of women."[33] Hays tells of the decline of the Polynesian taboo civilization in Hawaii in 1819 after a "strong-minded" wife of Kamehamcha the Great saw European women enjoying banquets from which the Hawaiian women had been excluded and persuaded her husband to eat with the women of his family.[34]

In the United States today, outright cooking and segregation taboos are just a cultural memory. The emphasis is on behaving normally during the menstrual period, and be she housewife or career woman, or both, today's woman is determined to prove that she can do her job "like a man" even when she is feeling most like a woman.

Afterword

Since the first edition of *The Curse* was published in 1976, more women anthropologists have based their research on the experience of women in preindustrial societies, expanding anthropology's basis of inquiry and yielding new kinds of information about menstrual taboos, their origins and uses. Anthropological research on the menstrual cycle has also led to other kinds of information about societies.

A 1983 World Health Organization (WHO) study examined attitudes toward menstruation among women of all socioeconomic classes in ten countries (Egypt, India, Indonesia, Jamaica, Mexico, Pakistan, Philippines, Republic of Korea, the United Kingdom, and Yugoslavia). Its point was not to understand the taboos themselves as reflections of a society's attitudes toward women, however, but to assess patterns of menstrual attitudes in order to obtain better information on birth control practices, since population and health workers throughout the world know that disturbances in the menstrual cycle will invariably affect the way a woman chooses and uses birth control. The WHO study found that, despite the physical and emotional disturbances women suffer during menstruation and the changes they must make in their patterns of living because of cultural taboos, the women in the study see menstruation as a positive event—even in India, where three-quarters of them refrain from household chores because of concepts of pollution—and the vast majority of them would not voluntarily submit to induced amenorrhea, such as might result from the pill.[35]

Another contemporary study, on Mexican-American women, yielded its results as an afterthought to a study on family size. The reason so many women in this population had such large families, the researchers discovered, was that most of them thought they were most likely to be fertile when they had their periods and avoided intercourse then. So by observing the traditional intramenstrual taboo, these women thought they were prudently regulating the size of their families. This study too found that women perceived menstruation to be a positive event, one which "cleanses" the body. Unless they were pregnant, an absence of periods would mean to these women that the "dirty" blood was still in the body, creating an unhealthy state.[36]

Anthropologist Denise Lawrence found an economic and social rationale for the menstrual taboos in force in a small Portuguese village. Each family in this village butchers a pig once a year, with much cooperation from its neighbors during the traditional week of curing the meat and making the sausages which feed the family for the year ahead. The woman of the household exercises great care, influence, and selectivity over which of her female neighbors may assist, since there is a strict taboo against menstruating women coming into contact with, or looking at the meat while it is being cured (a contemporary example of the ancient taboo against menstruating women being around food in states of transition). But in reality more than menstrual contamination is at stake: the pig kill is in some ways a family's "annual report"; the size of the pig, the condition of the house, the availability and evidence of accumulated goods all reveal the family's economic status. So the housewife uses the menstrual taboo to guard the privacy of her family, keep face with her neighbors, yet maintain a village tradition. Lawrence concludes that the women's continuing strict observance of this menstrual taboo has little to do with concepts of pollution but instead shows how women exert power by manipulating the fears associated with menstruation in order to achieve their own ends.[37]

The power of women shines again in the menstrual habits of a contemporary hunting/gathering tribe of the Kalahari Desert in Africa. In *Nisa: The Life and Words of a !Kung Woman*, anthropologist Marjorie Shostak reports on the !Kung, one of the last societies to live as their human ancestors had done for 90 percent of the 100,000 years of human history.[38] In a series of interviews with the !Kung women, Shostak found that because they held positions in their society almost equal to men, sharing decision-making as well as labor, their menarches and menstruations were not objects of fear or taboo, beyond the almost universal prohibition against menstruating women and the hunt. The menarcheal hut is within the village and the men are free to watch the bawdy antics of the women as they celebrate. Regular menstruation is given minimal attention, as cotton cloth and water are scarce, and it is often neither possible nor necessary to conceal the blood. The !Kung do believe, however, that if a woman sees menstrual blood on another, she will start menstruating herself. This "synchronous menstruation" has been an object of curiosity to many cultures, including our own, and late in 1986 American researchers offered the first "evidence" that the phenomenon has a physiological basis (see afterword to Chapter 5.)

The !Kung's disregard for menstruation as "a thing of no account" [39] is paralleled in their evident freedom from what women in industrialized societies know as premenstrual syndrome (PMS). In a test designed to assess the presence, level, and quality of PMS among the !Kung, Shostak interviewed selected women every other day during at least two consecutive menstrual cycles, while her husband drew blood samples from them. The blood was tested for the hormonal variations common in women at different stages of their cycles, variations that are known to produce psychological as well as physiological changes. The interviews showed that the women did not "have any expectation or belief comparable to that held in the West of a premenstrual or menstrual syndrome. Nor did they recognize any effect of the menstrual cycle on women's moods or behavior. They were surprised when asked about it." But the blood samples revealed the !Kung women to be undergoing the same fluctuations in hormonal patterns as women everywhere else.[40]

Some may use these findings to show that we in the West are too suggestible and experience the emotional component of PMS because our culture now expects us to. But incontrovertible physical evidence of premenstrual symptoms—and of relief—negates that theory. It is far more likely that the absence of PMS symptoms reflects the superb physical conditioning of the !Kung women, an effect of their arduous life, and of course the relative infrequency of menstruation in these women during pregnancy and long periods of lactation.

Barbara Harrell, a sociologist, studied lactating women in a pre-industrial Taiwanese village that in the late 1970s was moving slowly but inexorably into the modern age. As in all such societies, women had normally breastfed their babies, but with prosperity, industrialization, and new opportunities for employment, they were nursing less frequently and for shorter periods of time and consequently having more menstrual cycles. This gradual redefining of what was a "normal" female state of being in this village led Harrell to reflect that because menstrual cycling is today the condition most common to our Western experience we overlook the fact that pregnancy and lactation have long been the norm, here and elsewhere.

Harrell forces us to look with new eyes at what really defines our womanhood, pointing out that women's ambivalence about menstruation (she even notes the irony of *The Curse* in which we extoll menstrual extraction while proclaiming the need to pass on "Eve's blessing") may be caused by the fact that "continuous menstrual cycling is not a natural attribute of human females. Perhaps 'the curse' can be explained as an artifact of the Age of Technology, something imposed upon women by a society of plenty which needs no more children."[41]

Or perhaps we need to reflect that opinions of what is "natural" to women historically have tended to go beyond describing a bodily function and have instead been used to define their place in the universe. That, after all, is the subject of *The Curse*. The absence of menstruation during the childbearing years in, say, Victorian England was accompanied by its own "natural" corollaries: it was then "natural" for women to lose many infants to "natural" causes. Today an infant death or deformity is frequently cause for a lawsuit, so accustomed are parents to expecting a "naturally" perfect baby every time. It was equally "natural" for such women to die in childbirth themselves. And let us not forget those well-intentioned nineteenth-century reformers who tried to convince women that higher education would dangerously divert blood from the reproductive organs to the brain, thus damaging the "natural" purpose of their lives.

In her introduction to *The Real Menstrual Cycle* Doreen Asso deftly explains the "rise" of menstruation and the decline in childbearing as a shift of focus, not of function. In this excellent book she shows how "every month the cycle turns through a myriad of changes which for most of the time create in women an entirely positive physical and psychological climate." She notes "the positive aspects of living with a marked rhythm of change" and so orients her book to a clinical look at the entire month-long cycle and the unique aspects of each part of it.[42]

In much the same way do we in this book try to put the cycle itself in its cultural context. The new kinds of anthropological studies examined here help fill in the picture of menstruation as a *cultural* phenomenon, and the new angles of approach are interesting and useful. But they must not make us mistake the part for the whole. Menstruation is not "womanhood" and women must not be defined or limited by it.

Chapter 2

"Not Tonight, Dear":
Taboos of Sex

Food and sex are still inseparable as evidenced by the subtitle of a recent best seller: *The Joy of Sex: A Gourmet Guide to Love-Making*. Menstruation is listed in the table of contents under "Main Courses," instead of where we might expect to find it, under either "Sauces and Pickles" or "Problems." Dr. Comfort advises that this is a good time of the month to find variant sexual experiences; clothed intercourse and femoral intercourse (between the thighs) come highly recommended. In *The Sensuous Woman*, we find no such alternative. Avoid orgies during your period, "J" advises.

What is so remarkable about the sex taboos against menstruating women is that they have not faded into vestigial reminders of a primitive past; they are still very much a part of everyday life for most people. Thus, we cannot present this taboo in a vacuum, as a primitive curiosity; we must deal with it wherever it appears. It will readily be seen that the more sophisticated the society, the more scientific the explanation for the intercourse taboo.

We have already mentioned that the male treats the menstruating woman with ambivalence; he both envies her ability to create and fears her power to destroy. The love-fear relationship is nowhere so potent as when it involves the act of love itself. A man is as likely to be sexually aroused by a woman when she is menstruating as he is at any other time. But the blood of the menstruating woman is somehow dangerous, magical, and apparently not something he wants to get on his penis. It is thus necessary to protect the penis from the menses.[1]

Although the menstruating woman is still considered to be magical, the primary reason for the dread of intercourse during menstruation appears to be the blood itself, which has associations in the male mind with pain, death, battle, injury, and castration. It has been found that in those cultures where the intercourse taboo is most strictly enforced, there is a significant degree of castration anxiety (fear of losing the penis) among the males.[2] But official explanations for the intercourse taboo range from the holy to the hygienic, and they do not acknowledge that the male is afraid of *anything*.

For example, in certain patriarchal cultures, the dread that the male feels toward the menstruating woman becomes a part of his worship of his gods. In some societies, violations of sexual taboos are seen as sins against the god of fertility; in ancient Persia, the offense was so serious that it warranted burning in hell until Judgment Day. In the Koran, the sacred text of the Islamic religion, it is written: "They will also question thee as to the courses of women. SAY: They are a pollution. Separate yourselves therefore from women and approach them not, until they be cleansed. But when they are cleansed, go unto them as God hath ordained for you." Yet, in the Islamic account of the Creation, blood is seen, not as a source of pollution, but as the substance of creation: "Recite, thou, in the name of thy Lord who created;—/ Created man from CLOTS OF BLOOD:—/ Recite thou!"[3] Blood, like the menstruating woman, is *sacra,* both sacred and accursed.

The rule against intercourse with a menstruating woman in Judeo-Christian scriptures appears first in Leviticus 15:19: "And if a woman have issue, and her issue in her flesh be blood, she shall be put apart seven days: and whosoever toucheth her shall be unclean until the even." In Leviticus 20:15, the punishment is more severe than the curse of uncleanness until the evening. Here it is warned that *both* offenders "shall be cut off from among their people."

The taboo described in Leviticus is still observed among Orthodox Jews. If a bride is menstruating on her wedding night, one tradition requires that a little girl accompany her to the bridal bed lest the young lovers get carried away. There is evidently enough violation of the taboo to have prompted Isser Yehuda Unterman, chief rabbi of Israel, to issue a statement in 1972 on "Family Purity," a statement that goes to every couple in Israel who apply for a wedding license. In his pamphlet, Rabbi Unterman repeats the precautions against intercourse with a menstruating woman that appear in the Torah, and he recalls the punishment for violating the law, the penalty of *Karet,* the "cutting of life on earth and the denial of a life to come." Unterman tells of one woman who came to him with the complaint that despite her unclean state, her husband had forced himself on her sexually. The rabbi comments, "In my humble opinion, the cause of such unbridled behavior is due to modern conditions of life, which both incite and nauseate."[4]

We have mentioned the Mae Enga belief that contact with a menstruating woman can make a man vomit, can "kill" his blood, waste his flesh, darken his skin, ruin his "vital juices," and "dull his wits." A South African clan believes that intercourse with a menstruating woman will make a man's bones get soft. In most cases, the punishment and physical suffering accompanying the violation of the intramenstrual taboo are borne by the male members of the community. That sexual intercourse during the period is of danger to *men* is the dominant belief of the forty primitive societies studied by William Stephens in 1961. It is also a dominant belief in European culture.

In the nineteenth century, it was widely thought that a male could get gonorrhea from contact with a menstruating woman. There seems to be a confusion between gonorrhea and such infections as trichomoniasis, both of which can be communicated to a man by a woman and vice versa. Trichomoniasis does become worse during menstruation because of lower vaginal acidity, but its most noticeable symptom is itching, not death or insanity. Augustus Kinsley Gardner, author of *Conjugal Sins* (1870), saw menstrual blood as corrupt and virulent, threatening an unwitting penis with "disease,""excoriations," and "blenorrhagias." ("Blenorrhagia" is now known as gonorrhea.) Another nineteenth-century idea was that the menstruating woman was likely, during intercourse, to regain from a man's lifeblood what she herself was losing.[5]

In the twentieth century, man's punishment from menstrual intercourse is said to be a disease called urethritis, an inflammation of the urethra, the duct that conveys both urine and semen. Such attacks are not very common, however; it is the rare medical practitioner who encounters a case. According to the best evidence available today, coitus during menstruation is generally harmless for men.

If men are free from the dangers of soft bones, vomiting, or venereal disease during menstrual intercourse, women are similarly unthreatened. In fact, menstrual intercourse is good for women because it temporarily relieves cramps by increasing the flow. Yet, it has long been argued in medical circles that the combination of menstruation and intercourse is harmful for a woman. Soranus (second century A.D.) writes that it should be avoided because the uterus is already "overburdened and is in an unresponsive state because of the ingress of material and incapable of carrying two motions contrary to each other, one for the excretion of material, the other for receiving."[6]

A 1935 sex manual implies that during her period a woman is sick anyway and that she could get even sicker from indulging in sexual activities. "The female sexual organs are more or less congested, therefore more irritated and subject to pain, and vigorous sex relations would no doubt cause a greater loss of blood by increasing the menstrual hemorrhage."[7]

Women seem to have accepted these pseudoscientific taboos. In a study of 109 women conducted in 1950, most reasons for abstinence listed by the participants had to do with a fear that intercourse during menstruation would be physically harmful, that it might lead to "hemorrhage, injury, or infection."[8] Even today, the most commonly argued reason is medical: The woman does have a decrease in vaginal acidity during her period and is at this time more likely to get vaginitis.

Among aboriginal peoples, a woman is occasionally in real physical danger for having violated the intramenstrual taboo. Among the Reindeer Chukchi, it was believed that a woman would eventually become sterile because of such action. In anthropological writings, there is the rare example of a woman suffering irregular menstruation as punishment for having intercourse with a harmful "hot" male (one whose blood is not cooled down). But this belief, found among the Kgatia of Beuchanaland,[9] is the only example we could find in any culture of a male's blood being the cause of a female's illness.

The consensus of contemporary medical experts is best expressed in this statement from a 1969 article: "There appears to be no established reason to abstain from coitus during the menses on patho-physiologic grounds."[10] Those who do abstain for such stated reasons are either ill informed or masking a deeper cultural dread of woman's blood.

A lesser fear is that intercourse during menstruation can harm the potential child. The Romans attributed the deformity of the god Vulcan to menstrual intercourse between Juno and Jupiter. In France, it was long believed that an infant conceived during the menses would be "puny, languid, and moribund, subject to an infinity of fetid maladies, foul and stinking as a result of the matter from which it was conceived." The child would be subject to a number of horrible diseases, among them leprosy, syphilis, scrofula, and virulent ulcers of the skin. Mentally, it would be "entirely stupid, dull, loutish, silly, deprived of sense and understanding, and entirely unskilled to do anything good."[11]

We have found no medical evidence that a child conceived during the mother's menstrual period will be deformed, ulcerous, or rotten. Chances are, in fact, that neither a diseased child nor a healthy one will be forthcoming. One definite advantage to having intercourse during the menses is that it is relatively "safe"; few women ovulate during days 1 to 5 of their cycle.

Of course, medicine and psychiatry have perpetuated the myth that women are the sexually passive members of the species and that they are the least interested in sexual activity while they are menstruating. Clinical studies usually show that the peak of a woman's sexual desire is during or immediately following ovulation. Fred Robbins stated in 1953 that the "menstrual blues" interfered with sexual desire.[12] Mary Jane Sherfey claims that women are most capable of multiple orgasms during the luteal, or postovulatory, stage;[13] Luschen and Pierce (1972) found, through studying women's reactions to pictures of sexually attractive males, that women are more easily aroused during ovulation than during menstruation.[14]

A few authorities are now beginning to recognize, however, that many women are most aroused during the flow itself. Masters and Johnson see arousal during the menses as an occasional happening.[15] This finding has been supported by others in the field. In still another study, 36 percent of the women noticed increased sexual desire during menstruation. "One patient reported that she experienced sexual desire only during menstruation, and on one occasion, felt so overwhelmed by passion that, although a shy and inhibited girl, she resorted to intercourse with a stranger."[16] Sexual arousal during menstruation has also been recorded among the Ngulu of eastern Tanzania. During her period, a Ngulu woman is "thought to attain her peak of fertility and passion," writes one anthropologist, "but precisely for this reason, men should avoid her."[17]

Not all women, it is true, experience the peak of sexual desire during the menstrual period. There seems to be sufficient evidence, however, that for a lot of women this is indeed the case, despite the persistent observation in medical literature that women find intercourse during the menses objectionable. It is noteworthy that, perhaps as a consequence of the much-ballyhooed sexual revolution, women's stated attitudes are changing. A 1938 study found that only 2 percent of women polled claimed to enjoy menstrual intercourse.[18] By 1969, 75 percent of Georgia medical students responding to a questionnaire had occasional intercourse during menstruation; another study conducted around the same time by Masters and Johnson revealed that 90 percent of 331 women said they had no objection to this activity as long as they were not at the peak of their flow and their partner expressed no aversion to it.[19] These terms *no objection* and *aversion* bring us to the currently fashionable aesthetic argument against menstrual intercourse.

The most commonly given reason for avoidance of menstrual intercourse, even among "liberated" men and women, is the couple's aesthetic sensibilities. Seldom do we hear today of the man's disinclination or dread. The word *aesthetic* seems to be a way for male doctors and sociologists to disguise what they really mean: that intercourse with a menstruating woman is messy, sloppy, and possibly frightening; it is also a subtle reinforcement of the message that woman is the "unclean" sex.

But if a *woman* does not wish to engage in sexual intercourse, her period is her one legitimate out. Using "the curse" as an excuse, many a woman has enjoyed a dinner date free from the bothersome knowledge that she herself might be the dessert. Katharina Dalton notes in this regard that some women actually develop prolonged menstruation as a way to avoid sex.[20]

But the menstruation excuse is not merely a modern device. Unterman tells of the Jewish woman who was taken by the Romans and sold into a "house of shame." "She repelled all those who sought to lay lustful hands on her with one cry: 'I am experiencing my menstrual period!' with the result that none molested her."[21]

Among the Tswana of the Beuchanaland, the intercourse taboo is so strong that "many a girl has been able, temporarily at least, to escape the attention of an ardent unwelcome lover by pleading her monthly illness as an excuse."[22]

Occasionally, however, one meets an unusual kind of man, a person who, instead of being put off by menstruation, is aroused by it. *Tits & Clits,* an early feminist West Coast "comic" book, did a piece on menstruation, really the first attempt of its kind to expose publicly the earthy, uninhibited things women think about the gurgling aesthetics of the menstrual flow. The result is bizarre and funny and consciousness raising in the extreme.[23] One male reader was so excited by what he read that he wrote to the editors and shared his sexual fantasies with them. He speaks of himself as "the Kotex Kid," describes a Danish sex film that features a menstruating woman, and recounts the various ways he and his girlfriend violate the intercourse taboo. He is stimulated when she makes dinner "in a flimsy nite gown and black high heels and a belt and Kotex," and the smell of menstrual blood on a pad or in a Tassaway turns him on for a week.

The Trakese of the Caroline Islands and the Maori of New Zealand also find nothing aesthetically unpleasant about intercourse during menstruation, and the New Guinea Manus "attach a positive value" to it.[24] Among the A-kamba, an East African clan, "married people usually perform coitus when the woman is menstruating, because of the belief that she can be impregnated only at this time."[25] The A-kamba people must have an extraordinarily low birth rate.

Among prostitutes, whose living depends on their being sexually available at all times, the menstrual intercourse taboo is not generally observed. Gail Sheehy, author of *Hustling,* told us that prostitutes who are controlled by pimps must use birth control pills to eliminate the flow altogether because "the show must go on six days a week, every week of the month." Constant use of the pills, of course, will ultimately have a devastating effect on their health. Some prostitutes stuff themselves with cotton; others service their customers orally or manually. Call girls can make their own rules, as can "house" girls under the control of a madam. "Yet, since they cater to all tastes, some of their clients (johns) may *prefer* intercourse during their periods."

Karen Paige has discovered that the intercourse taboo is not consistently observed among Protestants. The women whom Paige interviewed included fifty-six Protestants, eighteen Catholics, and thirteen Jews. Most of the Catholics and Jews said that they "would never have sex during menstruation," but only half the Protestants so responded.[26] In the only study we could find on blacks, statistics indicate that they are *not* exceptions to the rule. In an exploration of the attitudes of over 100 "medically indigent women" in Georgia, all but 3 of whom were black, the intramenstrual taboo was overwhelmingly observed. The women said that menstrual intercourse was "unclean and not right," "undignified," and "not polite." The 3 women in this group who did enjoy sex during menstruation said they did so because they were free from worry about pregnancy.[27]

Despite these exceptions, the rule remains. The intramenstrual taboo is widespread and affects people from all classes and all cultures. The California study shows that of 960 families, "half of the men and women had never had sex during menstruation."[28] Perhaps the vast majority of human beings are just being faithful to their animal ancestry; during the menstrual cycle of female apes, one authority claims, the males "scrupulously avoid serious copulation." The male may mount the female, but he does not try to penetrate. The mounting is no more than a friendly gesture.[29]

Among human beings, it is often difficult for women to ask a sexual partner, especially a new one, "What's wrong with a little blood?" The husband of one woman we talked to, who is sexually experimental in every other respect, prefers to avoid intercourse during her period. So she uses sheets with a red floral pattern. Except for the first day, when the flow is heavy, he doesn't seem to notice that she is menstruating.

Another friend wrote to us about the most extreme case of noncommunication in this area we've heard. A woman who didn't want to alienate her husband during her period had a voluntary hysterectomy:

> She is evidently pleased . . . the operation is accomplished . . . no more birth control . . . no, there was nothing *wrong* with her organs . . . simply quietly she explains that she chose *this* method of birth control so that she won't have to say no to her husband at *that* time . . . about the number 28 they see eye to eye . . . no honey not tonight . . . it's *that* time . . . .

"No honey, not tonight: it's *that* time." The majority of men and women still believe in the inviolability of this taboo, building menstrual huts of fear and superstition wherever and whenever they live.

Afterword

In 1983 Barbara G. Walker put together a wonderful collection of facts about women. *The Woman's Encyclopedia of Myths and Secrets* examines a goodly host of women's mysteries, among them menstruation, and argues that certain women's rituals honored during the "matriarchal age" degenerated or became falsified under the reign of the patriarchs. Much of the material listed under "menstrual blood" sheds new wisdom on the menstrual intercourse taboo. We learn, for example, that Vishnu's punishment for having intercourse with the menstruating goddess Earth is a reflection of the male fear of women in Vedic mythology. In the Golden Age, on the contrary, the menstruating goddess Kali was the sacred copulating participant of the "Great Rite," and menstrual blood was the essential ingredient in that regenerative ritual. As time passed, the celebration of menstrual blood became a lost secret; in its place appeared taboos against intercourse, as in the Zoroastrian belief that "any man who lay with a menstruating woman would beget a demon, and would be punished in hell by having filth poured into his mouth." The compiler of *The Woman's Encyclopedia of Myths and Secrets* connects these ancient taboos to the more recent fear of women among nineteenth-century doctors, who, as we noted, shared the superstition that sex with a menstruating woman caused gonorrhea.[30]

Once again, however, medicine is pointing the finger at the menstruating woman as potentially dangerous (or in danger) during intercourse. The disease in question is not gonorrhea but the more fatal AIDS (acquired immune deficiency syndrome). In 1985 Barbara Visscher, a California researcher, discovered, in her work on homosexual men, that AIDS could be transmitted to women. Visscher suspected that a woman could contract the virus through vaginal abrasions or possibly during menstruation. "That's when the blood vessels in the lining of the uterus open up, and could let the virus slip in." These tentative connections between menstrual intercourse and AIDS were reported by science writer John Langone in a "Special Report" in the December 1985 issue of *Discover*.[31] A month later Jonathan Lieberson made similar claims in the *New York Review of Books*: "If AIDS is to be passed on in vaginal intercourse, mixing of blood or contact between sperm and blood must take place, and this is unusual." Such transmission, said Lieberson, "would require either that the female were menstruating or that a tear occurred both in the vaginal wall and the penis so that blood could be passed."[32] Langone, in a follow-up to his special report on AIDS, again discussed the possibility, under "special circumstances," of a woman contracting AIDS. "If sex occurred during menstruation, the virus might have invaded the body through the blood; there are apparently times during the menstrual flow when the disintegrating blood vessels are open exactly like a cut to microorganisms."[33]

To our knowledge, however, the larger medical community has not made a major case for AIDS being transmitted to or by a woman during menstrual intercourse. *Index Medicus* and *Psychological Abstracts,* two of the major bibliographical sources on medical research, do not list any titles on AIDS and menstruation from December, 1985, through November, 1986—the time of this writing. Compared to the fear of toxic shock associated with the tampon, the fear of AIDS associated with menstrual intercourse *seems* minimal, but until this deadly disease is better understood, nothing is certain.

Sexual denial during menstruation still appears to be a matter of taste. And despite Germaine Greer's remark that in our age "refraining from sexual intercourse during menstruation is deemed fainthearted," the majority of married couples seem to be refraining.[34] A 1983 study by Naomi M. Morris and J. Richard Udry elicited daily reports from 85 husbands and wives over three menstrual cycles. Morris and Udry conclude that "intercourse and orgasm are reduced during menstruation, in association with impressively less female desire for intercourse during menstruation."[35] The reasons for this decrease were primarily religious or aesthetic.

The Morris-Udry conclusion that women have less desire for sex during menstruation opposes the findings of a report done two years earlier by Gold and Adams that *men* are the cause for the decline of sex during menstruation.[36] Many researchers would probably agree with Gold and Adams, however; the male partner is the one to resist sex during the woman's period.

One investigator has found that men fear the sexual aggressiveness associated with a woman's premenstrual and menstrual phases. Immediately preceding menstruation, he claims, the woman exhibits sexual assertiveness, thus creating both dread and attraction in the male. Menstrual bleeding further confirms this dread, serving as a reminder both of the woman's assertiveness and of the male's fears of castration.[37]

Menstruation, then, continues to be a barrier in heterosexual relationships, whether the barrier be erected by the male or by the female. And, in one of the rare studies on lesbian sexuality and the taboo of menstruation, we learn that among female partners sexual intimacy is on the decline during the menses.[38]

In reviewing the literature on the intercourse taboo we have found no evidence that sexual intercourse is on the rise during a woman's period. People are still faint-hearted, it seems. And "Not tonight, dear" is still likely to be heard monthly in the bedrooms of America.[39]

Chapter 3

Putting Her in Her Place: Rites of the Menarche

One of the reasons taboos die so hard—in all types of civilizations—is that they are rigorously taught to youngsters, who dare not question them. To the uninitiated, they represent the status and privilege of adulthood. The concentration with which today's pre-pubescent girl ponders the menstrual manuals supplied by the napkin manufacturers and probes the mysteries of the tampon box is only a pale vestige of the rituals observed throughout history and earlier to mark the onset of menstruation.

In most native cultures the world over, the first period is accompanied by rites which give formal notice to the menarcheal child that woman's place in society is indeed a special one. The most widespread practice is the seclusion of the menstruating girl from the tribe for periods lasting from a few days to a few years. During this seclusion, the girl is taboo. She may be prohibited from seeing the sun or touching the ground; she may not feed herself, handle food, or eat certain foods considered dangerous to her in this state. The circle of bushes or whatever barrier is placed between her and her people will probably also serve as her isolation hut during later periods. At the end of her seclusion, the girl is considered marriageable.

Among the more extreme devotees of this practice were the Carrier Indians of British Columbia, who caused a girl to live in the wilderness in complete seclusion for three or four years, far from all the beaten trails, believing that even her footsteps would defile a path.[1] Natives of New Ireland kept their girls at home for the same period of time, but in cages, where they would get fat and pale, in accordance with the tribe's standard of beauty. The richer or more powerful the father, the longer the girl was likely to remain caged; the poor could not afford to lose the labor of their daughters for such a long period.[2] Mohave Indian rites involved the first four menstrual periods,[3] and the Kolosh Indians of Alaska confined pubescent girls in a tiny hut, completely blocked except for one small airhole, for one year, during which time they were allowed no fire, no exercise, no company.[4]

In Cambodia, some girls were put to bed under a mosquito curtain for 100 days. Other Cambodian maidens were said to have "entered into the shade" and were required to observe strict seclusion for up to three years, during which time they would have to observe the traditional prohibitions against seeing the sun (with time out during eclipses).[5] Throughout India, girls became untouchable at puberty and were also forbidden to see the sun during their four-day seclusion.[6] Some Australian tribes were inclined to bury their girls in the sand,[7] as did the Mohave Indians of North America.[8] The Indians of British New Guinea, Brazil, and Bolivia swung their daughters in hammocks for the duration of the menarche.[9]

Sir James Frazer has interpreted such practices to mean that the society believed the newly menstruating girl to be in such danger from the magical powers of the menstrual flow and consequently so great a danger to the society at large that the safest place for her was in a state of suspension between heaven and earth. (Even those girls who were buried in sand observed ceremonial distance from the earth by means of special wraps or shoes.) He noted that this seclusion and suspension are the same for girls at menarche and sacred priests and kings. Both are *sacra;* both are charged with powers so precious to the entire society that they must be carefully guarded from harm. The seclusion and suspension are for their own protection as well as for the protection of the society, so that there will be no tampering with the divine power in them.[10]

The common association of the sun with "father" may also contribute to the reasons for seclusion of girls at menarche. Torres Strait maidens were enjoined from contact with men, especially their own fathers. This was for their mutual protection. The girl was believed to be in danger of sexual assault by her father, but the father was also facing the same dangers that would befall any man in contact with a menstruating woman: loss of his masculine powers.

At the same time, the father was experiencing a new status in the community. His role in the rites and doctrines of the menarche, suggests

Karen Paige, might have come from the economic advantage and bargaining power of a marriageable (barterable) daughter.[11]

Yet another important function of the menarcheal seclusion is its
suggestion of time "in the womb" as the girl prepares for her rebirth as
a fully functioning member of the society. The strict taboos during seclusion might be necessary because the initiate is in a "marginal" condition
(between her ritual death and ritual rebirth) and, like a child in a womb,
cannot help or protect herself from raging supernatural influences.[12] Among
the societies that emphasize the rebirth symbolism in their rituals are the
Navaho and Mohave nations. Both Navaho and Mohave girls are believed
to be physically and spiritually malleable during their seclusion. Their
female attendants actually massage their backs, arms, and legs, as women
of those cultures do with newborn infants, so that they will grow strong
and straight. The instructions the girls receive during their seclusion are
designed to shape their minds so that as women they will conform as
closely as possible to their cultural ideal.[13]

The rebirth notion is also prevalent in India, where it is compatible
with the Hindu belief in reincarnation. Just as a newborn child is believed
to be an ancestor reincarnate and is given the ancestor's name, so do some
initiates receive a new name at puberty. This emphasizes the seriousness
of the rebirth symbolism in initiation rites. A highlight of the puberty rite
in parts of India is often a magical representation of the act of dying and
being born again from the womb. Some candidates for initiation are
mourned by their mothers as dead and behave like infants when they
return from their seclusion.[14]

Because the appearance of the menses signals that a girl is ready for
a productive marriage, many societies use the occasion of the menarche
for a ritual defloration, either actual or symbolic. This practice stems from
the idea that the menarche is itself a defloration; often, no distinction was
made between menstrual and hymenal blood in the primitive mind. It was
also employed as a deterrent to the magical spirits and creatures who were
especially apt to be hovering around the girl at this time and likely to
have intercourse with her.

In Thailand and among certain African societies, it was believed that
a girl's first menstruation is a result of her defloration by one of a host
of aerial spirits, with each subsequent menstruation caused by further
intercourse with these spirits. Thus, at her menarche, a girl was often
referred to as a "bride."[15] A similar belief prevails in parts of India. There,
ritual defloration or marriage takes place before puberty so that the girl
is not placed in the danger of having her first intercourse with a super-

natural spirit. This defloration is often performed by a priest, a member of a higher caste, or perhaps a foreigner. Because it is considered dangerous for ordinary members of the society to have intercourse with a menstruating woman, being the cause of the menstruation would be even more dangerous. Frequently, a symbolic defloration satisfied the requirements. The Nayar peoples' menarche rites featured a ceremonial "husband" who tied a small gold plate shaped like a fig leaf around the neck of the prepubescent girl and was paid for his services.[16] And in South Africa, parents of a newly menstruating girl in the A-kamba tribe are bound to cohabit, either actually or symbolically (husband jumps over wife). It is believed that this practice is a relic of an older ceremonial defloration of the daughter, with her mother fulfilling her role instead.[17] (This is one of the few instances where a mother takes an active part in her daughter's ceremonies.)

As if the uncontrollable magic of the spirit world were not enough, a newly menstruating girl was, in many societies, considered to be in special danger from snakes. In the Australian myth of the Wawilak women, the stimulus of menstrual blood is so powerful that the "great snake" is impelled to symbolic intercourse with the women of the myth.[18] Another Australian tribe warns a girl against eating anything that lives in salt water, lest she be killed by a snake.[19] And Mohave Indian girls, during the ritual cleansing of the vulva after the first menstruation, are not to let any water enter the vagina so that they are not overcome by a dread disease caused by "supernatural snakes."[20] The common association of snake and penis indicates that the taboos relating to snakes are another expression of primitive belief that the menarche is the result of a magical defloration. Eve herself gained carnal knowledge and lost her innocence to just such a creature.

Fear of women's blood is, again, at the root of these various fantastic notions about the evils of intercourse with menarcheal girls. Much has been written about the psychological impact of a bloody penis; intercourse with a girl who is experiencing her first menstruation confronts a man with the added onus of the unknown and is therefore doubly dangerous. These feelings are probably at the root of the ambivalent reverence for virginity in most societies.

Even when the distinction between menstrual and hymenal blood is realized, their association in the male unconscious continues. Simone de Beauvoir writes in *The Second Sex*:

> According to whether a man feels himself overwhelmed by the encircling forces or proudly believes himself capable of taking control

of them, he declines or demands to have his wife delivered to him a virgin. In the most primitive societies, where women's power is great, it is fear that rules him; it is proper for the woman to be deflorated before the wedding night.[21]

Thus, we find that in societies which consider defloration especially repellent, a surrogate, usually an elder or a midwife, makes the passage for the husband. Although the Catholic church places an extremely high value on virginity and believes that consecrated adult virginity is a superior vocation to marriage, Tertullian, an early church father, writes: "No one is a 'virgin' from the time when she is capable of marriage; seeing that, in her, age has by that time been wedded to its own husband, that is, to time."[22] Tertullian apparently believes, with all primitive peoples in all times, that menarche and deflowering are inextricably linked. The blood itself is the problem, not its fountain of origin.

Symbolically linked with ritual defloration at puberty are all those aspects of the initiation ceremonies that involve pain, mutilation, or modification of the girl's body. Like defloration, bodily modification represents still another attempt by the society to control the dangerous emanations from the menarcheal girl for her own good and for the safety of the society. They are also in many instances designed to prepare the girl for marriage by enhancing her docility, fidelity, or sexual attractiveness.

Common practices among aboriginal peoples of South America are incision, stinging with ants, beatings—all carried out as a form of "purification," to expel those malignant influences brought about by the menarche.[23] In Australia, certain tribes "smoke" the girls like hams, then rub their bodies with opossum fat and ground charcoal.[24] But the Uaupes of Brazil really go to peculiar lengths to ready their daughters for the responsibilities of marriage. At her menarche, a girl is confined to her house for a month, with only a little bread and water for nourishment. When her seclusion is complete, she is brought out naked to be beaten with sticks by her relatives and friends of her parents until she falls senseless or dead. Hutton Webster notes:

> If she recovers, the flagellation is repeated four times, at intervals of six hours, and it is considered an offense to the parents not to strike hard. Finally the sticks are dipped into pots of meat and fat and given to the girl to lick. She is now considered a marriageable woman.[25]

The strongly patriarchal Semitic (Arab) tribes of the Middle East used the menarche as the occasion to remove the girl's clitoris or sew up the lips of the vulva to reduce her sexual pleasure and reinforce her need to be dependent on one man. And then there are the Peruvian Iquito, who perform excision of the clitoris and labia at the ages of nine and ten, respectively,"in the presence of men in full war regalia: feathers, paint, and spears."[26] The Bambara tribes also excise the clitoris "to allow the wanzo, the dangerous sexual principle which comes from the female spirit, to drip out with the blood lost by the operation."[27]

Bruno Bettelheim sees these practices as a sign of men's "aggressive enmity," a hostile expression of their fear of women's blood and sexuality. He distinguishes between clitoridectomy (removal of the clitoris) and infibulation (sewing up the entrance to the vagina), acts generally performed by men, and the manipulation of the female genitals that many societies apparently encourage in their girls. He notes that among the Baganda and the Shaheli of Africa, girls are taught by older women to enlarge their labia even before they reach puberty; in Dahomey, pubescent girls are given instruction in massaging the vagina to cause thickening and muscular development of the lips.[28] Such practices are designed to increase the woman's as well as the man's sexual pleasure.

Tattooing is another form of body modification practiced throughout the world in connection with both male and female rites of puberty. There are reports of societies in Paraguay and Brazil in which a girl at her menarche was gouged on the back, breasts, and stomach with a sharp fish or animal tooth and then ashes rubbed in the wounds for a permanent tattoo.[29] Because the purpose of tattooing is usually sexual attractiveness, it is considered part of a puberty rite. Similarly, ear piercing, a universal custom, has, in India, a sexual function: The hole in the ear is supposed to have a sympathetic effect on opening the womb for easier childbirth.[30] Nor is the length of an adolescent's hair a recently developed symbol of passage. In some primitive cultures, it was the custom to cut a girl's hair at her menarche and continue her seclusion until the hair had grown below her ears.

Not all aboriginal societies inflict such painful reminders of the menarche on their daughters. Contrasted with the cruelty of some South American natives is the beauty of the Navaho ceremony of *Kinaaldá,* the most important of all their religious rites. This menarcheal celebration finds its origin in Navaho mythology; its purpose is to make sex relations holy and effective, and to produce children to carry on the work of the tribe. Features of *Kinaaldá* include seclusion, instruction of the girl in the taboos she must observe as a menstruating woman, and a large tribal celebration when the seclusion and instruction are complete. A girl may undergo

Kinaaldá more than once during the first year she is menstruating.[31] This ceremony continues today, with modifications.

In India, with its thousands of ethnic groups, the menarche is universally a time for rejoicing, even though the customs of the different peoples continue to involve seclusion, taboo, and the prohibition against seeing the sun or touching the ground. High and low castes observe similar rites. Among the Deshast Brahmins, for example, the first menstruation is a time for seclusion; but at the completion of the seclusion, the girl, seated on a little throne, is visited by neighbors and relatives, given presents, and washed in ceremonial oil. Similarly, a Nayar girl of India will be visited by neighbor women at the end of the seclusion and dressed in new garments, usually the womanly sari, instead of the short dresses she wore as a child. Later, the menstruating girl and her friends undergo a ceremonial bath, followed by a great feast, where "drums are beaten and shouts of joy are given."[32] Among the Manus of the South Pacific (who believe that menstruation is caused by intercourse and therefore conceal each menstruation between the menarche and marriage), the ceremonies of the menarche involve large exchanges of food, splash parties in the lagoons, good times among the women, and the exclusion of the men.[33]

Anthropologists continue to question the origins of female initiation rites. The prevailing view is that, like the taboos against the menstruating woman, the rites are devised and perpetrated by men on women; for in no known society have women ever achieved positions of power significant enough to place them in control of these (or any other) vitally important religious ceremonies. Although there have been attempts, as early as the 1870s and as late as the 1970s, to prove that once, in a golden age, women ruled a peaceful world, there is no real evidence that such a society ever existed and, according to a group of feminist anthropologists, "a good deal of evidence to indicate that it did not."[34]

It has also been commonly believed that girls' puberty rites, being a function of the lesser sex, have been designed to imitate and complement the initiation rites for boys, which have intrigued social observers for decades. Unlike girls' rites, which are individual, boys' rites tend to be conducted in groups. This may be attributable to the absence of a single dramatic sign of puberty in the male, or it may be another way of teaching the children what society expects of them. Boys must endure the pains of circumcision and other ordeals in front of their peers; competition to endure the trials more stoically than the other boys thus becomes an important aspect of the ceremony. Girls, meanwhile, are being instructed by their older relatives—and by the very nature of their ceremonies—in the virtues of passivity. In this sense, the rites do complement each other. But it is unlikely that the girls' rites were developed as an afterthought; there is, rather, internal evidence showing that the boys' rites are designed to imitate menstruation (see Chapter 26).

One anthropologist, Judith Brown, made a cross-cultural study in 1961 of menarche rites and their relation to the position of women in a society. She found that girls' puberty rites occurred most frequently in those societies that observed matrilocal residence (the husband moves in with the wife's family). Such rites are more honorific and less painful than many we have described here. Brown finds instead that the painful rites are related to conditions of child rearing that foster a conflict in sex identity:

> Painful female initiation rites are also related to male initiation rites characterized by both a genital operation and seclusion. Since male rites are also strongly related to the presence of a conflict in sex identity, perhaps the latter condition makes it necessary for society to force both sexes to accept their respective roles.[35]

Although her theory has been both attacked and defended by others in her field, Brown seems to be one of the first anthropologists to seek an explanation for girls' puberty rites that does not equate them with the inferior position of women in most societies.

Afterword

Rites of the menarche may be joyous or humiliating, painful or soothing, depending on the cultural bias of the observer and the religious convictions of the participants, but they all share a common thread: an emphasis on the entrance to a sexual life and on the importance of the procreative function to the life and welfare of the society. But even the least culturally condescending among us would have a hard time reacting without shock to a 1985 story by Blaine Harden in the *Washington Post* about the widespread genital mutilation of African women today.[36]

Female circumcision—clitoridectomy and infibulation—which we described earlier as peculiar to a few isolated societies, is actually practiced today on millions of women in twenty countries throughout Africa. Premenarcheal girls, some as young as seven, undergo surgical excision of the clitoris, labia minora, and inner walls of the labia majora and suturing of the sides of the vulva. The operation, which except for the rich or educated is performed without benefit of hospital, anesthesia, or sterile instruments, may bring on shock, infections, urine retention. Throughout their lives the women suffer chronic infection, painful menstruation, complicated childbirth, sexual fear and pain.

Men and women alike accept female circumcision as a way to preserve the purity of unmarried women and to curb the sexual appetites of married ones. In *The Politics of Reproductive Ritual* (1981), Karen Paige and Jeffrey Paige describe infibulation as a father's means of protecting the "marriage value" of his daughter, who, in many of these societies, is likely to be betrothed well before her menarche and married soon after it occurs. Infibulation insures that the intended bridegroom gets the virgin he has bargained—and paid—for.[37] Although many Moslems believe circumcision is a requirement of Islamic law, no doctrinal justification for it exists, and it is not done in Saudi Arabia, the center of Islam. It is practiced by Africans who are Catholics, Protestants, Copts, animists, and nonbelievers and, as an ancient African puberty rite, probably predates all the religions predominant in the area now.

Harden filed his *Washington Post* story from Somalia, in a report on African specialists in female circumcision gathering in Nairobi for the United Nations Women's Decade Conference. For ten preceding years, African women had been writing and speaking out about it, with little effect. Nurse-midwives and other witnesses to the suffering endured by women in childbirth and the damage to their babies frequently caused by infibulation are fighting an uphill battle against centuries of custom, fervent belief in the value of female "purity," and the conviction that circumcision is the only way to maintain it. American and European efforts to force Africans to stop the practice are regarded as yet another attempt at cultural domination and patronization. Even today the Africans opposed to female circumcision wish Westerners would refrain from using the words *cruel* or *barbarous* and focus on it as a health problem. Edna Ismail, a Somali nurse-midwife, herself circumcised, wants non-Africans "to be only as horrified by female circumcision as they are by measles or cholera. We need to deal with this as a medical problem, and as a medical problem, western money can help us to educate people."

Americans are frequently accused of insensitivity to the torture and other "violations of human rights" common to other countries—Western, Eastern and third world—and are not asked by the oppressed in those societies to understand such things as medical problems. While we can empathize with the herculean task faced by those who would eradicate such an ancient and pervasive puberty rite, we cannot refrain from calling female circumcision what it is—torture, mutilation, cruelty, and the most extreme form of fear of female sexuality yet to be uncovered.[38]

Chapter 4

Woman Unclean: Menstrual Taboos in Judaism and Christianity

Codified, organized discrimination against menstruating women in the Jewish and Christian cultures begins in Genesis. God tells Eve he will "multiply thy sorrow and thy conception" (3:16). The Book of the prophet Micah refers more directly to menstrual pain: "Be in pain, and labour to bring forth, O daughter of Zion, like a woman in travail" (4:10). To biblical authors, the process was not only painful but also taboo. In a later chapter of Genesis, Rachel keeps her father's household gods from him by claiming she is menstruating. Sitting on the camel's saddle where she has hidden the stolen images, Rachel tells her father, "Let it not displease my lord that I cannot rise before thee; for the custom of women is upon me." (31:35).

A menstrual rag is used as an image of something loathsome to be discarded; in the Book of the prophet Isaiah, "Ye shall defile also the covering of thy graven images of silver, and the ornament of thy molten images of gold; thou shalt cast them away as a menstruous cloth; thou shalt say unto it, Get thee hence" (30:22).

The words of Leviticus 15:19-33 speak most clearly of the horrors of menstruating women and what they must do to erase the stain:

And if a woman have an issue, and her issue in her flesh be blood, she shall be put apart seven days: and whosoever toucheth her shall be unclean until the even.

And every thing that she lieth upon in her separation shall be unclean: every thing also that she sitteth upon shall be unclean.

And whosoever toucheth her bed shall wash his clothes, and bathe himself in water, and be unclean until the even.

And whosoever toucheth any thing that she sat upon shall wash his clothes, and bathe himself in water, and be unclean until the even.

And if it be on her bed, or on any thing whereon she sitteth, when he toucheth it, he shall be unclean until the even.

And if any man lie with her at all, and her flowers be upon him, he shall be unclean seven days; and all the bed whereon he lieth shall be unclean.

And if a woman have an issue of her blood many days out of the time of her separation, or if it run beyond the time of her separation; all the days of the issue of her uncleanness shall be as the days of her separation: she shall be unclean.

Every bed whereon she lieth all the days of her issue shall be unto her as the bed of her separation: and whatsoever she sitteth upon shall be unclean, as the uncleanness of her separation.

And whosoever toucheth those things shall be unclean, and shall wash his clothes, and bathe himself in water, and be unclean until the even.

But if she be cleansed of her issue, then she shall number to herself seven days, and after that she shall be clean.

And on the eighth day she shall take unto her two turtles or two young pigeons, and bring them unto the priest, to the door of the tabernacle of the congregation.

And the priest shall offer the one for a sin offering, and the other for a burnt offering; and the priest shall make an atonement for her before the Lord for the issue of her uncleanness.

Thus shall ye separate the children of Israel from their uncleanness; that they die not in their uncleanness, when they defile my tabernacle that is among them.

This is the law of him that hath an issue, and of him whose seed goeth from him, and is defiled therewith;

And of her that is sick of her flowers, and of him that hath an issue, of the man, and of the woman, and of him that lieth with her that is unclean.

The position of women in all of the books of the Bible, both Old and New Testaments, depends upon these rules in Leviticus. The fact of menstruation kept women out of the temples and out of the political and economic life of their times. A biblical heroine like Queen Esther could say proudly, "Thou knowest that I abhor the sign of my high estate [her crown] . . . as a menstruous rag" (Esther 14:16).

Obviously, the practices of the ancient Hebrews parallel the taboos and practices of many of the other early societies we have mentioned. The difference is that Judaism has never abolished the taboos; even today, an Orthodox Jewish woman is required to abstain from sex until seven days after her period has ended and after she has immersed herself in the *mikveh,* or ritual bath. There is an interesting defense of this practice in the July 1974 *Ms.,* written by Bracha Sacks, who calls herself both an Orthodox Jew and a feminist: "We do this because God commanded it. One thing is certain though: We are NOT unclean . . . . The woman is not kept out of the synagogue, nor is she forbidden to carry out most of her activities. Only the sexual relationship is forbidden." In speaking of the *mikveh,* she says, "The purpose of the ritual is completely spiritual . . . it hasn't anything to do with physical cleanliness, as we bathe and shower first. If menstrual blood suggests the death of the potential fetus, the *Mikveh* waters suggest a life-giving element."[1]

Christianity did little to improve the status of women, although Jesus himself was said to be far more enlightened than his successors. In an episode related in John 4:1-42, Jesus is traveling through Samaria on his way to Galilee and asks a woman drawing water at a well to let him drink from her vessel: "Then saith the woman of Samaria unto him, How is it that thou, being a Jew, askest drink of me, which am a woman of Samaria?" (4:9). Jesus then instructs her in the "living water" he will offer and convinces her that he is the Messiah.

Customarily interpreted in the light of political hostilities between the Jews and the Samaritans, this story takes on a new meaning when one is aware of the Rabbinic regulation that, from the viewpoint of Leviticus, the Samaritan women are, from birth, considered as unclean as menstruating women. Thus, Jesus, in asking to share the same drinking cup with this woman who was both religiously and politically anathema to his people, was flagrantly violating the laws of his nation. The surprise of the apostles and the woman's friends attests to the bizarre nature of his actions. A contemporary writer about women and Catholicism uses this incident to show that Jesus "repudiates centuries of thought and legislation which would define woman in her *specific mature womanliness* [italics ours] as unclean and unfit for direct association not only with the divine, but even periodically with the human."[2]

Jesus' best-known encounter with the menstrual taboo is the miracle he performed on the woman with the "issue of blood." This poor soul had been bleeding from the genitals for twelve years. Aware that she was thus ritually unclean, she dared not approach Jesus directly but came up behind him and touched the hem of his robe. Immediately, she was cured, Jesus saying to her, "Thy faith hath made thee whole" (Matthew 9:20-22, Mark 5:25-34, Luke 5:43-45). Here, as at the well, Jesus was using the most elementary and important aspect of the purification laws to demonstrate the new spiritual purification he preached.[3]

But those who made Christianity a worldwide religion listened less to Jesus than to the urgings of their own cultural predilections. Instances of the continuing viability of the laws in Leviticus spot the history of Christianity from the earliest centuries to the present. Even a 1953 edition of *The Interpreter's Bible* takes note of the relative invalidity of the purification laws in the modern world with the comment that "a sense of *natural disgust or shame* [italics ours] has been developed into an ethical and religious feeling of uncleanness."[4]

Of special concern to the church fathers of the first millennium was the question: Should a menstruating woman enter a church or receive communion? In an incident related in the Venerable Bede's *History of the English Church and People,* Augustine, bishop of Canterbury, sent a series of doctrinal questions to Pope Gregory I. Among them were the following: May a woman properly enter church at certain periods? And may she receive communion at these times? Gregory's reply was yes: "The monthly courses of women are not their fault because nature causes them."[5]

By 1963, however, a shade of remonstrance colored the reply. *The Handbook of Moral Theology,* intended for men in Ireland studying for the priesthood, has this to add to the echoes of Leviticus: "Involuntary pollution and the menstrual period do not render the body so unclean as to prevent the receiving of Holy Communion when there exists a right reason for approaching the sacrament."[6] And in 1970, the Levitical injunctions were among the arguments used to justify an American Roman Catholic prohibition against women serving in the sanctuary as lectors and commentators during Mass.[7]

Not even the Mother of God was spared. Popular tradition recalls that when Mary reached puberty, "There was held a council of the priests, saying, 'Behold, Mary has reached the age of twelve years in the temple of the Lord. What shall we do with her, lest perchance she defile the sanctuary of the Lord?' "[8] The reference is to the expected appearance of the menses in Mary and the sacrilegious possibility that she might be present in the temple, where she had been raised and educated since birth, when the menarche occurred. The answer was to betroth her to Joseph and get her out of the holy place. This interesting bit of fancy put Mary in the same position as the scores of girls whose societies believed the menarche to be a defloration by aerial spirits or who were ritually deflowered by human agents at that time. The immediate birth of Jesus suggests another primitive belief, that the firstborn of a young woman was the strongest of all children because it was formed from menstrual blood at its most powerful—right after the menarche.

So, throughout its formative years, during the development of the great intellectual and doctrinal systems, Christianity clung to the Old Testament belief in the uncleanness of woman and the basically imperfect nature that was a consequence of the menstrual flow. Menstruation was even involved in one of the many heresies that plagued the early church, this one perpetrated by one Bishop Valentinus. In an elaborate scheme involving numerology as well as ancient Middle Eastern religions, the "woman with issue" of the Gospels was seen as a precursor of a spirit named Sophia (wisdom), who attempted a direct relationship with the source of all knowledge, sidestepping the wisdom of her brother spirits. Sophia failed in her quest, however, and brought forth an amorphous substance "such as her female nature enabled her to produce." When she saw it, it is reported, her reaction was "one of grief, on account of the imperfection of its generation."[9] Sophia's emanation (menstrual blood) is an example of the Aristotelian belief that menstrual blood was the *matter* of creation, to which the sperm gave *form*. As a menstruating woman, Sophia could not hope to produce knowledge because knowledge was formal and hence masculine. Aristotle's theories of the matter and form of creation kept a tenacious hold on Christian doctrine for centuries thanks to Thomas Aquinas and his codification of the Aristotelian tenets. He described woman as a "misbegotten male":

> As regards the individual nature, woman is defective and misbegotten for the active power in the male seed tends to the production of a perfect likeness according to the masculine sex; while the production of woman comes from defect in the active power or from some material indisposition, or even from external influence, such as that of a south wind, which is moist.[10]

The inferiority of women is once again explained as being a result of her menstrual flow, believed to be the passive, "moist," therefore imperfect agent in procreation.

Christianity played a large part in the perpetration of yet another crime against women: the witch-hunts of medieval Europe and colonial America. During the terror known as the Inquisition, the vast majority of the hundreds of thousands of persons put to death for "heresy" were women, women who were accused of being witches on the same evidence that men since the dawn of human life had been using to taboo and isolate the menstruating woman.

Pliny's list of the disastrous effects of menstruating women on men, cows, gardens, bees, milk, wine could be a catalog of the evil effects of witchcraft as it was understood by church and state in Europe. The infamous *Malleus maleficarum* ("hammer of witches") comes down to us today as the handbook of witch-hunting and provides a documented link between the church's attitudes toward women's bodies and their persecution of the witches. The *Malleus* urged Inquisitors to look to a woman when witchcraft was suspected in a neighborhood "because she is more carnal than man as is clear from her many carnal abominations."[11] For "carnal abominations," read "menstrual blood." The *Malleus* itself was inspired by the famous 1455 Bull of Pope Innocent VIII, which, in its list of the horrors of witches, reads like Pliny on the evils of menstruating women:

> [Witches] have slain infants yet in the mother's womb, as also the offspring of cattle, have blasted the produce of the earth, the grapes of the vine, the fruits of trees, nay men and women, beasts of burden, herd-beasts, as well as animals of other kinds, vineyards, orchards, meadows, pastureland, corn, wheat and all other cereals; these wretches furthermore afflict and torment men and women, beasts of burden, herd-beasts, as well as animals of other kinds, with terrible and piteous pains and sore diseases, both internal and external; they hinder men from performing the sexual act and women from conceiving, whence husbands cannot know their wives nor wives receive their husbands.[12]

In many respects, organized religion is still in the Middle Ages when it comes to women. But there are indications that at least some of the faithful are exploring the old taboos in a new and exciting way.

In his 1973 play *The Prodigal Daughter,* set in a Catholic rectory in England and centering on the young housekeeper who is repenting an abortion, David Turner introduces the concept of an androgynous Jesus. The youngest of three priests in the rectory is disturbed by the church's indifference to the plight of women such as the heroine and an unseen old nun who is dying of cancer of the womb, cursing God. The young priest cries out in anguish that Christ must have been a woman. God incarnate could not have denied to itself the full experience of humanity; it could not have refused to partake in woman's nature, "in her gestations, her menstruations, her orgasms." Twenty centuries of Christianity have only now brought us to this concept. For if God menstruates, then menstruation becomes godly. If menstruation is godly, then woman has at least a chance of becoming godly herself.[13]

Afterword

In 1984 we met another dead nun, in another play about faith, miracles, and women, written by a man. John Pielmeier's *Agnes of God* probes the mysteries of faith and the possibility of miracles through a metaphor of blood, as does the 1986 film.

The play is about Sister Agnes, a young nun who has apparently "miraculously" conceived, given birth to, and murdered a baby within convent walls, and the struggle of her mother superior to preserve Agnes's otherworldliness from the probings of the court-appointed psychiatrist who aims to ferret out the "truth" (for Agnes denies it all happened). The unfolding of the plot—the unlayering of Agnes's soul—is punctuated at critical moments by blood: blood of the stigmata, blood of intercourse, blood of childbirth, and most importantly the blood of menstruation, its absence and miraculous reappearance.

On the night the conception was supposed to have taken place, Agnes burned bloody sheets. When Mother Miriam Ruth admonishes her about the "naturalness" of menstruation, Agnes blurts out that "it wasn't my time of the month." But if no man could have been in the convent that night, what kind of blood was it, hymenal or menstrual?

At the play's climactic moment, when Agnes, under hypnosis, reenacts the birth of the baby, there is much talk of blood, bloody sheets, too much blood to conceal from the other nuns. When Agnes comes out of the hypnosis, she begins to bleed from her hands—a shocking sight on the stark gray stage—as if the stigmata of Christ's wounds were appearing on her body, even as she has symbolically given up the child she claims (and no one can disprove) was fathered by God.

Throughout the play a counterpoint to the blood of Agnes is the *absence* of the blood of Martha, the middle-aged, ex-Catholic psychiatrist, scorner of miracles and faith, who symbolizes the rationality of psychiatric/scientific thought. In their first conversation Martha tells Agnes that she, Martha, will never have children because she has stopped menstruating. Further into the play, as Martha is becoming more sympathetic to the mystery of Agnes and unwittingly growing more open to the possibility of the miraculous conception, she mentions in an aside to the audience that she has begun to menstruate again. By the end of the play she is menstruating regularly, has been to confession, and returned to the church. But Agnes, found by the courts to be insane, has been sent to a mental hospital where she has stopped singing (her special form of prayer), stopped eating, and died.

So Agnes lost her faith and her life, while Martha regained her faith and the blood that signals her potential to create life. Throughout the play Martha's menstrual blood is trying to appear, along with her lost-but-not-forgotten faith, while at the same time Agnes's various bleedings signify the dying of the faith that keeps her alive.

Rarely has menstrual blood been used in so powerful a way in fiction, poetry, or drama. By symbolically uniting it with the most fragile of all gifts—faith—the author posits a feminine presence or principle in all people who struggle to understand God (as the author of *The Prodigal Daughter* says that God must be able to menstruate in order to partake of humanity). The playwright also shows the growth of godliness in a woman who, as a psychiatrist, was accustomed to *playing* God, as a return of her most "feminine" quality—the one which has been forever used to deny the godliness of women in the Judeo-Christian tradition.

Chapter 5

Menstruation and Medical Myth

When we move from myth to medicine, we see that even the scientific explanations for menstruation have been colored by the same fear and wonder of the most primitive peoples on earth. By the late nineteenth century—when political and social revolutions had irrevocably altered the course of world affairs and *The Origin of the Species* had successfully and finally challenged man's solipsistic view of his universal worth—menstruation was still a mystery to men.

We can hardly be surprised that menstruation remained a medical mystery for so long. Those studying it—men—didn't menstruate, and as these men of science pursued their objective explorations into the female reproductive system, few (if any) thought to ask a woman for basic facts and figures about the monthly cycle. The weird theories put forth in the advancement of menstrual knowledge reveal at least as much about the men as they do about the menses.

Aristotle was one of the earliest to tackle the problem: he saw menstruation as a sign of female inferiority, related to the passive part he felt women played in reproduction. Aristotle's *On the Generation of Animals* was enormously influential and became the standard treatise on embryology from the fourth century B.C. until William Harvey's work on embryology in the seventeenth century A.D.

In *On the Generation of Animals*, Aristotle explains the contribution of male and female to the production of a child: "The female always provides the material, the male provides that which fashions the material into shape; this, in our view, is the specific characteristic of each of the sexes: that is what it means to be male or to be female."[1] The male, then, is the active partner; the female is passive.

Aristotle adds that "the physical part, the body comes from the female, and the Soul comes from the male, since the Soul is the essence of a particular body" (2. 4. 185). Again, the male performs the more valued part. Lest one see the sexes as complementary in creating a child, Aristotle makes it clear that they are not: "We should look upon the female state as being as it were a deformity, though one which occurs in the ordinary course of nature" (4. 6. 461). (This is the source of the sexual theology of Thomas Aquinas discussed in Chapter 4.)

The outward sign of female inferiority is menstruation. The female is deficient, says Aristotle, in performing the task of "concoction." (The Greek word for concoction, *pepsis*, is the same word used for ripening or maturing fruit or corn with heat.) Because the female does not have enough natural vital heat, her concocting achievement proceeds only as far as menstrual blood. This forms the embryo's "Nutritive Soul." The male, however, can transform matter with heat and produce semen, the end product of concoction. The colder female, in other words, is a case of arrested development. She cannot go beyond menstrual blood to produce semen.

Hence, says Aristotle, a residue of useless nourishment gathers in her blood vessels (in fact, menstrual bleeding is from the capillaries in the uterine lining, not from major blood vessels). When the blood vessels are full, an overflow is necessary; this overflow is menstruation (4. 5. 451).

Later writers did not question Aristotle's beliefs. Menstrual blood was the passive female matter; semen was the outward sign of the active male principle. The Roman historian Pliny, for instance, concluded in the first century A.D. that women who do not menstruate "are incapable of bearing children because it is of this substance that the infant is formed. The seed of the male, acting as a sort of leaven, causes it to unite and assume a form, and in due time it acquires life and assumes a bodily shape."[2]

Seventeen hundred years later, the French naturalist Georges de Buffon agreed with Aristotle on the supremacy of the male role: "The male semen is the sculptor, the menstrual blood is the block of marble, and the fetus is the figure which is fashioned out of the combination."[3]

Aristotle's theory had stated, in effect, that the menses is a substance intended to nourish the fetus. Because believers in this nutritive theory were ignorant of or uncertain about the ovum's existence (until the nineteenth century), they assumed that the nutritive substance was the only female contribution to reproduction.

Another popular theory suggests that women have an overabundance, that they have more of something than men do, not less. But the standard of health is still a male one from which women may deviate in either direction.

According to this theory, women have a unique need for "evacuation." This need is explained in several different ways. Pythagoras (sixth century B.C.) saw the menses as eliminating extra blood. According to Empedocles, a century later, this need for evacuation stemmed from the different densities of flesh; the male flesh, denser, has no need for evacuation. Parmenides, also in the fifth century B.C., stated (in opposition to Aristotle) that woman is "hotter" than man and therefore contains more blood, of which she eliminates a part each month. Through the course of her life, she becomes progressively "colder" until she reaches menopause.[4]

Galen (second century A.D.) saw in menstruation an evacuation of the fluids or juices women accumulated in an idle life: "I imagine that the female sex, inasmuch as they heap up a great quantity of humours, by living continually at home, and not being used to hard labour, or exposed to the sun, should receive a discharge of this fullness, as a remedy given by nature."[5] Even today, there are those who, like Galen, seem to believe that woman's work, housework, is not hard work.

Soranus, in the same era as Galen, mentions the popular belief that the menses get rid of surplus matter in women in the same way that men eliminate it in athletics.[6] That belief, unlike the others, sees the sexes as complementary; the female is not a deviation from the norm. But for the most part, a certain denigration of women is suggested in both the nutritive theory and the plethora theory.

Avicenna, the eleventh-century Arab physician, agreed that menstruation was caused by an overabundance of blood in women, but he added his impression of the female body. According to Avicenna, menstrual blood is eliminated through the womb because that organ is the weakest and the last formed.[7]

In the seventeenth century, Regnier de Graaf (after whom the ovarian follicle is named) agreed that the uterus is the weak point of the female and hence the outlet for the menses. He also added an analogy to Avicenna's formulation: "The menstrual blood escapes by the feeblest parts of the body, in the same way that wine or beer undergoing fermentation escapes by defective parts of the barrel."[8] This, then, was the concept of menses as ferment (or womb as defective barrel).

John Freind (eighteenth century) attempted to reconcile plethora and ferment. According to Freind, women are more moist and have more blood than men, and this is a reason for their attaining full growth sooner. If a man did have a plethora of blood, Freind says that it would escape, through hemorrhoids or bloody urine. If this discharge were kept inside, however, a "distemper" would ensue, the man might become "hysteric," and he might die.[9]

Freind argued in part against de Graaf's theory of ferment or "vehement effervescence" because the theory did not explain where the ferment was hidden, only its means of escape. Instead, Freind attempted to prove that the plethora exists in women. With mathematical similes, diagrams, and analogies from physics, Freind explained the belief for this plethora through the periodic discharge of blood. He also insisted that the length of menstrual cycles is a multiple of seven: usually fourteen, twenty-one, or twenty-eight days. Freind's work is admirable for its symmetry, but it makes little sense.

The idea that the amount of blood circulates rather freely, yet escapes where it might most easily do so (the womb as weak point) also becomes a part of "Stephenson wave" explanation for menstruation. Dr. William Stephenson, who described his wave theory in the *American Journal of Obstetrics* in 1882, felt that menstruation is associated with a "wave of vital energy" shown in the body temperature, the daily amount of urine, and the pulse rate. This wave is varied but works in cycles, menstruation coinciding with the average body temperature. When the excessive nutritive material and vital energy are not used in reproduction, they are used in menstruation.[10]

The Stephenson wave theory also explains vicarious menstruation. If there is an obstruction, the wave is thrown to whatever point of the system is weakest. Hence, says G. Stanley Hall after citing Stephenson in his own *Adolescence* (1908), every trouble in woman demands special attention to the pelvis.[11] Hall, like many of his predecessors, seems to adopt the ancient definition of woman: *Tota mulier in utero* ("Woman is a womb").

Most menstrual theorists did glimpse a portion of the truth. The lining of the womb becomes menstrual fluid unless it is needed for an embryo's nutrition, so the nutritive theory is partially vindicated. There is a sort of plethora when conception does not occur, in that the lining is no longer needed. The womb is the convenient place for the escape of this fluid.

But nearly all menstrual theorists also imposed their own order upon their material observations, and their ordering was shaped by patriarchal preconceptions. They reasoned that menstruation was a sign of woman's otherness, hence a sign of her inferiority; their next step was to rationalize this inferiority through whatever science was at their disposal. And that kind of rationalization is hardly dead in our own era.

From the inferiority of all women, the early theorists moved easily to the idea that the age at which a woman first menstruates may be a sign of the inferiority of her ethnic group or an indication that she has been leading a wicked life. The fact is, the age at menarche (first menstruation) depends greatly on good food and good health. Those who eat well mature earlier. Today, the average American girl first menstruates when she is 12½ years old. Figures from Norway, where the oldest such records are kept, show that in 1850 the average girl had her first period at 17; by 1959, at 13½.[12] For each generation since 1850, then, a girl's period has come about a year earlier than her mother's.

The association of the lowering menarcheal date with modern nutritional advances is today a popularly acknowledged "fact." But this statistic, too, may be questionable. Nineteenth-century women, laboring under the old equation—menarche equals first intercourse equals fallen woman—may have given a later date for their menarche out of modesty or embarrassment.

The earliest researchers gave only impressionistic testimony about age at menarche. Soranus claimed that menstruation first appears in the fourteenth year.[13] The great medieval scientist Albertus Magnus, in the thirteenth century, said that 14 was the most frequent age at menarche.[14] However, the Virgin Mary, according to medieval tradition, was 14 when she conceived. Because the ancient and medieval minds did not always distinguish myth from what we call scientific fact, Albertus's sources of information could be theology rather than observation.

By 1869, the empirical method of data gathering was more generally used, and an enterprising scientist named Wieger classified the age of young women at menarche according to country. In Lapland, for instance, girls bled first at 18; in Germany, at 15 years, 7 months, and 6 days; in Egypt, at 10.[15] Wieger's figures are suspect because he probably depended on the memories of the women he interviewed, but the vast body of such studies, by Wieger and others, reveal a number of cultural prejudices disguised as scientific fact.

Climate was one obsession of the researchers. Although the later and more reliable studies indicate no correlation, scientists as early as 1704 wanted to believe that the hot-blooded wenches near the equator bled first. Richard Mead, one of George II's physicians, wrote in that year that "everyone knows how great a share the moon has in forwarding those evacuations of the weaker sex" and that near the equator the lunar pull toward menses would be the greatest.[16]

Over a century later, August Bebel agreed with the earlier age for tropical women, claiming that warm climates stimulate the sexual drive but that the unfortunate Eskimo girls do not menstruate until age 19.[17] The nineteenth-century American physician Pye Henry Chavasse added that in warm climates, "such as in Abyssinia and India," girls menstruate at 10 or 11 but that in Russia menarche does not occur until 20 to 30 years of age, and even then only three to four times a year.[18] And Eskimos, according to the nineteenth-century doctor George MacDiarmid, menstruate only during the summer months.[19]

Such generalizations seem based less on observations (which often invalidate them) than on cultural assumptions about the relationship of climate and sex, with the menarche, even in scientific terms, a continuing symbol of sexuality. One cultural assumption is an old Anglo-Saxon one: that the darker races are more sensual than the fair. The slave traders, entertaining the prejudices of their own societies, assumed that Africans were more sexually inclined because the latter (sensibly) wore fewer clothes than Europeans. In the European and American minds, the torrid regions were expected to produce early sexual maturity. As late as 1920, it was common belief that early sexual experience and/or early marriage (i.e., an early stimulation of the genitals) would cause an earlier menarche. Studying women of India who married very young, another researcher found the belief was totally false.[20]

Similarly, a 1951 American textbook by K. C. Garrison, *Psychology of Adolescence,* asserts without proof that "colored children in America mature earlier than white children of the same age."[21] C. L. Henton tested this hypothesis and found no significant difference between black and white girls. Again, Garrison's text may have reflected a common cultural preconception: that blacks have more and earlier sexual activity than whites and hence must menstruate earlier.

It is not only with the darker races that the menarche and sexual morality are linked. A similar association about white American girls appears in nineteenth-century texts. Dr. Carpenter, in his *Physiology,* observed that "girls brought up in the midst of luxury or sensual indulgence undergo this change earlier than those reared in poverty and self-denial."[22] The *New Warren's Household Physician* insists that the menarche is "hastened by high living; by the whirl and bustle and excitement of city life; by reading novels which are full of love incidents; by attending balls, theatres, and parties; and by mingling much in the society of gentlemen."[23]

To such writers, the menarche appears to be both a literal and a figurative stain, a sign of a badly ordered existence.

Whether the age at menarche does, indeed, involve either moral turpitude or moral grace is doubtful. Nor does maturity correlate with hair color. One study asserts that blondes menstruate about a year earlier than brunettes. Another argues that redheads are first and have a peculiar smell; still another gives the nod to brunettes.[24]

Weber, who studied Russian women in the nineteenth century, argued for a relationship between profession and periods. He claimed that teachers, singers, actresses, and other women who showed an inclination for the professions menstruated exceptionally early; but again, he is ascribing to women who worked, no doubt because they had to, an attribute commonly linked with immoral behavior.[25]

Menstruation before age 9 is *precocious puberty*. Extremely early menarche may be caused by tumors or other abnormalities, such as dwarfism or rickets. Most literature on the subject has more the aura of folklore than of medical report. Cases of menstruation at age 7 days, 6 weeks, and 2, 3, and 7 months are among the earliest recorded.[26]

The first precocious case reported by name is Anna Mummenthaler, a patient of G. E. Von Haller (Bern, 1751). She had her menarche at 2, gave birth to a full-term child at 9, reached menopause at 52, and died at 75.[27] Menstruating for nearly fifty years may in itself be a record.

Rather less fortunate was her contemporary Eva Christine Fischer of Eisenach.[28] Born in 1750, she was as developed as a woman of 20 by 1753. She was "exhibited" in the Easter Fair at Leipzig, it is reported, and died not long afterward, in May 1753. Perhaps as a reward for her pains, she is depicted in the Leipzig anatomical school.

In the nineteenth century, *pubertias praecox* took on moral overtones. *Lancet,* the British medical journal, reported a mother under 11 years old, the youngest example the writer was aware of. The writer hoped the age would not be surpassed, "for it manifests a depraved precocity which is truly lamentable in a Christian country."[29] Although a male was surely involved, the girl's early maturity seems to be all that is considered depraved.

In the present century, precocious puberty is more likely to be probed than exhibited or condemned. In Peru, in 1939, Lina Medina, 5½ years old, gave birth to a normal healthy boy. The girl had menstruated from the age of 8 months. Lina was regarded neither as a fallen woman nor as a sideshow candidate, but as a rather unfortunate little girl whose menarche was extremely early.[30]

The age of menarche has long fascinated medical researchers, nearly all of whom were male. The fascination may be with what makes a woman different from a man, but it may also be read as an attempt to control that difference by analyzing and defining it.

Afterword

Age at menarche, a subject which intrigued so many nine-teenth-century scientists, is now generally explained as a matter of nutrition and not, as some moralists thought, as punishment for promiscuity. Sharon Golub puts a number of such menstrual myths to rest in her essay "Menarche: The Beginning of Menstrual Life." The old belief that women living in the tropics menstruate early is not verifiable. Their periods come later than myth would have it, claims Golub, and they have more to do with diet than with climate. Women who exercise and are involved in high-energy activities "have a later age at menarche and a high incidence of amenorrhea," says Golub (see our discussion of menstruation and sports in Chapter 6).

Golub cites two apparent factors affecting menarcheal age: skeletal growth and the accumulation of fat, with strong influences from the hypothalamus and the follicle-stimulating hormone (FSH) (see Chapter 7). In addition Golub states that the first menstruation is most likely to occur in "late fall or early winter," thus dispelling the myth prevalent in popular fiction and in advertising: it happens in summer and the girl is wearing white.[31]

One scientific theory publicized at the time *The Curse* went to press involves the belief that women sharing the same living quarters will eventually get their periods at the same time of month. This phenomenon, called synchronous menstruation, has actually been around for centuries, as women observed these changes in their cycles and the folklore spread. In the early 1970s psychologist Martha McClintock observed identical menstrual patterns among 135 women and suggested that the menstrual synchronization had to do with chemical substances named pheromones.[32]

The idea of menstrual synchrony is an appealing one, particularly since it expresses the (repressed) desire for shared menstrual experience among women. We have always tended to be skeptical that synchronous menstruation had a scientific basis, if only from our own observations: sometimes we have been in groups that bled together and sometimes not (Mary Jane is the mother of identical twins whose menarches occurred almost eleven months apart and who, despite their living together for five menstrual years, have not had identical or even similar patterns).

But in December 1986 scientists announced the first apparent evidence that pheromones can affect the menstrual cycle, isolating the pheromones themselves in the armpit sweat of men and women. Researchers George Preti and Winnifred Cutler of the Monnell Chemical Senses Center in Philadelphia demonstrated that an alcohol solution containing essence of a woman's sweat extracted during her menstrual cycle, rubbed under the noses of ten women several times a week, caused their periods to synchronize after several cycles. Ten women treated with simple alcohol solution showed no such effect. Another experiment revealed that women treated in the same way with essence of male sweat tended to have more regular periods, leading the researchers and other observers to conclude that the presence of a man is important for a woman's reproductive health. Women who had intercourse with a man at least once a week also tended to have more regular and trouble-free periods.[33]

"The effect of a sweaty male would hardly surprise a monkey or a rodent," says Stephen Budiansky, reporting on the research in *U.S. News and World Report*. His comment refers, of course, to the sexual aromas given off by males of many species that are necessary for female arousal and mating. What is new in Cutler's research is the discovery that females also emit pheromones, thus the long-awaited "proof" of a physiological basis to menstrual synchrony. Zoologist John Vandenbergh of North Carolina State University suggests that menstrual synchrony could have led to synchronized births, an advantage for our prehistoric ancestors in coping with a hostile environment.[34]

Thus a long-standing medical myth becomes medical fact, at least until the next medical facts emerge to disprove it.

Chapter 6

Modern Menstrual
Politics

It was the last day of the long Senate debate over Joint
Resolution 208, otherwise known as the Equal Rights Amendment. The
leader of the opposition, the self-proclaimed protector of women from
the implications of their equality, took the floor to offer still another set
of amendments designed to weaken ERA. As was his custom, Senator
Sam Ervin, later to be a hero of Watergate but now little more than an
anachronism to the hundreds of women who lined the galleries, cited
what he considered to be the ultimate authority for his argument:

> We find in Chapter 1, Verse 27 of the book of Genesis this statement
> which all of us know to be true: "God created man in his own image.
> In the image of God created He him. Male and female, created He
> them . . . ." When He created them, God made physiological and
> functional differences between men and women. These differences
> confer upon men a greater capacity to perform arduous and hazardous
> physical tasks.[1]

Even on March 22, 1972, forty-nine years after the amendment had
first been proposed to Congress, one of the most respected U.S. senators
was linking the Bible with the old question of equal rights for women.
The final vote that day, approving the resolution 84 to 8, reflected the
legislators' ability to divorce religion from reality in matters of state. But
Senator Ervin's use of the Bible (as well as a staggering number of articles
in scholarly and legal journals) to prove women do not deserve to have
equal protection and responsibilities under law is a perfect illustration of
the power of one religious tradition to keep the "physiological and func-

tional" differences between men and women in the forefront of all debate
about women's intellectual and professional freedom.

Since the advent of modern science, the fears and prejudices surrounding menstruation have given way to an acceptance of it as a normal
bodily process—at least in print. But the habits of centuries are not easily
unlearned by men, who depend on woman's manifest physical differences
to give a rationale for their belief in her emotional, economic, and social
otherness. That is why the system we call *menstrual politics* has by no
means disappeared with the twentieth century and the "emancipation" of
women from their biologically determined roles.

For the sake of argument, in reviewing the last hundred years or so,
we are going to leave in the background the multiple movements in U.S.
history that produced the drive for full female equality and concentrate
instead on the one constant fact about women: their menstruation. The
resulting picture puts in sharp focus how far we've come—and how far
we have yet to go.

Practitioners of menstrual politics have one basic tenet in common:
They are convinced that women are naturally and irrevocably limited by
the menstrual function. Since the early nineteenth century, menstrual politics has taken two positions with regard to menstruation and economic
life: first, that *factories and businesses pose a fatal threat to women's
reproductive life;* second, that *the menstrual cycle threatens the health of
American capitalism.* The progression of ideas has been from the first to
the second; as medicine began paying more attention to the facts of the
menstrual cycle and medical excuses for the exclusion of women waned,
the idea that menstruation was bad for business gained in popularity, and
that is where we are now. In this second wave of the American woman's
movement, at a moment in history when man has so mastered his universe
that he is beginning to redefine even life and death, women are still hearing
from people like Edgar Berman, a physician and Democratic party func-
tionary, who announced in 1970 that he would not like to see a woman
in charge of this country at a time of national crisis because her "raging
hormonal imbalances" would threaten the life and safety of all.

But the first phase of American menstrual politics was no less insidious
for all its creaky chivalry. On the one hand, it was instrumental in getting
some legislative relief for the thousands of women employed in the sweatshops and "dark satanic mills" of the nineteenth century. On the other,
the bodily weakness attributed to the menstrual function became a favored
argument for restricting the participation of women in higher education
and national affairs. A continuing monument to the politics of menstrual

exclusion in this country is the body of "protective" legislation that restricts women's working hours, women's duties, and ultimately, women's pay and prestige.

Women had been working in the factories and mills since the industrial revolution. England and New England alike exploited young women and children, working them as much as sixteen hours a day for as little as a dollar a week. Only very gradually did women organize in the nineteenth and twentieth centuries to change these conditions. The fledgling labor movement, then as now, was more concerned with stabilizing conditions for men. Few women had power in the American Federation of Labor; perhaps their Victorian sense of obligation to their paternalistic employers prevented them from getting any real power on their own.[2]

Meanwhile, some states, alarmed at the appalling working conditions endured by *both* sexes, had tried to legislate humane practices. One such law, a New York statute setting maximum hours of work for bakery employees, had been declared unconstitutional by the U.S. Supreme Court in 1905 (*Lochner v. New York* 198 U.S. 45). But in 1908, the Court sent down a decision whose implications would have a significant effect on the ratification of the ERA. It upheld the constitutionality of an Oregon law that restricted the employment of women in any mechanical establishment, or factory, or laundry to ten hours a day. What the Court believed set this law apart from the New York statute was the question of sex:

> That woman's physical structure and the performance of material functions place her at a disadvantage in the struggle for subsistence is obvious. This is especially true when the burdens of motherhood are upon her. *Even when they are not, by abundant testimony of the medical fraternity continuance for a long time on her feet at work, repeating this from day to day, tends to have injurious effects upon the body,* and as healthy mothers are essential to vigorous offspring, the physical well-being of women becomes an object of public interest and care in order to preserve the strength and vigor of the race. (*Muller v. Oregon* 202 U.S. 412 [1908], italics ours)

Regarded as a stunning victory for women in 1908, and progenitor of many state protective laws, *Muller v. Oregon* was still being cited in the U.S. Senate in 1972 as an argument for the defeat of ERA. It made no distinction between pregnant and nonpregnant women and classified all women as mothers or potential mothers. The state's interest in the bodies of all women was established—for the good of the preservation of the race.

Labor-union women and others who fought for the protective laws were principally interested in gaining a minimum standard of working conditions. They believed that minimum standards for women would be merely a first step toward humane conditions for all. But because the Court made its decision on the basis of "woman's physical structure" and the "strength and vigor of the race," the laws that followed the 1908 decision tended to restrict women more than help them; whereas men's hours—and salaries—remained limitless. Laws after *Muller* restricted the number of pounds a woman might lift, the kind of place she might work in, the number of rest breaks she must take during the day.

The debate in the courts was accompanied by strident debate among doctors over the effects on menstruation of living an active life. One controversy threatened to undo the progress of higher education for women, which had also been gaining momentum early in the nineteenth century. In 1874, a small book by one Edward F. Clarke, M.D., proposed that educating women would mean the end of the human race. Titled *Sex in Education*, its thesis was that American girls were generally feebler than their European sisters because of the deplorable trend toward higher education for women. The college years, Clarke believed, followed too soon on the menarche, when the debilitating effects of the newly flowing menstrual blood made the body susceptible to disease and outside influence. Studying forced the brain to use up the blood and energy needed to get the menstrual process functioning efficiently. Allowing young women to continue their studies would thus result in the weakening of women and consequently the weakening of generations of Americans as yet unborn. For of course, woman, to Clarke, was defined by her uterus, as she was to the 1908 Supreme Court: "Let the fact be accepted that there is nothing to be ashamed of in a woman's organization, and let her whole education and life be guided by the divine requirements of her system."[3]

The uproar caused by Clarke's book is a measure of the extent to which thinking people were in favor of the education of women and were willing to answer Clarke in his own language. Several rebuttals were published, among them *Sex and Education*, a collection of essays by distinguished educators and public figures, edited by Julia Ward Howe (author of "The Battle Hymn of the Republic"). Most significant in this volume was the testimony from colleges admitting women, Vassar, Antioch, Michigan, Oberlin among them. Alida C. Avery, Vassar's resident physician, assured Dr. Clarke that students were forbidden to attend gym classes during the first two days of their periods and were denied physical education if they suffered from dysmenorrhea (painful menstruation). But the reports from these institutions all supported the thesis that education and discipline and regular exercise improve menstrual health and general vigor, thus contributing to a healthier and more intelligent population of mothers.[4]

While declaring the halls of ivy off limits to any female person, Clarke had not shown similar concern for the mills, factories, and sweatshops that were the college of thousands of unfortunate young women. Clarke had, in fact, declared that factory work was not so damaging to young girls as studying, for bodily strain did not tax the fragile new menstrual process the way mental exertion did. But in 1875, Dr. Azel Ames, in *Sex in Industry,* spoke of the evil results of "co-ordinated mental and physical activity on the menstrual function."[5] He called for laws that would prevent the exploitation of cheap female labor. Nonetheless, the message of both men was the same: If you let women out of the home and into the man's world, their reproductive lives would be so damaged that the future of the human race would be irrevocably jeopardized.

And so the arguments went. The major theme seemed to be that emancipation of women would mean the destruction of their menstrual cycles and thus the end of the human race, for woman exists to bear children. Even the real need for labor reform could not mask the determination to keep woman "in her place" and to provide a physical basis for doing so, so that competence, skill, strength, or intelligence could have no bearing on her advancement.

The turning point seems to have come around the time women gained the vote; large percentages of the female population were gaining advanced degrees, entering the professions, and in general reaping the benefits of the "century of struggle" for legal and political equality. An enormously liberating factor in these advances was the mass marketing of disposable sanitary napkins after World War I. Before Kotex came on the market in 1921, women had been wearing garments similar to babies' diapers, which they washed and reused. Imagine the effect this cumbersome and unhygienic garment must have had on the average woman's workday outside the home, whether in a factory or in an office, and you have some idea of why women probably did not venture out of the house when they menstruated. Imagine, too, the real courage and determination of those who did enter the work force despite this handicap. Significantly, women nurses, not men, were the motivating force behind disposable sanitary protection.

Turn-of-the-century studies succeeded in convincing many women (and a few men) that their menstrual cycles need not be considered a disability. Clelia Duel Mosher's *Health and the Woman Movement* (1916) attempted to disprove the belief that increased activity would damage woman's health. Citing centuries of old wives' tales, she said:

> Certainly, there is no disputing the fact that the mind has a powerful, if unconscious, control of organic processes. Now for generations, if we have taught girls any thing at all in regard to menstruation, we have been instilling the idea that it is a periodic illness involving suffering and incapacity.[6]

An especially convincing part of Mosher's thesis was her denunciation of women's clothing. Fashions, she found, were directly related to cramps. The heavy skirts and waist-pinching corsets of the nineteenth century would increase congestion and pain in the uterus, but "as the skirt grew shorter and narrower and the waist grew larger, the functional health of women improved." She also devised a set of exercises to accompany the flapper fashions and free girls and women from menstrual pain.

Twenty years earlier, Mary Putnam-Jacobi, M.D., had also spoken out against the listlessness and enforced rest for women during menstruation, claiming that nothing but custom and the wishes of men were at the root of it:

> Thus one of the most essential apparent peculiarities of the menstrual process, its periodicity, that formerly was supposed to indicate the periodical increase in the vital forces of the female organism, has come to be considered as a mark of constantly recurring debility, decidedly as a fracture or paralysis.[8]

In their work, both women were actually trying to persuade women that no one need suffer menstrual pain against her wishes. This must have been a revolutionary idea for women, who had been convinced that ill health at menstruation was "woman's lot." The fact that women themselves perpetuated this belief is related to the eternal question of menstrual isolation: Who makes and enforces the taboos: men or women? In the industrial nineteenth century, just as in some prehistoric villages, menstrual malingering may have been subtly encouraged by men to ensure their dominance in the social and economic hierarchy. Woman, caught in this vicious circle of cause and effect, accepts her lot and makes the most of the benefits men see fit to extend to her, such as the protective labor laws, even if their real effect is to protect society from the achievements of women who work.

By the twentieth century, society showed more concern for the dollars and work hours lost because of menstrual and premenstrual absences than for the health and vitality of unborn children and their mothers. The protective laws themselves were used as evidence that women were incapable of holding responsible positions, from factory forewoman to company president. Grace Naismith, in *Private and Personal* (1966), uses unsupported statistics to prove that billions of dollars are lost each year because of women staying home from work with dysmenorrhea. She says:

> Since one out of every three workers in American industy today is a woman—24.5 million in our labor force—menstrual problems assume major significance. Eight percent of absenteeism is due to dysmenorrhea. The economic loss is said to be equivalent to an entire year of work by 5800 women.[9]

To combat such waste, she suggests expanded use of industrial programs in which female employees are sent routinely to gynecologists ("sometimes a woman") to answer questions about their periods. She claims that Paramount Studios and United Artists require a gynecological exam for each employee, as do many other enlightened companies. If a woman (always an employee, never the boss) is absent too much, her (male) boss has a right to ask if she is menstruating or is "really sick," for "it is in the business world that menstruation plays havoc with men and their money."[10]

Naismith's book suggests that absenteeism caused by dysmenorrhea is all but out of control in twentieth-century America and that only the patient, kindly, fatherly bosses and gynecologists can save the economy from these bleeding subversives. Yet, every year, the U.S. Department of Labor statistics on absences from work prove this argument to be unfounded. In 1971, for example, men lost 5.1 days because of sickness or injury, and women lost 5.2. These figures remain about the same from year to year. That hardly heralds a massive breakdown of American industrial life, especially when coupled with the fact that women bear the responsibility for staying home with sick children—and husbands.

Another book with a similar argument is Katharina Dalton's *The Menstrual Cycle* (1969), which treats exhaustively the alleged effects on the economy of the emotional aspects of the premenstrual syndrome. Like Naismith, Dalton emphasizes an unproven correlation between menstruation and work loss but overlooks those studies and tests that tend to prove the opposite.[11] Especially important are the myriad of tests conducted in the private sector and the public as early as the 1920s, all showing little or no difference in efficiency and absenteeism among women during fluctuations of the menstrual cycle.

This same approach prevails in women's athletics. Historically, the menstrual cycle has been the root of discrimination against women in sports, despite the fact that in the last three Olympics, says an article in the September 1974 *Ms.*, "women won gold medals and established new world records during all phases of the menstrual cycle." Although there is a dearth of research involving women's psychological endurance or performance in sports, those studies that do exist find that menstruation has little or no effect. A recent study by the American Medical Association of sixty-six Olympic sportswomen showed that 75 percent continued regular training during menstruation, and only 5 percent stopped entirely. Unless a woman's period is unusually painful, says the AMA, "there seems to be no medical reason not to train or compete during menstruation."[12] Obviously, the menses did not interfere with the American Olympic swimmer who broke a world record and won three gold medals at the height of her period.

But, again, most of the popular reasons for discrimination are based on the *effect of the menstrual cycle on the sport*. For example, Dick Butera, owner of the Philadelphia franchise of the World Team Tennis League, was quoted in *Philadelphia* as saying that he plans to hire more women athletes than he needs at any one time: "What happens if Billie Jean wakes up the morning of a big match and she's got her period bad? What are you going to tell the fans?"[13]

One thing that an athlete *can* do if she "gets her period bad" is take hormones to delay it until after an important contest. Birth control pills can be used for this purpose, or the male hormone testosterone can be administered. Both Dalton and Naismith refer to the latter practice, but Dalton points out that the effects of testosterone on a woman's bodily strength and endurance are so extensive that the injection is illegal in most athletic contests. At Olympic Games, hormone tests are required of all athletes to make sure men aren't competing in women's contests.

Most women who are nonprofessional athletes probably formed their attitudes toward menstruation and sports in their high school gym classes, where they shared the experience of a character in Alice Munro's *Lives of Girls and Women:* "We had hidden in the girls' toilet together when we had the curse at the same time and were afraid to do tumbling—one at a time, in front of the rest of the class—afraid of some slipping or bleeding, and too embarrassed to ask to be excused." Such fears have bothered young women for centuries and originate in the two principles of menstrual politics we have been discussing: Girls in any condition do not participate in strenuous exercise because it might harm their female organs, and women cannot compete successfully in sports because their menstrual blood might "stain" the playing fields.

It is impossible to escape the conclusion that menstrual politics has dominated social and economic relations between the sexes since the beginning of time. In all their struggles for equality—the suffrage movement, the labor movement, the struggle for ERA—women have been obliged to fight against an enemy who will not contend with them in the halls of Congress or the courts of law. The enemy is within every woman, but it is not her menstruation. Rather, it is the habit of mind regarding menstruation into which she has been led by centuries of male domination. She has been taught that menstruation is disabling, and so she has been disabled.

Even in terms of twentieth-century life, it is inaccurate to say that women "invented" menstrual politics. Neither in machine-age America nor in contemporary Stone Age societies have women had enough control over their own lives to manipulate and control the lives of the ruling men. As the servant learns to reinforce the prejudices of the master, so woman has learned well to echo the male menstrual prejudice born in fear of her mysterious functions.

Afterword

Talking about menstruation does not necessarily make it less mystifying, according to *The Tampax Report,* a statistically valid major national study on menstruation conducted in 1981 for Tampax, Inc. by Research and Forecasts, Inc.[14] *The Tampax Report* finds that menstruation remains a taboo subject for many Americans, that two-thirds of them, in fact, believe it should not be talked about at social gatherings or in the office, and that one-quarter of them think it "an unacceptable topic even for the family at home." Other findings in *The Tampax Report:*

—one-third of American women were not prepared for menstruation, and two-fifths of them report their first reaction to it to be a negative one;
—one-quarter of Americans think women cannot function normally at work while menstruating;
—one-half the population thinks that women should not have sexual intercourse while menstruating;
—one-third believe that menstruation affects a woman's thinking ability;

—one-third think women should restrict their physical activity during menstruation;
and
—nearly one-quarter think menstrual pain is all in a woman's head.

Men and women tend to hold similar attitudes about menstruation, but in certain key areas they disagree. For example, 56 percent of women but 39 percent of men say menstruation is painful; 88 percent of women but only 66 percent of men think menstruation has no effect on job performance; and, oddly, more men than women believe it is socially acceptable to discuss menstruation (38 percent vs. 27 percent).

Where are the myths and misconceptions about menstruation learned? Mostly in the home, the report finds, although 30 percent of teenagers today learn about it in school—and a whopping 91 percent of Americans think school is just the place for it.

If 91 percent of the American people think menstruation should be taught in schools, but two-thirds of them think it shouldn't be discussed at home or in the office, then attitudes haven't really changed at all. These figures tell us that people are comfortable discussing menstruation when it is treated as a clinical, perhaps pathological, condition, apart from ordinary experience, but that it remains taboo when it is considered a natural part of the life of half the people in the world.

One wonders how the responses would have compared if the questionnaire had included attitudes toward social discussion of diet or flu or sports-related injuries—"personal" conditions one can hardly escape hearing about in the living rooms of America these days. *The Tampax Report* tells us, in fact, that despite the presence of menstruation in books, movies, and television programs, despite the publicity about toxic shock syndrome, the mainstream thinking in America has not changed since the 1976 publication of *The Curse*.

But women have changed. They are participating in public life today to a degree unforeseen in the early 1970s. They comprise almost 70 percent of the work force and are excluded from virtually no job or profession except the Catholic priesthood and the orthodox Jewish rabbinate. And despite the limitation, as Susan Brownmiller put it in *Femininity*, of "playing the jock with a bloody cloth between one's legs," women are obviously in sports, professional and amateur, to stay.[15]

This enormous jump in athletic participation, combined with the need for statistical information on women's bodily strengths in relation to men's when women entered West Point, Annapolis, and the astronaut ranks, has caused a small growth industry in testing women athletes, and more is known every day about how women's bodies react to the pressures of training and competition.

On at least one aspect of this the experts agree: the highly individualistic nature of athletics precludes any generalities about how a woman's menstrual cycle will affect her performance. Each woman is different. A woman whose premenstrual syndrome or dysmenorrhea impedes her performance will probably not reach the Olympic level of competition (and thus will probably never be part of one of these studies). Some researchers posit that PMS will affect concentration, visual acuity, or precise movements, with postmenopausal women in a position of greater safety when diving or swimming "presumably because they do not experience hormonal swings" suggests Dr. Albert W. Diddle in a 1983 report.[16] But the consensus of the experts seems to be that a far smaller percentage of woman athletes than women in general perform less well when menstruating and that for the rest menstruation may be a bother but probably has no more effect than other biorhythms.[17]

The bigger story is not how menstruation affects sports, however, but how sports training affects the menstrual cycle. One hundred years after doctors Clark and Ames worried that higher education and factory employment could threaten the reproductive health of women, medical science is beginning to take seriously the effects of both mental and physical stress on menstruation.

It is by now well known that menstruation disappears under certain conditions of weight and fat loss, brought about by rigorous athletic training or rigorous dieting, of the kind experienced by, say, fashion models or victims of anorexia nervosa. Recent theories suggest that when women lose between 10 and 15 percent of their total body weight they also lose about one-third of their fat, and when that happens, the menstrual cycle may stop. It has been shown that estrogen is produced in the fatty tissue of women as well as in the ovaries and adrenal glands, and when the fat goes, so does the estrogen and thus the menses.

Doctors Rose Frisch and Janet McArthur of Harvard are among those who believe that fitness for sports at the highest levels thus leaves the female body totally unfit for pregnancy, when the body needs all the reserve energy it can store.[18] Lest we think this a new syndrome of stress-filled American society, anthropologists have known for a long time that during periods of famine and stress a people's birth rate drops, rising when times get better—agreeing with Dr. Frisch's conclusions that diminished fat ratios are responsible.[19]

But other researchers emphasize the stress component of amenorrhea in athletes and are reluctant to state unequivocally that the fat/estrogen loss is responsible. Dr. Mona Shangold, professor of obstetrics and gynecology at New York Hospital-Cornell Medical School and a leading expert in the field of menstrual physiology, noted in 1982 that during any training program an athlete is subjected to the "physical stress of training, the emotional stress of training and/or competing, weight loss, low weight, loss of body fat, and low body fat," each of which, alone or in combination, could cause amenorrhea, and that many athletes experienced amenorrhea before they began training.[20] Dr. Diddle also recommends full gynecologic exploration before a diagnosis of the cause of amenorrhea is made, noting that "the causes of menstrual dysfunction appear to be the same for athletes and nonathletes. Emotional stress is a predisposing factor in both."[21]

As early as 1978, when the phenomenon first began to be noticed because of the dramatic rise in women runners, Dr. Dorothy Harris, director of the Research Center for Women in Sports at The Pennsylvania State University, observed that women whose periods are irregular before athletic training begins are likely to experience irregularity as a result of the training; those who were regular, are not.[22]

So the "menstrual politics" in sports is still based on a dichotomy, but thanks to the volumes of medical research it is a dichotomy between the effects of menstruation on performance and performance on menstruation and not on whether women are fit to compete (we must humbly retract our indignation over the Dick Butera comment on cramps and tennis, since Grace Lichtenstein, who wrote *A Long Way Baby* after following the Virginia Slims Professional Tennis tour for a year said that "menstrual cramps were literally the curse of the women's circuit" and that more than one championship player had dashed off court in midgame to change a tampon.)[23]

But in other walks of life menstrual politics has not moved from the old "raging hormonal imbalance" canard, made more intense by the spotlight of public attention now focused on premenstrual syndrome and the consequent dispute among women over how far this syndrome should go toward defining women's competencies. We recall Ellen Goodman's view of President Reagan's firing of Margaret Heckler from her job as secretary of Health and Human Services, presumably because she wasn't "good" enough at her job. In an incisive analysis of Heckler's downfall and its connection to the nearly total absence of women in high positions in the Reagan administration, columnist Goodman reveals that incompetence might have been the public charge but that plain old sexism was the cause. Goodman quotes no less respected a person than Jeane Kirkpatrick on the same old story: talking about White House efforts to keep her ambitions in check while she was U.S. Ambassador to the U.N., she said, "One male colleague . . . said that I was too temperamental to hold a higher office. What do they mean—too temperamental once a month?"[24]

PART TWO

The Menstrual Cycle in Action

Chapter 7

The Menstrual Process

Menstruation is activated by the pituitary gland, which is located at the base of the brain. The pituitary releases a hormone called the *follicle-stimulating hormone* (FSH) at about midcycle. It also triggers the release of measured amounts of estrogen and progesterone in complementary curves throughout the month (so that when the level of one is the highest, the other is at its lowest). FSH also stimulates the ovaries, two glands about the size of almonds, as they prepare to release the eggs.

Each month, the left or the right ovary brings forth a ripening ovum, which bursts out of its sac, the graafian follicle. The egg's journey down the fallopian tube to the uterus is called *ovulation*. As the egg passes down the tube, it may meet with a sperm, unite, and form an embryo. This embryo will then imbed itself in the endometrium, the lining of the uterus, or womb. The imbedding is called *nidation* (literally, "nesting"). During the early stages of its development, the nested egg takes food from the endometrium, which has become thick and plushy, filled with watery fluids and blood. The neck of the womb will be sealed; no menstruation occurs during pregnancy, nor for as long as three to six months afterward. Breast-feeding may prevent the return of menstruation for an even longer time.

But if the egg travels down the tube unaccosted by a fertilizing sperm, then the enriched endometrium is not needed for food. The hormone estrogen, which supported the lining, soon stops its work. Progesterone takes over, stimulates the contraction of the uterus, and assists the velvety lining to leave through the vagina as menstrual "blood."

Menstrual fluid actually consists of more than blood; real blood makes up about one-half to three-quarters of the fluid, which also contains mucus, fragments of uterine mucous membrane, and scaling cell tissues from the vagina. Menstrual fluid has thirty times as much lime as regular blood and lacks ordinary blood's power to clot.

About midway between two periods, a physically mature woman will usually ovulate. The biological connection between menstruation and ovulation is a fairly new discovery and one that distinguishes the woman from other mammals. Less than a century ago, the menstruating woman was thought to be like an animal in heat (estrus). Animals at such times experience a discharge; they are also ovulating and are in their fertile period. But now we know that it is ovulation, not menstruation, that is closest to heat.

A woman may not be aware of any of the profound changes in her body over the course of her monthly cycle, but the possibilities for contrast are remarkable. Various studies have shown, for example, that a woman is less sensitive to pain while she ovulates, that her sense of smell improves, that her feelings of aggression and anxiety are low. Her hearing and sight are at their best, and she is more likely to feel elated. According to Kinsey's (disputed) study, 90 percent of women rate their own sexual arousal highest at midcycle. All these facts suggest that a woman will be most eager for sex at a time when she is most likely to conceive.

But about two weeks later, the menstruating woman might have cramps. She will be more prone to skin diseases, the most common being herpes (cold sores); acne, too, can be aggravated. Dark circles may appear under her eyes, and if she is susceptible to vaginal infections, this is the time when they may thrive because the vaginal atmosphere is less acidic.

Most of this monthly drama goes unnoticed by the average woman; a pimple on the nose will be lamented, of course, but the internal temperature and anxiety changes are more easily measured by scientific tests than by a woman's reactions. Sexual arousal is such a personal thing that many more women note their peak to be immediately before the menstrual period, possibly because of engorgement of genital tissues. The vast majority of women, in other words, regard the menstrual process in the proper light: as a normal, unremarkable biological process that may serve as a continuing reminder of their potential motherhood or may, on the other hand, be a nuisance welcome only at those times when motherhood, potential or actual, is merely an option in a woman's future program. Dark centuries of fear and taboo to the contrary, women, as opposed to men, are for the most part cheerfully and resignedly realistic about their periods.

Afterword

The menstrual process itself, as we describe it here, has not changed in the last ten years. But the scientific approaches to this physiological process have. Many of the recent medical studies on menstruation are inaccessible to the lay reader; they are concerned with genetic factors, hormone levels, and endrocrinology—with placental proteins, gonadotropin secretions, and biochemical bases for mood change.

As writers about literature and culture, we are not in the position to speak with authority on the medical intricacies of the menstrual process. We would instead suggest to the reader the following books and journal articles for further information:[1]

BOOKS

Doreen Asso. *The Real Menstrual Cycle*. New York: Wiley, 1982.

Boston Women's Health Book Collective. *The New Our Bodies, Ourselves*. New York: Simon and Schuster, 1984. Particularly useful is an appendix to Chapter 12, "Anatomy and Physiology of Sexuality and Reproduction," called "Hormones of the Menstrual Cycle Simplified."

Alice Dan, Effie A. Graham, and Carol P. Beecher. *The Menstrual Cycle: A Synthesis of Interdisciplinary Research*. New York: Springer, 1980.

Richard C. Friedman, editor. *Behavior and the Menstrual Cycle*. Grand Junction, Colorado: Dekker, 1982.

James R. Givens. *Endocrine Causes of Menstrual Disorders*. Chicago: Year Book Medical Publications, 1978.

Sharon Golub, editor. *Lifting the Curse of Menstruation: A Feminist Appraisal of the Influence of Menstruation on Women's Lives*. Binghamton, N.Y.: Haworth Press, 1983.

———. *Menarche: The Physiological, Psychological and Social Effects of the Onset of Menstruation*. Binghamton, N.Y.: Haworth Press, 1983.

Karen E. Paige, et al. *The Female Reproductive Cycle: An Annotated Bibliography*. Boston: G. K. Hall, 1985.

Ann M. Voda, Myra Dinnerstein, and Sheryl R. O'Donnell. *Changing Perspectives on the Menopause*. Austin: University of Texas Press, 1982.

Rudolf F. Vollman. *The Menstrual Cycle*. Philadelphia: Saunders, 1977.

ARTICLES IN MEDICAL JOURNALS

Anthony W. Clare. "Hormones, Behavior, and the Menstrual Cycle." *Journal of Psychosomatic Research* 29:2 (1985): 225-33.

M. Julkungen et al. "Secretory Endometrium Synthesizes Placental Protein 14." *Endocrinology* 118:5 (May 1986): 1782-6.

K. N. Muse et al. "Calcium-Regulating Hormones Across the Menstrual Cycle." *Journal of Clinical and Endocrinological Metabolism* 62:6 (June 1986): 1313-6.

R. L. Reid et al. "Oral Glucose Tolerance during the Menstrual Cycle in Normal Women and Women with Alleged Premenstrual 'Hypoglycemic' Attacks: Effects of Naloxone." *Journal of Clinical and Endrocrinological Metabolism* 62:6 (June 1986): 1167-72.

W. W. Tam, Mo-yin Chan, and P. H. Lee. "The Menstrual Cycle and Platelet 5-HT Uptake." *Psychosomatic Medicine* 47:4 (July-August 1985): 352-62.

Chapter 8

The First Pollution: Psychoanalysis and the Menarche

Psychoanalytic studies of the trauma of the menarche and subsequent menstruations have been limited to patients, that is, women whose reactions are significantly aberrant from the normal woman's. In transposing these studies to generalized theories about women's attitudes toward menstruation, the assumption has been that menstruation itself is the aberrancy, that it is a bloody sign of women's loss of a penis, that it remains for all women in all times a sign of their uncleanliness and inferiority. In the major psychoanalytic writings, the menarche is generally seen as a curse associated with penis envy, castration anxiety, female masochism, and a potpourri of other psychic disorders. The psychoanalyst Otto Fenichel calls the menarche "the first pollution."[1]

Sigmund Freud makes a number of references to menstruation, although he develops no extensive theory about it. Early in his career, he used hypnosis to regulate a patient's menstrual cycle (2: 57).[2] In his essay "The Taboo of Virginity" (3: 198-99), he suggests that some women make a subconscious connection between the menstrual flow and defloration, thus implying physical violation or damage. In *Interpretation of Dreams*, he views red camellias as a symbol for menstruation. Freud's most imaginative statement about menstruation, however, is in *Civilization and its Discontents* (1930). Here, he examines the unpleasant effect of menstrual odor on the male psyche, a phenomenon that he attributes to man's shame when he began to walk on two legs; now that his genitals were out in the open, they became (logically?) something to be concealed, and any pleasure previously obtained from the sense of smell during intercourse now became taboo (21: 99). It would seem that at this historic moment, man's shame became woman's shame.

When Freud speaks specifically about the menarche, he usually compares it with the menopause. He views both events as internal (as opposed to external) crises in which the dammed-up libido, the source of psychic energy, can release disturbances ordinarily held in check (12: 236). Freud more or less expects someone who was not normally neurotic to become so at those moments. Thus, one psychoanalytic view of the menarche comes to parallel the instinctive fear of primitive peoples that menacing spirits, uncontrollable except by taboo, hover around a menarcheal or menopausal woman.

One of the earliest psychoanalytic works about menstruation is Mary Chadwick's *The Psychological Problems in Menstruation*, published in 1932. The section on the menarche describes the fears that Chadwick claims usually accompany the first menstruation. The adolescent girl is ashamed of her growing breasts and of her pubic hair, but her greatest shame is her menstrual blood: "She believes that she has injured herself, that it is some horrible disease, or that divine punishment has fallen upon her as retribution for former misdeeds."[3] After the first flow stops, the girl may fantasize that she is pregnant. She often revives the anal hate of childhood, the need to keep clean during the menses evoking painful recollections of diaper soiling and bed-wetting. She may indulge in self-torture or "morbid masturbation," although Chadwick does not specify exactly what morbid masturbatory techniques are most prevalent. The blood itself creates other fears: fears of castration, of separation, of blood-sucking, vampires, penis-breast identification, and witches.

A girl's ignorance of the menstrual process could surely cause some of this distortion. Despite the barrage of educational materials now available to children, approximately 20 percent of adolescent girls are still uninformed about the menarche when it happens. We must also remember that Chadwick wrote this book more than forty years ago, when girls were generally more secretive and unknowledgeable about body functions than they are now. Yet, what to this day remains disturbing about Chadwick's book and others like it is the virtual absence of any positive statement concerning what to most pre-teens we know is an exciting, long-awaited, and much-discussed event.

One of the most influential theorists writing in the 1930s was Helen Deutsch. Like Freud, Deutsch regards both the menarche and the menopause as agitated periods during which previously repressed feelings are released.[4] The menarche is a disturbing event, she says, because for the first time in her life a girl is faced with "the double function of the female as a sexual creature and as a servant of the species" (1:172), that is, as mother of the race. Deutsch views the adjusted adolescent as the one who accepts her subordinate status and, consequently, her female sexuality. But, Deutsch argues, if the menarche is met with resistance, the adolescent may have difficulty with what she calls her "final decision to be a woman" (1: 162).

The menstrual blood that brands the female as "servant of the species" is interpreted by Deutsch as an exclusively negative symbol. It represents, first of all, symbolic castration. The genitals bleed, reminding the adolescent that she has forever lost her wished-for and imagined penis. Deutsch constructed a theory based on her patients' fantasies without challenging its implications for her own sex, although she replaced Freud's "female castration complex" with the somewhat milder term *genital trauma*.

A second interpretation of women's psychological reaction to the menstrual flow, the one for which Deutsch is most noted, is the equating of lost blood with lost children. She assumes that all women want to be mothers. Thus, each menstruation is a dreadful disappointment because it indicates the failure to become pregnant. We find this idea restated by numerous analysts, among them Erik Erikson, who writes in his famous essay "Womanhood and the Inner Space" that a woman is most hurt when she is most empty: "Each menstruation . . . is a crying to heaven in the mourning over a child."[5]

Deutsch also notes that the first menstruation can signify a child's punishment for having played with her clitoris. Underlying this interpretation is the now-discredited Freudian assumption that clitoral stimulation is a regressive and self-indicting act which must eventually be abandoned for the mature, womanly vaginal orgasm.

Melanie Klein's discussion of the menarche in *The Psychoanalysis of Children* is based on equally negative assumptions. Klein says that the adolescent unconsciously identifies menstrual blood with urine and feces and thus with all their negative connotations. This is a fairly consistent idea in psychoanalytic theory, and it was probably first expressed by Ernest Jones, who discovered that girls who had never explored their vaginas often imagine that the menstrual flow and urine emanate from the same place.[6] Fear of bodily mutilation may also be experienced at the first sight of menstrual blood. Klein suggests that this phobia may arise because the girl has fantasized copulating with her father and fears her mother's revenge. Like Deutsch, Klein speculates that the blood is a sign that the potential child has been destroyed or, relying on Freudian theory, that the clitoris is an atrophied penis, that the clitoris is "the scar or wound left by her castrated penis."[7]

Castration anxiety is thus another common theme in psychoanalytic writing. Perhaps the most fear-ridden description of the castrating-castrated menstruating woman appears in Norman O. Brown's *Love's Body*, a book greatly influenced by the writings of Melanie Klein: "The vagina as a devouring mouth, or *vagina dentata;* the jaws of the giant cannibalistic mother, a menstruating woman with the penis bitten off, a bleeding trophy."[8]

Klein's single positive contribution to the psychology of menarche is that it may alleviate anxiety because it signifies the achievement of sexual status. The catch here is that the "feminine position" must have been carefully nurtured in the child as she grew to sexual maturity. It seems that in order to arrive at the "feminine position" a young girl must say to herself, "Yes, I'm mutilated. I'm a castrated male. I don't have the penis I always wanted. But I am very fortunate. I have the privilege of being a total woman. I shall bleed in the service of mankind."

This insistence on a total feminine identification is maintained by many recent theorists, among them Judith Bardwick, whose essays have been anthologized in *Woman in Sexist Society* and other feminist publications. Bardwick wrote in 1971 that although the "normal" adolescent will value the first menstruation as a sign of her femininity, the "neurotic who has rejected her sex will find the physiological changes of puberty traumatic because they challenge her repudiation of her sex."[9] Fleeing femininity, she may increase her efforts to gain a penis or castrate a male—at least symbolically.

When examining the causes of menarcheal disorders, most analysts tend to view the girl's mother as the chief source of the daughter's disturbance. Chadwick observed that children learned about menstruation from their mothers, many of whom spent two or three days a month in bed having headaches, being irritable, emitting foul odors. The realities of twentieth-century health and hygiene have probably obviated many of these traumas by now, but Chadwick suggests another idea that may still have some validity: because so many females are narcissistically concerned about staying young, they may resent their daughters' coming of age as a dismal reminder of their own approaching menopause.[10]

Deutsch, like Chadwick, states that the mother's uncleanliness and bad odor can create reactions of disgust in the daughter. Deutsch, however, also observes the mother's secrecy about her own menstruation, an attitude that seems far more prevalent than conscious carelessness. According to Deutsch, many mothers are more likely to talk to their daughters about conception, pregnancy, and birth than about menstruation (1: 152-157).

The analysts Karen Horney and Clara Thompson see society as the root cause of destructive attitudes in women. Horney also suggests that the mother's menstrual blood can reinforce the girl's discovery that women's bodies are extremely vulnerable; the girl may think that her mother has been injured in sexual intercourse.[11] (We wonder if the child who doesn't understand the meaning of menstrual blood is likely to know about sexual intercourse.) Thompson noted that learning about the menarche from an embarrassed or worried mother can cause negative reactions in the daughter, particularly when the mother uses the occasion to warn the girl about the dangers of becoming pregnant.[12] Probably the most extreme example of regarding the mother as the chief source for the daughter's menstrual difficulties occurs in an essay by Natalie Shainess, who argues that girls receiving no advance knowledge have experienced "castration by the mother—the result of her omission of information."[13]

The mother is, of course, involved. Mothers who have learned to fear and resent their own bodies are likely to transfer negative feelings concerning menstruation to their daughters. However, it is crucial to emphasize, as few analysts do, that the society itself is primarily responsible for this internalized dread and that the mother, because she is presumed to be an exclusively sexual, childbearing, castrated, second-class animal, is herself a victim.

It is hard to find, in the psychoanalytic discussions of the menarche, a balanced conceptualization, one that presents the potentially positive as well as the inherently negative aspects of menstruation and one that accounts for the societal attitudes that underlie many of our feelings of disgust. We do find some ambivalence in the writings of Fenichel. While agreeing that menstrual disorders can signify "I have neither child nor penis," Fenichel nevertheless also stresses the purely biological aspects of menstruation that might cause discomfort or stress. In listing some of the unconscious meanings of menstruation, Fenichel includes the positive aspects of relaxation, genitality, and love, along with the more negative attitudes of "Oedipus guilt, castration, the frustration of wishes for a child, and humiliation."[14]

As early as 1926, Horney began to challenge some basic Freudian ideas about female sexuality, particularly the concepts of female castration and female masochism. Horney found among the patients she was treating a universal negativity toward the menstrual process; however, she is convinced that, although menstrual disorders can at times be an outlet for masochistic tendencies, this self-inflicted pain is not rooted in female anatomy alone but must be seen as "importantly conditioned by the culture-complex and social organization in which the particular masochistic woman has developed."[15] In other words, society has chosen to reward the bearer of the penis, not the loser of the blood, and then has interpreted the woman's unease with her inferior status as a "problem" that requires realignment of her personality in accord with the "norms" of society. Among the common traits of menarcheal girls, Horney lists lack of self-confidence, emotional detachment, the fear of being unattractive to men, the fear of being punished for masturbating, a loss of interest in work, and a development of homosexual tendencies.[16] The menarche, Horney admits, is a period of anxiety and stress primarily because the girl recognizes for the first time her vulnerability as a woman.

What distinguishes Horney's theory of the menarche from those of the other analysts is not, then, a positive attitude toward the menstrual process. Rather, it is her viewing menstrual difficulties within a broad social context. According to Horney (in the same paper), man devalues woman's functions in order to keep her out of his domain, creating an ideology that will keep him powerful and her inferior. The male sees the female as biologically incapable of assuming positions of power. This certainly is the theme that dominates intersexual relations among the primitives, and it clearly conditions the economics of the contemporary world.

Like Horney, Thompson calls into question the concepts of female castration and female masochism. Thompson insists that female sexuality must be discussed in nonmale terms, that women's bodies and minds must be seen in their own right. She points out, for example, that Freud based his observations of female masochism on a study of passive male homosexuals.

Among Thompson's own patients, there were a number of adolescents who were troubled during the menarche. One was an active, healthy child who, upon reaching puberty, was no longer allowed to go camping or hiking with her brother. "She was filled with bitterness and envy of her brother and for several reasons centered her whole resentment on the fact of menstruation. This seemed to be the sign of her disgrace, the sign that she had no right to be a person." This girl suffered, not from any fantasied hate or scarred and imagined wound, but from the fact that her first menstruation meant that her body and mind were to be restricted. She had not lost an imagined child or imagined penis. She had lost freedom, equality, and "the right to be aggressive."[17]

Thompson notes that positive advantages to reaching puberty, such as initiation into the important work of society and the passage into adulthood, have been devalued by our culture. Contemporary analysts suggest a few additional advantages. Judith Kestenberg, for example, speculated that the onset of menstruation "makes it possible for the girl to differentiate reality from fantasy." The regularity and "sharpness" of the menstrual experience leads to clear thinking and to a reorganization of the previously chaotic ego.[18] We find Kestenberg's account of renewed intellectual development at the menarche a phenomenon noted by many educators, more satisfying than the Freudian explanation offered by Chadwick and others: namely, that any marked intellectual achievement is a defensive reaction against the loss of the imagined penis.

Yet, the most influential psychoanalytic literature concerning menstruation continues to view this common and at times bothersome process as a "monthly neurosis" fraught with fears of castration, maternal revenge, anal repulsion, and lost children. The menarche, the first stage of this anxiety-ridden history, appears to be the first encounter in an intense psychic battle. The only "acceptable" action a woman can take is unconditional and immediate surrender to society's expectations.

Afterword

A 1986 catalog distributed by International Universities Press, Inc. lists hundreds of titles available in the fields of psychoanalysis and psychoanalytic psychology. Many of these titles pertain to the adolescent girl; all of them touch on some aspect of therapy or analysis. Yet in none of the annotations to this comprehensive catalog does the word *menstruation* appear. As in the past, menstruation tends to be ignored as a significant factor in the development of the female psyche.

When Freudians discuss the process of sexual differentiation between boys and girls, they invariably do so by focusing on the concept of penis envy. Boys fear girls because girls lack a penis; the boy is then threatened, fearing castration—fearing to become a girl. The girl, on the other hand, always wants the penis that she realizes she lacks. Always desiring, she can only be fulfilled by giving birth to a boy child—a child with a penis.

This oversimplified review of Freudian theory is meant to suggest that, in the vast psychoanalytic literature on sexual development, there is barely any attention given to what the girl has that the boy definitely lacks, namely, a menstrual cycle. We have seen Mary Chadwick's views of the first menstruation: the adolescent girl is tortured by fears of separation and of vampires. We have not seen menstruation used in a conceptually aggressive way, however, as a way to develop an in-depth theory of sexual difference based on this special distinction between women and men.[19]

In Chapter 18 we refer to Claude Dagmar Daly, a psychoanalyst who in the 1930's posited a theory which he named "the menstruation complex." Over the years we have been reading Daly with considerably greater attention, puzzled at the fact that a concept so important could have been so consistently ignored by the psychoanalytic establishment.

Daly was one of several analysts in the late 1920s and early 1930s who called into question Freud's concept of penis envy as it related to female castration anxiety. He was particularly involved with the work of Karen Horney, whom he occasionally quotes. In his earlier essays Daly is concerned with menstruation only as it affects the mother's impact on her sons; not until later did his theory of menstruation evolve to include the influence of menstruation on the adolescent girl and on her prehistory.

To argue his menstruation complex Daly had to chip away at the classical Freudian view of the Oedipus complex, replacing the castrating father with the menstruating mother. This was a formidable job, since psychoanalysis in its formative years was not open to ideas about menstruation, having literally eliminated the sexual development of the female from its deliberations. If Daly was to convince anyone, he first had to place feminine sexuality within the phallocentric system and *then* talk about menstrual blood.

So Daly went on to attack Freud's notion, so often quoted by today's feminists, that "a little girl is a little man." But what makes Daly's argument so unusual is his use of menstruation as the distinguishing point between male and female, a distinction that pre-exists in childhood: "The girl in the positive phase of her Oedipus complex is a little woman just as the boy is a little man, and the fact that she does not menstruate and produce ova is only parallel to the fact that the boy does not produce sperm."[20] The girl menstruates. In Daly's argument the mother, through her menstruation, is a reminder of castration and death. What saves Daly's theory from being a bleakly morbid account of the female is his insistence that she is both separate and powerful—hardly the victimized figure that dominates the Freudian vision of womanhood.

Many feminists of the last decade have been critical of Freudian and post-Freudian theory, especially of the phallocentrism that underlies the works of French theoretician Jacques Lacan. The ideas of Claude Dagmar Daly would seem especially valuable in reconstructing a theory of feminist psychoanalysis. Unfortunately, Daly's essays remain in obscurity, his menstruating mother a forgotten dream. What is more, menstruation itself is forgotten, repressed by those very women whose critical voices are potentially the strongest in challenging a male-dominated psychoanalysis.

French feminist Luce Irigaray is perhaps the best example of this silence. Irigaray, renowned internationally for her essay "When Our Lips Speak Together," eloquently celebrates the flow of blood—of language and of female sexuality—in that essay.[21] But in her major philosophical text, *Speculum of the Other Woman,* on the subject of menstruation Irigaray's lips are sealed.

Her own speculating, her own constant questioning of phallocentrism, reflects an omission of menstrual consciousness. In "The Blind Spot of an Old Dream of Symmetry," for instance, she challenges Freud for his idea that the phallic stage is a necessary step in normal female development. "And even more, why, if stages there be," Irigaray wonders, "is there no question, for example, of a vulvar stage, a vaginal stage, a uterine stage, in a discussion of female sexuality?"[22] Irigaray's questions are of course legitimate; they need to be asked and to be responded to. But what strikes us as strange is her neglect of menstrually related stages in this open string of possibilities. Menstrual absence in this instance is its own signal.

More puzzling is the section, in the same text, called "How to Conceive (of) a Girl." Irigaray opens this rather brief chapter with four citations from Aristotle. Two of them are about menstrual fluid. Yet Irigaray refuses to comment on Aristotle's menstrual notions in her own text.

In *This Sex Which Is Not One* Irigaray states her purpose: "It is thus a matter of examining the texts of psychoanalytic discourse in order to read what they express—and how?—of female sexuality, and even more of sexual difference."[23] Irigaray desires to separate the masculine from the feminine, to question certain prevalent phallocentric concepts: the woman is a mirror of maleness; the little girl is a little man; the clitoris is a little penis.

What better place for this separation to occur than in menstruation? Men cannot enter or even entertain the language of menstruation, with its fluidic periodicity, its mood-signing, its cyclical reminder of the feminine real. Some men, the Wogeo of New Guinea, for example, can simulate menstruation. But men do not actually menstruate, have no conception of the anxiety or hormonal fluctuation or physical bleeding that accompanies each and every menstrual cycle for a woman's reproductive life.

Menstruation has its own language, its own images. It is woman's special blood, often alluded to by Irigaray but rarely specified. Irigaray's denial of menstruation is a denial of the very non-system that signifies female difference. It is the fluid matter at the center of femininity, the one possibly tangible female difference on which to base a separate feminist psychoanalysis.

Chapter 9

The Storm
Before the Calm:
The Premenstrual
Syndrome

Perhaps in reaction to the negativism of traditional psycho-analytic thought about women, there is today a growing interest in the physical basis of menstrual disorders. Indeed, many researchers are convinced that all menstrual problems can be traced to a physical source, such as hormone-related water retention by the body's tissues. Others, however, insist that even if a psychological problem has a physical source, it remains necessary to treat the mental symptoms as well as the physical.

Two major groups of symptoms bother women immediately before and during menstruation: the physical sensations of cramping, bloatedness, backache, and pain and the mental symptoms of irritability, mood swings, or depression. All these symptoms, physical and emotional, are part of the total biology and psychology of the menstruating woman and indeed may spring from the same physiological source.

In the second century A.D., when Soranus wrote his treatise for midwives, it was recognized that women were tense right before their periods. Not until 1931, however, did scientists invent a name for the tension. Karen Horney called it *Die Premenstruellen Verstimmungen* and said that women got it because they were denying the wish to be pregnant. The American gynecologist Robert Frank called it *premenstrual tension* and said that women got it because of an increase in the production of the female hormone estrogen.[1] It has also been called *premenstrual distress* (a minor disorder), the *premenstrual syndrome* (a generally more serious disorder), and the *premenstrual tension syndrome* (PTS). To avoid confusion, we shall call the difficulties experienced immediately before the period the *premenstrual syndrome* (PMS), and we include in that category both major and minor symptoms.

We believe that premenstrual symptoms are experienced to a lesser or greater extent by most women and that these symptoms are real rather than imaginary. We do not think, however, that PMS is, as some have argued, either a disease or a neurosis. It is so widespread a phenomenon, in fact, that the absence of the most common symptoms during the premenstruum would be unusual.

The premenstruum occurs shortly before the menstrual flow begins, usually within two or three days. The most common mood indicator for this phase is a feeling of tension, rather like a clock that has been wound too tightly. Besides feeling tense, women in their premenstrual phase are reported to feel irritable, faint, restless, sluggish, crabby, impatient, depressed, lethargic, deluded, indecisive, dizzy, nervous, nymphomaniacal, and irrational—although not all at once. The most common physical symptoms include swelling of the breasts, feet, abdomen, and vulva; hoarseness; constipation; hemorrhoids; skin eruptions such as cold sores or acne; weight gain (around three to six pounds); easy bruising; migraines; backaches; graying of hair; and peeling of fingernails. Dr. Katharina Dalton, who for the last decade has been accumulating statistics about the perils of premenstrual women, says that a tendency toward puffy skin and rings under the eyes has led some film stars to prohibit close-ups during menstruation or the premenstruum. Office assistants, on the other hand, slop coffee in saucers on these "off days," according to Dalton.[2]

A less common disorder associated with the premenstruum, but one of significance in the attempts to establish the syndrome as legal grounds for insanity, is spontaneous hypoglycemia. This condition, caused when blood-sugar values fall below the normal level, is similar to an overdose of insulin. Symptoms of hypoglycemia are nervousness, sweatiness, trembling, a craving for sweets; in extreme instances, which are rare, the spontaneous hypoglycemia of the premenstrual phase is marked by disassociation and other mental disturbances, coma, convulsion, and even death.

Frequently, the premenstrual woman will experience a tremendous surge of energy, coupled with an inability to direct this energy into productive channels. Some women take on huge tasks immediately before their period, tasks that are nearly impossible to complete. Housewives often display an intense urge to do major housecleaning. This increased spurt of energy is less characteristic of the phase, however, than the symptoms of sluggishness or lethargy.

During the premenstruum, women's dreams may reflect more anxiety and frustration than at other times. In 1968, Judith Bardwick and Melville Ivey studied twenty-six "normal" female college students during two consecutive cycles in order to determine the extent of premenstrual anxiety. They found that twenty-one of the twenty-six women scored higher in death anxiety, diffuse anxiety, mutilation anxiety, and shame anxiety during the premenstrual as opposed to the ovulatory phase of the cycle. They also noted among their subjects certain "premenstrual themes": inadequacy, hostility, incestuousness, death, fear of accidents; whereas the same subjects during ovulation expressed joy, peacefulness, achievement, fertility, and self-confidence. In one unusual instance, a subject expressed anxiety on the fourteenth day of her cycle. The next day she menstruated, two weeks early.[3]

For most women, the symptoms of the premenstrual phase are minor. They do not always occur, and when they do, they are almost unobservable. The most universal discomforts are bloatedness, irritability, and depression. In some instances, however, the woman may become violent, psychotic, or suicidal during the two to three days preceding her period. More commonly, she may be quarrelsome or irrational, characteristics that in the popular mind are erroneously associated with the menstrual rather than the premenstrual phase, as in the familiar observation, "She's acting crazy; she's got the rag on." Women who have severe premenstrual symptoms would be wise to consult a physician, although not necessarily Dr. Steincrohn, who writes in his health column (*Baltimore Sun*, June 14, 1973):

> This almost unbelievable change from a Sweet Sue to Horrible Hannah for one week before her periods is what breaks up many homes. If, instead of making a beeline for an attorney's office, the couple would first consult an understanding doctor, they might save themselves much grief.

How universal is so-called premenstrual tension? Estimates of sufferers range from 20 percent to 100 percent of women. But (and this is the same problem found with the psychoanalytic studies of menstruating women) many of the statistics on the severity of PMS do not adequately reflect the society at large because they are based on doctors' evaluations of their patients, frequently women in mental institutions. And of course, a major problem with premenstrual studies is that they fail to account for environmental pressures, which in many cases intensify the symptoms.

Several studies show that PMS is most intense in women between the ages of thirty and forty; others find it intensifies with successive pregnancies. Common sense would show that this is the age when women are "making it" (or not) in their careers and in their families. The children of

a thirty-three-year-old mother are old enough to be making constant demands on her time; she may be involved in community affairs, the PTA,
and cub scouts; and if she also is struggling to finish a degree or establish
herself in her profession, the pressures on her are enormous. On the other
hand, a Washington, D.C., gynecologist told us that he almost never sees
severe cases of PMS in women who work outside the home; nor do the
young daughters of these women experience any dysmenorrhea. The psychologist Karen Paige has found that women who are most distressed
premenstrually are the ones most tied to home, children, and traditional
maternal roles.[4]

Just as many psychiatrists have said that painful menstruation is in a
woman's head, so have they said that premenstrual symptoms are "nervous" disorders and reflect a failure to adjust to woman's role, which they
see as primarily reproductive. In the pioneer psychoanalytic essay on PMS,
Karen Horney suggested that the tension preceding the period is caused
by the unconscious denial of a desire for a child. Horney found the
premenstrual phase to be a burden only for those patients who had con-
flicts about mothering.[5]

Treating PMS as a psychological problem goes back to the nineteenth
century, but not until 1942 were the first extensive psychological tests
conducted on menstrual and premenstrual women. Therese Benedek and
B. B. Rubenstein examined the emotional and hormonal swings of the
menstrual cycle and found a tendency toward acute emotional response
and dependent behavior during the premenstruum, which they attributed
to changes in the production of estrogen and to certain psychological
factors.[6]

Since 1942, many attempts have been made to evaluate the premenstrual symptoms, but psychologist Mary Brown Parlee later concluded
that there is *no* established proof that a measurable PMS even exists.[7] The
correlational studies and the *Premenstrual Distress Questionnaire* results
of Moos in 1968 often predict, through their wording, the very symptoms
that they expect to isolate. Most of the studies on violence and PMS fail
to place women in appropriate subgroups (for instance, criminals or artists).
And in almost every case that involves proving PMS, a nonmenstruating
(i.e., male) control group is absent. Parlee suggests, as do Lennane and
Lennane,[8] that menstrual dysfunctions are more likely to have physiological than psychological origins.

Looking more widely for the causes of emotional changes during the
premenstruum, the psychologist Karen Paige argues that premenstrual and
menstrual blues are the result of cultural conditioning. Paige interprets

menstrual distress as a social response to menstruation rather than a re-action to shifts in hormonal balance. Paige found that when her subjects' actual flow decreased, their anxiety also decreased. She also found that religious training had a significant effect on PMS, which was most severe among Catholic women in her group. The women most likely to suffer dysmenorrhea or PMS were found among those Catholics interviewed who believe that "a woman's place is in the home" and who are not interested in careers for themselves. Jews were the next most anxious group, with Protestants the freest from menstrual pain. Paige's observation is in opposition to the most frequently given psychological explanation for painful menstruation: that it is a sign of woman's failure to establish a "feminine identity." It seems to us that a woman who spends all day in the house concentrating on her "womanly" duties will be much more inclined to notice and think about her changes in weight and emotion than one whose mind is occupied with extra-female things. Another point made by Paige is that none of the symptoms associated with premenstrual or menstrual depression is unique to menstruation or, for that matter, to women.

Yet, the fact remains that many women do get headaches or the blues right before their periods, even those who are convinced that woman's place is not exclusively in the home. The sociological theory of PMS too readily dismisses undisputed evidence of hormonal changes triggering water buildup in the tissues, a physical condition that can produce most of the emotional conditions we have enumerated.

The most plausible theories about the origins of PMS center on the production of and tenuous balance between the hormones estrogen and progesterone in the female body. We have already noted that the pituitary regulates these hormones and that, as the level of estrogen peaks and then falls just before the onset of the period, the level of progesterone also rises after ovulation. While progesterone levels also drop immediately before menstruation, it is progesterone that is the water-retaining hormone. And fluid retention seems to be at the root of many of the evils of the premenstruum.

When there is too much water in the tissues, it shows up as general bloatedness, swelling of the hands, feet, and legs; it can also cause dark, puffy rings around the eyes. Even the brain tissues retain water, and the accumulated body tension from all these causes produces a pressure that is easily translated into emotional stress, especially, we think, when combined with the nuisance of menstrual bleeding and the sexual abstinence that usually accompanies the period. Although there has been some con-

fusion in the medical literature over which hormone (estrogen or progesterone) has the more direct effect on a woman's emotions, a gynecologist
told us that balanced concentrations of the two hormones help preserve,
rather than disturb, a woman's emotional equilibrium during the premenstruum.[9]

A consensus of medical experts shows that the easiest and most sensible solution to the problems of premenstruum is to eat well, particularly
to reduce the intake of salt and fluid during the premenstruum. One's
food should be high in protein, low in carbohydrates; a high-protein diet
will do as much as any other regimen to maintain a normal fluid balance
in the body by facilitating the oxidation and excretion of food. A high-
protein diet will also help keep the blood-sugar level stable. The reduction
in blood sugar that accompanies the premenstruum can produce an irresistible urge for sweets, which provide only temporary relief of fatigue
and listlessness. And the same blood-sugar drop can make women more
susceptible to the effects of alcohol.

Regular exercise will help carry off body fluids in the form of perspiration. Exercise also keeps the abdominal muscles in good working
order and prevents the congestion that so often leads to cramps during
the first or second day of the period. And both good diet and regular
exercise will help prevent constipation, another source of misery to the
already full and bloated abdomen.

Birth control pills can reduce PMS. One gynecologist told us that
approximately 25 percent of his patients who take the pill do so primarily
to ease PMS or dysmenorrhea. The usefulness of the pills is based on the
fact that they establish a false pregnancy in the reproductive organs, so
that although a woman continues to menstruate, she is not really experiencing a menstrual cycle.

Basically, the pills employ a combination of estrogen and progesterone
in proportions that approximate the hormonal conditions of pregnancy.
As in pregnancy, the pituitary gland is not stimulated to release FSH;
therefore, no egg is released; therefore, the ovulation part of the menstrual
cycle never occurs. Because there is no ovulation, there is no corresponding
rise in progesterone; with no rise in progesterone, the body's fluid level
remains more or less constant. Furthermore, the lower progesterone level
also prevents the contraction of the uterus that normally produces menstruation and possibly cramps. When a woman stops taking the pills after
twenty days, the accumulated blood and tissue leave her uterus because
there is nothing there to hold them, but the flow is not a true menstruation
if we consider menstruation to be one part of a complex monthly cycle.

Although many different types of pills are on the market, each with a different combination of the two hormones, they all work in this basic way. Obviously, the absence of fluid buildup and uterine contraction alleviates the most common symptoms of the premenstruum and the early days of the period. Although there is well-documented evidence that these pills have dangerous side effects, and some women find that they diminish sexual pleasure, for those who are willing and able to take risks, the pills are definitely beneficial in treatment of the normal but annoying symptoms of menstruation.

On the other hand, caffeine and epsom salts are two nonprescription drugs that help to reduce water retention. There are a number of premenstrual remedies on the market, including Trendar, Pamprin, Midol, Aqua-Ban, and Aquatabs. These pills are diuretics, and their major ingredients are caffeine and ammonium chloride. Some of them contain aspirin. Diuretics, although they relieve the physical symptoms of PMS, do not affect the mental symptoms. The pill docs both.

Removing the menses altogether through drugs has been suggested as a treatment for PMS, particularly for the severely retarded or for mental patients. If we remember Karen Paige's findings that the more diminished the flow, the less intense the premenstrual symptoms, menstrual suppression would seem a valid alternative to the menses in some cases. Of course, continued use of birth control pills can help a woman achieve this same effect; this practice, although relatively harmless on occasion (one's wedding day, a big sports competition), would undoubtedly increase the risks of dangerous side effects if prolonged. As far as we know, there have been no extensive studies or tests of such continuous usage.

More than a few gynecologists practice still another form of menstrual suppression: hysterectomy. A woman whose PMS is severe can easily find a doctor who will remove her uterus, thus eliminating the organ that is the focus of menstrual and premenstrual problems. Even though a hysterectomy may not be indicated for a serious medical reason, such as cancer, a precancerous condition, or deterioration of the endometrium, the operation has been performed to eliminate PMS.

Some clinicians see PMS as a response to anticipated sexual denial. Because women usually refrain from intercourse during their periods, they feel nervous or frustrated immediately before, and of course during, their days of abstinence. Paige's research would support this hypothesis. Paige found that women who had few negative attitudes toward sexual intercourse during their periods (about 50 percent of the Protestants in her sample) were the ones with the lowest incidence of PMS.

Whatever the causes of PMS, and in spite of the increasing possibility of alleviating it for most women, the argument that the menstruating woman poses a threat to her society is still heard. The following statistics and studies proving the incompetence of some premenstrual women are cited repeatedly as evidence that all women function in inferior fashion when subject to Eve's curse.

The "Women at Work" chapter of Dalton's *The Menstrual Cycle* is a compendium of aches and pains experienced by premenstrual women who work outside the home. Secretaries fill wastebaskets with spoiled work, executives fire the wrong people, forewomen slow down the assembly line, and factory workers stay home. This chapter gives apparent scientific support for Dr. Edgar Berman's widely publicized remark: "If you had an investment in a bank, you wouldn't want the president of your bank making a loan under these raging hormonal influences at that particular period."[10]

In 1959, a study was done in England of 102 uteri collected from one of Her Majesty's morgues in order to determine at what phase of her cycle a woman is most prone to fatal accidents and to suicide. By examining the cells of the endometrium, the investigators found the peak danger phase to be not the premenstrual phase, as we might suspect, but rather what is called the *midluteal* phase (days 17 to 23). In the bleeding phase itself, there was only 1 suicide and *no* accidental deaths.[11] Dalton found, however, in a study of hospital admissions, that 53 percent of women admitted for emergency accident treatment were in the menstrual or premenstrual phase.[12] But one author has suggested with refreshing logic that the accident-proneness of the premenstrual phase might be caused by the drugs women take to reduce the symptoms.[13] Statistics, as usual, can be marshaled to support either side.

One early study of accidents and the menstrual cycle teaches us a lesson in how scientific "evidence" can lead to discrimination against women. The investigator, who worked for the U. S. Department of Commerce, was disturbed by an increasing number of accidents among women pilots: "The United States have been practically depleted of women pilots by accidents," the investigator claimed. Of the three specific accidents he looked into, the three pilots were in fact menstruating (rather than *premenstruating*). In one, the plane was so demolished that "no satisfactory examination could be made of the control system." Of course, the control system would not have been menstruating.

The investigator did not insist that women be banned from the skies during their periods, but they should, he suggested, be aware of their weaknesses and ground themselves if they have problems. "If they are not able to evaluate their frailties while on the ground," he asks, "how are they going to evaluate them in the air?"[14]

The essay includes no assessment of the premenstrual phase, perhaps because it would have been harder for the investigator to establish proof. Nor does he compare the ratio of female accidents with that of male accidents. Nor does he consider such contributing factors as weather or control system malfunctions. Yet, in 1934, when this essay was written, women were being removed from the skies as pilots and going back up as stewardesses.

Of the 102 women whose uteri were subjected to Her Majesty's microscopes, most of those who committed suicide did so during the midluteal phase, with carbon monoxide poisoning being the leading cause of death. In a 1965 study of fifty-nine (live) women who had deliberately injured themselves, the researcher found a "premenstrual excess," defining premenstrual to include the seven days before the menses.[15] The most enlightening fact of this study is that premenstrual suicide attempts were most frequent among women who lived with a man. Fifty-six women who called the Saint Louis Suicide Prevention Center in 1971 also were predominantly premenstrual.[16]

The most statistically convincing connection between suicide and menstruation comes from Nairobi, Kenya, where, between 1955 and 1960, a doctor performed necropsies on twenty-two Hindu women who burned themselves to death and found that nineteen were menstruating at time of death and two were pregnant. Of three African women who hanged themselves, the same doctor discovered that all three were menstruating.[17]

In evaluating any demonstrated relationship between suicide and menstruation, we must keep in mind the fact that suicide rates among women are considerably lower than suicide rates among men. The 1973 *Information Please Almanac,* for example, lists not one country in which female suicides exceed male suicides. The highest percentage of female suicides among the places listed is in West Berlin, and even there, only slightly over 30 percent of total suicides are females. To our knowledge, no studies have been made of periodicity in male suicides.

In none of the studies of suicide and the menstrual cycle does the investigator examine the environmental situation surrounding the suicide. Had the premenstrual or menstrual woman been beaten by her husband or lover before attempting suicide? Had she been fired from her job? Had she been drinking? Had the Hindu women set themselves aflame for political reasons? Had it been raining for several weeks? We learn from A.

Alvarez's book on suicide, *The Savage God,* that the poet Sylvia Plath committed suicide during one of the coldest winters London had ever known. She was suffering from sinus problems, loneliness, depression, and cold. All the pipes in her flat had frozen solid. She had just come back from a weekend. She had no telephone. She was unable to reach her psychiatrist. There were at least fifty-nine other suicides in London that week, the weather being a major factor.[18]

Emile Durkheim, in his classic study *Suicide* (1897), *does* consider the effects of women's rhythms (along with the effects of aging, childlessness, widowhood, and divorce) on female suicides. He finds that the "sexual cycle" does *not* affect the suicide rate among women and offers a sociological explanation: "Woman kills herself less, and she kills others less, not because of physiological differences from man, but because she does not participate in collective life *in the same way.*"[19]

In her study "Menstruation and Crime," Dalton interviewed newly convicted women and women in prison who had been reported for bad behavior while jailed. She found that 49 percent of the crimes were committed menstrually or premenstrually, with theft being the most frequent (56 percent), alcoholism second (54 percent), and prostitution third (44 percent). Dalton explains that criminals were convicted most frequently in the premenstruum because slow reaction time and "mental dullness" made getting caught more likely.

Most other studies of the type support some correlation between menstruation and crime. But it is crucial to emphasize, as in the suicide studies, that women's crimes are far fewer than men's crimes. From a 1973 FBI report published in the 1975 *Information Please Almanac,* we learn that men commit 94.6 percent of all burglaries and 92.0 percent of all crimes involving possession of dangerous weapons. Women, on the other hand, commit 75.5 percent of crimes involving prostitution and commercialized vice, 31.5 percent of all larceny and theft, 26.7 percent of forging and counterfeit crimes, 34.2 percent of vagrancy crimes, 31.2 percent of all frauds, and 55.5 percent runaways. In all other areas, from a total of thirty categories, women commit well under 25 percent of the crimes in this country. In light of these statistics, the menstrual cycle becomes a minimal consideration.

Menstrual irregularities have frequently been associated with insanity, particularly with postpartum depression and schizophrenia. In a study conducted in the early 1930s, it was discovered that acutely disturbed women are often "exhibitionistic" about their menstrual blood. One "cyclothymic" woman had a habit of throwing "blood-stained sanitary napkins out of windows to boys"; another woman liked to smear herself with menstrual blood, which she called "the blood of Jesus Christ."[20] Many contemporary psychiatrists would argue that a schizophrenic's actions have meaning in terms of the society which oppresses her. These napkins, then, become a mark of defiance against a world that devalues and oppresses women.

Among women who have experienced extreme postpartum depression, there is sometimes a tendency for the psychotic episode to recur premenstrually once the menses has resumed. Repetition of psychotic behavior during the premenstrual phase was also observed in a twenty-one-year-old black college student who was declared "sick" when she became abusive to her teachers and "began to use words in German which she had incidentally learned." The student was given shock treatment by her white male doctors for her premenstrual disorder. Another black woman, a patient of the same doctors, was given a series of eight shock treatments to cure her premenstrual disorientation. The symptoms nevertheless returned during her next premenstruum but eventually disappeared after she was treated with drugs.[21]

Because of long-established connections between psychosis and PMS, some forensic psychiatrists have argued that severe and ascertainable premenstrual disorders should be considered grounds for the insanity plea. The French have long viewed PMS as grounds for temporary insanity, although Americans have not.

In 1953, a New York law professor made a strong case for the premenstrual syndrome as a legal defense. Arguing that the hypoglycemic factor of the premenstruum can account for "impairment of self control" and for "moral insanity," the professor insisted that the law must deal with PMS, just as it must deal with "the phenomenon of insanity or gravity."[22] In a counterargument, another lawyer claimed that it is "totally misleading" to connect "a procedure such as a vaginal smear with a person's legal responsibility."[23] A vaginal smear, it seems, is one of the proofs of PMS that the defendant would be expected to produce in court.

In a lengthy essay written in 1971,[24] Aleta Wallach and Larry Rubin analyze medical data and legal precedent in order to establish PMS as a plea for "diminished capacity," meaning that the defendant did not at the time of the crime have a specific criminal intent. They also suggest that PMS would be useful in plea bargaining (pleading guilty to a lesser charge in order to get a reduced sentence). Wallach and Rubin base their argument on a number of complex issues and past rulings. One of their strongest points is that the chromosomal imbalance known as the XYY syndrome, a genetic defect in men, has been successfully used as a defense; yet PMS, which they define as an organic disorder, has been largely ignored in legal writings. They emphasize that the defense would have the most chance of success in the state of California, where the attitude toward temporary insanity is more flexible than in other states and where the plea of "diminished capacity" has legal precedent.

Wallach and Rubin anticipate one of the basic objections to their argument: namely, that PMS would then become a *legal* justification for discrimination against women. They stress that PMS is an organic disease only for some women, not for women as a class, and that those women who do have severe mental disturbances during the premenstrual phase deserve the protection of the law. Nor do they think that a woman would have to provide a case history of premenstrual disorders before the court. Because the medical profession has for years been treating the syndrome as imaginary, they argue that it would be unreasonable to expect a woman to provide evidence of treatment in establishing the syndrome as an alibi.[25]

We think it likely that a judge would demand proof if PMS were used as a defense. The defendant would probably be asked to furnish evidence of a past history of premenstrual disorders, and she would have to prove that she was in the premenstrual phase of her cycle when the crime was committed. This record would entail visits to a psychiatrist and submission to laboratory tests. But perhaps the greatest discomfort would occur in the courtroom, where the woman's menstrual cycle would become public information. Given the public silence on this subject, a defendant might be reluctant to employ PMS in her defense. If she bravely spoke about her menstrual cycle in court, the jury, which would be likely to believe many of the cultural myths about menstruation, might be unsympathetic.

Real as the premenstrual symptoms are, it seems to us that enshrining them in the legal system of the United States would pose more problems than it would solve. At a moment in history when the Equal Rights Amendment is looked upon as the great eraser of all statutory distinctions between the sexes and the only hope for women's equality before the law, such a step would be regressive.

There is one final alternative to the problem of PMS, one that is diametrically opposed to menstrual suppression. Rather than reduce or eliminate the menses, that visible sign of woman's otherness, we could instead psychologically embrace the blood that is ours, making of menstruation an affirmation instead of a denial. There is at work in our bodies a menstrual dialectic, a complicated shift of rhythms, a tension and then a release from tension. The more conscious we become, the more fully we can sense these rhythms, the more self-knowledge we shall achieve. As Nancy Milford has written: "There is something of unalterable value in woman's experience: the very cyclical motion of her body makes her life marked by upheaval, change and discharge. I am not willing to say that she is more vulnerable because of it, but that it is instead a source of potential strength; change need not stun her or threaten her, for she is in constant flux."[26] To reject and eliminate the body processes, to let our moods be dampened through progesterone or estrogen or testosterone, is in part to agree with those who hold that womanhood is an inferior state of being.

One of the acknowledged symptoms of PMS is a sharp increase in drive and energy. Some women enjoy this drive and energy; they find it creative. Premenstrual tension can mean, depending on who is defining it, an acuteness of sensibility and a sharpening, rather than a dulling, of intelligence. It can be a time for directing our hormonally induced irritability into significant social action that will challenge the society that would curtail our movement and keep us grounded.

Tests, graphs, and questionnaires by the dozens have been designed to show the extent of woman's premenstrual or menstrual misery. Yet Parlee is one of the few researchers to question the soundness of such questionnaires, which she claims reflect a bias toward treating menstruation as a problem and which in effect measure stereotypical beliefs. Parlee is working on new kinds of psychological tests, ones that would measure a woman's premenstrual strengths rather than her premenstrual tensions.[27]

We believe that with a more positive attitude toward female processes, researchers could begin to view PMS in an altogether different framework. In the case of the *Menstrual Distress Questionnaire* devised by Rudolph H. Moos in 1969, for example, the title reveals quite clearly that the attitudes will be negative. Of the forty-seven items in the questionnaire, only five predict positive results, for example, "feelings of well-being" or "bursts of energy or activity." The other forty-two questions measure menstrual distress, for example, "avoid social activities" or "decreased efficiency."[28] The questionnaire, because of its overwhelmingly negative emphasis, is bound to show negative results.

If the questionnaire were called the *Menstrual Joy Questionnaire,* if the majority of items asked for responses such as "happiness" or "feeling great" or "able to plot effective strategy" or "increased creativity," the end results would inevitably be different. We have learned from the many studies on suicide that women's suicide attempts occur at a "certain" time of the month, although at what time is rarely consistent. There are no

MENSTRUAL JOY QUESTIONNAIRE

Name _____   Occupation _____
Age _____   Today's date _____

Below is a list of pleasures which women sometimes experience. Kindly evaluate your experience of these pleasures during the three different states listed below:

    A. During your most recent menstrual flow
    B. During the week preceding your menstrual flow
    C. During the remainder of your cycle

Write the number in each space which corresponds most accurately to your experience:

    1 = none
    2 = hardly noticeable
    3 = mild
    4 = moderate
    5 = strong
    6 = acute

NOTE: In answering the questionnaire, reflect the experiences of your *most recent* cycle.

	A. most recent flow	B. week before	C. remainder of cycle
1. High spirits			
2. Increased sexual desire			
3. Vibrant activity			
4. Revolutionary zeal			
5. Intense concentration			
6. Feelings of affection			
7. Self-confidence			
8. Sense of euphoria			
9. Creativity			
10. Feelings of power			

studies, to our knowledge, of creativity or good works during the pre-menstruum. Who knows what suffragist and feminist strategy was initiated during Elizabeth Cady Stanton's or Lucy Komisar's premenstrual phase? What day did Billie Jean King have circled on her calendar when she massacred Bobby Riggs with her drive, energy, aggressiveness, and self-control? (It is said that King had hypoglycemia a week before the match.)

These questions, which cannot be asked in a vacuum or answered in a laboratory, are the kinds of issues that historians and psychologists must bring into the open if they are to assess the effects of PMS on women's public and private lives. Tests, graphs, and questionnaires by the dozens have been designed to determine the extent of woman's incompetence. Now we need to measure a woman's premenstrual strength.

Afterword

BEWARE: I AM ARMED AND HAVE PREMEN-STRUAL TENSION   So reads a button from a novelty store, sent us by an understanding friend. It is a sign that the world may finally be getting interested in women's premenstrual "strength."

PMS: a flyer from a vitamin store promises to cure it with a smor-gasbord of vitamins and minerals; ads in popular magazines offer "PRE-MESYN PMS" and other pills with catchy names which are really nothing more than mild diuretics plus over-the-counter painkillers, dressed up to serve the 1980s version of the curse. Another flyer, this from a tampon manufacturer, solicits membership for a national nonprofit organization devoted to its sufferers' interests.

PMS has become a growth industry, with all the implications for good and ill that term implies. On the one hand, medical research into the causes and "cures" for PMS has increased dramatically. On the other, "PMS profiteers" are relieving sufferers of millions of dollars with false promises of unproven "cures." The sad fact is that in the past ten years the ever-expanding knowledge about the origins of the syndrome has not led to much in the way of significant relief but has tended to reinforce the value of a strictly controlled diet as the most beneficial "treatment." Michelle Harrison's *Self-help for PMS* was the pioneering work in this area.[29]

Judith Green, a contributor to the 1982 *Behavior and the Menstrual Cycle*, reviewed the tests conducted on diuretics, progesterone, lithium, bromocriptine, pyrodoxine, physical activity, neuroleptics, psychotherapy, and bellergal and found them *all* inconclusive for relief of PMS. Oral contraceptives (as we noted on pages 88-89) did the most good, and prostaglandins looked promising.[30]

Here is a digest of what we *have* learned, from the literally hundreds of books and articles circulating on the subject, about new developments in causes, treatment, legal effects, and social implications of PMS (no need to update our readers on the symptoms—they remain depressingly the same).

The consensus today is that PMS has a physiological origin but that it is accompanied by certain psychological symptoms. Further, that it is not one disorder but many, which at least one researcher, Guy Abraham, thinks can be classified into four subgroups according to their symptoms and recommended treatments: PMT-A afflicts women with anxiety, irritability, and nervous tension, occurring as early as mid-cycle and intensifying as menstruation approaches. PMT-H causes women to experience premenstrual weight gain and bloating. PMT-C describes those who succumb to increased appetites and cravings for sweets, followed by fainting spells, fatigue, and headaches. And PMT-D afflicts those who experience premenstrual depression or suffer suicidal thoughts or attempts.[31] Dr. Abraham's categories are tidy ways to pigeonhole PMS for medical and other practitioners. But any woman suffering from PMS and looking at those symptoms would probably find that she experiences at least one or two from *each* group every month.

Yet with the overwhelming evidence that the premenstrual syndrome has real physical symptoms, physicians are still not sure how to treat it. Often the theories and experiments of one researcher are not borne out by the work of another. The theory of British doctor Katharina Dalton that the drop in progesterone levels immediately before the onset of the flow is responsible for the symptoms is still the basis for her course of treatment,[32] although in thirty years only one study has emerged to find progesterone useful in PMS treatment. One study cited by Dr. Penny Budoff, a family practitioner and pioneer in menstrual pain relief, actually disproved Dalton's results.[33]

Budoff tried harder, however, to find causes for and relief from premenstrual pain. She noted that during the premenstruum increased prostaglandin levels, which affect brain chemicals, have a direct impact on mood and produce the congestive pain many women associate with PMS. She then tried the antiprostaglandin medicine used for the spasmodic pain of arthritis to treat dysmenorrhea and PMS, experimenting first on herself. While she had much success with these drugs (now marketed over-the-counter as Motrin, Advil, e.g.), she cautions that we remember that PMS is such a complex set of symptoms that there is no "magic bullet" to cure them all.[34]

Eleven years ago we told you to watch your diet, get plenty of exercise, restrict salt, and be careful how you use tranquilizers or oral contraceptives. The same advice is being dispensed today (though the use of caffeine as a diuretic may exacerbate breast tenderness and hypoglycemic-type symptoms). If you do go to a doctor for PMS relief, however, a wide variety of therapies may be tried, according to the knowledge, interest, or bias of the practitioner you see.

According to its fans, the most effective of these is progesterone therapy. There are no known significant adverse side effects of long-term progesterone use mainly because no conclusive studies of long-term users had been revealed, as far as we knew, as of 1986. But any long-term hormonal manipulation must be considered risky, and "*no* treatment currently available can be cited as unconditionally suitable for sufferers of premenstrual syndrome." Dr. Dalton treats patients with synthetic progesterone, usually administered in suppository form. Pharmacists in the U.S. may make up the suppositories according to a doctor's prescription, but although they have been legally available in Great Britain for years, the suppositories may not be *manufactured* in the U.S. until the many tests required by the Food and Drug Administration are completed. Progesterone therapy has never been implicated as a cause of cancer, for example, but many reasonable people wonder if all the votes are in on its safety.[35]

Antiprostaglandins, along with thyroid treatment and prolactin suppression, are some of the medical therapies for PMS relief. Prolactin, the substance which releases the milk in nursing mothers and which tends to rise in women around the premenstruum, is known to be increased in the blood by a group of commonly prescribed tranquilizers—thus the dubious value of treating PMS with Valium or Librium. Many doctors prescribe diuretics for women whose water retention is high, although Budoff believes that most of the diuretics prescribed—medicines that lower blood pressure and deplete the body of potassium—are unnecessarily powerful for use in PMS treatment and may bring their own set of problems. Naturally occurring diuretics in foods like grapefruit and others high in vitamin C, or an over-the-counter drug like Aqua-Ban, can usually do the job.

Because the physiological etiology of PMS has documented psychological implications, much attention has been given in recent years to the identification and treatment of the effects of PMS on the sufferer's mental state. Mary Brown Parlee—one of the many researchers today actively studying PMS and the brain—cites the various studies showing psychological correlations between PMS and aberrant behavior, beginning with Dalton's statistical findings on PMS and crime, accidents, and hospitalization. Parlee focuses on one of Dalton's early studies showing that college students facing an examination actually began to menstruate just before the exam, owing, she concludes, to the stress induced by the test.[36]

Like medical research, however, psychological research also remains inconclusive. Norris and Sullivan's thorough study of PMS treats the subjects of psychoanalysis, psychotherapy, and, especially, psychotropic drugs (tranquilizers and others). Norris and Sullivan point out, through analysis of the literature and case histories known to them, that there is an unknown correlation between PMS and depression, the mental illness that affects so many more women than men. Many times a woman presenting symptoms of clinical depression may actually be suffering from PMS, which is, by definition, a periodic disorder, disappearing when menstruation starts. Or a woman who actually has the disease of depression may be diagnosed by her physician as a PMS sufferer, because the symptoms of PMS so closely follow—and often mask—the symptoms of depression. Why this problem is so difficult to pinpoint, moreover, may be seen in Norris's comment that "research into the causes of depression . . . has indicated that hormones may play a role in triggering the [depression] episodes. It may well be that the hormonal changes critical to the orchestration of the menstrual cycle spark the mood swings and depressed states."[37]

Perhaps this ambiguity has something to do with Parlee's discussion of and ultimate questions about the Menstrual Distress Questionnaires (MDQs) pioneered by Rudolph Moos, which are still very much in circulation and remain a large influence on his findings about PMS.[38] Parlee notes that the MDQs frequently get the same responses from men as from women, reflecting either the expectations of both sexes about the menstrual cycle or the male respondents' reflection of what the women in their lives experience rather than an unbiased and uninfluenced clinical account of symptoms. Therefore, she says, "*Particular patterns of responses on menstrual distress questionnaires cannot be interpreted as accurate reports of personal experience without further research* using other measures or responses to establish the validity of women's responses and self-reports."[39]

All of the ambiguity surrounding the origins and treatment of PMS as a "disease" of the body or of the mind comes to the foreground when PMS goes to court. Since the first edition of this book, at least two murderers in England received reduced sentences because they successfully pled that PMS precipitated the mental imbalance that caused their crime. Dr. Dalton was the expert witness in both of these cases.[40] The PMS defense has not been used *per se* in the U.S., although in a civil suit arising from a stabbing incident in Colorado the defendant tried unsuccessfully to win her case based on a plea of diminished capacity (similar to the defense in England, diminished responsibility) due to PMS.

Thoughtful people—male and female, in the legal profession and out—are troubled by the implications of PMS being enshrined in law as a *pro forma* defense, like the insanity defense. While PMS may be accompanied by wildly erratic behavior, it differs from insanity in significant ways, the obvious one being the cyclical nature of true PMS behavior. Norris thinks PMS falls into a "legal no-man's land between insanity and 'automatism,' the condition in which an individual acts automatically and without conscious knowledge of his acts."[41] If PMS is given the test of the M'Naughton Rule, the 1843 British case in which insanity was established as a condition or disease of the mind in which the individual acts without being aware of what he or she is doing, it fails to match up. PMS is a condition arising from changes in the body, not a "disease of the mind," for one thing, and for another, there is no evidence that PMS sufferers do not know what they are doing. They may be acting under an irresistible impulse, like kleptomania, but they are not insane according to the law.[42]

The American Psychiatric Association entered the dispute over PMS in 1986 with its revisions of the third edition of the Diagnostic and Statistical Manual of Mental Disorders (DSM-III), the most widely accepted criteria for diagnosing mental problems. The APA is considering listing something they call "premenstrual dysphoric disorder" in the next printing of this manual (to be called DSM-III-R) as a description or definition of some of the behavioral symptoms associated with PMS. Many in the profession believe that labeling PMS as a mental disorder would ultimately label all women—just as would establishing PMS as a legal defense. It is especially dangerous coming at a time when the etiology of PMS is still unclear and when new connections are uncovered every day about the relation of premenstrual symptoms to activity in the brain.[43]

Some of the most significant work being done in this field, in fact, is questioning the bias of the research. Randi Daimon Koeske, for example, eschews those methodologies that try to relate "bad" emotions to biologic imbalances or the no-effect approaches to PMS research that say there is no consistent relationship between the cycle and emotional behavior. She tries instead to differentiate explicitly between beliefs about premenstrual emotionality and the sources of the emotionality itself, asking the same question we have asked elsewhere in this book: why are the positive emotions associated with the premenstruum never studied as a clue to premenstrual behavior or to the real nature of women and their cycles?[44]

The many attitudes towards PMS, its treatment, and its sociological implications were illustrated on that great small world of television in March 1984, when Janice Delaney was one of fourteen women who discussed the PMS "controversy" on the nationally syndicated show, *woman to woman*. The participants included Dr. Katharina Dalton and several PMS sufferers who swore by her progesterone therapy; Virginia Cassara, who as the founder of PMS Action runs one of the most widespread and successful PMS support and referral organizations in the U.S.; Andrea Boroff Eagan, the author of the October 1983 *Ms.* article, "The Selling of Premenstrual Syndrome,"[45] which was highly critical of both progesterone therapy and Cassara's group; the defendant in the stabbing incident mentioned above and her attorney; Judith Ramey, a San Francisco attorney specializing in employment discrimination cases (and coincidentally, the daughter of Estelle Ramey, the Georgetown endocrinologist we cite on page 268 for her work in the cycles and rhythms of men); Carol Downer, the menstrual extraction pioneer (see page 255); and other women who, as social workers and feminist organizers, had helping and sharing relationships with PMS sufferers.

The discussion was more than lively; it was occasionally bitter and accusatory. As the group debated the merits of therapies and the publicity generated by PMS as a legal defense, it illustrated the "PMS dilemma": how far can medicine go to recognize, treat, and "legalize" PMS as an exclusively female condition without endangering the extremely tenuous position of women in the economy and the political arena in the 1980s and beyond? Women are becoming publicly divided on this problem, with many of those who call themselves feminists generally seen as opposing the publicizing and dramatizing of PMS symptoms, not only because of the impact such ideas could have on women's progress in the world, but also because they see women being exploited in a new way. As we have shown, no one therapy for PMS has been proved overwhelmingly effective, and few have been tested for long-term side effects.

If in 1976 a woman had responded to our advice in *The Curse* to "psychologically embrace the blood that is ours" and look upon the fluctuations and mood swings of the menstrual cycle as a potential source of strength, she would have found herself nearly alone in her self-affirmation. Today, however, she would be supported, not to say beset, on all sides by people who want to help. "PMS societies," support groups, clinics, and centers exist in nearly every state. Books and articles on the subject appear as regularly as menstruation itself. While these organizations must do some good in steering women toward appropriate therapies, one can't help but think that they too might be looking to PMS as a source of strength—strength to the financial positions of their sponsors.

And throwing a monkey wrench into the whole debate is this news from the *New York Times* in June 1985: "Biologists studying wild primates in Kenya have found that premenstrual female baboons display symptoms resembling those of premenstrual syndrome in women. In the days just before onset of menstruation, female baboons eat more and are less social than at other times."[46] This startling finding reinforces the growing conviction among professionals and laywomen that PMS is an overwhelmingly physical fact of life. The baboons, which have reproductive systems similar to humans' and are frequently used in research, may ultimately provide the "missing link" between premenstrual physiology and premenstrual behavior, and release all women from the chains of their own and society's expectations about premenstrual "madness."[47]

PART THREE

The Menstruating
Woman in the
Popular Imagination

Chapter 10

"What Every Girl Should Know"

There is a community of experience among women who have come of age in twentieth-century America. Conversations about The First Time seem to be punctuated with "You, too?" or "Wait'll you hear how I found out . . . !" We release our precious "dirty" secrets and laugh in relief when we are understood, for those adolescent attempts to understand what the "glory of womanhood" was all about were thwarted on every side by euphemisms. From the anxious comparisons among the eleven-year-olds to the tight-lipped acknowledgments of some mothers that, "Yes, Virginia, you are a woman now," the play unfolding within our bodies has been spoken largely in whispers.

The coming of our periods might have been relatively normal events in the mixed-up teen years. But we learned quickly that however frankly menstruation might be discussed at home, the world did not want to hear of it. We live in a greeting-card culture where, for twenty-five cents, we can purchase socially approved statements about childbirth, marriage, or death. But Hallmark manufactures no cards that say, "Best Wishes on Becoming a Woman." Rather than celebrate the coming-of-age in America, we hide the fact of the menarche, just as we are advised to deodorize, sanitize, and remove the evidence. Even the booklets from Modess and Kotex (themselves monuments of greeting-card blandness), which we giggled over and learned by heart in the forbidden hours at slumber parties, were sent in plain brown wrappers.

We who grew up in the fifties think that these booklets were as important in shaping our permanent consciousness about menstruation as the attitudes of our mothers and our friends. The message from the manufacturers, of course, was aimed at getting us to use more and more napkins, to send for "training kits" so we'd be prepared, paraphernaliawise at least, for the big day (becoming a woman in the United States involves education for consumerhood as much as the kiddie shows and their paper cereals do). But the message behind the ads was hard-sell shame: *Cover it up.* Use our product because "nothing will show"; "no one will know"; "your secret will be safe."

The information about menstruation available to our daughters, compared with what our mothers might have read, shows few changes: deodorize, sanitize, hide your shame, although some companies seem to be groping their way toward a more positive educational message.

In 1934, a female "Voice of Experience" gave the following advice to young readers: Girls should not exercise, play tennis, or wear high-heeled shoes during their periods; such activity can cause a prolapsed uterus. Girls should wear tight-fitting bloomers during the winter menstrual cycles; otherwise, they are likely to develop a "catarrhal condition" in the delicate vaginal tissues. The Voice of Experience discouraged cold or hot baths, swimming, horseback riding, "athletic dancing, lifting of heavy weights, doing arduous household duties, etc." The punishment for this sort of activity during the menstrual period includes fallen organs, irregular menstruation, and a "critical menopause."[1]

Most current advice books, far from forbidding exercise and baths, recommend lots of fresh air, exercise, and personal hygiene. In a pamphlet distributed by Kimberly-Clark, the makers of Kotex, a girl is assured that she can do everything during her period that she does during the rest of the month: shampoo her hair, go to gym class, shower, and dance. The pamphlet does not mention "arduous household duties." The booklets also tend to de-emphasize the actual bother of menstruation, although most perceptive adolescents can readily conclude, from all the instructions about keeping clean and changing napkins, that it can indeed be a messy business.

Another common theme in advice books is that menstruation means motherhood. In *A Doctor Talks to Teenagers* (1948), the doctor urges his readers to view the menarche as a time for strengthening the maternal instinct. Men and women are equally intelligent, the doctor conceded, but "man's world is in the economic and industrial field, while woman's domain is in the higher spiritual activities of society and the home."[2]

But recognizing the childbearing aspect of menstruation when you are thirteen does not bring personal fulfillment, any more than a boy's first wet dream signals the glorious achievement of potential fatherhood. In

You and Your Daughter, a pamphlet published by Kimberly-Clark in 1968, ovulation is discussed realistically, with the bearing of a child treated as a future possibility rather than an immediate joy. "The mere fact of menstruation does not always mean that a girl is mature enough to have babies—either biologically or psychologically" is the advice. "A young girl cannot become a mature full-fledged woman overnight."

The napkin manufacturers also obtain wide circulation for their educational films, which are generally based on their major pamphlets and are designed to be shown in schools. Kimberly-Clark has for about twenty years been floating a Walt Disney production called *The Story of Menstruation.* In the Disney world, the menstrual flow is not blood red but snow white. The vaginal drawings look more like a cross section of a kitchen sink than the inside and outside of a woman's body. There are no hymen, no clitoris, no labia; all focus is on the little nest and its potentially lush lining. Although Disney and Kimberly-Clark advise exercise during the period, the exercising cartoon girls (who look like Disney's Cinderella) are drawn without feet; bicycles magically propel themselves down the street without any muscular or mental direction from the cyclist. The film ends happily ever after, with a shot of a lipsticked bride followed immediately by a shot of a lipsticked mother and baby.

In *Naturally . . . a Girl,* a film produced by the Personal Products Company (Modess) for "girls 9–14 and their mothers," the drawings are more realistically done; however, there are still no cervix, clitoris, or labia. Boys as well as girls are included in the filmed discussions. The film ends with a series of shots of working women: lineswomen, cops, mothers, secretaries. The last words are: "It's better than being a boy!"

The minute sex becomes the school subject, boys and girls are separated. In the juvenile novel *Are You There God? It's Me, Margaret* (written by Judy Blume, who has also written the Personal Products Company's updated *Growing Up and Liking It*) an appropriately satiric treatment is given to these separate sex-ed classes. The sixth-grade girls attend a film, *What Every Girl Should Know,* sponsored by the PTA. "The film told us about the ovaries and explained why girls menstrooate, but it didn't tell us how it feels, except to say that it is not painful, which we knew anyway. Also it didn't really show a girl getting it. It just said how wonderful nature was and how we would soon become women and all that."[3]

During the PTA lecture, Nancy, one of Margaret's friends, asked the shocking question, "How about Tampax?" The advice giver's flustered response is, "We don't advise *internal protection* until you are considerably older." Prohibiting tampons to youngsters probably has little to do with discomfort or lack of accommodation but, rather, most likely reflects the fear that a girl may ruin her hymen, that magical tissue of flesh that never gets shown in the how-to-insert folders. In the book *Our Bodies, Ourselves,* an illustration actually shows six different hymens, or maidenheads. The Boston Women's Health Collective, which wrote the book, takes aim at the myth that tampons can be used only after losing one's virginity. They explain that there are openings in the hymen through which the fluid flows and through which it is, except in rare cases, quite possible to insert a tampon.[4]

Few advice books or pamphlets are so honest. Few films or illustrations show, as *Our Bodies, Ourselves* does, a hymen or a clitoris, both of them parts of a woman's anatomy. And few books are so direct in talking about the realities of the menstrual process.

Are You There God . . . and *Our Bodies, Ourselves* indicate a possible change of direction. Another is the attempt, albeit thwarted, to initiate a To Be a Woman badge for girl scouts. This badge was proposed by the Philadelphia Girl Scout Council and would have included the scouts' learning about a number of topics of vital importance to them: menstruation, abortion, contraception, rape, and job discrimination. As one of their assignments, they would have been required to discuss menstruation with their mothers and grandmothers. One of the mothers who helped defeat the proposal commented: "Being a Girl Scout means baking cookies for old ladies on Christmas and watering the plants at the railroad station."[5]

This controversial matter will emerge again, not only in Philadelphia but in rural areas, not only among the Girl Scouts of America but among the 4-H clubs, the Y-Teens, the Camp Fire Girls. For, like Margaret, young women know that they can swim and dance and use tampons if they want to without any serious physical or psychological damage. But even this minimal amount of knowledge and openness about menstruation has had to break through strong barriers of innuendo and taboo.

Afterword

Among the things every girl should know today is how to avoid contracting toxic shock syndrome from tampons stuffed with untested ingredients by an industry as determined to sell tampons to teenagers now as it was reluctant to do so before (see chapter 14 for a full discussion of the history of and current thinking on TSS). While Personal Products Company's *Growing Up and Liking It* was revised in 1983 to include information about TSS and what to do if its symptoms appear—still in Judy Blume's delightful epistolary text—Tampax, Inc.'s 1983 booklet for nine- to fourteen-year-olds, "Accent on You," does not mention TSS. Even though teenagers are at statistically highest risk for contracting this disease, Tampax's booklet states flatly, "When you begin to menstruate, you are old enough to use Tampax tampons and can use them right from the start." Promoting the line especially developed for the youth market, the booklet notes, "Junior and Slender Regular Tampax tampons are perfect for beginners. They're slim as can be . . . ." Tampax in 1985 was also promoting its New Petal Soft Tampax—"It's perfect for beginners like us"—in such teenage markets as *Seventeen,* with no mention of TSS in the ad.

Tampax's complete package of educational materials, including a TSS-less teacher's guide, does contain one large sheet of information on TSS and one reproduction of the federally mandated tampon box warning. But not to include information and warnings on the actual books used in the classroom or in the home throws into clear relief the less-than-educational nature of these publications. Selling the product, we are shockingly reminded, is the bottom line.

Undoubtedly this climate of corporate irresponsibility was one of the factors that prompted the U.S. Food and Drug Administration to send posters warning about TSS to junior and senior high schools all over the country in the fall of 1985. According to a July 1985 report in the *Washington Post,* the agency believed that many girls just entering their menstruating years were too young to remember the enormous publicity surrounding the discovery of TSS and its link to tampons in the late 70s and early 80s and that their mothers, no longer barraged daily by reports of new cases and new recalls of products, might think the disease had gone away.

The FDA poster warns "TOXIC SHOCK SYNDROME IS SO RARE YOU MIGHT FORGET IT CAN HAPPEN," lists the symptoms and immediate action to be taken on the front, and on the back includes lesson plans and other teacher aids so that discussion of the disease can become part of the regular sex-ed curriculum. To emphasize the value of such classroom conversations, Dr. Lawrence D'Angelo of Children's Hospital National Medical Center in Washington, D.C. told the *Post* about a twelve-year-old TSS patient of his who recognized her symptoms (her mother thought she had the flu), immediately removed her tampon and called her doctor, and ultimately saved her own life because she had been taught in school what to do.[6]

Despite this negative climate surrounding menstruation in relation to TSS, many people, parents as well as educators, are seeking to make the menarche a happier experience for this generation than it might have been for the ones before. Recalling our report about the abortive girl scout efforts in Philadelphia in the 1970s to encourage discussion among mothers, daughters, and grandmothers about the menarche, we find the work of Byllye Avery in Atlanta to be a reassuring sign of progress. Mrs. Avery is the executive director of the National Black Women's Health Project, which focuses on the many health issues pertinent to black women. But she is also very much the mother in her sensitivity to her daughter and other menarcheal girls.

To help mothers and daughters confront the changes in their bodies and talk about them, she instituted a workshop for mothers and daughters called "On Becoming a Woman." These workshops give mothers and daughters an opportunity to talk about first periods. Then every aspect of the menstrual function—from paraphernalia to plumbing to the ultimate choices women face for responsible sexuality—is discussed between the generations.

It is significant that these workshops are free from association with school or church. Those who criticize the teaching of reproductive biology in the schools—to our way of thinking, *one* of the places it belongs—have rarely offered concrete suggestions to mothers and fathers as to how they properly may communicate this vital information to their children. Mrs. Avery is one of the few persons actually to give the family some help in carrying out its responsibilities. As she says, "Motherhood is a difficult job and frequently requires on-the-job training."[7]

And yet the subject of menstruation remains encumbered with the emotional baggage brought by mother and daughter, teacher and student, bags not easily unpacked just because a celebrity discusses her PMS on television and perhaps clears the air for others. We wrote in 1976 of the ambivalence with which mothers sometimes greeted their daughters' menarche. Since then, we have learned more about the daughters' fears and anxieties.

For example, Wellesley College psychologists Elissa Koff and Jill Rierdan tested the validity of the hypothesis that for preteens, "becoming a woman" was cause for joy. They asked forty-three white, middle-class seventh and eighth graders to complete this thought: "Ann just got her period for the first time. Her first reaction was . . ." The sixteen girls in the group who had not yet menstruated imagined that Ann felt proud, happy, excited. The eighteen who had, however, opined that Ann wanted to cry, die, or throw up. Nine girls were so embarrassed by the question they wouldn't tell the researchers whether or not they had menstruated, while the sixteen-year-old daughter of one told her mother she was "humiliated" by her research.[8]

Another study by Susan Stoltzman found that adolescent girls reported more symptoms and negative feelings about menstruation than did their mothers, probably because, Stoltzman found, their mothers' long experience with menstruation makes them less likely to notice monthly disturbances. Her study also shows that teenage girls get far more messages from the media about menstruation than they get from their mothers, leading us to infer that even a mother with a healthy, positive attitude towards menstruation may be stymied in her attempts to communicate the "friendly monthly nuisance" attitude to her daughter.[9]

These findings are supported by conversations we have had with educators and parents and, indeed, by the experience of living through our own daughters' menarches since 1976. One director of a private elementary school for girls told us that the fourth and fifth graders are usually much more interested in the sex-ed component of the science curriculum than are the sixth graders—many of whom have begun to menstruate. The director speculated that the children are more disturbed about the loss of their childish bodies than grownups think and cited the sloppy big shirts and sweaters common to this group—no matter what the prevailing style— as evidence of their anxieties.

But personal experience also tells us of the imaginative menarcheal celebrations of the 1980s—mothers and fathers, sisters and brothers, sharing the day with the "new woman" with red roses; the special gifts of watches and calendars; the happy, funny meals of spaghetti with red sauce, strawberry ice cream, and a grown-up glass of red wine.

So it was with great pleasure that we learned that the excellent *What's Happening to My Body?*, a book for young teens, was a mother-daughter effort. Lynda Madaras, a women's health writer, decided to write this book as a response to her daughter Area's troubled early adolescence. Correctly linking the sullen or wildly emotional behavior at home with the exclusionary "playground politics" of preteen girls, and both with the children's confusion and bewilderment about their changing bodies, she began to realize that celebrating the menarche or knowing how to wear a sanitary napkin may not be enough to support girls through the storms of adolescence. So she and her daughter collaborated on a two-hundred-page book that speaks directly to girls between nine and fourteen, in their language, but does not patronize.

There are forty pages on menstruation alone, including drawings of paraphernalia and discussion of PMS, TSS, and symptoms of less serious fluctuations of the cycle. *What's Happening to My Body?* explains the four phases of the monthly cycle and helps readers anticipate their first period by showing them how to make charts chronicling the five stages of breast and pubic hair development. Lots of attention is given to the impossibility of all girls looking like "the cultural norm," whatever that happens to be this year, and to the importance of liking one's own body. It also details the sexual development of boys, thus removing yet another layer of mystery from the human body.[10]

All in all, Lynda Madaras's and Byllye Avery's work is a welcome addition to a field that, in the past, probably was dominated by the sanitary products manufacturers because ordinary women were too firmly in the grip of their society's taboos and their own ignorance to reach out collectively to their daughters.

Chapter 11

The Monthly Euphemism

One of the notable qualities of menstruation is its democracy. No respecter of class lines, no quibbler with standards of decency, it strikes all women in all walks of life.

The menstrual consciousness expressed in literature and psychoanalysis is likely to be that of an individual sensibility, that is, the response of one artist or doctor to a woman's monthly bleedings. But the materials of popular culture, the jokes and advertisements, because they are anonymous or at least unattributed, are much better clues to mass psychology, to what "the people" think.

Several common themes appear in popular verbal expressions used with menstruation.[1] Time and regularity, blood and redness are the most obvious factors, but expressions are also likely to refer to visitors, to illness or inconvenience, and to male or female persons. And especially in American slang—more open, less inhibited than that of most other cultures—there are references to menstrual paraphernalia and to the taboo against sex during menstruation.

The number of menstrual expressions in a language often indicates the society's attitudes toward women's periods. The more openly the subject is accepted, the more words there are. In a study made in 1947 and 1948, Natalie F. Joffe found that Irish, English, Polish, and Yiddish had very scanty menstrual vocabularies, but that there was an abundance of expressions in German, Italian, and French and a flood of Americanisms.

If common expressions indicate what is most obvious and noticeable, then one of the most obvious facts about menstruation is that it keeps coming back every month, as in the Italian "the month," the Yiddish "the monthly time," the Polish "every month," the Irish "in season," the German "the time," the English and American "it's her time of the month" and "the monthlies." In French, menstruation is *les règles* ("the rules"), for its regularity.

The monthly visitation is frequently referred to as a visitor, particularly a red one, such as a "red aunt." In German (as in Yiddish) the visitor is "the red king" or the "tailor" or is called by a name, Frederick Barbarossa. Visitor expressions may date back to the Middle Ages; Frederick Barbarossa (red beard) lived in the twelfth century. Although their country no longer has an official ruling family, Italian women may still visit "the magnificent marquis." The French may say, "I have Jacques" (or "François" or "Martin"), or "I am going to see Sophie," or "I am having the painters," or "I am going to see my relatives at Montrouge" (literally, "red mountain").

The French sometimes use phrases that express their xenophobia. A Frenchwoman may "have the English" ("red-coats") or "Garibaldians" ("redshirts"), or she may see the "landing of the English," an ironic expression also stemming from the Middle Ages, when an English debarkation usually meant a bloody massacre.

Redness and blood are recognized in ways that are devious and ways that are explicitly crude. The French speak of periods as "cardinals" and "tomatoes" and of the menstruating female as *la femme fraise des bois* (literally, "the strawberry woman"). Italian women may travel "the red road" or may say they are "losing blood." Polish women have "leakage" or "flow."

American women may visit "my redheaded aunt from Red Bank," may have "a red-letter day," say "I'm Bloody Mary today," or "the Red Sea's out." Yet, American males are more likely than females to refer to red or blood; in the 1940s, they used jive talk: "The chick is a Communist"; "dirty red"; "her cherry is in sherry." And although the French might say *les fleurs* ("flowers") and American Indians "time for flower," preserving the very old association between periods and flowers, American navy men after World War II reduced flowers to the lowest common denominator; in their vernacular, the menstruating woman was characterized as "a snatch box decorated with red roses."

Nineteenth-century expressions tend to hide the physical facts of menstruation behind euphemisms: "sickness," "unwell," "poorlies," "indisposed." But modern American popular language is apt to be much more graphic. Although "the curse" and "falling off the roof" are not very explicit, other expressions openly celebrate menstrual paraphernalia or bemoan the intercourse taboo. A tampon may be simply a "plug," but sanitary napkins are more grandly described: "cotton horsies," "Mickey Mouse mattresses." The menstruating woman may be "riding the rag" or "have the rag on"; she may bear a "manhole cover"; she may also "ride the cotton pony" or "the cotton bicycle." Because "ketchup" is used as a term for the blood, and "sorority juice" was once a college students' term for ketchup, an astute observer in the 1940s might have remarked, "Too much sorority juice down there." Other implications of sexual unavailability are "the flag is up" (referring to the red flag on rural mailboxes), "ice-boxed," "Mickey Mouse is kaput," and "flying baker" (a navy reference to the signal flag for *B*, which is red and which signals "Beware, keep off").

Although most expressions, especially American ones, have a certain crude ingenuity, they are rarely positive. They seem intended either to hide the subject entirely (to some minds, the word is as shameful as the thing it signifies) or to defend against embarrassment by being overtly gross. We were unable to discover any new, more positive expressions, but we hope the emerging feminist sensibility will do so. Perhaps, then, American English will have an equivalent for the lovely ancient Indian expression for a girl's first menstruation, "flower growing in the house of the god of love."

Afterword

In *The Wise Wound* Penelope Shuttle and Peter Redgrove cite a number of euphemisms for menstruation that do not appear in this chapter: "woman's Benefit," "gal's at the stockyards," and "she's covering the waterfront" are a few examples. They also provide an inventive interpretation for the term "falling off the roof." This, they claim, is "sometimes a dream-image for menstruation, roof-tiles are often red, and it could reflect the falling-off from a premenstrual high."[2]

We would suggest that "falling off the roof" is essentially a crude description of menstruation itself. For a woman lacking medical knowledge of the process, the menstrual flow could seem to be "falling off" from some higher place (the "roof" of the womb). The monthly euphemism, which is meant to disguise the physical reality of menstruation, is surely open to interpretation.

One critic has gone beyond minimal explanations, however, and has actually converted the menstrual euphemism into a substantive literary argument. In an essay on Nathaniel Hawthorne's "The Birthmark," Jules Zanger explores the implications of the curious red mark (a tiny hand) on the heroine's cheek. Zanger traces the meaning of Georgiana's imperfection to nineteenth-century menstrual attitudes, demonstrating that because of its tabooed nature, menstruation demanded "a set of euphemisms." Since one could not "name" menstruation, one had to supply the appropriate substitute. Thus Hawthorne's "crimson hand" is similar to "vapours" and "headaches": these "evasions" can be understood as concessions to what the female body privately and personally required and as resistances to what was required of it socially, familially, and maritally."[3] The monthly euphemism, then, to this male critic and to women everywhere, is an evasion of menstrual reality, a denial of menstruation achieved through renaming the unmentionable. Positive expressions are not yet a part of the menstrual vocabulary.

Chapter 12

Red Humor:
The Menstrual Joke

What does a man do when he's about to bed his ladylove and she tells him she has "the curse"? If he's like Tina's lover in Sue Kaufman's *Diary of a Mad Housewife* (1968), he may say, "I don't mind that," and go ahead with his plans. If, however, he observes the common taboo on intercourse during menstruation, he may relieve his frustration with a joke.

Those who hold power are those who decide what is serious and what is a worthy target for a joke, a form of subtle verbal aggression. Usually, the target of the joke will be someone who is other than those in charge: Pole, black, homosexual, woman. And the jokes are often directed against what makes the target unavoidably different from the jokester; in a woman, her anatomy. Compared with jokes about breasts, vagina, and buttocks, menstruation is a minor and less common subject. Yet, with the exception of puns, menstrual jokes almost invariably reveal male hostility toward women and their periods.

The pun is the most innocuous form of menstrual humor. The joke turns on words rather than on the deep-seated feelings other kinds of jokes seem to mask or displace. The word *menstruate* provides the basis for some of the wry word play. There is, for instance, the cockeyed seamstress. What was her problem? She couldn't "mend straight."[1] There's also the young woman whose boyfriend brags, "I have a Honda." She retorts, "I have my menstrual cycle." Both these jokes have little or nothing to do with the physical fact of menstruation.

A little closer to bodily reality is the remark in *Still More from Sex to Sexty:* "They're always talking about the Little Red School House back in the country . . . but you'd be red, too, if you had eight periods a day!" There's also the tale of the two unusual vampires: "They sat around chewing the rag." Still, unlike most menstrual jokes, these make no judgment on the menstruating woman.

Two jokes that are really aural puns turn on the lack of a period as a sign of pregnancy. In one, the joke teller's audience is asked why the sentence "Sister Mr." struck terror into the hearts of priests. The audience is expected to read the sentence as punctuated, making it read "Sister missed her [mister] period." We are not told the sentence's effect on the sister, only on the priests.

In a similar joke, the audience is asked to punctuate this group of words: Fun fun fun worry worry worry. The correct answer is: "Fun period fun period fun no period worry worry worry!"

The aim of puns is to demonstrate the verbal dexterity of the teller, not embarrass the listener. Most menstrual jokes, however, provide examples of the two purposes Freud saw in noninnocent jokes: to be hostile (aggressive, satirical, defensive) and to be obscene (exposing or denuding another, usually a woman). These jokes may further be classified as "smut," which according to Freud is "the intentional bringing into prominence of sexual facts and relations by speech."[2]

Hostility toward women appears most openly in jokes about the intercourse taboo, the idea that a woman should not engage in genital relations during menstruation ("3/4 jazz time, 1/4 ragtime"). In jokes, the woman's condition is almost invariably regarded from the man's point of view: as his defeat. For instance:

> A drugstore clerk who is given a black eye by a customer explains that he was only trying to make a companion sale. The customer asked for a box of Kotex for his wife, and the clerk suggested, as a companion sale, "a deck of cards for a dull weekend!"

Obviously, the clerk assumed that the customer followed the intercourse taboo and that the customer needed another form of play to assuage sexual defeat. The customer preferred not to be reminded of his loss.

Another joke combines two all-American pastimes: football and bragging about sex.

> Three football players decided to get married on the same day and to spend the wedding night at the same motel. They had worked out signals in advance: At the moment of climax, the players were to yell, "Touchdown!"

The big night finally arrived. From the star quarterback's room, after five minutes, came the yell, "Touchdown!" Five minutes later, the all-state tackle yelled, "Touchdown!"

In the center's room, all was silent. Finally, the other two players heard the center muttering, "Game postponed. Muddy field."

The farmer's daughters pretend to have their periods in order to avoid the salesman in one version of that perennial series of jokes. Staying overnight at the farmer's house, the salesman tries to climb into bed with the eldest daughter, who has put red ink on the sheets. Deflated, the amorous salesman moves from her (presumably) bloody bed to that of the second daughter, who performs the same trick. Feeling even smaller, the salesman finally gets to the bed of the youngest daughter and finds *green* ink on the sheets. Realizing the trick that's been played on him, the salesman asks why *green* ink. The young girl responds, "Because I'm not ripe yet."

Still another defeated lover is the man who "got Mary Lou as high as a kite, in the mood, and spread abed, but then he discovered there was a string attached to it."

In these jokes, the woman is seen in a passive or asexual role. She has to be sexually aroused by the man because she lacks the natural desires he has; she would rather pour ink than make love. The jokes correspond well with the Western classification of woman into two categories: the lady, the chaste woman to whom sex is distasteful, and the tramp, the bad woman who revels in sex. Both are defined with respect to men's view of them: The lady becomes the man's passive wife and mother; the tramp, his active mistress or prostitute.

Jokes may be directed against both kinds of women. A passive woman tells her story in a parody to the tune of "Bye Bye Blackbird." She is a young girl whose boyfriend taught her not to be a lady: to stop wearing underwear and to begin to "shake that thing." But romance died when

> You took me to a cottage in the wildwood,
> There you took advantage of my childhood.
> Put your hand beneath my dress,
> There you found a redbird's nest.
> Boyfriend, bye-bye.

We have found only one intercourse taboo joke in which a woman is active. Of course, she is a tramp. "One night all the gals in Hattie's Cat Flat were sick at the same time, so Madame Hattie decided to put on a menstrual show." The joke turns both on a pun and on the intercourse taboo but at least provides the woman with more than a passive role in men's eyes.

Obscenity (in Freud's sense) appears in jokes about the paraphernalia women must use during their periods. In these jokes, women are portrayed as somewhat unpleasantly tied to their physical processes.

One jingle advises a girl to remedy her problem:

> Rosie's is red,
> Her two lips are, too.
> Try Tampax, Rosie,
> That's what to do.

A riddle indicates the loathing with which female smells are regarded: "Why doesn't an elephant use a Tampax? If the average girl had to change them with her nose, she wouldn't either!" Every woman knows how fearful she is about spots and smells during her period. In the presence of these jokes, she is more likely to feel exposed and embarrassed than amused. Clearly, she is the butt of the joke, and her discomfiture can contribute to man's pleasure.

A 1946 nightclub act in Florida is said to have brought down the house. In the performance, as recounted by G. Legman,

> The master of ceremonies' stooge pretends that he is drunk and con-
> fides that there is a slot machine in the ladies toilet. "Sure, there is,"
> he insists when the master of ceremonies disagrees. "Where do you
> think I got this collar for my tux?" (Pulls out a woman's Kotex pad
> and hangs it around his neck, bringing down the house. Then as
> topper:) "Well, maybe it isn't a collar. I could use it as a simonizing
> rag for my car, except for these two pins." (Dangles the pad and belt-
> pins before the audience.) "I only went for cigarettes anyway."[3]

It is difficult to say what the audience found so amusing in this act. It may have been the association of a man with a female article of dress; men dressed in women's clothes have long been regarded as comical, as have whites in blackface. When those who control society ape their social inferiors, it is considered humorous, a voluntary—and only temporary—relinquishing of power.

The nightclub comedian was not alone in using the paraphernalia of menstruation in a supposed comic manner. Such joking has been used elsewhere as a form of obscenity against particular men, exposing and disparaging them by linking them to female objects. The famous country singer Tex Ritter was once reportedly silenced by a man who cracked, "Where's your Kotex?" ("coat, Tex"), implying that the star was weak, "effeminate."

A man in another joke pointedly rejects the association with female paraphernalia, even to the point of irrelevance.

Noticing a man smoking on the bus, the driver turned around to him and asked, "Didn't you see the No Smoking sign?"

The passenger replied, "Yeah, it's right below the one that says, Use Our Tampons. I didn't pay any attention to that one, either."

Peculiar associations between menstrual paraphernalia, scatology, and sexuality appear in this anecdote:

Having a great need, Mr. Turdington Thudd found the men's room locked, so dashed in and occupied the ladies' room. Then he noticed a bunch of fancy buttons on the wall by the commode. Foolishly, he pushed one, blacked out, and awoke in the hospital.

"Which button did you push?" he was asked. "The ATR button."

"That explains it. *That* button was the Automatic Tampax Remover!"

The diminution of the man to a lesser being is assumed. A real he-man controls his bowels, never uses the ladies' room or manifests undue curiosity, a stereotypical female trait.

A menstrual joke recounted in Marilyn Coffey's novel *Marcella* turns on another allegedly female trait: cattiness. Three society matrons were "sipping their tea with little fingers curled, and bragging about who was the daintiest."

"I have such tiny feet," said the first. "Only size three. I can't get shoes small enough to fit me anywhere."

"With me it's my hands," said the second. "My hands are so small I have to have my gloves 'specially made."

The third lady excused herself, and went to the bathroom. When she came back, she said, "Oh, sorry to bother you, but do either of you have a Band-Aid? My period started."[4]

Menstrual bleeding itself, like paraphernalia, is used in jokes as a sign of women's inferiority. In one anecdote, the moron is told to ask his blind date "How about it?" She answers, "Not tonight. I have the rag on." He doesn't understand. "You know. I'm bleeding." He's still uncomprehending. She shows him. He answers, "Gee, no wonder you're all bloody. They cut your dick off." The joke defines woman as an incomplete man.

Homosexual men are also seen as incomplete males in many jokes. In one menstrual joke, two lovers are chatting together, and one gets a nosebleed. He cries to the other, "I'm bleeding! I'm bleeding!" His lover responds, "Thank God it came!" Like many other homosexual jokes, it seems to reveal the teller's anxiety about his own maleness.

Perhaps menstruation jokes are no more critical of women than many other kinds of jokes, such as women-driver jokes are. But the driver jokes disparage a certain *class* of women: those who drive. Menstrual jokes degrade women as a *caste:* All women menstruate for a large part of their lives, and there is thus no way they can escape the ridicule and insult directed at them by this kind of humor.

One would like to think that feminism will help women develop a different sense of humor, one that is warm, loving, egalitarian, compassionate. But the one menstrual joke that seems to amuse women and men equally is the most perverse one. It combines punning, paraphernalia, and peculiarly American varieties of ethnic stereotype. Perhaps the black (or red) humor lies in the democracy of it all; unlike the jokes having women as the sole victims, this one spares hardly anyone.

> A black man was walking down a street and kicked a can. A Jewish genie arose from it in a cloud of smoke and said, "Okay, to you I'll give two wishes!"
>
> Delighted, the black man quickly announced his choices: "First, I want to be white; and then, I want to be surrounded by pussy." Immediately, he found himself transformed into—a tampon.
>
> The moral of the story: Never take anything from a Jew. It always comes with a string attached.

Afterword

Menstrual jokes may come and go. Their patterns, however, have remained fairly consistent during the last tasteless decade. A number of the jokes which we cited in this book have been reborn, in slightly altered versions, in three best-selling joke collections that we are using here as a sample of the updated material.[5] Now a million people can be exposed to the Jewish Genie joke—but without the feminist analysis.

Like many of the menstrual jokes, several in these collections are harmless puns, for example:

> What's the best sanitary napkin for girls who go dancing? Discotex.[6]

The dancing reference, while simply a play on words, does, however, communicate the idea of a woman being active during the period—as does the menstrual cycle/Honda pun on page 119, above.

Menstrual elephant jokes, while amusing, are less flattering to women, since they imply largeness and grossness. The old elephant/mattress joke has been surpassed by this one:

> What does an elephant use for a tampon?
> A sheep.[7]

The elephant brand of menstrual jokes usually belongs in a category having to do with menstrual paraphernalia, with the often embarrassing aspects of the physical process.

Some paraphernalia jokes disparage men by associating them with female functions, as in the question-answer joke:

> When you order a Bloody Mary, how can you tell if the waitress is mad at you?
> She leaves the string in.[8]

Tampon-tasting, which is treated as delightful in Erica Jong's *Parachutes and Kisses* (see the Afterword to chapter 19), is considered disgusting both in menstrual humor and in the minds of the millions who buy these collections. Thus in one joke we learn that the only use for discarded sanitary napkins is "tea bags for vampires." In another we are told that tampons have strings "so you can floss after you eat."[9] All three represent the menstruating woman as truly tasteless-but-tasty.

It is surprising that menstrual jokes against homosexuals, so prevalent in our 1976 survey, do not appear in the otherwise extensive homophobic selections found in these three books. We do find one joke directed against lesbians. Again we have the typical question-answer format:

> How do you identify a bull dyke?
> She kick-starts her vibrator and rolls her own tampons.[10]

This joke, meant to insult the woman who doesn't need men, is actually flattering in its portrayal of self-sufficiency and independence.

As was true in the past, the most insulting menstrual jokes are directed against ethnic groups, particularly the Polish. Two of these involve paraphernalia.

> How can you tell a Polish woman is having her period?
> She's only wearing one sock.

The second emphasizes foulness and filth along with the inept use of menstrual products.

> Why are hockey goaltenders and Polish girls alike?
> They both change their pads after three periods.[11]

If these jokes stereotype Polish women as stupid and smelly, the Italian counterpart represents the menstruating woman as a heavy drinker.

> Did you hear about the Italian girl who thought a sanitary belt was a drink from a clear shot glass?[12]

Although these jokes are aimed against Italian or Polish "girls," they are in effect directed against all women, since all women at some time menstruate and since all women are forced to deal with the physical realities of pads and tampons and strings.

There has recently appeared a whole new subclass of menstrual jokes, one not around to be laughed at ten years ago. This is the toxic shock joke. Because toxic shock is still mysterious, and because toxic shock syndrome is known to affect men, postmenopausal women, and children, these jokes are unfocused. Of the three we uncovered, all exist on the level of the pun, and none specifically attacks a bodily function or female characteristic. The first of these is, inevitably, Polish.

> What's the latest disease in Poland?
> Toxic Sock Syndrome.[13]

This piece of red humor, which reiterates the sock-as-tampon insult of the previous Polish joke, exists merely by virtue of sound association. So too does the joke about the New Wave group, the Toxic Shock Syndrome, with its hit "Ragtime."[14] The last pun in this category names a new feminine hygiene product—Toxic Shock Absorbers.[15]

It is discouraging to see so little wit in so many years. None of the jokes related here treat the menstrual process with affection. Only one or two treat it with anything resembling humor. These dismal efforts at menstrual drollery just don't knock our socks off.

What we need for truly red humor is a sense of irony. And this we get in Gloria Steinem's classic essay, "If Men Could Menstruate."[16] Steinem looks at some of the basic problems of menstruation; but by reversing the process so that it affects men rather than women, she points out the comic incongruities should those in power (men) have to deal with "the curse." Men would boast about their flow. New products would appear on the market, like "John Wayne Maxi Pads." Napkins would be federally subsidized. And so goes Steinem, chopping away at male privilege in the manner of Florynce Kennedy's famous statement: "If men could get pregnant, abortion would be a sacrament." In her jokes about males and menstruation, Steinem does not resort to the nastiness that we find in so many of the tasteless menstrual jokes. Rather, she exposes the sexist assumptions about menstruation, using her brains without hitting below the belt.

"If Men Could Menstruate" appeared, along with several other pieces of menstrual humor, in a 1980 collection of feminist humor and satire called *Pulling Our Own Strings*.[17] The tamponesque title carries into the first chapter, "Periodic Hysteria," where most of the menstrual humor appears. There is a cartoon about two girls learning the insertion process, a theme which appears elsewhere in the collection, for example, in a piece that describes a tampon as a "cardboard Tootsie Roll." Other selections include a newsflash on menses and mosquitoes, a satirical how-and-why tale called "Splat," and a clever spoof, presented from the point of view of an unliberated male doctor, which explains why the menstrual cycle disables women three weeks out of four. There are also three menstrual jokes, under the heading "Ragtime."

In another area of popular culture, menstrual humor is also asserting itself. Greeting cards are now promoting menstrual aches and pains as cause for amusement. One card from California Dreamers (1985) pictures a woman draped across a sofa, drugs at her feet, spilling their contents over the rug. The caption reads: "Lonnie Gets P.M.S." A similar card created by Nicole Hollander for The Maine Line Company shows a fairly happy looking but "painted" woman. The cover of the card reads: "Midol relieves the special pain that women get . . ." Inside comes the punch line: "When they realize they picked the wrong man, again." Neither of these cards is a howl. Neither presents a positive image of the menstruating woman. Nonetheless, this kind of product, by visually exposing what for so long has been kept secret, can help to change the climate of menstrual repression still so prevalent among the general public.

For one-quarter of our menstrual lives, the authors of *The Curse* have been joking about our periods, in our internal correspondence and sometimes in public, where we credit menstruation with our relaxed moods, our cheerfulness, our swift flow of wit. Sometimes people laugh with us. Sometimes they are horrified, a situation which Dale Spender has amusingly described: "You do feel a bit like a leper when everyone round lowers his eyes, looks away, coughs and changes the conversation."[18]

For those who do not cough or look away, red humor is a form of liberation. Through shared laughter one realizes that menstruation is a common female experience and not some secret shame. The moral of the story:

> Never take anything from a menstruating woman. She often comes with a joke attached.

Chapter 13

Periodic Parade: Menstruation in Advertising

Del Jordan feared well-groomed girls, for "never, never would they feel that little extra gush of blood, little bonus that no Kotex is going to hold, that will trickle horrifyingly down the inside of their thighs. No indeed; their periods would be discreet; nature served and did not betray them." Del, the protagonist in Alice Munro's *Lives of Girls and Women,*[1] fears exactly the kinds of girls who appear today in menstrual paraphernalia ads: ones who are always "confident," "safe," "secure," even during "those difficult times of the month."

The advertising image of the menstruating woman has shifted at times in response to national needs and ideology, for example, according to whether women are wanted in the home or in the war plant. Recent ads have become much more explicit and have moved from women's magazines onto television. Yet, the underlying message has been fairly consistent, playing on both hopes and fears: hopes that the woman will not have to change her ordinary life too much during "that time of the month"; fears (like Del Jordan's) of betrayal by dripping blood, revealing outlines, or odors.

Kotex "sanitary napkins" were invented at the end of the First World War and appeared on the market in 1921. Women who could afford them quickly substituted them for their "diapers," which usually had been washed and reused each month. But women's magazines did not immediately advertise the new products. Although *Ladies' Home Journal* carried an ad for "Amolin—the personal Deodorant Powder" for women's "intimate personal uses," as early as 1920, there were no ads for napkins. *Good Housekeeping* carried ads promoting Lysol for "every purpose of personal hygiene" but did not advertise Kotex. Questions of discretion and/or prudery seem to have been involved.

By the 1930s, however, Kotex had penetrated *Good Housekeeping*. It took four years to convince *Ladies' Home Journal* to run the ads. In a 1933 *Good Housekeeping* ad, a woman in a shadow advertised "the new Phantom Kotex . . . no revealing outlines." The new Phantom Kotex, still low priced, had "the same thickness, the same protective area," but the tapered ends helped "eliminate those tell-tale outlines." The ad's language stresses the hush-hush nature of menstruation: The pad must not be outlined; it must be "protective." No one must know the woman's guilty secret. Menstruation in the 1930s was, as it is today, a subject for concealment and euphemism, yet one for which "new" products must constantly be created.

In the 1940s, menstrual paraphernalia advertisers participated in the war effort. Because women's labor was needed, women were taken more seriously than they would be in later advertising. Ads called them women (i.e., adults), rather than girls; the language stressed utility and purpose and the ability of women to assume responsible and competent positions. Women were used to advise other women.

The ads for Lotus De Luxe "New Air-I-Ated Flow Napkin" show a nurse speaking about the product; Meds goes farther, showing an absorbent tampon "perfected by a woman's doctor," who is also pictured. San-Nap-Pak ads emphasize saving time and money: "No time to mince words—less time out for changes!" The product reportedly gave "hours of extra service . . . without extra bulk!" To the extent that bulkiness is a physical, not a psychological, problem, the ad is a practical one; it meets a serious physical need for comfort without trying to create psychological tension.

Fibs ads from 1943 show women doing secretarial work, getting dressed for work, and wearing slacks, carrying a lunchbox, and punching a time card. Tampax ads stress that the product is "not limited to 'special' users. Many swimmers, bikers and movie stars have adopted Tampax, but it is designed every bit as much for the less strenuous woman at home or in the office."

A laudable feature of this ad, and most menstrual ads, is the absence of competition among women. Whereas most advertising appeals to one's desire to "be the first on your block" and "get ahead of the gang," ads for menstrual products generally do not draw lines between women. In this respect, modern advertising has not changed from that of decades ago.

A wartime Kotex ad stresses the need for cooperation. A teen-aged girl sits brooding, her broom and mop in front of her, apparently having deserted the household tasks because she has her period. The ad chides,

> Who would have thought you'd turn out to be a deserter from a dustmop and a few dishes ... when Mom's counting on you? When your country's counting on you? As Mom explained—it's girls like you taking on "homework" who release a whole army of mothers for rolling bandages and selling war bonds and driving drill presses!

The 1940s ads glorify bravery and competence, the qualities needed by women on the home front.

Betty Friedan has noted the remarkable changes in the contents of women's magazines after World War II. Once, the woman who combined career and marriage, who worked hard for her country as well as her man, had been praised. But in the late 1940s and throughout the 1950s, the "feminine mystique" prevailed: the postwar idea that a woman's primary and only fulfilling roles were those of wife and mother, her place in the home. Friedan documents the change in national ideology from the 1940s to the 1950s in magazine articles; a similar change can be seen in menstrual product ads.

Women's faces, without bodies, are shown more frequently in the 1950's than they were in the 1940s; to show a woman working is no longer important. Women are more often called "girls," indicating that the adult female is no longer taken so seriously. Instead of useful arguments, the advertisers use coy language arranged in short sentences. When women are less needed in the work force, their IQ automatically decreases, if we are to judge by advertisers' practices.

A typical example is a Tampax ad showing four women's faces. All of them say, "We all use Tampax, of course." Each gives her reason: "Such big difference! ... So ingenious. ... Daintiness plus. ... Gives me confidence." The hardworking woman of the 1940s was not worried about daintiness and ingenuity; she sought a useful product enabling her to carry on needed chores.

The more ornamental view of women also appears in the 1953 Kotex ad. Ten years after exhorting young girls to do the housework so their mothers could drive drill presses, the Kotex advertisers show an impeccably dressed mannequinlike woman standing in front of an art gallery. "Not a shadow of a doubt with Kotex," says the text. Kotex is soft, "dainty," with no outlines. In the corner of the page is a description of the woman's Herbert Sondheim dress, made in a "soft silk twill of tiny geometrics." The woman obviously does no useful work; a lady of leisure, she gazes and poses.

Also influencing the women of the 1950s were the "Modess, because . . ." ads, showing elegant, perfectly dressed models, often in voluminous swirls of lush fabric. The expression dated from a 1943 nationwide contest offering $25,000 in prizes for the best twenty-five-words-or-less completion of the sentence "I'm glad I switched to Modess because. . ." In 1949, the Modess . . . because ads were named the best national ads of the year. They were so attractive that Del Jordan's boyfriend in *Lives of Girls and Women* used them as pinups; along with movie stars' pictures, he had "ladies in lovely ethereal dresses advertising sanitary napkins."

The woman of the 1940s bore burdens; in the 1950s, her burden was to be beautiful. A narrowing of woman's sphere came in every respect in that decade, as Friedan shows. In menstrual product ads, the woman's aspirations became individual and inner-directed (sleekness, beauty) rather than collective and outer-directed (the war effort). Even as late as 1970, the feminine mystique was not dead; a Kotex ad instructed women to "Be his. Be home. Be hard to forget. But be sure. Sure as Kotex napkins."

In the ads of the 1960s and early 1970s, menstruation is still usually discussed with euphemisms: "those special days," "those difficult days," "that time of month." "Special" is double-edged, used to imply both "noteworthy" and "problematic." One of the noteworthy or "special" problems is that women are not supposed to be able to talk directly about their periods. Unless they use Tampax, they may be forced into embarrassed excuses: "Tampax Tampons. So you won't have to make excuses. You're free to enjoy the magical water world. Anytime. No need to make excuses. Like 'I have this bad cold.' Or 'I have this awful hangnail.'" Equally covert is the treatment of what to do with used menstrual paraphernalia. "Now—one more thing *not* to worry about . . . that little discussed disposal problem. Now—neat, discreet, disposal bags come in each box of new Scott Confidets." Menstruating women should be embarrassed, say advertisers.

Even those ads that promote their products with a more positive tone tend to stress psychology over technology. For instance, the word *absorbent* appears far less frequently than the terms *secure, confident,* and *free.* Sometimes, advertisers seem to suffer from a poverty of vocabulary: "The way you feel is free. Today and everyday, you feel free, confident, unhampered. Tampax tampons worn internally make this possible. Keep you feeling good and comfortably confident, in or out of the water . . . for total freedom, total comfort . . . Tampax."

In the last decade, the pictures accompanying menstrual ads are usually of young women, no older than twenty-five. They are more active than in the 1950s, although their activity is usually a sport (swimming, tennis playing) rather than gainful employment. Except for ads in black magazines, the women are usually white. Even when the model's color changes, the ads are exactly the same—same layout, same text. The women are all smiling, well-groomed, confident—the kind Del Jordan feared.

Within the last few years, however, there have been some changes in the advertising. In line with the general cultural trend toward the natural look and natural foods, recent ads have begun to substitute *natural* for words like *confident* and *free*. For instance, Kotex tampons "are a lot like you. Soft and natural. Soft, natural shape. Natural insertion guides instead of bulky tubes."

There is also greater explicitness in advertising, perhaps in recognition of the sexual revolution. Ads for tampons now say "young girls" more frequently than they say "unmarried girls" when discussing the tampon's effect on a hymen. Pursettes, which used to call itself "the tampon that's right even for single girls," now advertises itself as "the comfort tampon."

In recent years, a new product has appeared on the menstrual market. Tassaway is a small, soft cup used to collect menstrual blood. Its ads are factual and appeal to the intelligence, using the word *menses* and *uterus*. Whereas other ads say coyly that there's "nothing hard" about insertion, Tassaway is more positive and less authoritative, quoting a satisfied customer: "Once you get the 'feel' of it you can't go wrong." Tassaway ads also say "women" rather than "girls"; the ad's sentences are longer and more complex. The Tassaway ad shows a respect for women's minds and points to a direction in which ads for menstrual products might go.

Very recent magazine ads, probably influenced by the women's movement, have returned to the 1940s practice of showing women at work. A Tampax ad stresses

> on-the-job security. It's your job and you love it. It's hectic—it's hard work—it's a ball! But no matter how busy you are, you always feel in charge, confident, calm. Even if it's the wrong time of the month .... And that's important when your job means more to you than just a paycheck.

No doubt because menstruation is considered a taboo subject, the product itself is shown much less frequently than a woman is. Although Pursettes tampons were introduced to women in 1955, an unwrapped tampon was not shown until 1968.[2] Pursettes ads in late 1973 show a size comparison between a Pursette and lipstick. Other advertisers are still keeping their products under wraps and in a box.

Although television and sanitary napkins are about the same age, until November 1, 1972, ads for sanitary protection products were banned from TV and radio. Tassaway worked hard to break the ban, for without the electronic media, it had no sure way to inform and educate women about the product. By running ads on stations that do not subscribe to the code of the National Association of Broadcasters, with little adverse public reaction, they eventually helped convince the NAB to lift the ban. Scott's Confidets also tested ads on noncode stations and was the first menstrual hygiene product to receive code authority for a television commercial. Modess was first on radio and is now also on television. Interestingly, Kimberly-Clark fought the lifting of the television ban, claiming the products "too personal," but now uses the medium for competitive purposes. Perhaps they didn't want any new information that might spoil Kotex's impressive share of the market to reach the consumer.

Of course, the companies are restricted in what they can say on the air and when they can say it. The ads may make no reference to absorbency, cleanliness, anatomy, comfort, insertion, application, duration or efficacy. This leaves "generalized statements relating to grooming, femininity, freshness" and "statements related to supplemental aspects of a product and general product description" such as packaging and disposability, and the like.[3] Perhaps this latest directive is responsible for the disposal bags, towelettes, and other gimmicks. The ads are usually shown during "women's hours" (daytime television) or late-night programming, when the children are in bed.

A good example of the kind of thinking that animates these restrictions is shown by the remark of a Kimberly-Clark executive. "Menstrual care is such a very personal thing to a woman," he said. "For example, she equates changing her brand of tampons almost with committing adultery."[4] No such Neanderthal thinking obscures advertising in Europe. We have been told of a German television commercial for o.b. Tampons in which a stewardess's skirt is snatched from her by an overeager passenger. In the flash of fabric and fadeout are heard the words: "I'm glad I'm wearing my o.b. Tampon!"

Afterword

O.b. is on American television today, doing penance for its sexist German ad. Judith Esser, the grandmotherly gynecologist credited with inventing the o.b., is shown with a group of upscale young women. "O.b. expands with you, to give the best protection," she says. "That's important to me," says one of them. "Yes, so you can get on with the important things," says Dr. E. In this message for today's thinking woman, menstruation is indeed the friendly monthly nuisance and must be managed so that it doesn't interfere with "the important things," whatever they may be.

And that's the style of most of the menstrual product advertising today, a hundred-thousand-dollar-a-year business, spending 80 percent of that budget on television. Women are sold convenience, comfort, security and, since toxic shock syndrome, safety. They are shown presumably menstruating women in all the familiar settings of the eighties: health spas, ballet studios, jogging tracks. Women's magazines, a category greatly expanded since the first edition of this book to include such periodicals as *Savvy* and *Working Woman*, carry print ads in the same style. The copy is informative, clinical, and frankly useful, discussing absorbency and comparing brands.

The frequency and style of the advertising is still determined by the magazine's audience, of course. Upscale *Vogue*, read by at least as many postmenopausal women as those still menstruating, has only two ads for sanitary protection in its massive (756 pages) September 1985 issue. The first is a straightforward, clinical explanation of "why o.b. prevents accidents better than any other tampon," with a line drawing of a (bloodless) o.b. conforming to the shape of what we presume to be a vagina. The other is a low-text, nonexplicit picture of two napkins, showing "new" maxithins with a "new longer length, new quilted softness, new level of confidence." We presume this pad has been to charm school.

A *Seventeen* of the same autumn has seven ads for napkins and tampons and three for "cramps" medicine (Advil, Nuprin), taking advantage of the new, over-the-counter availability of ibuprofen, the ingredient promoted by Penny Budoff for its antiprostaglandin effect on menstrual cramps (see chapter 9). *Seventeen*'s o.b. ad is identical to the one in *Vogue*, as is the one in the May 1985 *Ms*. (We admire o.b.'s respect for the intelligence of women of all ages and persuasions). But *Seventeen*'s specialty is ads that appeal to its very young audience. It runs the Tampax ad we discussed in chapter 10 for pink "new petal soft Tampax—perfect for beginners like us" with no mention of the dangers of TSS for teenagers. In 1987 it was speaking "frankly" to its young readers with a Tampax ad featuring one teenager asking another, "Are you sure it won't hurt?" in a school bathroom setting and with a Playtex ad showing a young woman in a ballet leotard telling us, "I felt funny about using a tampon." The Tampax ad still carries no mention of TSS, but the Playtex one does, including the note that "the reported risks are higher for women under 30 years of age and teenage girls." *Seventeen* also runs an eye-level shot of a pink-checked fanny on a bicycle, pushing Sure and Natural, the "practically invisible Maxi" with the legend that "she's not wearing a tampon." We can probably thank the designers of jeans advertising of the last ten years for that particular angle of vision. Interestingly, none of the napkin ads seek to capitalize on the TSS scare by urging their customers to shun tampons. No doubt the manufacturers want to avoid connecting *any* of their products with disease and death.

Some of this "new" frankness in menstrual product advertising was forced by the public discussion of the dangers of TSS, as well as the mounting medical advances in treatment of premenstrual symptoms. But some of it is brought about by the realization that menstruation and its necessities are no longer to be hidden, despite the occasional letter to Dear Abby like this one:

> Dear Abby: Please tell me what can be done to stop the advertising of personal feminine products on television. . . . I find such commercials embarrassing in mixed company, and degrading to women. Is nothing sacred anymore? My daughter says it's impossible to watch TV with her boy friend because of these commercials. . . .
> Disgusted

Instead of addressing herself to "Disgusted's" obvious sense of shame and degradation about her own body, Abby merely responded with the names and addresses of the manufacturers of the products and the television networks.[5]

"Disgusted" wrote that letter in 1984. What must she have thought in 1985 when Tampax broke the ultimate taboo and said "period" in a TV ad? A healthy-looking woman in a ballet studio talks about how Tampax makes you "feel cleaner," while a (female) voice-over says "Tampax will change the way you feel about your period."[6] The implication, of course, is that you used to feel dirty. (We find the frequent use of ballet studios another attempt to "clean up" the product's image. Although dancers sweat as much as any other athlete, one is inclined to think of them in their incarnation as white swans bathed in blue light, even when they are surrounded by exercise bars and damp towels.)

Mark Miller of William Esty, Tampax's ad agency, said, "We used the word because it happened to fit the campaign. We asked the networks to let us prove that it wouldn't be offensive. . . . It's a natural evolution. Over the past five years everyone has gotten more straightforward. It just doesn't make sense any longer to show a woman in a long white dress, drifting through a field of wildflowers, saying something like, 'It makes me feel fresh.' "[7]

Chapter 14

Rags to Riches:
The Menstrual Products
Industry

We do not know what Eve wore as sanitary protection after she was "cursed." European artists often show her wearing a fig leaf, not a very absorbent material. We are told that in some cultures women wear no protection and have few taboos;[1] whereas in our own society, there are now approximately fifty different brand-name napkins and tampons, and "feminine products" is a half-billion-dollar industry.

Through the ages, women have used either tampons or bandages as sanitary protection. But until World War I, the only significant improvement over the basic bandage was that the "civilized" matrons of the Roman Empire used cloth bandages; whereas their "savage" sisters in Africa and Australia used bandages made of grass or vegetable fiber.[2] Thrifty Frenchwomen were still washing out their menstrual rags in the 1940s; in parts of South America, disposable napkins are only now being mass marketed.

Among tampon users, there was more variety. In ancient Japan, women used from eight to twelve paper tampons a day, held in place by a bandage called *kama* ("pony"). For centuries, Indonesian women made tampons from vegetable fiber. Roman women wore tampons of soft wool; and Egyptian women, rolls of soft papyrus. Rolls of grass and roots served women in Equatorial Africa.[3]

Until about 1925, American women wore a diaper of bird's-eye or outing flannel, which they were obliged to wash and reuse. These were cumbersome, uncomfortable, and apt to cause soreness. Johnson and Johnson manufactured "Lister's Towels" in 1896, the first commercial disposable pad, made of gauze-covered cotton. But because turn-of-the-century morality prevented advertising these "unmentionables," the pads did not reach many women and were eventually withdrawn from the market.

Then, during the First World War, French nurses discovered that the cellulose material used for bandaging wounds absorbed menstrual blood better than cloth diapers. In 1921, Kimberly-Clark made the first successful disposable sanitary napkin, Kotex, which like the same company's Kleenex, has become a generic name. Johnson and Johnson returned to the market in 1927 with Modess, manufactured by its subsidiary, the Personal Products Company. Kotex and Modess had the field more or less to themselves until 1961, when Scott Paper Company came out with Confidets. Today, Kotex products command approximately a 55 percent share of the total napkin market, Modess reaches about 35 percent, and Confidets is in third place with 10 to 11 percent.

Between 1921 and today, the sanitary napkin has undergone constant improvement, but the basic design remained the same until the advent of Stayfree Mini-pads, a Personal Products innovation, in 1970. These smaller pads, designed to be fastened to panties with a thin strip of adhesive, found a ready audience. Fan letters (which we have seen) extolled their use for everything from bladder problems and vaginal discharge to emergency lifts inside a pair of shoes. One writer went so far as to say the pads "almost make me wish I weren't ready for menopause!" Kotex is now in this zooming market with New Freedom Small Pads and Lite-Days Oval Pads, and both Kotex and Modess have regular-size pads with the strip of adhesive, for "beltless freedom."

The ecology movement spawned a school of "flushable" products, another innovation on the basic napkin. Stayfree Maxi-pads and Modess Flush-able claim to be both flushable *and* biodegradable. As one researcher explained to us, you can flush even a steel ball down the toilet; the key to an ecologically responsible product that won't create a tornado in the plumbing is biodegradability.

Tampons are not biodegradable, but in most households, they are eminently flushable. Disposable tampons have been on the market in the United States since the invention of Tampax in 1933, but from the myths, misconceptions, and dark mutterings about spoiled virginity, you would think they had sprung full-blown from the forehead of Jack the Ripper. When they were first introduced, even the churches got into the act, in a rare show of concern for women's bodies, and disputed for some years over the tampon as an engine of contraception, masturbation, or defloration (even though the napkin, with its constant pressure on the clitoris, is a more likely candidate for devil's disciple). Happily, all now agree on the product's harmlessness, and tampons are fast overtaking napkins, with an average 12 percent growth over the past five years (although the majority of women still use pads exclusively).

As might be expected, Tampax has the lioness's share of the tampon market and is the largest advertiser. Playtex is the number two; Kotex tampons, three. The tube-applicator tampon is favored by 80 percent of all tampon users, for reasons probably having to do with our Puritan heritage. In Europe, however (where the major U.S. manufacturers have factories and subsidiary companies), applicatorless tampons do extremely well.

In 1969, the Tassett Company of California introduced the first truly new menstrual product since the fig leaf. A plastic cup that looks like an upside-down Liberty Bell, the Tassaway, when properly folded, fits into the vagina and collects the flow. Because there is no absorption, there is no leakage; because it can hold more volume than the average tampon, the danger of overflow is minimal; because it is made of plastic, no bacteria can grow on it. Some women find the Tassaway uncomfortable; others find it messy to remove. Although the company's literature says otherwise, it can be used more than once. But most women dispose of the Tassaway immediately after emptying it, which makes the package scarcely "the equivalent of 25 to 30 tampons or napkins," as advertised on the box.

The most advanced development in monthly protection, still in its experimental stage, is period extraction: the removal of the entire flow at once by inserting a suction tube (cannula) into the uterus. This "fifteen-minute period," when perfected, could be the most efficient method of dealing with the menstrual period; but right now, the risks of infection or tissue damage are high. Changing attitudes toward fertility and a reluctance to accept "woman's lot" in all areas of life would seem to make this technique a logical next step.

In their journey from rags to riches, the manufacturers have relied heavily on gimmickry to liven up sales. The huge success of vaginal deodorant sprays (the manufacturers first created the need and then rushed to fill it) inspired napkin and tampon makers to capitalize on the odor mania and "deodorize" their products. What passes for deodorant in most napkins is, of course, perfume. The exception to this is the Modess napkin-with-deodorant-protection. The gridlike construction of the napkin (similar to that of Kotex Plus, which also incorporates a small extra napkin within the larger), spreads the flow over a larger internal area, with the surface remaining drier and therefore less odorous because the menstrual flow develops an odor only when it hits the air.

But that fact makes the deodorized tampon a useless innovation—and an example of just how gullible the public can be. The Food and Drug Administration has already begun receiving reports that question the safety of these products, but as in the case of sprays, such reports will probably have no effect on their success or failure in the marketplace.

Other gimmicks include individual disposal bags (Confidets) and, most recently, "towelettes" in boxes of Kimberly-Clark's Fems.

One other method of sanitary protection remains to be mentioned: the household sponge. Following the advice of Alicia Bay Laurel in *Living on the Earth*,[5] we made our own tampons out of a sponge. One 12-cent O-Cel-O kitchen sponge (3½ by 4¾ inches) divided widthwise into four equal strips makes four perfect tampons. One sponge, we found, lasted for as long as 6¼ hours during a heavy flow, as opposed to only 4 hours with Pursettes Plus. The sponge is economical and, if it is sterilized by boiling, reusable. It is by far the best protection not on the market, but it would probably not find overwhelming favor with the millions of women brainwashed by the manufacturers to "change often" to ensure "daintiness."

Retail sales of feminine hygiene products exceed $500 million annually. Vaginal sprays and certain birth control products pad the figures somewhat, so it is not a completely accurate representation of sales of menstrual products. But it does give some indication of the size of the market.

We wanted to get the most complete picture possible of the sanitary products industry, so we visited the Personal Products Company in Milltown, New Jersey. We chose this company purely for reasons of time and distance; to avoid bias, however, we wrote to every other manufacturer in the country, seeking information on the history of the company, product testing research, finances, advertising, and other details relevant to the individual companies. Tassaway, Kimberly-Clark, Tampax, and the Campana Corporation (Pursettes) responded.

Tampons and sanitary napkins are made from rayon and wood pulp. The more compressible rayon is used for tampons; the wood pulp, which is more absorbent but noncompressible, is used in napkins.

No federal agency governs product specifications in the sanitary products industry, nor are there industry-wide boards of standards. "House" brand napkins and tampons, for example, which are usually not made by the major manufacturers, may be cheaper than the name brands, but they are also of lower quality. The government monitoring of advertising claims is the only official pressure applied to the companies, but the response of the public is a steadily effective deterrent to the production of shoddy goods. At Personal Products, both salaried and wage employees participate in quality control. Explicit product specifications are followed along the route from tree to container, and there are several in-process checks of the napkins and tampons at the machine, the packing table, and the shipping platform. Such items as quality of adhesive, length of tabs, and compactness of fibers are checked, and the threat of pay loss is a further incentive to employees at all levels to produce quality products. In the positive-reinforcement department, plant employees see the complimentary letters from the satisfied users of their product, attend screenings of the company's educational films, and are made to realize that they have a stake in the company's success.

Although its products have the world's largest captive audience, the industry gave us a pleasant surprise at the amount of money it spends on product improvement and education of the public. Ingenious contraptions are used at Personal Products constantly to test the rate of absorption and fluid capacity of products from all manufacturers in simulated use situations, and a group of women test the products themselves under the supervision of a doctor. In both cases, the used napkins and tampons are carefully studied for fluid patterns and amount of fluid retained. Both Personal Products and Campana Corporation, which were the only companies to give us detailed information on their test methods and procedures, claim test results showing the superiority of their own products over other brands. We were convinced of the honesty of the testing and the sincerity of their claims, and we urge readers to look more closely at certain tampon ads. Because of the shape of the vagina, tampons that expand in width, such as Pursettes and Carefree, are more likely to give better protection, as the ads say, than tampons that expand only in length, such as Tampax.

Tampax supplied us with an impressive set of medical studies, dating from 1945 through the late 1960s, proving the safety of the tampon. Despite the fact that tampons are as old as civilization and had long been used for contraception and medication as well as for menstrual protection, they were suspected of causing such conditions as endometriosis, cervicitis, and vaginitis. A 1965 study by the Rock Reproductive Clinic found, however, that the "use of vaginal tampons has no physiological or clinical undesired side effects. This is true even when tampons are used in the presence of injury or inflammation." Another study tested the use of tampons after childbirth, beginning at ten days postpartum, and found no evidence of "increased vaginal irritation, or delay in healing of either episiotomy or the reproductive organs." (It must be said, though, that many women who have vaginitis or inflamed or irritated cervices do not use tampons because the tampons hurt.)

Similar tests preceded the introduction of Tassaway into the national market. The Tassaway had previously been used successfully to treat certain disorders of the bladder and reproductive organs. A 1963 study from the vulvovaginitis clinic of Mount Sinai Hospital found that the Tassaway prevented infection and odor and was comfortable to use.

The manufacturers of menstrual products for the most part serve their customers well. They supply a product for which a real need exists, and they look hard for ways to improve it. But in one serious way they fail.

The basic sanitary napkin is no better than menstrual protection used thousands and thousands of years ago. Absorbency, disposability, comfort do not change the basic design. The napkin is still a breeding ground for bacteria (not from the menstrual flow itself, which is bacteriologically "clean," but from the anal and urinary tracts, contributing to vaginal infections). In our hygiene-oriented society, it is amazing that such a product is so widely accepted. Nowhere does the literature from companies making both napkins and tampons attempt to dissuade women from continued use of the pad. Nor has any company yet made a tampon that a woman with a heavy flow can wear with complete security, so that she will not need even the mini-pad "just in case." Instead of adding disposal bags to an over cluttered world, these companies should be using their talents to develop new ways to deal with menstruation, whether menstrual extraction or some process as yet undreamed of. As long as the sanitary napkin is applied like a bandage to a wound, women cannot forget the cover-up approach to menstruation.

Afterword

"The manufacturers of menstrual products for the most part serve their customers well," we said in 1976. But during the next four years a series of decisions made within the legal, scientific, and marketing communities sent our trust and optimism fleeing and raised new and undreamed-of anxieties about menstruation and its management. The cause: TOXIC SHOCK SYNDROME.

Toxic shock syndrome was named in 1978 by Dr. James K. Todd of the Children's Hospital in Denver. The disease is said to involve a bacterium, *Staphylococcus aureus*. Current researchers have connected it with a protein (TSST-1) and possibly with an enzyme capable of breaking down the tissue during an infection. It has also been connected with the tampon, not only by researchers at the Centers for Disease Control since 1980, but also in a June 1985 report from the Harvard Medical School. Most recently, TSS has been connected with influenza: six people contracted TSS after a bout with the flu in Minnesota in 1986, the year we also learned that flu-induced TSS could have been responsible for a plague in Athens around 430 B.C.[7]

And yet for all the research, much of it funded by the tampon industry itself, the specific causes for TSS remain uncertain. Todd, actively involved with the etiology of toxic shock for almost a decade, was quoted in a major essay in *Science 85* as saying, "I would bet that it will take another five years before the scientific community will be able to say that it has found the cause of toxic shock."[8]

In the meantime the disease continues to claim victims. The Centers for Disease Control (CDC) report a total of 2,814 cases between 1979, when reporting began, and June 1, 1985. Of these, 122 were fatal. The actual number of cases peaked in 1980, and the numbers reported since then have declined by 70 percent. Yet researchers at the CDC are concerned that as many as 90 percent of toxic shock cases are *not* reported and in 1986 were conducting a study to try to determine the real facts on the disease's spread.[9]

The symptoms of the disease are by now household words, inserted in all tampon boxes as a monthly reminder of what could happen. The following list is from Playtex:

WARNING SIGNS

WARNING SIGNS OF TSS FOR EXAMPLE ARE: SUDDEN FEVER (USUALLY 102 OR MORE) AND VOMITING, DIARRHEA, FAINTING OR NEAR FAINTING WHEN STANDING UP, DIZZINESS, OR A RASH THAT LOOKS LIKE A SUNBURN. IF THESE OR OTHER SIGNS OF TSS APPEAR, YOU SHOULD REMOVE THE TAMPON AT ONCE, DISCONTINUE USE, AND SEE YOUR DOCTOR IMMEDIATELY.

If the disease advances beyond the initial stage, the victim is also likely to experience peeling skin on the palms of the hands and the soles of the feet, paralysis, gangrene, and the loss of fingers and toes.

Our major concern here is, of course, the link between toxic shock syndrome and menstruation. This link became official in 1980, when Senator Edward Kennedy held hearings on TSS and charged the CDC to find its cause.[10] Research has continued to this day. A 1982 study from the Mayo Clinic, for example, concluded that there was no toxic element in tampons among the six brands sampled. Tampons have "been around the environment for a long time, and should have been linked to problems long ago if they were causative factors," researcher Dr. Miles J. Jones told reporters.[11] Yet a team of scientists headed by Dr. Edward H. Kass of the Harvard Medical School and funded by Tambrands, Inc. (makers of Tampax) announced in June 1985 that they had discovered how tampons "caused" toxic shock: the major ingredients in the super-absorbent tampons are polyacrylate rayon and polyester magnesium. When so concentrated, they can enhance the production of the bacterial toxin that leads to TSS.[12]

After this discovery most manufacturers began to recall existing supplies of their super-absorbent tampons while working to redesign the tampon with different ingredients. Tampax placed ads in major newspapers offering refunds for its super-plus tampons, perhaps hoping to avoid the embarrassment suffered by Playtex in March 1985, when U.S. district judge Patrick Kelly offered to reduce an 11-million-dollar jury verdict against the company if they would acknowledge that Playtex Super Plus tampons were "killing people" and take them off the market.[13] Of significance to the users of tampons is that the Tambrands-funded study did not receive widespread publicity and, in fact, was known to the manufacturers four months before it was announced to the general public.

Nonetheless, it is crucial to stress that TSS has no exclusive claim on tampon users. It also afflicts children, men, and post-menopausal women. No one who read reporter Nan Robertson's chilling account of TSS, told from the point of view of the victim, could possibly forget it. Robertson vividly described the fever, nausea, and loss of circulation, which ultimately cost her several fingertips. And Nan Robertson was fifty-five, beyond the menopause.[14]

Health writer Jane Brody wrote in July 1985 that whereas in 1980 almost 98 percent of the toxic shock victims were using tampons, today about 30 percent of all cases involve people who have never used them. Although the risk is still greatest for menstruating women, the disease can affect people having surgery or using diaphrams or being bitten by insects or (and this is the most disconcerting) "people with no apparent source of infection at all."[15] Brody attributes the decline of tampon-associated

TSS to medical research, improved standards in the industry, and better feminine hygiene. Her advice to tampon-users is consistent with policies advocated by the American Medical Association for the past several years: avoid continuous use; change frequently; insert carefully; avoid synthetic fibers; use the tampon with the least absorbency necessary; and change sizes as the menstrual flow decreases.

But many women believe that the tampon industry can play a much larger part than it has until now in improving the safety of its product and the health of its customers. From the beginning of the toxic shock discoveries the sanitary products industry's posture has been one of re-action to disaster rather than thoughtful planning to prevent harm. The first product to disappear under public scrutiny was Proctor and Gamble's Rely tampon, a totally new product introduced in 1979. Unlike the tra-ditional tampon, a tightly rolled cylinder of cotton and rayon fibers, Rely was a little bag containing clumps of polyacrylate fibers and polyester foam, two super-absorbent materials now linked to the disease. While other super-absorbent tampons on the market at the time (and since) also contained polyacrylates, Rely was the only one also to contain polyester foam, and many believe that was the reason for such a high incidence of cases involving that product (*all* tampon brands were known to be as-sociated with cases of TSS).

What has not been sufficiently acknowledged was that Procter and Gamble had market-tested Rely in the summer of 1979 by sending free samples to millions of women—most of whom were happy to try a product that claimed to "absorb even the worry." We believe that Procter and Gamble's aggressive promotion and distribution of Rely may have had as much to do with the disasters that followed as did the fact that the ingredients in the tampon had not been tested for safety.

Rely was taken off the market very soon after its association with TSS became known, and all tampon manufacturers began to meet with the CDC and other interested parties to find ways to cut their losses. Mean-while, stunned by the revelations that product testing for absorbency did not necessarily include product testing for safety, women began to demand that the U.S. government involve itself in regulating tampons as the "de-vices" (like IUD's) they had been classified under law in 1974.

Since 1979 representatives from the Food and Drug Administration (FDA), women's health and other public-interest groups, and the sanitary products manufacturers have been meeting regularly, concentrating first on the now-familiar warnings and subsequently on absorbency standards. Issues of biocompatibility (effects of tampons on living tissue); bacterial contamination and sterility; and the presence of other ingredients, such as perfumes and lubricants, are also of concern to the consumers' groups but have been pushed to the back burner by the industry.[16]

The first round of talks, while the relationship between tampons and toxic shock was known only to be circumstantial rather than causal, involved warnings in tampon boxes. During and immediately after the Rely crisis, the manufacturers agreed to a voluntary warning, with the encouragement of the CDC; but the warnings did not become federally mandated until late in 1982. While the warnings and the information about symptoms and first aid are probably familiar to most women, whether they give up tampons as a result is not clear. Industry figures in 1985 put the number of women using tampons at 55 percent; the National Women's Health Network believes the number is 70 percent; while a *Consumer Reports* study shows evidence that 65 percent is the latest figure. A study for the International Communications Association found that while 75 percent of a population of educated women over twenty-three used tampons, 26 percent did report having changed products since the tampon-TSS connection was made, a statistic that reflects an unusually high rate of response to the public information campaign waged by manufacturers, consumer groups, and the government.[17]

Potentially more useful to women than warnings, and consequently far more difficult to extract from the manufacturers, has been an industry-wide standard of absorbency, so that a woman could heed the medical advice to use the least absorbent product necessary. In 1985 tampons varied so widely in what they meant by the terms *super, regular,* or *super plus,* for example, that a Playtex Regular was twice as absorbent as a Tampax Original Regular and more absorbent than any other brand's super except its own.

A committee of the American Society for Testing and Materials (ASTM), including representatives from the FDA, consumer groups, and the manufacturers, could not agree on how to set a standard. In general, the consumer groups favored a simple definition of *super* or *regular* that would apply to all brands. The manufacturers preferred to retain their individual idiosyncrasies and use a numerical labeling system like the suntan-lotion makers use to inform the buyer of the "protection factor" of the product on a scale of, say, two to fifteen. Many consumer groups, among them the respected Boston Women's Health Book Collective, believe this would needlessly confuse the woman confronted with finding a tampon big enough to absorb her blood yet safe enough to reduce her risk of disease or death.

The talks ended inconclusively in 1984, with no action by the FDA. When Tampax announced in 1986 that it would voluntarily begin to use absorbency labeling, the FDA asked, rather than required, that other manufacturers follow suit. Because of different methods of testing for absorbency, however, the manufacturers will not be using the same kind of labeling. Kotex and Tampax will use standardized terms like *regular,* for example, to mean a tampon that absorbs six to nine grams of fluid. Playtex and o.b., on the other hand, will carry numerical labels, throwing right back into the consumer's lap the impossibility of any meaningful interbrand comparison.[18]

Hoping to seize some measure of control, feminist health workers and others for a time promulgated the use of sea sponges as a non-synthetic, economical, reusable alternative to the tampon. What they did not realize was that in their "natural" state the sponges contained such matter as sand, coral, bacteria, fungi, and trace amounts of eleven minerals, among them arsenic, barium, calcium, chloride, copper, iron, magnesium, potassium, sodium sulfate, and zinc. They also contained varying levels of the pollutants and chemicals present in the waters from which they were harvested and, a final irony, were implicated in at least two cases of toxic shock.[19] After a study of these sponges by the University of Iowa, the FDA stopped their distribution as menstrual protection by the small, woman-owned businesses that sold them but has not rushed to demand comparable speed or accountability from the tampon manufacturers.

In this new climate of skepticism about the safety of these and other consumer products, a growing body of research has linked tampons to other kinds of illness and vaginal injury. At the 1983 menstruation conference in Atlantic City, a summary of research into tampon-related injuried presented by Daniel Colburn, M.D., showed that women suffering from abnormal vaginal discharge or intramenstrual spotting were usually found to have ulcerations of the vagina, acute and chronic inflamation, and embedded fibers in the ulcers.[20] Because the same symptoms also present themselves in such diseases as herpes, syphillis, and cancer, many women suffer needless anguish because they are not aware of the more common and less serious probable cause of such symptoms. The response to this news confirms what the early research into TSS revealed: tampons are too popular to attract a bad reputation.

Yet incredible as it seems now, all the research done on tampons' safety has been voluntary, in the sense that the FDA never even got into the tampon-regulating business until 1974. The FDA then reportedly ignored the mounting evidence of tampon-related injuries in its files until the Rely-induced TSS crises of 1979 forced it to act. Meanwhile, the law still allowed tampon manufacturers to make changes in the composition and ingredients of their products without FDA approval. This is how the polyacrylate rayon and polyester foam, the substances responsible for the high absorbency of many of the super plus products, were able to be introduced into the market and into women's bodies with practically no research done on their safety as an internal absorbent.

This same spirit of laissez-faire governs what goes into the new, improved, and heavily promoted sanitary napkins. We asked the Personal Products Company if they used the same superabsorbent ingredients in their napkins (Sure and Natural) as in their tampons (o.b.), and they responded by saying they had never used synthetic ingredients in the o.b. tampon but did not, in effect, answer the question about the napkins.[21] A box of Carefree panty shields from the same company contains this fine print: "CAUTION: if irritation develops, discontinue use. Consult your physician if irritation persists." But no ingredients are listed, even though the box says the pads are "softly scented, too."

What is next for women and the sanitary products industry? Some extremists would ban the tampon. Or they might suggest that women sign a release in order to buy tampons, an idea promoted in Denver during the height of the Rely scare.[22] The appearance of toxic shock has generated a number of negative attitudes, not only against tampons, but against the menstrual process itself. One doctor from the Cornell Medical School, speaking against the tampon, went on to indict menstrual blood as "an excellent culture for bacteria" that should be eliminated immediately rather than be kept in place by a blocking device.[23] We are here approaching a medical myth that we tried to dispel earlier: such remarks are in the same league with Pliny's exhortations about menstrual blood withering the crops and spoiling the mayonnaise.

Given the choice, we would keep the tampon for its convenience, its security, its disposability—reasons we have lived with so long that it seems inconceivable not to have the tidy box in the bathroom cabinet. But we think there should be a far more widespread sense of outrage about the way the manufacturers of sanitary products do *not* serve their customers well—and continuous pressure on them to prove that their products are safe.

Since the Rely tampon changed the way women regarded the "friendly monthly nuisance," several lawsuits alleging injury or death from tampon-related causes have been filed against the sanitary products companies. The U.S. Supreme Court recently let stand a 1.1-million-dollar award won by a California woman who suffered TSS after using an o.b. tampon. The manufacturer had argued in its appeal that it should not have been required to pay punitive damages because it did not know of the risk from the tampon until after the woman had been injured.[24] Million-dollar reminders of their responsibilities to their consumers should go a long way toward keeping the manufacturers accountable and giving women a healthy sense of control over their bodies.

Chapter 15

Menstruation Goes Public

In the 1970s, a new explicitness is in the air; for the first time, menstruation appears openly in cartoons, in insults reported in the media. More positively, it becomes a subject for television, songs, and commercial movies.

The uses of menses-as-insult are not new; what is new is the public reporting of them—no more cover-up, no more "Modess, because . . ." The new menstrual insults appear in contexts both traditional and innovative. An article on pitcher Tom Seaver reports the standard clubhouse "ragging" (a pun?): "One player will pay attention to another by tying up his clothes or stuffing Tampax in his locker."[1] Athletes have always taunted one another with aspersions on the other's supposed (and dreaded) femininity; now, the paraphernalia of menstruation are used to make the same insult. Even transvestite singer Wayne County, himself dressing in feminine clothing, uses paraphernalia to insult men. Bothered by a ring-side heckler, County once responded, "Go stuff a Kotex down your throat, you asshole!"[2]

Nor are paraphernalia insults aimed only at men. *Village Voice* columnist Jill Johnston tells of a "jock on the plane out of s.f." who was insulting a woman. Johnston became especially incensed because he'd "brandished a Kotex at this woman," and Johnston planned to "crack the guy on 'is head" with her *Mainliner Magazine*.[3]

But it is the iconoclastic *National Lampoon* that finally gives a man his comeuppance. A Spanish dandy serenades a mantilla-wearing lady on a balcony. Instead of a rose, she flings down to him a bloody tampon (colored red in an otherwise black-and-white cartoon).

Not all examples of the new openness are insulting or even negative. Although television, songs, and film may allude to the discomforts of menstruation, there are also instances of pleasure and celebration of being a woman.

Jackie Gleason didn't think it should be done on television. Menstruate, that is. But the Great One was behind the times; 1973 was the year that the menses hit the tube.

All in the Family, TV's breaker of taboos, broke the menstrual barrier in an episode called "The Battle of the Month," first aired on March 24, 1973. Gloria is irritable because of her period and quarrels with her mother, Edith. Archie, conservative in all matters, objects to Gloria's talking about her period in front of him. Sally Struthers, the actress who plays Gloria, was allegedly the inspiration for this episode. According to one of the show's writers, "When Sally Struthers has her menstrual period, forget it. She can't work, she's headachy, she's irritable—we took it from her. And it worked." According to the writer, the "menstrual episode" was not done for shock value.[4]

But it did shock. It generated more mail than any other episode that season, most of it objecting to mentioning the menses. Viewers seemed to agree with Jackie Gleason, who argued in a *New York Times* interview that "there is nothing funny about a menstrual period . . . these are not suitable topics."[5]

All in the Family's sister show *Maude* treated periods in a more off-hand, casual way. In an episode aired on January 29, 1974, Maude, her husband, Walter, and friends are marooned in an out-of-the-way railroad station during a blizzard. The intrepid Maude looks for a candy machine and reports to the group, "The one in the ladies' room works: you can have a Clark bar or a Midol." Walter advises, "Buy a Midol—we might be here all month." The target of his humor, such as it is, seems to be the weather rather than menstruation; his remark, then, demonstrates a healthy nonchalance toward women's periods.

Even better than nonchalance is a feeling of sisterhood among women because of menstruation. On *The Mary Tyler Moore Show,* September 29, 1973, Mary and her friend Rhoda reminisce about the trials of puberty. Rhoda finds one of her old diaries and reads, "Today my mother came into my room and whispered that something wonderful is going to happen to me—once a month." Her conversation with Mary is easily integrated with the rest of the story: Mary and Rhoda are in New York for the marriage of Rhoda's friend. Their adolescent memories provide a bond between them.

By now, many casual references to menstruation have been heard on a wide variety of programs. But to date, the most positive image of menstruation on television we've encountered is *I Love You, Goodbye,* a made-for-TV movie first shown on February 12, 1974. The central character, Karen Chandler (played by Hope Lange), leaves her insensitive husband and three children. She then meets a potential lover, Alex, but she ends the relationship when she breaks a date in order to be with her daughter Julie, who is having her first period. Karen tells Julie her future is bright, she has many choices ahead of her, and that's what women's liberation really means. It is a remarkable episode. Not only does a woman put another woman's needs ahead of a man's (a rare choice in literature, as in life), but they both celebrate the menstrual process, seeing it as a fulfillment, not as something to be hidden or denied.

Menstruation is celebrated more often in story than in song. It is something to write home to your mother about but not something you sing about onstage. We have found very few songs mentioning the menses, and most are by men. The Rolling Stones seem to refer to it in their song "I Can't Get No Satisfaction" in which the girl says, "Baby, better come back, maybe next week." Does Bob Dylan refer to menstruation in "Just Like a Woman" when he writes these lines: "She aches just like a woman," and "your long time curse hurts"?

For Simon and Garfunkel in their "Big Bright Green Pleasure Machine," menstruation is one of a list of problems. Along with "Does your group have more cavities than theirs?" comes the line: "Are you worried 'cause your girlfriend's just a little late?"

These songs all treat menstruation as it impinges upon the male consciousness: as a sign of lack of pregnancy and as a reason for postponing sexual contact. New women artists can be expected to treat menstruation as women see it, and they are beginning to do so. At the first National Women's Music Festival, held in May 1974, a group called the Clinch Mountain Back-Steppers performed a song called "The Bloods" by Debbie Lempke. Funny and frank, the song acknowledges, "Some sisters get down for menstruation / Ain't no time for sad desperation." As if in response to the male songwriters' view, the third stanza asserts:

> Men keep sayin' that the bloods are bad
> Because it means you ain't fertile
> That you ain't been had

The refrain joyously proclaims the renewal of body and spirit that can be possible when a woman embraces the "natural rhythm" of her body:

There's a new day comin'
When you got the bloods again.[6]

The treatment of menstruation in film has followed a path similar to
that of television. First, there is the groundbreaking: the mention of the
periods, perhaps to shock, ultimately to be nonchalant. Then, there is the
probing into women's thoughts about menstruation, positive or negative.
And finally, there is celebration of the monthly bleeding as part of the
pleasure of being a woman.

In 1973 and 1974, mention of menstruation, previously rare, became
common. Most references, both in earlier and in later films, were of the
usual kind: missed periods and fears of pregnancy (*Images, Travels with
My Aunt, Saturday Night and Sunday Morning, The Lords of Flatbush*),
the intercourse taboo during menstruation (*McCabe and Mrs. Miller, Diary of a Mad Housewife*), women's unhappiness with cramps (*They Shoot
Horses, Don't They; Rosemary's Baby*). But two fairly recent foreign films
make menstruation, for the first time, a central event in film, one treated
not only verbally but also visually.

In Ingmar Bergman's *Cries and Whispers*, Ingrid Thulin plays a wife
who feels great antagonism toward her husband. In order to avoid having
sexual relations with him, she takes a broken wine glass to her genitals,
and the blood rushes out from between her legs in a false menstruation.
Smiling fiercely, as if achieving an orgasm through pain, she smears some
of the blood on her face.

The scene is difficult to interpret. Is it menstruating that is loathsome,
or self-mutilation? Is Bergman sympathizing with or humiliating his female
character? The sequence, in any interpretation, is an unforgettable one,
and the red of the blood is linked visually with other reds in the film, as
in the red-outs, rather than blackouts, sometimes used to end scenes.
Bergman is perhaps the first director to use menstrual red for its color, as
beauty, in the ways that other directors have used the red blood of killings
and woundings (compare, for example, *A Clockwork Orange*). Bergman's
scene is an affirmation of the color potential of menstrual blood but hardly
a celebration of its meaning for a woman.

The celebration is present in *Valerie and Her Week of Wonders*, a
Czech film written by Ester Krumbachova and Jaromil Jires and directed
by Jires. The film was shown in New York and at the Chicago and San
Francisco film festivals in 1972 and 1974. Valerie is a thirteen-year-old
girl entering puberty. Her first period leads to a week of wonderful sexual
awakening in which imagination runs into riotous fantasy. Discovering
that "she is no longer a child," she imagines tooth-chomping vampires,

lewd priests seducing wholesome virgins, weasels doing vanishing acts; plagues and murders occur. Lyrical music and surreal images flow together; the line between fantasy and reality is never entirely clear. There are even magic earrings, shaped like little silver bells, with "pearls" (perhaps a clitoral symbol) inside them, that save their owner from many dangers: incest (the vampires are very loving toward one another), rape, neck bites, death at the stake, and an actual partridge in a pear tree.

In the end, the whole family lives in a sort of vampire Valhalla, leading the good life of happiness and sensuality. Valerie walks about, watching it all calmly, now a "blood" part of this society. *Valerie and Her Week of Wonders* consists of beautiful images, and it celebrates menstruation as a gateway, an awakening to the new perceptions and possibilities in being a woman. It is the first truly feminist film about the menarche. Certainly, there will be more.

Afterword

Since menstruation went public, we've seen an increase in television ads for napkins. But except for spotty appearances by menstrual or menopausal women on certain series, like "*St. Elsewhere*" and "*Golden Girls,*" TV is silent about menstruation. As a character from Judith Krantz's novel *Princess Daisy* observes, women on television never have periods or ovaries or "any of their equipment—except in the soap operas when they're always taking out everything in the hospital."[7]

There are exceptions. One "*Santa Barbara*" episode used menstruation as a way to dramatize the estrangement between Eden and her mother, Sophia. Eden tells her mother, whom she had presumed to be dead: "When I was twelve, it took me almost a year before I would confess to Rosa [the Hispanic servant] that I been—I thought there was something wrong with me, I thought that I'd inherited something from you, and that I was going to die, just like you did. I had to be my own mother. You can't make up anything to me, because I already did it myself."[8] This sort of self-revelation is uncommon in soaps, which only on rare occasions connect a character's mood with her cycle.

Nor are ballads about menstrual blues flooding the airways or reaching MTV, despite such strong female presences as Cindy Lauper, Pat Benatar, and Tina Turner. In pop music women bleed only from the heart. Even the male singer Alice Cooper, who recorded "Only Women Bleed" in the mid-1970s, has denied that the words are about menstruation. For explicit menstrual music one has to look to the women's counterculture. Like The Bloods, other women's groups have menstrually associated names: Lost Cherrees, Mydolls, the Modettes.[9] One British women's group known as Friggin' Little Bits has taped a song that's a takeoff on a menstrual celebration.

Carol Erdman's poem of celebration, "Song for Sisters in the Moon Hut," is an involved set of incantations on the theme that "There is power in the blood of the woman."[10] Throughout the poem menstruation serves as the collective sign for all women, a process envied by men, who "gashed blood from each other" in emulation of the menstrual flowering. This poem, which includes ceremonies of song, eating, drinking, celebration, and purification, has been used in feminist rituals—in a Women's Spirituality Conference held in Baltimore (1977), for instance. Erdman's song, meant for women only, praises the hidden powers of menstrual blood:

> Let me lie in the Moon Hut.
> Let me tell of my visions, let my sister tell me her dreams.
> Lead me blind to the place where the wetleaf fern curls.
> Let me learn where the hidden spring finds its source,
> Let me float on my scarlet tide,
> Let the light sift through me—

The power of menstruation is also a theme in film, most notably in Brian de Palma's *Carrie* (1976). Blood is the central image of the film, the ads capitalizing on the face of Sissy Spacek, once lovely, now streaming with the blood of a pig. Carrie is all red except for her eyes. De Palma bathes the entire gory scene with a red filter, recalling the bleeding Carrie of the early shower scene, when she discovers her period and also her power.

In their Jungian study of menstruation, Penelope Shuttle and Peter Redgrove briefly describe *Carrie* as a film in which "a girl's terrifying poltergeist and telekenetic abilities are linked with her late menarche." They also discuss similar powers in *The Exorcist* (1974), linking Regan's vomiting to premenstrual tension, her swollen tissues to premenstrual edema, and her wounds to the continuity of the menstrual cycle.[11]

Of current film directors, Brian de Palma seems to be the one most intrigued by the menstrual process, centrally in *Carrie,* peripherally in two later films—*The Fury* (1979) and *Body Double* (1984). It is curious that both films involve vampires. Gillian of *The Fury* is a Carrie-like adolescent who makes people bleed from their noses and hands (what we have called vicarious menstruation). Before doing tests on Gillian and her psychic peers, the doctor warns, "If you girls are into your monthlies, I don't want you around when Gillian is testing." A woman colleague clearly grasps these dangerous, menstrual connections: "What is this kid, a vampire?" The Dracula/menses reference in de Palma's *Body Double* occurs late in the film. The hero, an unsuccessful actor, has a job playing a vampire in a porn movie. Before the final scene is to be shot, the actress cautions, "My breasts are very tender and I've got my period." Then follows a potent visualization of vicarious menstruation: the vampire buries his face in the actress-victim's bleeding breasts. Blood, biting, pain, periodicity—all of these horror motifs have menstrual implications. According to one film critic, the "vampire's bloodletting of women who suddenly enter into full sexuality, the werewolf's bloody attacks—which occur regularly each month—are certainly related to the menstrual cycle which suddenly and mysteriously commands the body of every adolescent girl."[12]

Other films of the eighties, none of which reached so large an audience as de Palma's, allude to menstruation. The movie *Top Secret,* for instance, contains a rather gross one-liner. A mad scientist is telling an American rock star to hide. "You must go now quickly. If they find out you've seen this [a discovery about magnetism and submarines], your life will be worth less than a truckload of dead rats in a tampon factory." In *Sixteen Candles* (1984), a film that looks affectionately at adolescent sexuality, menstruation is the cause for far lighter humor. A bride gets her period immediately before her wedding day. To relieve her cramps she takes a muscle relaxant and ends up staggering, then fainting. The mother, embarrassed, tries to hush up the bridal party. "Will you please be quiet. We don't want to announce to everyone that she has her period." Unfortunately, the mother's voice is heard on the church's public address system. In *Sixteen Candles* menstruation indeed goes public. The hush-hush attitude is exploited for humorous effects, as it is in the film *Mr. Mom,* where the liberated husband is so humiliated at having to purchase sanitary napkins that he cancels the order to avoid facing the public. Menstrual humor somehow fails in the popular comedy *Ghostbusters.* Bill Murray plays a paranormal psychiatrist. He asks a woman some questions about her family history: are there problems with schizophrenia, drug abuse, or alcohol? He then asks: "Are you, Alice, menstruating right now?" Puzzled, his partner asks, "Why that?" Murray's cool response: "I'm a scientist."

This scattering of references, however, does not indicate a generally open attitude toward menstruation in recent movies and videos. The film *Endless Love,* for example, totally eliminates the vivid menstrual intercourse episode so crucial to Scott Spencer's novel.

In our search for menstrual images in film, we were probably the most surprised to find menstruation treated, on both a literal and a symbolic level, in Prince's *Purple Rain* (1984), a film which many viewers disliked for its anti-woman attitudes. The plot involves the conflict between "The Kid," a rock star, and his girlfriend, who is being sought after by a competing group. This major male-female conflict is echoed in the subplot. Two women in the band, song-writers, are angry because the men won't take them or their music seriously. When Wendy insists that her song be played, one musician remarks: "God got Wendy's periods reversed. About every twenty-eight days she starts acting nice. Lasts about a weekend." This menstrual put-down, an expression of male hostility, is an attempt to separate the girls from the boys in the band. Ironically, this joke about the weekend period is rephrased in the famous title song, where it appears to represent unity rather than separation, women's values rather than male ones.

"Purple Rain" is Wendy's song. "The Kid" finally sings it near the end of the film, after his father has died, after he has come to terms with those emotions which, in his maleness, he has not released. The song, rendered from a male point of view, is reconciliatory; it praises women and attempts to establish friendship rather than domination: "I never wanted to be your weekend lover/I wanna be some kind of friend," Prince sings in the second lyric. In one sense this line reflects back on the earlier crack about Wendy's "nice" period: "Lasts about a weekend." In the song Wendy has written, however, such time distinctions are removed. Connecting the love/reconciliation themes of the song is the central image—the purple rain. The rain could represent the tears which Prince can now shed, having let go of his emotions. But our inclination is to see in the title two of the major symbols for menstruation, color (red/purple) and fluid (rain/flow).[13]

The song celebrates women. Women run, bathe, and laugh in the purple rain. Repeated again and again, the chanted words "purple rain, purple rain" echo the repetitious nature of the menstrual cycle as well as create the same kind of magic we find in Carol Erdman's incantations. Prince/Wendy invokes in "Purple Rain" a menstrual celebration experienced vicariously, through the women participating in their ritual of wetness. In this miraculous lyric, at least, the goddess seems to have gotten Prince's periods reversed.

PART FOUR

Menstrual Images
in Literature

Chapter 16

The Bleeding Tower: Menstrual Themes in Fairy Tales

Weaving in and out of the mythmaking imaginations of centuries are those symbols of the eternal feminine: blood, flowers, the witch, the moon. When these images appear in poetry, fiction, or mythology, critics are reluctant to associate them with that most female of attributes, the menstrual cycle. The same neglect has applied to the menstrual themes that seem to fill the universe of folktales. There is no mention of them in collections and codifications of folktale motifs.

Fairy tales told to children are built on ritual and myth, embellished with the narrative art. Because they occupy an intermediate position between true myth and high art, they show us human beings linking profound and unchanging myths about the meaning of life with the naive wish fulfillment of storytelling. Studies of repeating themes and motifs in folktales throughout the Indo-European language group and beyond reveal these homely tales to be rooted in common experience, fears, and misconceptions. It is thus logical that the terror of menstrual blood, one of the most profound imprints on the collective unconscious, should occupy a prominent place in these tales.

Many of the menstrual themes and allusions in fairy tales are filtered through the character of the witch, a figure who appears in some form in most Western tales and who is closely associated with fear of menstruation. But certain key elements of plot also recall the practices of menarcheal seclusion and avoidance of the menstruating woman common to primitive societies and to many advanced societies as well. Thus, the young heroines of fairy tales are inevitably pubertal maidens who must undergo some trial before being allowed to live happily ever after with Prince

Charming. Furthermore, the image patterns and repeated symbolic motifs rely heavily on the white-red-black color progression of the Great Goddess and on blood and flowers as essential components of plot development.

We shall limit ourselves here to some of the 200-plus *Household Tales* collected by the Brothers Grimm. They are familiar, and they are the stories most illustrative of our European-American heritage.[1]

In *The Fear of Women*, Wolfgang Lederer points out that witches usually are either very old or very young. The old ones deal in "envy and malice"; and the young specialize in "love magic," concocting potions from their newly flowing menstrual blood.[2] The old witch in Grimms' tales has the appearance of the menopausal woman of old: protruding nose and chin, facial hair, bowed back, coarsened voice. She specializes in malicious curses on the young and frequently has in her care a pubertal maiden. More than once in the stories, she is associated with child cannibalism. Black is her color, the color of death, decay, and the crone aspect of the Great Goddess.

The young witch is almost never the heroine but is frequently the natural daughter of the old witch (the heroine is usually her stepdaughter). Following Lederer's description, the young witch is usually found plotting to steal the bridegroom from the true bride and frequently uses some magic arts learned from her mother to assist herself. Examples of the young witch abound in Grimms' tales, but the most familiar are Cinderella's stepsisters.

Lederer suggests that something about the child-rearing function seems to dim both the white and the black magic of witches;[3] thus, the age of a witch must be one extreme or the other. We must emphasize further that at menarche and menopause the menstrual function is extremely influential in a woman's life, informing her attitudes and personality. During the childbearing years, however, menstruation is important more for its usefulness as a guide to fertility—that is, when it appears. Pregnancy and lactation combine to suppress menstruation for long periods of a woman's childbearing years. Thus, even in folklore, the conclusion is that menstruation causes a woman to act like a witch.

We discussed in Chapter 8 the ancient fear that a woman's "natural" feelings of destructiveness toward her children are intensified during her periods. Even worse, the mother of a pubescent daughter may experience barely controllable rage as the daughter blossoms and the mother decays. The dualism in the personality of the mother is expressed in fairy tales in Western culture by two mothers: the natural mother and the stepmother. The true mother is good and loving but dies prematurely, frequently at the birth of a longed-for daughter. The stepmother is wicked and seeks to harm the child or shut her away from the world.

Snow White is blessed with just such a pair of mothers. The true mother looks out a window and wishes for the birth of a child; the stepmother looks into a mirror and wills the death of the child. Arland Ussher, an Irish critic, has linked these two mothers to Eve and Lilith, Adam's fertile and barren wives, suggesting the archetype of all dual-mother roles in these tales.[4]

In "Sweetheart Roland," the envious stepmother hates the daughter's beauty and plots to cut off her head. She kills her own child instead, and the drops of blood from the severed head speak to her, suggesting that she is gaining self-knowledge from this "first bleeding" of the daughter. In "Brother and Sister" (also called "The Enchanted Stag"), the stepmother sends her stepchildren into the forest to die (as in "Hansel and Gretel"); when they survive, she then attempts to kill the stepdaughter and steal her child. Only the magical appearance of the real mother to nurse the baby defeats the witch's power (lactation suppressing menstruation).

The witches in "Snow White" and "Hansel and Gretel" are also devouring mothers, another problem for the analysts. Hansel and Gretel escape being roasted for dinner by Gretel's wits; Snow White's stepmother eats the lung and liver of a wild boar, thinking they are Snow White's.

Both the psychoanalytic theories of maternal destructiveness and the imagined crimes against children attributed to historical witches emerge in these children's fables. Both are tied in with the fear inspired by menstrual blood: the fear that the normal order of things can be reversed, and the life-creating womb become a bloody chamber of death.

There is extensive fear among all peoples that witches and menstruating women are the archetypal castrating females. Various anthropological studies claim that the extensiveness of menstrual taboos in a society reflects that society's degree of castration anxiety. Church decrees against witches in the Middle Ages accused them directly of causing impotence. And castration anxiety inspired by menstrual blood finds latent expression in Grimm in the mutilation of young men as they try to overcome a witch's curse and reach a young woman who is under her influence. So, we find that Rapunzel's lover is blinded when the witch throws him from the tower, and that all princes who tried to penetrate the briar roses around Sleeping Beauty's castle before the hundred years were up perished.

Somewhat displaced castrations occur in "The Twelve Brothers" and "The Six Swans." In the first, the birth of a thirteenth child, a girl,[5] means that the twelve brothers must die. This is the first castration in the story.

The brothers escape and set up house in the forest; when their sister, grown to puberty, reaches them, they live happily together until the girl plucks some flowers ("flowers" means menstruation in many cultures), an action that turns the brothers into ravens. In this nonhuman form, impotent to act as men, the brothers must remain for seven years. "The Six Swans" has a similar plot: Six brothers are turned into swans and can only be released by fulfillment of a trial of silence and work by their sister.

It is also possible to regard transformation stories such as "The Frog Prince" and "Snow White and Rose Red" as tales reflecting fear of castration by a menarcheal child. In both, a prince has been changed into an animal and is dependent on the unselfish love of a maiden to regain his human masculinity.

The unseemly haste with which nubile maidens were locked away in towers in the land of Grimm seems to be a direct narrative analogue to the custom of seclusion at menarche in most early societies. As we described in Chapter 3, newly menstruating girls in Africa, the South Pacific, India, and the Americas were commonly separated from their tribes at their first menstruation, some for a few days, some for four or five years. The purpose of the seclusion was to protect the girls and their societies from their *mana* at this dangerous time. Important during this seclusion were the instructions they received from the older women of the tribe in female matters. Their natural mothers, however, were almost universally excluded. At the end of the seclusion, the girls were considered marriageable and were welcomed into the adult life of the tribe.

Sleeping Beauty, Rapunzel, and Maid Maleen, to name a few, were kept from the eyes of the world during their adolescence and endured their seclusion at the behest of, or in the company of, a bad mother (a witch or other old person not their natural mother). In many stories of this type, a pointed reference is made to the age of the girl when her seclusion began: Sleeping Beauty was cursed at her birth by a fairy who said that on her fifteenth birthday she would prick her finger on a spindle and die. Bleeding at fifteen seems an obvious reference to the menarche. Rapunzel was shut in her tower at age twelve, another menarcheal age, although she had lived with the witch from birth.

The places of seclusion were impenetrable. Everyone, even the flies on the wall, slept for 100 years in Sleeping Beauty's castle. Rapunzel's tower had no stairs and only one tiny window; like the sacred priests and kings, she was literally suspended between heaven and earth. Maid Maleen's tower didn't even have a window; she and a waiting woman were shut away when she refused to marry her father's choice. When her seven-year seclusion was up, she chipped away some stones and found that the land had been ravaged and only they had survived. Here is an example of the menarcheal seclusion protecting the girl herself from the dangers of her state.

The frequent trials imposed on married women involving separation, actual or symbolic, from their husbands, is a lesser-known aspect of many fairy tales. It suggests to us the representation in folklore of the taboo against intercourse with a menstruating woman.

For example, after the witch found out about Rapunzel's tower assignations with the prince, she took her into the wilderness and forced her to live in great hardship. It took seven years for the prince to find her, handicapped as he was by the blindness (castration) he suffered when he fell from the tower. But Rapunzel had an eye-opening surprise for him: seven-year-old twins born to her in the wild. This suggests not only the menstrual intercourse taboo, with its attendant fear of castration or impotence, but also the seclusion imposed on women after childbirth, all blood from the genitals being considered dangerous to men.

In both "The Twelve Brothers" and "The Six Swans," to release her brothers from a charm, a bride must keep silent for seven years, during which time she is married and bears children. In "The Pink," a queen is shut away in a tower that neither the sun nor moon could penetrate for seven years following the kidnapping of her newborn son and the false accusation that she had murdered him. The bride in "The Lady and the Lion" must follow her enchanted husband all over the world for seven years when he is changed into a dove; every seventh step, he sheds a drop of blood and a white feather so that she will be able to follow.

In "Fairy Tell True," a fourteen-year-old girl, told to look behind only twelve of thirteen doors in the palace of the good fairy she lives with, fails the test of obedience and is permanently stained with gold on her finger from the thirteenth room. The gold is suggestive of the permanent stain of menstrual blood, and the fairy recalls the witches and other nonmaternal guardians of menarcheal girls. The child is sent into seclusion and struck dumb until she is willing to confess her transgression to the fairy. A king marries her, but she remains dumb through the early marriage and the birth of several children. This condition and the stain of gold suggest that she is expiating the stain of the menstrual blood and its evil connotations and keeping a tabooed distance from her husband as a prelude to living a normal life, just as the heroines of other stories underwent tests and trials to save their marriages from menstrual contamination.

The stain of gold is but one instance of precise descriptions of appearance or action. Some descriptive emblems and motifs recur constantly and point to associations that go back to the mythic and ritualistic origins of the tales. One such recurring motif is the use of the colors white, red, and black.

Snow White's mother pricks her finger while embroidering on an ebony frame at a snowy window. As the drops of blood fall on the snow, she wishes for a daughter with skin as white as snow, lips as red as blood, and hair as black as ebony. The mother of the little boy in "The Juniper Tree" stands under a dark tree in white snow, peeling a red apple. She, too, cuts her finger and bleeds on the snow; she, too, wishes for a child as white as snow and red as blood.

In these two tales, the colors associated with the Great Goddess are being used to suggest the eternal feminine life cycle. Lederer refers to Io, the cow, who changed her color from white to rose to black, and associates her with the new moon (the White Goddess of birth and growth), the full moon (the Red Goddess of love and battle), and the old moon (the Black Goddess of death and divination): virgin, nymph, crone, the three aspects of the Great Goddess. Most heroines of tales are presented to us first in their white, or virgin, state. After they fulfill conditions of seclusion and trial and ride off with the prince, they are associated with the color red, or nubility; and all have a brush with transformation or death, which brings them in touch with the black.

Snow White herself is first innocent, or white; she meets her apparent death from eating the red side of the poisoned apple, analogous to menarche (or sexual knowledge, like Eve's); she goes into the "seclusion" of death, although the dwarfs will not bury her in the "black" ground; and she is revived by a kiss on her red lips, signifying marriage and nubility.

The colors appear in "The Twelve Brothers" in a more displaced fashion. In this story, red first means death. The birth of a daughter is announced to the doomed brothers by a flag: "It was not white, but blood red, to warn them that they were to die." The daughter plucks white lilies when she is old enough to be married; her action turns the brothers into black ravens, signifying the death of their human form or perhaps the impotence brought about by the presence of a nubile (menstruating) woman. The brothers are also represented by the lilies, and had a boy been born, they would have seen a white flag. This gives us an interesting situation in which the males are emblemized by white and black but not by red, menstrual blood; only the sister has any association with red in this tale.

Red is the most prevalent color in the stories and frequently appears as a rose. The rose or any flower is a dominant menstrual image in literature and folklore. A flower is also an image for the hymen. Because old beliefs associated the menarche with the breaking of the hymen, these correspondences persist. Thus, the briar roses that grow around Sleeping Beauty's castle and cause the death of the would-be penetrators may be allusions to the fear of defloration prevalent among primitive peoples and their association of defloration with the dangerous properties of menstrual blood. Another instance of symbolic defloration occurs in "Jorinda and Joringel": a witch changes a maiden into a nightingale, only to have her released from the charm when the lover wields a "blood-red" flower.

Red blood is itself an ever-present element in most fairy tales, which are full of the casual violence of childhood itself. Beheadings are as common as finger prickings and serve the same purpose: to provide the blood that keeps the plot moving. Blood from the severed head of the ugly daughter in "Sweetheart Roland" speaks to the wicked stepmother; the blood from Snow White's mother's finger becomes a symbol of Snow White's birth. In "The Goose Girl," three drops of her mother's blood on a handkerchief go with the heroine on her wedding journey, symbolizing the passing of the menstrual magic from mother to daughter; the blood speaks to the girl, giving her comfort and protecting her from the machinations of an evil servant who travels with her. When the heroine loses the handerkerchief with the blood, she loses her power, and the waiting woman almost wins the bridegroom.

But the most beautiful and meaningful use of blood in these tales to symbolize the life-giving menstrual fluid occurs in "The Juniper Tree." The true mother cuts her finger peeling a red apple while she is standing in the snow under the juniper tree. The drops of blood inspire her to wish, like Snow White's mother, for a child as red as blood and as white as snow.

> And as she said it, it made her feel very happy, as if it was really going to happen. And so she went into her house, and a month went by, the snow was gone; and two months, and everything was green; and three months, and the flowers came up out of the ground; and four months, and all the trees in the woods sprouted and the tree branches grew dense and tangled with one another and the little birds sang so that the woods echoed, and the blossoms fell from the trees; and so five months were gone and she stood under the juniper tree and it smelled so sweet her heart leaped and she fell on her knees and was beside herself with happiness; and when six months had gone by, the

fruit grew round and heavy and she was very still; and seven months and she snatched the juniper berries and ate them so greedily she became sad and ill; and so the eighth month went by and she called her husband and cried and said, "When I die, bury me under the juniper." And she was comforted and felt happy, but when the nine months were gone, she had a child as white as snow and as red as blood and when she saw it she was so happy that she died.

This beautiful allegory of pregnancy and birth, encompassing the growth of life as well as the death that always lurks within the womb, is begun by woman's blood. The menstruation is the drops from the finger, which fertilize the ground under the juniper tree and cause both the baby and the tree to grow to fullness, making an indisputable connection between the mystery of woman's bleeding and the mystery of life that remains throughout the story.

Later, when the second wife murders the child born of the union between the woman and the tree, his sister, "weeping tears of blood," buries his bones under the juniper tree. This leads to an intensification of the blood-fertility correspondence. The spirit of the mother now inhabits the tree and receives new vitality from the bones of the child:

But the juniper began to stir and the branches kept opening out and coming back together again, just like something that is really happy. And then there was a sort of mist coming out of the tree and right in this mist it burned like fire and out of the fire flew this lovely bird that sang, oh, so gloriously sweet and flew high into the air and when it was gone the juniper tree was just the way it had always been and the cloth with the bones was gone.

In the original Grimm version of "Cinderella" (before Walt Disney), Cinderella's fairy godmother is her dead mother, whose spirit also resides in a tree. The tree grows over the mother's grave from a twig planted by Cinderella and watered by her tears. Cinderella prays to her mother for release from the cruelty of her stepsisters and for a gown for the prince's ball: "Shiver and shake, dear little tree/ Gold and silver shower on me." The mother, in the form of a bird, grants Cinderella's wishes.

This repeated correspondence between the woman and the tree—a source of life and strength, haven, refuge, and comfort—is consistent with the images of menstruation as flowers and of woman as flowering branch. It reflects one of the few positive attitudes toward menstruation in these stories from the childhood of our race.

Afterword

In the same year this book was originally published, Bruno Bettleheim brought out his compelling and insightful *The Uses of Enchantment: The Meaning and Importance of Fairy Tales.* In it he shows how fairy tales told to children function as guides for the growing-up process. While entertaining the child, they also feed his or her unconscious with information about the milestones of development ahead. In their solutions to the heroes' and heroines' dilemmas they show the child that growth involves changing oneself and that achieving adulthood involves risk and sometimes a kind of death of the old self.

While we did not have the benefit of Bettleheim's research, nor he ours, we were pleased to notice that he reaches similar conclusions about the importance of menstruation in many of the tales. Going beyond the mere identification of the menstrual themes and images in the stories toward an interpretation of them consistent with his thesis, he explains "Sleeping Beauty" in this way: "The story of Sleeping Beauty impresses every child that a traumatic event—such as the girl's bleeding at the beginning of puberty, and later, in first intercourse—does have the happiest consequences. The story implants the idea that such events must be taken very seriously, but that one need not be afraid of them. The 'curse' is a blessing in disguise."[6]

An even more dramatic encounter with puberty, sexual knowledge, and its consequences befell Little Red Riding Hood. This tale has a long and complicated history, with elements of the myth of Cronus swallowing his children and ultimately a stone, with traces of the werewolf cults of central Europe, and of a Latin story of 1023 in which a little girl wearing a red woven cap of great importance to her is found in the company of wolves.[7] Red Riding Hood has also been seen as an aspect of the goddess Diana, encompassing the triple aspects of the Great Goddess in the child, mother, and grandmother of the story.[8]

The popular versions of the story come from Charles Perrault's retelling in 1697 ("Le Petit Chaperon Rouge") or the brothers Grimm's version about a hundred years later. Perrault's is a fairly explicit tale of seduction and rape, in which Red Hiding Hood and grandmother are eaten by the wolf, with no rescue by the hunter, followed by a poem setting forth the moral of the story: nice girls don't. The Grimms' "Little Red Cap" is more complicated—in one version the grandmother is cut out of the belly of the wolf and saved; in another, Red Riding Hood and Grandmother save themselves by pushing the wolf into a vat of boiling sausages—and, in accord with Bettleheim's theories, allows the child reading or hearing it to make the appropriate unconscious connections between the story and her fantasies about life.

Recent studies have focused on most of the versions as examples of male approaches to the dangers of sexuality for women. One writer calls Perrault's version "a projection of male phantasy in a literary discourse considered to be civilized and aimed at curbing the natural inclinations of children."[9] What we find odd is that with all the emphasis on the color red, the presence of menstruation is ignored. The child is of pubertal age, and the color red is instead regarded as a symbol of evil, sexuality, or danger with no reference to the origins of these attributes of woman traceable to society's fear of her menstrual blood.

Chapter 17

Absent Literature:
The Menarche

Uniquely female experiences are missing from most of literature. We learn of a male's attaining manhood in sexual initiation; much less frequently, of a woman's feelings on losing her virginity. We commonly see men rejoicing in the birth of a son, accepting that of a daughter, but Anaïs Nin is one of the few writers to portray the physical agonies of childbirth. Discussions of menstruation are rare, and generally present the male's point of view.

Even more rare is literary depiction of the menarche. This peculiarly female experience barely appears at all until the twentieth century in Western literature. Like her counterparts in other cultures, the Western girl who becomes a woman is generally hidden from view.

She is shown more often in diaries, in which she confides her fear, pride, ambivalence; later fiction writers use the menarche as a focus for the girl's developing attitudes toward men, herself, and other women. Finally, in recent fiction (undoubtedly influenced by feminism), the menarche becomes an occasion for celebration, an initiation into female culture.

The earliest fictional treatments of the menarche that we have found are in French literature, in Edmond de Goncourt's "documentary novel" *Chérie* (1884) and Emile Zola's novel *La Joie de Vivre*[1] (1884). Goncourt conceived his *Chérie* while listening to the confidences of a princess's lady-in-waiting. Fascinated by the literary possibilities of female culture, he decided to write what would be his last novel about the life of a *jeune fille* growing up in fashionable Second Empire circles. Seeking the collaboration of women, Goncourt asked young girls to send him diaries, letters, confidences about growing up. He received many letters, some containing bizarre episodes or physiological details that would have appeared only in medical books in the 1880s.

The story he wove from the young girls' materials describes the life, coming-of-age, and death of Chérie Haudancourt, the daughter of a military officer and a Spanish mother who becomes insane. Not long after Chérie's first communion, she undergoes a transformation. Losing her childish grace, she becomes clumsy, awkward, almost comic; she trips over herself, does not know what to do with her hands and feet. She alternates between laughter and tears. Inwardly, she is changing from a little girl to *"une créature d'amour."* Goncourt interjects that although the medical profession insists that Parisian girls attain puberty at thirteen or fourteen, his letters from little girls mention numerous earlier cases, from nine to eleven; hence, his Chérie will menstruate early.

One day, Chérie awakens from a troubled sleep and finds unexpected and inexplicable blood. Five lines of dots follow, then Chérie's terrified thoughts: that she will have no more blood, that she will die because she cannot stop the blood from leaving her. She bursts into tears and is afraid to tell anyone what has happened to her.

The chambermaid enters, laughs mysteriously, and tries to remove the traces of Chérie's new state. For several months afterward, Chérie feels a little ashamed of her loss of blood, sensing it as a weakness and a strain, in her eyes having the disgraceful aspects that the Bible attributes to women in "that state." Chérie also becomes more timid and anxious around men.

Zola's *La Joie de Vivre* contains similar material about the menarche of Pauline Quenu, the cousin of the novel's hero. Zola's Pauline, once studious, becomes inattentive, temperamental, nervous. Like Chérie, she is motherless. Zola is more precise about her physical changes; she gains swelling curves that feel congested and painful and "a light down like a black shadow in the most secret and delicate parts of her skin." Her aunt, with whom she lives, shrinks from telling Pauline what is soon to occur.

One morning, Pauline, like Chérie, wakes up on bloodied sheets. Pauline, "white with terror," is "screaming continuously for her aunt: her bare, parted legs were stained with blood, and she was staring at what had come out of her, all her habitual courage driven away by the shock." Her aunt tries to find "some lie which would calm her without telling her anything" and explains that it's like nosebleeding, and happens to all women. Pauline, unbelieving, faints and is insensible for several days.

Later, Pauline (like Zola, her creator) learns the truth from research in books. Surreptitiously reading her cousin's medical books, she learns at fourteen "things that are hidden from virgins until their wedding night." She gains a lifelong pity for suffering people, as well as understanding why "that red stream, the sign of her puberty, had poured from her as from a ripe grape crushed at the vine-harvest . . . that full tide of life that she felt surging within her." Ultimately, she becomes proud of "the rising tide of blood that broke in red rain."

Zola's imagery, richer than Goncourt's spare *histoire,* resembles that of later writers about menstruation, especially Anne Sexton and Sylvia Plath. Zola and Goncourt together introduce motifs that continue in later literature about the menarche: the girl's ignorance and fear, the timidity or refusal of other women to tell her what is happening to her, and the stained sheets, the palpable sign that she has entered the realm of womanhood.

As realists, Goncourt and Zola sought a slice of life, and the truth of their portrayals is reflected in diaries and autobiographies. But few, if any, fictional works treat the menarche between the 1880s and the 1920s.

Emma Goldman, the noted feminist and anarchist, published her autobiography, *Living My Life,* in 1931, but her menarche came in 1880 in Russia, when she was eleven. Like Chérie and Pauline, she awoke one day "in great agony." She called her mother, who drew back the bedcovers and gave her the traditional slap Jewish mothers are expected to give their daughters.

> Suddenly I felt a stinging pain in my face. She had struck me. I let out a shriek, fastening on Mother's terrified eyes. "This is necessary for a girl," she said, "when she becomes a woman, as a protection against disgrace." She tried to take me in her arms, but I pushed her back. I was writhing in pain and I was too outraged for her to touch me. "I am going to die," I howled, "I want the Feldscher" [assistant doctor]. The Feldscher was sent for. He was a young man, a newcomer in our village. He examined me and gave me something to put me to sleep. Thenceforth, my dreams were of the Feldscher.

Emma Goldman's menarche, like Chérie's, led to her new awareness of men. Other diaries and novels, such as *A Young Girl's Diary,* include the central figure's changing consciousness about both men and women.

Freud was instrumental in the 1915 publication of *A Young Girl's Diary,* for which he wrote a prefatory letter. In the diary, a girl named Rita describes her life from ages eleven to fourteen and a half. Hers is an early description of what might be called *menarcheal competition:* girls' desire to be the first in their peer group to get their periods. But this competitive spirit is usually tinged with some embarrassment and ambivalence, as in Rita's report of her friend Hella's menarche.

Hella, bashful, does not want Rita to look at her. Hella's mother says, "Now you are not a child anymore, now you belong among the grown-ups." Hella is "a little puffed up about it"; like most of the schoolgirls, she feels herself entitled to "put on airs" now that it's happened. She swears her mother to secrecy so that her mother won't tell her father.

Not long afterward, in physics class, Rita's first period comes. She writes, "My goodness, to-day I have . . . , no, I can't write it plain out." Finally, she tells Hella, who kisses her on the street. But Rita dreads telling her aunt, with whom she lives, because she needs a "San- T-" (sanitary napkin or towel). She doesn't think she'll ever be able to buy one for herself, "even if I live to be 80. And it would be awful for Father to know about it."

Colette Audry, in her autobiography *Aux Yeux de Souvenir* (1947), is more than embarrassed about men's possible reactions. She feels "soiled" at her menarche, envies her younger sister's freedom. "Then I began to hate men, who would never experience that, who knew about it. And I detested women, who took it so easily, and who, if they knew about me, would gleefully think, "Now it is your turn."

Nearly all writers about the menarche have some sense that it is to be hidden from males and, as in Rita's case, from grown-ups. Ignorance at the first period seems to have been a fact of life for many girls until recent years, and reticence about discussion could lead to terror for the girls.

Or reticence could lead to comic misapprehension, as Mary McCarthy reports in her autobiography, *Memories of a Catholic Girlhood*. When she was twelve and living in a convent boarding school, she cut her leg in athletics and bled on her bedsheet during the night. The next day, she asked the nun for a clean sheet. Mother Slattery announced that young Mary would be excused from athletics, then produced a "sort of cloth girdle and a peculiar flannel object which I first took to be a bandage." The bandage was, of course, a sanitary napkin. Although Mary protested that the blood was from a cut, neither Mother Slattery nor the mother superior (who explained "becoming a woman" later in the day) believed her. In order to keep peace, each month Mary

> reopened the cut on my leg, so as to draw a little blood to stain the napkins, which were issued me regularly, not only on this occasion, but every twenty-eight days thereafter. Eventually, I abandoned this

bloodletting, for fear of lockjaw, and trusted to fate. Yet I was in awful dread of detection; my only hope, as I saw it, was either to be released from the convent or to become a woman in reality, which might take a year, at least.

Hence, even false menarche can be an occasion for anxiety.

A few diaries record girls' pride in becoming women. Anne Frank writes that "I have the feeling that in spite of all the pain, unpleasantness, and nastiness, I have a sweet secret." Thyde Monnier in *Moi* (1949) describes the pleasures of menarcheal competition: "Several of us had become 'big girls' during vacation; others reached that estate while at school, and then one after another we went 'to see the blood' in the courtyard water closets where they sat enthroned like queens receiving their subjects."

Menarcheal competition, like fear, pride, and ambivalence, is mentioned in fiction as well as nonfiction. So is generational tension and conflict between mother and daughter. In an early twentieth-century treatment of the menarche, Radclyffe Hall's controversial *The Well of Loneliness*, the heroine, Stephen Gordon, is very shy about discussing menstruation with other girls. Her attitude is a sign of her uneasiness with the female role, for she gradually learns she is a lesbian. Like many girls, Stephen wonders about her mother's female functions. "Had her mother shrunk back resentful, protesting when the seal of womanhood had been stamped upon her?" Stephen decides, with suggestions of both regret and envy, that her mother did not. For Stephen, however, the "seal of womanhood" may be a curse.

Within fifteen years after *The Well of Loneliness*, two other well-known novels handled the menarche in greater detail. One, by a man, treated the protagonist's resulting attitudes toward men, toward her body, and toward her memories. The second, by a woman, portrayed the heroine's subsequent attitudes toward other women.

The first girl, Christopher Morley's Kitty Foyle (1939), has her menarche on a train. She feels upset, but

> of course it proved to be the Curse, for the first time. I thought I was dying of tuberculosis, which in a vague way I knew caused hemorrhages. It must be a serious case because the hemorrhage had gone the wrong way.

She tells the porter, "I guess I'm sick," and "with the intuition of a great gentleman he must have guessed, for soon after a large black hand came through the curtains and handed me a package." She decides, as she later tells her lover, Wyn, that Pullman porters are the finest gentlemen she knows.

There is a curious outsiderness to the tone, as if events occur only to be told, later, to Wyn. Even Kitty's abortion, later in the novel, is treated in the same way as her menarche, an outside event that happens to her but does not greatly touch her except in very small glimpses, as in her response to later porters making beds on the train with the green curtains: "just the look of them always gives me the preliminary cramps."

Francie's first period, in Betty Smith's *A Tree Grows in Brooklyn* (1943), is described with a greater degree of inwardness and in a cultural context involving women. Kitty Foyle, contemporaries might say, is male-identified; Francie is not. Francie has looked forward to being a woman; when she turns thirteen, she writes in her diary, "Today I am a woman." Then seeing her chest "as flat as a washboard," she rips the page out of her book. Francie is becoming a writer as well as an introspective woman, but she is as yet unformed in either role.

On the day of her menarche, Francie sees a group of women throwing stones at Joanna, a neighbor girl who gave birth to a child out of wedlock after her boyfriend's family (especially his mother and sisters) persuaded him not to marry her. Very upset at the stone throwing by those who are not without sin, Francie goes to the cellar of her house and feels "waves of hurt." She aches all over. When she tells her mother, Katie, the mother sighs and says, "So soon?" Katie tells her, "It's a natural thing that comes to all women. Remember always be a good girl because you can have a baby now. . . . You mustn't let the boys kiss you. . . . Remember Joanna." Francie thinks Katie has read her mind about Joanna and is amazed at her mother's insight.

Francie remembers Joanna and remembers how the other women treated her. Francie respects her mother and her aunts, who are the strong and sincere persons in her world, but resolves not to trust any woman because of women's disloyalty and cruelty to each other. The pain of giving birth "should make a bond that held them all together," thinks Francie, "It should make them love and protect each other against the man-world. But it was not so." Francie's menarche, then, is a point of departure for her reflections on what it means to be a woman. She has a vision of a female culture that is sisterly, not competitive or cruel, with the virtues of love and compassion traditionally associated with women.

For other female protagonists, too, the menarche is associated with reflections on what is and what ought to be. In Rumer Godden's *Greengage Summer* (1958), the protagonist is thirteen-year-old Cecil, one of five English children unexpectedly spending the summer in a French hotel because of their mother's illness. Eliot, a man friendly to her and the other children, nevertheless turns out to be a jewel thief and murderer, and Cecil becomes confused about appearance and reality. Cecil's confusion about the world of adults is mirrored in her confusion about herself, when the "full tide" of her period appears. Eliot is the one who comforts her, telling her "now you are ready for love." Cecil is ecstatic at this unexpected male approval and thinks of Juliet, Cleopatra, Eve—and of her own plainness. But she later shows herself to be "manly," that is, brave and intrepid. The title of the book, like Zola's imagery in *La Joie de Vivre,* may refer not only to Cecil's physical ripeness but also to her sinking her teeth into unknown and previously forbidden knowledge.

When their first menstruation comes, most girls cry (if they can) for their mothers. One of the few treatments of the menarche from the mother's point of view is Jay Kennedy's *Prince Bart.* Valerie is the daughter of Bart, an actor, and his wife, Mollie, who are on the verge of divorce. Mollie tells Valerie, "This is an important event for you." Valerie nods and answers, "It's an awfully stickly feeling." Mollie shares her daughter's pride in being the first among her friends and tries to get Valerie not to refer to her condition as "the curse." Mollie wants Valerie to be proud, and yet Mollie feels her own life is in ruins. What can she say to make Valerie happy about being a woman? The sequence is a remarkable treatment of a mother's conflicting feelings about her daughter. Finally, Mollie pours wine for herself and Valerie, and they toast the girl's becoming a woman and then toast themselves.

In novels of the 1960s and early 1970s, the first menstruation frequently reveals cultural as well as generational tensions. Mother-daughter relationships are often the focus. In Ella Leffland's *Mrs. Munck* (1970), the menarche provides proof positive for the lack of closeness between mother and daughter:

> When the change did occur—and by that time I had grown used to the idea, had bowed, almost gracefully to the inevitable—I was careful to keep it a secret from my mother. But that was not difficult, for by that time she had given up all hope of the smallest intimacy.

Similarly, in Joyce Carol Oates's *them* (1969), Maureen and her mother are unable to communicate about the "cramps." Maureen's menarche occurred at school with "a hot flow of blood, a terrible sickening surprise." Maureen's terror at her menarche is part of her general fastidiousness, her aversion to dirt and blood and sex.

In *Shadi* (1971), a juvenile novel by Margaret Embry, Emma's menarche becomes a symbol for the gap between the older and younger generations and cultures. Emma, a Navaho girl, is reluctant to participate in the *kinaaldá*, the traditional welcoming ceremony for girls who have their first period. Emma's grandmother, however, refuses to let her go to the Apache girls' dance, in which all the "girls who come to womanhood" are celebrated together. The grandmother insists on the separate, traditional *kinaaldá*. The grandmother tells Emma the legends about Changing Woman, who was found by First Man and later fell in love with the sun. Emma listens, so she'll remember how to tell the story to her granddaughters, "though she wasn't sure they would think it very important."

Emma's celebration, which takes four days, concludes with a conflict between her family and local missionaries. *Shadi* records the folkways of another American culture in conflict with more modern standards. Emma's friend Ruby and other girls mock her for having the "old-fashioned" and "square" ceremony, and Emma feels torn between the old and the new. Her menarche is a rite of passage revealing a cultural split.

Cultural conflict over the menarche also appears in Toni Morrison's *The Bluest Eye* (1970). Pecola's initiation into womanhood has meaningful consequences in fixing her hatred for whites. Her sisters, Frieda and Claudia, attend Pecola, bringing her water and a napkin. Rosemary, a white girl, spies on the black children and tells Mama that the girls are "playing nasty." Mama begins to beat Pecola until she realizes the child is "minstratin'." Later that evening, Claudia and Frieda view Pecola with new respect. "Lying next to a real person who was really minstratin' was somehow sacred. She was different from us now—grown-up-like."

Some very recent fiction about the menarche treats it with comic deference, if not joy; possibly the influence of modern feminism has muted or eliminated ambivalence. The young narrator in Penelope Street's short story "The Magic Apple" sees a whole world of new possibilities surrounding her menarche. "My first day in Ann Arbor my first menstrual period began with a flourish. Some people call it a curse, but I called it a blessing. I was still a virgin, but I swore that wouldn't last for long. My breasts were starting to grow!"

Menarchal competition in recent fiction becomes fierce, fast, and funny. Getting an early period is a mark of unambivalent distinction. Myrna in Peter Marks's *Hangups* tells her friend Sidney: "That was a very big summer. They gave me my first camera, and I got my first period. They all thought I was a genius for getting it so early. . . . You may think it's funny, but it's a very important moment in a woman's life."

The heroine in Julia Whedon's *Girl of the Golden West* is quite competitive: "It was at this time that I learned that Gay had just had her first period. I was devastated. Where was mine? What if I had to wait until I was fifteen or something? The Onset of the Menses. It had a noble ring."

In Sandra Hochman's *Walking Papers,* Eleanore Fishback is the first in the crowd to "fall off the roof." The others are jealous, and Eleanore, like Hella in *A Young Girl's Diary,* lords it over them.

> Eleanore came down the steps of Girls' Quarters swinging a sanitary napkin around her head as if it were a lasso and all the time yelling, "I've got it! I've got it" and we all huddled around her locker and made her tell us, in detail, what it was like. Yes, we were all grand inquisitors of the menstrual mystery.

Also new among recent women writers is an interest in the technology of handling menstruation. In *The Bluest Eye,* Pecola is taught how to use a sanitary napkin. In Lois Gould's *Such Good Friends,* there is a comic-horror episode in which the protagonist learns to insert a tampon, aided by two friends in the school lavatory. The instruction folder is horrifying: "The diagrams—terrifying cross-sections of the female interior, full of squiggly Suez canals—showed a cute little cotton wad nestled in there like an eensy white mouse with its tail hanging down and out."

Already scared, Julie can't find the spot. Then she's afraid it won't work because she's a virgin; the instructions say "unmarried girls" and nothing about "hymen." The girls are very anxious that no one should come in during Julie's lesson, although what they are doing is a bathroom function. When Julie is afraid she'll fail, her friend Peggy says, "Just don't tell me how you hate sanitary belts and how icky it all is." Whatever mystique there is surrounds the act of using a tampon, not the menstruation. After all the graphic groping, Julie finally succeeds and writes in her memory book: "Today I became a woman."

Sasha Davis's initiation into womanhood in Alix Kates Shulman's *Memoirs of an Ex-Prom Queen* is also a comic adventure suitable to an explicit and technological age. When her first period comes, Sasha emits the primal scream for her mother. "I knew for sure I was a freak," she confides to the reader. She's afraid her solitary hobby will be discovered: "I was sure my curious finger had injured something." She gets blood on the bath mat, in the bath water, on her fingers, on her towel—"everything I touched was getting soiled."

Her mother proceeds to give her a lesson in the use of sanitary napkins, like "a stewardess demonstrating the oxygen mask." Sasha is sure no one else has this awful bleeding, and everyone will know she bleeds "down there." After her menarche, Sasha reports, "I tried to pass as normal, but inside I knew I was a freak."

Shulman and Gould, although humorous in their treatments of menstrual nitty-gritty, seem to regard periods as laughable out of a slight desperation: Periodic bleeding is an inevitable occupational hazard of being a young woman. There is one book, however, that presents an entirely positive view of the menarche and may point a new direction. The book is a juvenile novel we mentioned earlier, Judy Blume's *Are You There God? It's Me, Margaret.*

Margaret Simon is a girl waiting, with her three close friends who form the "Pre-Teen Sensations Club," for their periods to come. They enjoy visiting the sanitary napkin displays in the drugstore but run when the male clerk looks at them. There is a friendly but not frantic menarcheal competition, and Margaret tries to get an edge on her opponents by praying to God. She offers a deal: She'll be good around the house if He'll give her some breasts.

A week later, "Gretchen got it." The others, shrieking, want to know all about it: What did her mother say? How could she stand to keep a washcloth in her pants while her mother was going to the drugstore to get pads? How did it feel? Did it make her feel older? Gretchen is very calm.

When her friend Nancy is next, Margaret sees Nancy, who has lied and said she's had a period before, become scared and hysterical. Gretchen and Nancy appear as positive and negative role models. As other women usually do in fiction, they serve to define the possibilities and limits of action for the central female character. Margaret can be calm or frantic.

Finally, when Margaret is packing for camp, "it" comes. She sees blood on her underwear, "not a lot—but enough." She starts to laugh and cry at the same time, and so does her mother, who brings her some "Teenage Softies." Her mother offers to show her how to use the napkin, but Margaret stops her. "Mom, I've been practicing in my room for two months!" Both of them laugh. Reverently, Margaret locks the bathroom door, attaches a Teenage Softie to the little hooks on her pink belt, gets dressed, and looks in the mirror. Then she thanks God that it came.

Although *Are You There God?* is an odd book (girl-gets-napkin), it is an exceptionally warm one in the attitudes expressed toward women. The mothers are understanding and good-humored. Margaret's grandmother, who carries a shopping bag filled with corned beef and pickles from New York because she's sure such delicacies cannot be had in New Jersey, is a lovable eccentric. Margaret has the kind of friends and family Francie, in *A Tree Grows in Brooklyn,* would have liked.

Furthermore, *Are You There God?* presents some clues to why the menarche is usually absent from literature. Not only are women writers underrepresented in literature, but males have had, since Adam named Eve, the power of defining reality, that is, of saying what is important and what is not. Confrontation with a white whale, though unlikely, is at least a possible experience for males and therefore of possible significance. Having a first period is neither possible for men nor does it affect them. Hence, it can be dismissed—and usually is.

Are You There God? insists on the centrality of the female experience. The protagonist and the significant characters are all female, and they define what is and what is not important in their universe. Female culture consists of those experiences that are not accessible to men and that until recently have been undervalued by both women and men.

A survey of menarcheal literature reveals the shifting emphasis and the interplay between art and life. When female experience is more valued in life, it takes on more positive roles in art. The menarche, once an event surrounded with fear, terror, and ignorance, can today be seen as a treasured moment, the moment of becoming a woman.

Afterword

Once absent as a theme in literature, the first menstruation became in the 1970s an important feminist issue, but today's women novelists seem to be treating this theme less frequently in their depiction of young women characters. For one male writer, on the other hand, the menarche has swollen to mythic proportions. We did not know of Stephen King's novel *Carrie,* published in 1974, until it splashed onto the crimson screen two years later.

King opens *Carrie,* the novel, with a violent portrayal of the menarche. Carrie is showering in the gym when she discovers her first blood. In derision her classmates deluge her with tampons. King admits to having had no practical knowledge of the menstrual process when he fabricated this scene: "I suddenly realized that I (1) had never been a girl, (2) had never had a menstrual cramp or a menstrual period, (3) had absolutely no idea how I'd react to one."[2] But mere lack of experience doesn't stop King from turning the menarche into a bizarre event, a cosmic unleashing of the Primal Flow. The cruel classmates later bathe Carrie in pig's blood.

The blood is everywhere, an emblem of the inescapability of menstruation and, for King, of its inherent power.

In the novel (but not in the film) menstruation serves a dual role, through Carrie's menarche and through her friend Susan Snell's worries about a late period. At the end of the novel Sue finds Carrie dying in a parking lot. The last words of *Carrie* belong to Sue, "as she felt the slow course of dark menstrual blood down her thighs."[3] Though King naively exaggerates the physiological process—a trickle is more normal—he is quite clearly connecting Carrie with Sue through the reinitiation of that process which in this novel represents the core of female sexuality.

In *Time of Desecration* (1980), another male novelist, Alberto Moravia, links the menstrual process of his teenaged heroine with the ritual defloration of ancient societies. Early in the novel Desideria goes to a whorehouse to sell herself. The excitement brings on her period. In her fury the madam says: "And what will he find instead of a virgin? A pack of sanitary towels." At the end of the novel, in an ironically parallel scene, Desideria loses her virginity. Her lover, presuming the hymeneal blood to be menstrual, turns away in disgust and calls her an "absolute turd."[4] This rejection of the heroine in her phase of menarcheal adjustment underlines the themes of blood, death, and revolution which for Moravia are emblems of an unstable modern Italy.

Women writers tend to be less cataclysmic in their treatment of the menarche. Generally, they continue to write about the first menstruation in ways similar to the ones analyzed earlier in this chapter—as a source of shame, knowledge, failure, surprise, conflict, and achievement.

We thank Susan Koppelman for recently bringing to our attention a growing-up novel written in 1971 by Merrill Joan Gerber, *Now Molly Knows*. The menstrually naive Molly, unable to insert a tampon, receives advice from a more "experienced" woman, who tells Molly that it's easier if you're not a virgin: "Your sense of geography is better then." Molly fails the tampon test but achieves, like Judy Blume's Margaret, a heightened menarcheal consciousness, a joyful awareness of becoming a woman: "What she is really thinking is that this function of her womanhood deserves complication, inconvenience, attention. Even cramps. Molly doesn't want to dismiss it, ever. She wants to savor it. She didn't wait for all those years to wish it invisible now."[5]

In a 1982 short story, "The Facts of Life," Maxine Kumin treats the psychological complications of the menarche, connecting the first menstruation of the narrator's daughter with the last breath of the narrator's mother. The narrator ponders these contradictions: "On the face of it, the etiquette of sex information and the etiquette of dying have little in common. In truth the same prurience, the same resentments obtain in both." Although the story ends in menarcheal celebration, the "facts of life" are complicated emotionally by the cold fact of death. The grandmother dies. "Two weeks later my daughter's first blood comes. She is terribly happy, terribly sad; terribly hungry, overstuffed. Women together, we try to keep the celebration down to a dull roar."[6]

In Rosa Guy's *A Measure of Time* one finds another somber treatment of the menarche by a woman writer. As Kumin associates the first blood with death, so Guy associates it with racial oppression. The young heroine, Dorine, is being driven home by her seducer-employer, Master Norton. "I remembered his hand on my leg, him playing with me while he drove, and I thought of the day when his hand came way with my first blood."[7] The "first blood" is undetermined, suggesting (as in Moravia's *Time of Desecration*), both menstrual and hymeneal violation. Dorine recalls the episode abstractly; it is the master's hand rather than Dorine's body which experiences the menarche. Dorine's dehumanization has occurred long before puberty.

The first menstruation also has negative cultural associations in Maxine Hong Kingston's *The Woman Warrior*. As the heroine reaches menarche, her mother tells her the story of "No Name Woman," an aunt from China who became pregnant and drowned herself and her infant, "plugging up the family well." The scandal caused rioting among the villagers. The mother uses this legend to warn her daughter about the dangers of pregnancy: "Now that you have started menstruating, what happened to her could happen to you."[8]

These episiodes from *A Measure of Time*, "The Facts of Life," *The Woman Warrior*, and *Now Molly Knows* are only a few examples of the menarche in contemporary women's fiction. But we have not discovered among recent women writers a novel which makes the menarche and early menstrual adjustment absolutely central to the development of the heroine. And Stephen King's portrait of a Menarcheally Mad Prom Queen is not exactly the fictional model we would wish to emulate.

There are, however, some promising collections of shorter fiction and poetry organized around the theme of the menarche. One, in progress, is being edited by Dena Taylor, a California woman who became fascinated several years ago by the celebratory rituals of Native Americans. Taylor began to talk to women about menstruation, especially about the menarche, requesting poems and artwork. "At first," she wrote us, "I was asking for materials on the pain, the power, and the celebration of women's bleeding. My feeling was that this subject is so hidden, so shame-ridden, that I wanted to put together a book of women's actual expressions of what they feel, so that other women could read it and hopefully become de-mystified about this important aspect of our lives." Presently she is trying to emphasize the more positive aspects of menstruation, under the working title "Red Flower: A Celebration of Menstruation."[9]

There are similar projects going on in women's studies groups, in small presses, in writing collectives, among individuals. One collection, published in 1983 by Avon Books, is a splendid gathering of menarcheal pieces; it contains chants, poetry, rituals, autobiographical accounts. Also inspired, like Taylor's, by Native American rituals, the anthology *I'm on My Way Running: Women Speak of Coming of Age* is an impressive record of adolescent awareness from a multiracial perspective. One of our favorite pieces is a poem by Penelope Scambly Schott, told from the mother's point of view. It gives the menarcheal experience the cosmic/geographical importance it deserves. In addition, it explores, like Maxine Kumin's story "The Facts of Life," the psycho-sexual closeness between mother and daughter at the heart of menstrual repetition.

> "When you phoned home from California
> to tell me it had started"

> A brilliant globule of blood
> rolled out over the surface of the desert
> up and down the Continental Divide
> through the singing prairies
> parting the Mississippi
> leaping the Delaware Water Gap
> until it spilled into this tall red kitchen
> in Rocky Hill, New Jersey
> where it skittered across the linoleum
> and cracked into hundreds of little faceted jewels.

> I will not diminish this day with labeling
> I will not say foolishly
> "now you are a woman"
> I will never tell you
> "don't talk to strangers"

> because we are each of us strangers
> one to another
> mysterious in our bodies,
> the connections between us
> ascending like separate stone wells

from the same dark waters
under the earth

But tonight you delight me like a lover
so that my thigh muscles twitch
and the nipples of my breasts
rise and remember
your small mouth
until I am laughing to the marrow of my bones
and I want to shout
Bless you, my daughter, bless you, bless you;
I have created the world in thirteen years
and it is good.[10]

Chapter 18

The Miracle of Blood: Menstrual Imagery in Myth and Poetry

Direct references to menstrual blood are uncommon in myth and poetry. Usually, the unmentionable is not mentioned. Or else, the menstrual flow, when it does appear, invariably appears in disguise, as an image or symbol, ranging from the full moon to the garbage dump. Literary critics have been either unconscious of or uninterested in the possible menstrual significance of certain myths and poems. Claude Dagmar Daly and Clark Griffith are two exceptions.

In 1935, Daly published a psychoanalytic essay entitled "The Menstruation Complex in Literature." He argued that the menstruation complex, the revulsion toward and denial of the menstruating woman, was at the root of the Oedipus complex. The menstruating woman is a continual reminder of the male's fear of castration and death, a figure so threatening that she is buried deep in the unconscious mind. She emerges nonetheless in myth and dreams.

Daly's theory of the menstruation complex has received scant attention both from psychoanalysts and from literary critics, presumably, he would have argued, because the idea is too unpleasant to face. Yet, menstrual imagery is "everywhere," claimed Daly, who concentrated his own analysis on the poetry of Charles Baudelaire and the poetry and stories of Edgar Allan Poe. Daly thought that Poe's story "The Masque of the Red Death" fully captured the menstruation trauma. The red, disease-bearing visitor comes like a "pall of death, shutting out the pre-historic past."[1]

In 1964, another male critic, Clark Griffith, found menstrual themes in the poetry of Emily Dickinson. Griffith buried this insight in the epilogue of his study of Dickinson, *The Long Shadow*. Although Griffith viewed menstrual cramps as Dickinson's major problem, he kept his secret until the end of the book, and he kept "menstruation" out of the index.

Griffith contended that the "rhythm of suffering" so prevalent in Dickinson's poetry was the menstrual rhythm. Because she wanted to be a man, because she desired a penis, Dickinson saw menstruation as "an affront and a burden." Her main poetic voice, said Griffith, is "the helpless, abused, harassed, tormented female," who expresses her menstrual problems through a trio of images: the clock (a symbol of the repetition of pain), the father (the envied male who doesn't menstruate), and childhood (the only state in which pain could be escaped). The menstrual theme, of which Dickinson was utterly unconscious, was greatest in her thirties and forties, "when her spinsterish prejudices and their consequences were probably most demanding." By universalizing her pain, by moving from the personal to the tragic, Dickinson turned her "sickness" into great art, "while another woman, confronted with the same grave issues, might have become hysteric, a feminist, a lesbian, a religious tractarian, or an aggressive shrew."[2]

Clark Griffith is not alone in explaining Dickinson's achievement as a poet in terms of her penis envy, her Oedipus complex, her failure at femininity. His mention of the unmentionable, however, sets him apart. Unfortunately, Griffith's understanding of the psychology of menstruation is based on the works of Helene Deutsch and Mary Chadwick rather than on the more reasonable conclusions of Karen Horney and Clara Thompson. His evaluation of Dickinson displays a negative attitude toward menstruation and female sexuality. Daly's examples of menstrual imagery (redness, fluid, and the moon) seem more to the point than Griffith's psychology.

A number of poetic symbols may at times signify menstruation: sickness, mud, volcanoes, the arrival of a visitor, bathing, dumping garbage, falling from a high place, odors, leakages, stains, clocks, swamps, rags, tamps, tidal rhythms, and the colors red, pink, and purple. But the most universal images are flowers, fluid, witches and the moon. Like other images, the ones suggesting menstruation do so only at times and only within a particular context. Red can sometimes represent the menstrual flow, but it is also open to a variety of other interpretations, such as anger, jealousy, war, adultery, and suffering. Or it may have no symbolic meaning at all. Dickinson uses the word *red* in thirty poems, usually to describe the setting sun. In only four of her poems does red seem to signify menstruation. Nonetheless, an openness toward menstruation as a symbolic possibility in poetry can lead to a fresh reading of some familiar works.

Of all menstrual symbols, the one most clearly connected to the monthly flux is blood. At times, however, the mythmaker or dreamer or poet disguises the blood, converting it into a sacred river, a tide, a flood, or some other liquid. This process of conversion is vividly conveyed in a speech by the nineteenth-century feminist Victoria Woodhull, who saw the menstruation as a river of waste. In Woodhull's vision of the New Jerusalem, menstruation would cease, and the "perverted" flow would become "a pure river of the water of life proceeding out of the throne of the God."[3]

Some of the early Flood myths may have been in part a response to the dread of the menstruating woman. Although there is no evidence of this meaning in the Flood myths of the Hebrews or the Greeks, it seems fairly obvious in the Babylonian myth of the creation of the earth.

In that myth, Tiamat, the Mother of All and the symbol of chaos, creates monsters whose blood is poison and unleashes them on the world. She is defeated by her son, Marduk, who "cut channels for the blood to flow out of her, and he bade the winds bear her blood away into the secret places." He then splits her body in two, sending half of it into the sky and bolting it in place to prevent floods and from the other half making the earth. Marduk is the ordering principle, who must destroy chaos before he can govern. The emphasis in this myth on chaos, flooding, and blood suggests that before he himself can come into power, the male must subdue and divide the body of woman, whose danger lies in her unpredictable fluid.

Emily Dickinson occasionally uses fluid images in a way that suggests menstruation:

> The name—of it—is "Autumn"—
> The hue—of it—is Blood—
> An artery—upon the Hill—
> A Vein—along the Road—
>
> Great Globules—in the Alleys—
> And Oh, the Shower of Stain—
> When Winds—upset the Basin—
> And spill the Scarlet Rain—
> It sprinkles Bonnets—far below—
> It gathers ruddy Pools—
> Then—eddies like a Rose—away—
> Upon Vermillion Wheels—

Red is the dominant hue of this poem about autumn, the time of death and of witches.

In Edna St. Vincent Millay's poem about menstruation, called "Menses," the fluid comparisons are to "ugly" snake venom and "innocent" oil; menstrual blood is "poison." The venom motif is carried throughout the poem with references to "coiling," "fangs drawn," and "strike again." The final two lines recall the Satan-snake plunging into the abyss, or menstrual hell. Millay's "Menses" is one of the few poems in English directly about menstruation. As the subtitle indicates, the images derive from a male point of view: "(*He speaks, but to himself, being aware how it is with her*)." The snake and poison images reveal unequivocally the male fear of the menstrual process.

Another poem specifically about menstruation is Nadine Mac Donald's "On Menstruating in the Middle of a Lecture on the Fall of the Roman Empire," which we quote in its entirety:

> Three weeks late, three weeks of wearing
> clean Kotex as a guard, three weeks
> of looking behind me as a [sic] I walked, three
> weeks of renouncing sex; of not wearing
> white pants. And yet it started, recapitulated
> somewhere between Caesar and the coliseums,
> a spot minute, like a leak in a dike.
> It spread like a chest wound under a toga.
> During the rhetoric there were stirrings
> in me, like history. It betrays me
> like Brutus; my monthly let; late,
> released upon my yellow taffeta:
> My mark remains, slowly conquering
> the white velvet of the wing chair,
> leaving the cradle of civilization in its wake.

The menstrual imagery here is unconventional. Rather than a tide or a flood, the menstrual fluid is a "leak in a dike." The dominant image is of battle; the menses spreads "like a chest wound," conquers the wing chair. The word *let* means an obstacle, something that must be overcome; yet, the word also contains the idea of release of flow, as in "to let blood." In the context of Roman (and male) history, menstruation is the betrayer of Caesar.

Mac Donald has captured in this poem the ironic contradictions between traditional male and female roles. Woman wears taffeta, stains her white pants, looks behind herself as she walks; man fights battles, builds empires, records history, looks ahead. In "On Menstruating in the Middle of a Lecture on the Fall of the Roman Empire," Mac Donald assimilates both roles with great discomfort but emerges victorious, leaving her menstrual mark on Western culture.

Another rich and important symbol for the menstruating woman is the flower. Flowers symbolize fertility and delicacy. They are pretty and decorative rather than useful. They give off odors. They easily wilt and decay. In the Bible, the word *flowers* means menstrual blood: "if any man lie with her at all, and her flowers be upon him, he shall be unclean seven days" (Leviticus 15:24).

Flowers have similar meaning in the Greek myth of Persephone. This myth, first mentioned in Hesiod's *Theogony,* has been treated by Ovid, Spenser, Milton, and Shelley, among others. The versions vary, but in each, Persephone is seduced while gathering flowers.

In Ovid's version, Persephone (Proserpina) and the daughters of Ocean pick violets and white lilies. "And while with girlish eagerness she was filling her basket and her bosom and striving to surpass her mates in gathering, almost in one act did Hades (Pluto) see and love and carry her away; so precipitate was his love." In the abduction, Persephone's garment is torn. Her flowers fall from her tunic, "and such was the innocence of her girlish years, the loss of her flowers even at such a time aroused new grief." Hades chariots her through deep lakes and pools until he reaches a bay inhabited by the water nymph Cyane, who tries to stop him. But Hades opens Cyane's pool and plunges with his bride into the underworld. In her grief, Cyane melts, limb by limb, into the water. "And finally, in place of living blood, clear water flows through her weakened veins and nothing is left that you can touch." Cyane's changing from blood to water, from the threatening to the subdued, is similar to Tiamat's blood flowing underground into secret places and to Victoria Woodhull's dream of a New Jerusalem.

Bullfinch, who records the legend in his *Age of Fable,* comments that Persephone "signifies the seed-corn which when cast into the ground lies there concealed." Yet, in Bullfinch's version, flowers, not seeds, fall from Persephone's apron. The fallen flower is on one level an emblem for defloration, the breaking of the hymen. The flower may also be a symbol for Persephone's wasted menstrual blood.

In *Interpretation of Dreams,* Freud records a dream of flowers, which he interpreted as having menstrual significance. The patient dreamed that she was descending from a high place. "As she climbs she is carrying a *big branch* in her hand, really like a tree, which is thickly studded with *red flowers.*"[4] As she descends, the flowers, which look like red camellias, begin to fall. Freud reads both the blossoming branch and the falling flowers as symbols for menstruation. The patient, in analysis, had associated the bough with a lily and herself with the angel of the Annunciation. The dream, Freud argues, represents both sexual purity, symbolized by the lily, and sexual guilt, symbolized by the red camellia. The bough is an allusion to Dumas's *La Dame aux Camélias,* in which Camille wore a white flower except during her period, when she wore a red one. This interpretation seems applicable to the Persephone myth as well. Persephone is both pure and sexual, the virgin and the temptress. In most versions of the myth, the flowers she picks are white and purple, the lily and the violet. (Freud, who often went to Greek mythology to explain human behavior, makes no reference to the Persephone myth in this context.)

What finally attracts Hades to Persephone is her flowers. In the Homeric hymn, flowers are Persephone's temptation as well; she is raped after being drawn away from the group in pursuit of a "most marvelous flower, with a hundred blooms and a delicious fragrance." The fragrance is compelling. In his essay on "The Taboo of Virginity," Freud speculates that in the prehistoric past, menstrual blood was a sexual stimulus. Men were once, like animals, sexually drawn to the smell of menstruation. But when man assumed an upright gait, he repressed this attraction. In Ovid, it is clear that Hades "falls in love" at the same moment that he sees the flowers, as if Hades were sexually stimulated by the scent.

The flower is the key symbol in the poetry of Baudelaire. Daly, in his study of Baudelaire and Poe, quotes from several poems that show a repugnance for flowers and for women. In "The Martyr," for example, a bleeding, decapitated corpse lies, like a flower, in a warm, perfumed room. In his analysis, Daly views the perfume as the mother's menstrual odor, the corpse as the bleeding (menstruating and castrated) vagina.

Applying Daly's insights to *Les Fleurs du Mal,* we have noticed a snake or an odor or a ruined flower or a secretion on almost every page. In "The Blessing," for instance, *"boutons empestés"* (blighted buds) fall from a branch. In "Beacons," Baudelaire refers to Delacroix's *"lac du sang hantée des mauvais anges"* ("lake of blood haunted by evil angels"). The title of his best-known collection, *Les Fleurs du Mal,* is translated as *Flowers of Evil.* But the word *mal* also means "sickness," and the flowers appear to represent, on a secondary level, flowers of sickness, of menstruation.

Some women poets have likened the ripening of flowers to the ripening of their bodies. In a poem called "Moonrise," Sylvia Plath contrasts white, symbol here of purity and death, with red, symbol of life and ripeness.

At the poem's conclusion, Plath equates the berry's redness with her own fluids, its fertility with hers: "The berries purple / And bleed. The white stomach may ripen yet." In a poem called "Gardener," Erica Jong describes the inside of her womb in colors of poppies and bougainvillea.

Anne Sexton also uses the bleeding flower image, for example, in "The Wedding Night," where a twelve-year-old flower girl is compared with more "sure-bodied" buds: "Not one of them had trickled blood." The reference is to the potential budding-bleeding of the flower girl and to the breaking of the bride's hymen. In another poem about her own childhood, Sexton recalls how, at the age of six, she "lived in a graveyard full of dolls," unaware of her flesh, of the "exotic flower" that would soon bloom inside her. Sexton's most specific reference to menstrual flowers is in her poem "Menstruation at Forty." As her birthday approaches, she longs for a son, but it is too late; it is the "November of the body," and the year and the harvest are finished. Sexton is approaching menopause; menstrual blood comes as a sign of the womb's failure to bear a male before the end of her fertile season. The two days of menstrual bleeding are deathdays, symbolized by flowers bleeding from her wrist. The flowers are also funeral wreaths, emblems of the death of her womb. The bleeding corsage, fallen rose petals, blighted buds, spotted geraniums—these menstrual images dominate in poetry concerned with woman's fertility and with her seasons of harvest and death. Rarely does one find a poet comparing menstruation with the cycle of the mighty oak or the spreading chestnut. The flower, both perishable and reproductive, has traditionally worn woman's color and shared her perfume.

In a poem written by May Sarton in 1937, woman is strong, her seed the seed of the tree of life.

> There were seeds
> within her
> that burst at intervals
> and for a little while
> she would come back
> to heaviness,
> and then before a surging miracle
> of blood,
> relax,
> and re-identify herself,
> each time more closely
> with the heart of life.
> 'I am the beginning,

the never-ending,
the perfect tree.'
And she would lean
again as once
on the great curve of the earth,
part of its turning,
as distinctly part
of the universe as a star—
as unresistant,
as completely rhythmical.

If the tree in Sarton's "She Shall Be Called Woman" represents the strength and resilience of the menstruating woman, her "surging miracle of blood," so the witch traditionally represents her wickedness, her demonic excretions. The fearful ugliness of the traditional witch is an appropriate symbol of the woman whose life-giving blood has dried. The season of the witch is autumn, what Plath calls "the month of red leaves"; Dickinson, "the hue of blood"; Sexton, the "November of the body." In autumn, Demeter punishes the world for the rape of Persephone. Flowers decay and fall. Witches ride the sky to the dark light of the old moon.

The witch is a major symbol in Sexton's poetry. In "The Double Image," a poem that begins in November, she recalls her suicide attempt following the birth of her daughter. The "green witches" in her head remind us of hags traditionally associated with destroying mothers' milk, causing madness, carrying away children. Here they are related to bodily flow, to leaking doom. The witch-fluid image combines the ideas of blood, milk, and the suicidal poison: "The white men pumped the poison out."

Plath also associates witches with autumn and sickness. The time for witch burning is October, "month of red leaves," of burning dry sticks in the marketplace; the "hag" in Plath's poem "Maudlin" is also a menstruating witch, eternally linked with the moon's "curse."

Muriel Rukeyser writes about witches in "Mrs. Walpurga." (The name comes from Saint Walpurga, an eighth-century British nun who became, in the Middle Ages, a protector against magic and incantations.) In her Walpurgis Night dream, the persona sees and psychologically embraces the spirits that had seemed dead in her: the lost years, the children, the couples copulating in the dark. At the climax of the poem, in a passage rich with images of fluid, flowers, and the moon, Mrs. Walpurga is reborn into the life-giving night.

The complex "Mrs. Walpurga" presents the persona of a withered witch against an affirmation of woman's moon-linked periodicity. In myth and poetry, much depends upon the association of menstruation with the moon.

The word *menstruation* means "moon change." German peasants have long referred to menstruation as "the moon"; in France, it is called *le moment de la lune.* In non-Western cultures, we find similar associations. In Saibai and Yam, two islands off the northern tip of Australia, people believed that menstruation was caused by the moon, who came in the form of a man to seduce the pubescent girl. Their word for moon, *ganumi,* is often used as a substitute for *nanumud,* or menstrual blood.[5]

Menstrual seclusion rituals are frequently determined by the phases of the moon. Women in one African clan are isolated for two moons: "For one moon and another moon you have hidden yourself away from profane eyes, you have whitened your bodies so that death will not carry them off to his village," the people chant as the girls return from their menstrual huts.[6] The Juluo, from the district of Kavirondo in East Africa, believed that menstruation came with the new moon and that only then could women become pregnant.[7] Darwin, observing that both moon and menstrual cycles were of twenty-eight days' duration, actually theorized that menstruation was directly related to the action of the moon on the tides and began when we were all sea creatures.

In some cultures, the moon is a bridegroom responsible for causing the first menstruation. The bridegroom-moon of a New Guinea legend pursued women without success until one took pity on him. After she became pregnant, the jealous husband threw the moon man into the fire. His blood flew to the sky and became the moon. As punishment, from that time on, all women were condemned to bleed at his apparition except for the very young, the very old, and the pregnant.[8] Among the Maori of New Zealand, menstruation is called *mata marama* ("moon sickness").

For poets, the moon is an eternal symbol—of death, of the mother, of the imagination, of virginity, of immortality. The moon is also, for many, a menstrual image. William Butler Yeats constructed a vision, a culture, and a poetic mythos around the cycles of the moon. "Twenty-and-eight the phases of the moon,/ The full and the moon's dark and all the crescents," Yeats writes in *A Vision.* The birth of the hero occurs in phase twelve; the thirteenth phase "sets the soul at war." Phase seventeen, shortly after the full moon, is the phase of "Unity of Being," the phase of Shelley, Dante, and Yeats himself. Yeats turned his lunary visions into poetic symbol.

One source of Yeats's symbolism was his uncle George Pollexfen, who shared his dreams and his residence with a "second-sighted servant" named Mary Battle. Mary had frequent dreams of blood, as did Yeats's uncle. One night, the uncle had an infection, a "blood-poisoning" following vaccination for smallpox. At the peak of his delirium, George saw "dancing red figures." A little later, he told Yeats, "There is a river running through the room." Yeats advised him to get rid of the figures by invoking Gabriel, the "angel of the Moon," who could command the waters. When the red men reappeared, the uncle was able to send them away. This metacommunication between Yeats and George Pollexfen, recorded in *The Autobiography of William Butler Yeats,* is remarkably similar to what Daly, in discussing the poetry of Poe and Baudelaire, calls the "menstruation complex" images: redness, rivers running in and out of rooms, the tide-controlling moon.

In his poetry, Yeats uses many of these images, most fully in the 1933 volume *The Winding Stair and Other Poems,* which includes one of his greatest poems, "Byzantium," with its haunting refrain "mire or blood." Blood and mire are for Yeats symbols of the flesh and change, contrasted in the poem with the permanent, hard images of "bird and golden handiwork." The moon of "Byzantium" is associated with the cyclical blood and change of human life. In "Blood and Moon," the tower and the moon represent nonchange or art; whereas the blood symbolizes frenzy and impermanence. The word *blood* is used eight times in "Blood and Moon," most memorably in the line "Odour of blood on the ancestral chair!" In the poem "Oil and Blood," there is reference to the odor of violets and to "bodies of the vampires full of blood;/ Their shrouds are bloody and their lips are wet." "Oil and Blood" is followed in *The Winding Stair* by a strange poem, "Veronica's Napkin," which ends with the line "A pattern on a napkin dipped in blood." (Veronica is the woman in the New Testament who wiped Christ's face with her veil.) The various napkin, blood, mire, oil, and stain images running through Yeats's poetry—literally hundreds—are bound together by the overwhelming presence of the moon, whose biological significance Yeats makes apparent in "The Crazed Moon": "Crazed through much child-bearing / The moon is staggering in the sky." Depending on her cycle, the moon is staggering or crazed or pure or arrogant, as are the rough beasts under her influence.

In his last volume of poetry, the poem "The Circus Animals' Desertion" traces the various themes and images of Yeats's poetry to their primal source, "the foul rag-and-bone shop of the heart." It seems possible that Yeats's images were born from the rags and refuse of the bleeding slut-mother, who is cyclically purified as she goes through her phases—from old to new to full moon, from Crazy Jane to the Holy Virgin to Helen, from crone to virgin to whore.

For Plath, as for Yeats, the moon is a major symbol, one that she uses quite often in conjunction with two other menstrual images, the tide and the witch. The menstruating moon appears in the poem "Lesbos." In "Childless Woman," she presents the idea we found in Sexton's "Menstruation at Forty": that menstrual flow means the failure of the empty womb. In "The Munich Mannequins," after describing the purposeless, monthly "unloosing" of moons, she writes, "The blood flood is the flood of love, the absolute sacrifice."

Gary Snyder, in "In Praise of Sick Women," uses most of the menstrual images discussed here: falling rain, blighted fruit, berries, bleeding tides. The poem concludes with a reference to the age-old ritual of menstrual seclusion: "in a bark shack." An untitled prose poem by Edgar Allan Poe is another work by a man that seems rich in menstrual images, not only the red fluid but also flowers and the moon:

> It was night, and the rain fell; and falling it was not rain, but, having fallen, it was blood. And I stood in the morass among the tall lilies, and the rain fell upon my head—and the lilies sighed one unto the other in the solemnity of their desolation.
> And, all at once, the moon rose through the then ghastly mist, and was crimson in color.

In "Planetarium," a poem commemorating the astronomer Caroline Herschel, Adrienne Rich uses the moon-tide image to convey the time-lessness of the female experience.

We can expect new incantations from women as well as from men as they struggle to find new means of poetic expression. As the old mythology encounters the new menstrual consciousness, a new vision of woman should inform the poetry of our age.

Afterword

In this chapter we have given a close menstrual reading to certain mythic figures, among them the Babylonian goddess Tiamat and the Greek flower-gatherer, Persephone. In *The Wise Wound,* published two years after *The Curse,* Penelope Shuttle and Peter Redgrove explore related ideas, finding menstrual significance in a number of sources, among them the Hebrew "Song of Songs," the Greek legend of Medusa, and the quest for the Holy Grail, a chalice "brimming with blood."[9] Amateur paleontologist and mathematician Bart Jordan has recently uncovered a wealth of menstrual symbols in his explorations of Venus or the Great Mother.[10] It is becoming increasingly clear that buried in the myths and dreams of numerous cultures is a menstruating woman with the power to create and to destroy, to bless and to punish, to poison and to replenish the earth. In *The Innocence of Dreams* (1979) psychoanalyst Charles Rycroft lists "Dreams about Menstruation" as one of the categories for interpretation. Rycroft relates the menstrual symbolism in dreams to such concrete experiences as fear of pregnancy, the feeling of being unattractive, feelings of resentment against menstruation itself. Most importantly, he links dreams of menstruation to ideas of creativity: "A woman dreamt that she was removing a tampon in order to allow her menstrual blood to flow; two days later she found herself writing poetry."[11]

Indeed, the flow of words discharged at menstruation is something we ourselves have experienced from time to time and a phenomenon which we earlier observed in Virginia Woolf's diary. A recent example of the menses/writing fusion appears in a poem by Erica Jong called "Inventing My Life." Jong compares writing to bleeding; parchment becomes, in this analogy, "a tampon to the muse's womb."

Other poets have been less loving in their treatment of menstruation. Marge Piercy, for example, separates the positive and the negative attitudes in a poem called "The Watch." Some women, she writes, see menstruation as the "red splash of freedom." Others see it as a sign of infertility, "Another month, another chance missed." For poet Safiya Henderson, Tampax is just one of many burdensome objects, like phone bills and Lestoil, that she would take with her if she were jumping off a bridge. "One less stain, one less line./ one less bundle of dirty clothes" ("Portrait of a Woman Artist").

Also ambivalent in her attitude towards menstruation is Audre Lorde, whose poem "NEED: A Chorale of Black Women's Voices" shows a particularly powerful use of menstrual blood as poetic metaphor. The poem opens with a statement about black women's blood being "shed in silence." While blood is in fact a prevailing image in poetry by black women since the 1960s, few, like Lorde, relate that blood to the universal female process of menstruation. Lorde makes this connection in a vivid passage:

> Dead Black women haunt the black maled streets
> paying the cities'
> secret and familiar tithe of blood

> burn blood beat blood cut blood
> seven-year-old child rape victim blood blood
> of a sodomized grandmother blood blood
> on the hands of my brother blood
> and his blood clotting in the teeth of strangers
> as women we were meant to bleed
> but not this useless blood
> my blood each month a memorial
> to my unspoken sisters falling
> like red drops to the asphalt
> I am not satisfied to bleed
> as a quiet symbol for no one's redemption
> why is it our blood
> that keeps these cities fertile?

Here Lorde distinguishes between "useless blood"—the needless blood shed by blacks in Detroit and Boston and Harlem—and menstrual blood, which ironically becomes useless as well, when its nourishment is lost in death. The affinity between life-blood and death-blood is reinforced by the repetition of *blood, blood, blood,* repetition being a rhythmic technique of much Afro-American poetry and also a major aspect of the menstrual cycle. Lorde's words flow forth, like blood, forging a "memorial" to the continued periodicity of the creative process.

But the most comprehensive, all-encompassing poem on menstruation that we have yet discovered is by Ellen Bass. The poem, simply entitled "Tampons," touches on almost every major theme explored in this book: drugs, regularity, chemically treated tampons, tassaways, menstrual extraction, synchronic menstruation, the menstrual products industry, and, yes, even a bleed-in.

> The first day
> of our heaviest flow we will gather in Palmer,
> Massachusetts
> on the steps of Tampax, Inc. We'll have a bleed-in.
> We'll smear the blood on our faces. Max Factor
> will join OB in bankruptcy. The perfume
> industry will collapse, who needs
> whale sperm, turtle oil, when we have free blood?

The poem ends in a vision, with Bass reversing the old myth that menstrual blood is a poisonous substance which withers plants and makes bones brittle. In Bass's menstrual utopia blood restores the earth.

We'll feed the fish with our blood. Our blood
will neutralize the chemicals and dissolve the old car
parts.
Our blood will detoxify the phosphates and the
PCB's. Our blood will feed the depleted soils.
Our blood will water the dry, tired surface of the earth.
We will bleed. We will bleed. We will
bleed until we bathe her in our blood and she turns
slippery new like a baby birthing.

Here, in Bass's "Tampons" (as well as in a number of other poems, songs, and rituals discussed in this book), the old mythology has indeed encountered the new menstrual consciousness. And a new vision has emerged, a radical one, a prophecy that menstrual blood shall restore the earth.[12]

Chapter 19

Menstrual Madness in Drama and Fiction

Irrationality is the quality most commonly attributed to the menstruating woman in popular mythology. Most portrayals of menstruation are negative, evoking fear, disgust, loathing, or other hostile attitudes toward women. Only recently have writers given menstruation positive mythic overtones, as a heroic ritual shared by the community of women, connecting them both with the rhythms of nature and with each other.

The first overt mention of menstruation on stage may be in August Strindberg's *Miss Julie*. The title character forgets her station in life and dances wildly with her servants, her social inferiors. One servant explains to another, "Oh, it's just her time coming on. She's always queer then."[1] In more recent works, the myth remains: Helman in Alison Lurie's *Love and Friendship* asks why Emmy is carrying on: "Are you having your period?" In Clare Booth Luce's version of *A Doll's House*, Nora perceives a similar attitude in her husband: "He is saying to himself, she's not having her period, she's not pregnant, she's not jealous; it's *got* to be another man."

In John Fowles's *The French Lieutnant's Woman*, menstrual irrationality is associated with psychotic behavior. The naive Charles learns much about women's "nature" by studying the case of Marie de Morrell, who had accused an innocent man of rape. A physician later discovered that the obscene letters used to convict the rapist "fell into the clear monthly—or menstrual—pattern." Marie had written these obscene (psychotic, hysterical, irrational, monthly) letters to herself.

The myth that links menstruation and irrationality is not solely an old-fashioned idea, nor is it an idea confined to the community of men. Anaïs Nin uses it in *A Spy in the House of Love,* as do Alice Munro in *Lives of Girls and Women* and Joyce Elbert in *The Crazy Ladies.* These writers apparently share a belief that women are at the mercy of their menstrual flow.

The myth that menstruation means madness touches on another myth: the idea that the menstruating woman is disgusting, if not taboo. For several of Faulkner's characters, menstruation provides the negative definition of a woman. Quentin Compson's father in *The Sound and the Fury* sees women as a "delicate equilibrium of periodical filth between two moons balanced." In *Light in August,* a boy tells others about women: "the smooth and superior shape in which volition dwelled doomed to be at stated and inescapable intervals victims of periodical filth." A little later in the same book, Joe Christmas runs away from a girl who refuses sex because of "the day of the month"; he vomits.

The use of menstruation as a negative condition is not confined to male writers. In Janet Frame's *Faces in the Water,* a woman expresses her madness by hoarding used sanitary napkins, an action that links irrationality and loathing as two aspects of menstruation in fiction. (Aubrey Beardsley reportedly asked his female friends to send him their used menstrual rags.)

The taboo on intercourse during menstruation, a conscious embodiment of a more primordial fear, is mentioned in countless works, including Alexandre Dumas's *La Dame aux Camélias,* Sue Kaufman's *Diary of a Mad Housewife,* Gail Parent's *Sheila Levine is Dead and Living in New York,* Gisela Elsner's "The Initiation," Henry Miller's *Tropic of Cancer,* Joyce Carol Oates's *them.* Even O, the sexually experimental heroine in Pauline Reage's *The Story of O,* prefers to make excuses, not love, when her female lovers have their periods. All these examples are simply incidents in the books, not a part of the overall theme. In some books, however, the taboo on intercourse during menstruation pervades the entire work. Undoubtedly, the best example is the case of Yakov Bok in Bernard Malamud's *The Fixer.*

Yakov, a Jew, rejects making love to the crippled Za when he sees blood running down her leg. He tells her that she is unclean; he remembers that even his wife, who left him, was modest about her periods. Because he rejects her, Zina later charges him with assault. Yakov's disgust becomes, ironically, a part of his own destruction.

The Fixer is pervaded with disgust and fear surrounding blood. Yakov is accused of being a drinker of blood; he is said to be an example of the bloodguilt of the Jewish nation in Christ's death; he even has hallucinations about the czar and blood, and his gentile captors expect him to menstruate. Menstruation defines a woman as inferior, on the same level as a Jew. The menstrual taboo in *The Fixer* may be seen as the pattern for all the taboos in the book because it unites the fear and loathing of blood with similar attitudes or community myths about women.

Perhaps in an effort to counteract the "dangers" of the menstruating woman, many writers find it necessary to demystify menstruation. By treating it in a more matter-of-fact way, they strip away some of the fear and loathing. In Cervantes's *Don Quixote,* for example, menstruation seems to be a sign of earthly order, a touchstone of everyday reality. Cervantes's Don has a seriocomic, probably hallucinated adventure in the enchanted underworld Cave of Monestinos. While he is there, he sees the Lady Belerma; his guide, Montesinos, explains that she is under a spell, which causes the great rings around her eyes and her sickly complexion: "Do not suppose," he added, "that her sallowness and the rings round her eyes spring from the monthly disorders common to women, for it is many months, or even years, since these have even appeared at her gates. They arise from the grief in her heart." Enchantment, then, does not preclude real life processes; her age, not her enchantment, prevents her from menstruating.

Menstruation also functions as an unmasking in Joan Didion's *Play It as It Lays.* Maria Wyeth's abortionist tries to calm any possible emotional difficulties by telling her that the abortion is just "induced menstruation." Maria does not believe him, and later, she finds part of the placenta on the pad she is wearing. The doctor's saying it's menstruation is intended to diminish Maria's fears, but it also shows her what she knew all along: that few people can be trusted.

In both works, menstruation is demystified; the writers suggest that grief and abortion are more worthy of human concern. Menstruation is also demystified when it is mentioned inappropriately, as in a test of morality: in Dan Wakefield's *Going All the Way,* the reader learns that "Nice girls didn't do it when they had the rag on." Not loathing; merely custom.

Graphic details about menstruation tend to have a similar effect: If you know how it's handled, how can it be taboo or enchanted? Many modern writers describe the use of menstrual paraphernalia: Doris Lessing in *The Golden Notebook,* Lois Gould in *Such Good Friends,* Alix Kates Shulman in *Memoirs of an Ex-Prom Queen* (Sasha Davis brags that "my

Kotex disposal was down to an art"), Toni Morrison in *The Bluest Eye*. Such writers dispel male fantasies or myths surrounding female functionings, such as Erik Erikson's statement that each menstruation is "a crying to heaven in mourning over a child."

Some characters take menstruation into their own hands, using it or its paraphernalia for their own ends. In Lois Gould's *Necessary Objects,* a woman prominently displays a Kotex box so that her catty friends will know that she's still "young enough," has not reached menopause. A character in *The Crazy Ladies* does not like to wear underpants, so wears Pursettes to keep warm. In Marge Piercy's *Small Changes,* Beth uses ketchup to fake a period to avoid intercourse with her traditionalist husband. In Mario Puzo's *The Fortunate Pilgrim,* a young but not inexperienced bride uses her menstruation to fake the necessary virginal bleeding. What unites these disparate examples is the woman's control of the situation, her refusal to yield to myth, her insistence on shaping convention for her own uses.

Most mentions of menstruation in fiction and drama are brief. We have not even mentioned the countless works that show a missed period as a sign of pregnancy. These take us outside the realm of myth, although today they may involve a portrayal of greater female autonomy. In *Small Changes,* for instance, a group of women create a comedy skit in which a woman tells her beau she missed her period. What used to be tragic can be comic for them because of their shared community and their new power over their own bodies.

Only a few works make menstruation an important episode, one that defines the character of a woman and her relation to the world around her. Lessing's *The Golden Notebook* participates to a degree in the myth of female irrationality but eventually substitutes a sort of myth of female perspicacity. Erica Jong's *Fear of Flying* creates a new kind of myth with a female hero.

In *The Golden Notebook,* Anna Wulf's notebook entry for September 17, 1954, begins on the morning of her menstruation. Coincidentally, she had earlier decided to be very conscious of "everything" on that particular day—in order to improve her writing.

Lessing then proceeds to lay open Anna's wound. Anna describes her own tension, her irritability, her resentment. She records the "stale smell of menstrual blood," which she feels to be "an imposition from outside." She worries about the odor; she needs her co-worker Jack's "You smell lovely" to make her feel at ease and able to manage anything. Although she tries to see herself as a "free woman," she is nonetheless dependent upon male approval.

Her day at work, punctuated by frequent ablutions and changings of tampons, includes a quarrel with Jack. "I hear my voice shrill and stop myself. I realize my period has caught up with me; there's a moment in every month when it does, and then I get irritated, because it makes me feel helpless and out of control."

Anna's menstrual period also parallels moments of great change in her life. She decides she must leave the Communist party and thinks about the decision while washing herself between her legs. Because of her heightened sensitivity, she realizes that her lover, Michael, is leaving her.

Menstruation can be seen, then, as a sign of increased awareness of one's identity as a woman. During Anna's menstruation, she is stripped of the relationships that had defined her in others' terms: as part of the party, as part of Michael's life. But Anna's menstruation also makes her both resentful and dependent; she had wanted Michael to love her that night, to take away "the resentment against the wound inside my body which I didn't choose to have."

In *The Golden Notebook,* Lessing communicates a variety of attitudes toward menstruation: disgust, confusion, irritability, resentment, helplessness, alienation. Lessing is a woman giving candid expression to many women's ambivalent feelings about their periods. Anna is both more irrational and more intuitive. Both of these are, after all, qualities generally attributed to women; but in expressing both of them, Lessing allows for the emergence of a more complex mythic view of menstruation.

Jong's *Fear of Flying,* probably the most controversial neofeminist novel, involves menstruation in a reworking of the motif of the hero's quest, the pattern of Joyce's *Ulysses.* As critic Joseph Campbell describes it in *The Hero with a Thousand Faces,* the hero (Odysseus, Aeneas, or whoever) follows certain prescribed steps in his quest: departure from the world he knows in response to a call to adventure; initiation, usually involving temptation by a beautiful woman and a descent to the underworld; and return to his original starting point. Along the way, he gains self-knowledge and knowledge about the past, present, or future of other heroes like himself. We use the term *he* for the hero specifically, not generically; Campbell does not say that women can quest.

But Isadora Wing, Jong's protagonist, does follow the pattern of the male heroic quest. Isadora is called to adventure: a jaunt around Europe with a man other than her husband, from whom she separates herself. Like the hero Theseus, she goes through a labyrinth: a maze of pointless wanderings around Europe with her newfound lover, who plays the role of the temptress, like Circe. When her lover leaves her and she is alone, she has her psychological descent to the underworld: a dark night of the soul in which she reaches inside herself to puzzle out her destiny. She returns to her husband at the end of her quest: a quest that (like those of the male heroes) means a growth in self-knowledge.

But what is also significant is that at the time she decides to return from her descent, she gets her period (something Odysseus never did). The menstruation is part of her identity as female; finding her identity means finding herself as a strong person and a strong woman. When Isadora takes a bath in the last scene, simulating waters of rebirth and resurrection, she looks down and sees "the Tampax string fishing the water like a Hemingway hero" (the materials of female culture are as heroic as those of the male).

Jong shows that menstruation is not "the curse"; rather, it is a kind of blessing on the returning hero. Like Anna Wulf, Isadora Wing experiences acutely the modern woman's conflict: the competition between the claims of independence and love. Both Lessing and Jong use menstruation as a vehicle for showing women's expanding consciousness of themselves. For Anna Wulf and Isadora Wing are most rational—if by rationality we mean both reason and intuition—when they are most womanly.

Afterword

Earlier in this chapter we singled out Doris Lessing's *The Golden Notebook* for its mythic and complex treatment of menstruation, for its use of the menstrual cycle as a "vehicle for showing women's expanding consciousness of themselves." Lessing's achievement has been recognized by a few critics, by Elizabeth Hardwick and Rachel Brownstein, for example. Brownstein writes, "Deliberately or not, the style of Anna's pained prose breaks through the tradition of graceful novels about women whose menstrual periods are unmentionable."[2] One would have expected *The Golden Notebook* to generate a score of menstrually conscious novels, for it became in the 1970s the literary Bible of the new women's movement. From what we can judge, however, the menses is a less articulated theme in fiction than it was ten years ago. With the upswing of category romances and corporate romances, the menses goes back-stage. Menstruation simply isn't conducive to romance or to money and power.

One of the few category romances to mention the unmentionable is Jenny Bates's *Gilded Spring*.[3] Here the reference is the standard one: the menses means the presence or absence of pregnancy. This indicator is used frequently in popular fiction, for example in Emily Toth's historical romance *Daughters of New Orleans*. Toth also has one of her characters use menstrual cramps as an excuse not to leave her room: "She'd said that she had her monthly cramps, since no one ever questioned that."

Despite a general lack of menstrual consciousness in current literature, one does find important, scattered references. Two significant ones appear in novels by Afro-American women. Menstruation is a source of discomfort for Velma, a key figure in Toni Cade Bambara's *The Salt Eaters*. "She felt uncomfortable, damp. There'd been nothing in the machines—no tampons, no napkins, no paper towels, no roll of tissue she could unravel and stuff her panties with. So she slid carefully into the wide bowl of the wooden chair, the wad of rally flyers scratching against her panty hose."

Nettie, the missionary sister in Alice Walker's *The Color Purple,* writes to Celie about getting her "friend": "Just when I think I've learned to live with the heat, the constant dampness, even steaminess of my clothes, the swampiness under my arms and between my legs, my friend comes. And cramps and aches and pains—but I must keep going as if nothing is happening, or be an embarrassment to Samuel, the children and myself. Not to mention the villagers, who think women who have their friends should not even be seen." Nettie, who elsewhere in the novel pays considerable attention to the customs of the Olinka people among whom she lives, is typically silent on the matter of menstruation, as if she too were honoring the ancient taboo, hiding the embarrassment.

The hidden, embarrassing aspects of menstruation are given unusual treatment by Tabitha King in a horror fantasy entitled *Small World*. The book is about a doll-house collector who has the power to shrink people. She and her scientist-boyfriend shrink a beautiful journalist, who wakes up to find herself in a replica of the White House. Like *Gulliver's Travels* and *Alice in Wonderland, Small World* deals with the distortion of size and the problems therein. King, in her focus on bodily functions, outdoes Swift. The diminutive Leyna cannot get the faucets to work. She is surrounded by her own stench, her own vomit. In terror she thinks about menstruation: "What would she do when she did menstruate again? There was none of what her husband mockingly called feminine equipage in this bathroom. She would be compelled to ask for what she needed, a prospect that made her stomach ball with dread. . . . But the everyday plumbing of this house was more important than her monthly plumbing."

This menstrual thought, so succinct and paranoid, does not reappear. Yet the imagery of the novel supports the passage. Dolly the giant has hugh red fingernails, red like blood. Sick and depressed, Leyna slits her own wrists before her period ever comes. Dolly finds her victim in a "brick-red" puddle. "There was so much of it, Dolly thought, for such a tiny being." Like Stephen King's *Carrie,* so Tabitha King's *Small World* derives much of its dreadful strength from the menstruation complex—the fear and dread of menstrual blood.

Menstruation, then, is not totally ignored by contemporary writers. We were amused, in fact, to discover a direct reference to our own work in Gwen Davis's *Ladies in Waiting.* A character talks about having abandoned feminism after reading a *Ms.* article involving Titania's period in *A Midsummer Night's Dream.*[4] But of the various menstrual moments in current literature, only three novels seem to use the process in a major way, as Lessing did in *The Golden Notebook.* Two of these novels involve the intercourse taboo, while the third, Lawrence Sanders's *The Third Deadly Sin,* is a prime example of the fear of menstruation in fiction. Of these three novels, only one was written by a woman.

Famous for her ribald heroines and Zipless Fuck, Erica Jong has invented an even more amazing phenomenon in *Parachutes and Kisses*—the Tampon-Taster. Emily Toth and Mary Jane Lupton published an article on eating menstrual blood for a humor issue of *Women: A Journal of Liberation* several years ago. And there is tasting of menstrual blood in Caryl Churchill's play *Top Girls.* But not until Bean Sproul III do we find a character in literature who has tampon-nibbling down to a science.

> It was clear that he relished smells, juices, sweat, blood. He dove into her muff with great exuberance, parted it, found the white string that dangled chastely there and pulled her Tampax triumphantly out with his teeth.
> "Aha! A string!" he said between clenched teeth.
> He chewed on the Tampax lightly, savoring its taste, then tossed it to the floor and dove in again, tongue-first.

Later, while Isadora is on the phone talking to a less adventuresome love, Bean "picked up the discarded bloody Tampax from the floor and began to suck on it again."

Menstruation is the backdrop for the entire scene, which starts with oral tampon-removal and ends with Isadora hiding the bloody sheets in the washer, where the maid won't notice the mess. What Jong manages is a dark-red humor, the bizarre blood-sucking somehow undercutting the otherwise abundant soft-porn for which she is noted. In their violation of the menstrual intercourse taboo, these gymnastic lovers go the extra mile.

Scott Spencer achieves quite a different effect through similar material in his novel *Endless Love*. Whereas Jong, the liberated woman writer, stands outside of the scene smirking, Spencer, obsessive throughout in his treatment of heterosexuality, eroticizes sex during menstruation. The longed-for reunion between David Axelrod and his high school sweetheart, Jade, occurs in a seedy New York hotel room. Jade has just come from her father's funeral, for whose death David is largely responsible. In their love-making David identifies with Jade's blood. "I thought of *her* blood and in a dizzy leap of hunger and exhaustion I longed to *be* her blood, to be the stuff that made the constant circuit through every inch of her. Her menstrual blood." At first Jade resists intercourse: "Can't. Too much blood." David persists. And like Bean in Erica Jong's menstro-erotic passage, he drinks Jade's blood.

There is a desperate tone to the Spencer episode, an association of menstrual blood with endings and wounds. Jade leaves an oval of blood on the sheets, "the color of an apple bruise." Spencer seems, in the menstrual intercourse section of the novel, to be making a parallel to an earlier blood-letting—the death of Jade's father, Hugh, struck by a taxi while chasing David.

Spencer describes Ingrid, who kneels at her dead lover's body: "By now the pool of blood beneath him had spread out and she was on its rim, staring down into it as if to see her reflection. . . . Her loosely braided red hair dangled in front of her and her denim skirt was red and wet with Hugh's blood and now her hands were red too and her face when she touched it." The redness here is echoed in the menstrual scene, with blood transferred first from male to female, then from female to male. The movie *Endless Love*, which eliminates the menstruation element entirely, thus loses these profound connections between sex and death.

Sex and death are the subjects of the third novel under discussion, Lawrence Sanders's best-selling *The Third Deadly Sin*. The novel opens as Zoe Kohler, pale and saggy-breasted, lies in bed listening to her body sounds, to the "whispering course of tainted blood." Zoe is the victim of Addison's disease, a serious disorder involving the adrenal glands, and of severe menstrual cramps. Zoe sees menstruation as "the constant crucifixion." Mouselike, suffering, Zoe finds relief in murder. Once a month, when the cramps are most severe, she dresses in a wig and flashy clothes, picks up some unsuspecting hotel guest, and stabs him to death. Here we have another menstrual monstress, another embodiment of the menstruation complex. Like Dracula, like Carrie, so Zoe Kohler evokes in her readers the fear and dread of menstruation that, according to Claude Dagmar Daly, are continual reminders of death.

In one of the murder scenes Sanders graphically emphasizes the menstruation/death associations by having Zoe the menstruating victim become Zoe the Hotel Ripper. She has been violently seduced by a man whom she intends to kill. Finding her knife, Zoe stabs him. "His blood is smeared on her hands, arms, breast, stomach. Worse, she feels the warm course of her own blood on leg, knee, shin, foot." Her blood is two-fold: Zoe has cut herself getting away from the stranger; Zoe is menstruating. The deliberate parallel phrasing of this passage marks the fusion of male and female blood, the blood of sexuality and of death.

In developing his character Zoe, Lawrence Sanders is said to have spent two years researching premenstrual syndrome.[5] Indeed, many of Zoe's symptoms—depression, bloating, abdominal pain, irritability—can be associated with the premenstruum. But in *The Third Deadly Sin* these symptoms are confused with the rarer, far more dangerous problem of Addison's disease. Only near the end of the novel does Sanders differentiate between them. Thus *The Third Deadly Sin* gives one the false impression that the real deadly sin is menstrual cramping. Yet in fact menstrual cramps are treatable. And they occur, not (as Sanders imagines) before the period but at its onset. Like Stephen King before him, Sanders draws fictional material from the negative myths surrounding menstruation: menstruation represents madness, destruction, and death. That these myths sell is indicated by the Top Ten charts. That we buy them is a sign that the public is still entranced by the frightening powers of the menstrual process.

The narrative rhythms of Sanders's novel are set by Zoe's menstrual clock. In her terrible regularity she is reminiscent of Tiamat, Venus, the moon at high tide. Thus Zoe moves through the menstrual cycle, from serenity to violence. As the representation of order, the menstruating woman signifies rationality; so she does in *The Golden Notebook*. When, however, she shows her other face, like Zoe, the cycle-logical order disintegrates. It is the darker, violent side of the Goddess that so often appeals to writers of current fiction.

PART FIVE

The Menopause

Chapter 20

From Leeches
to Estrogen:
The Menopause and
Medical Options

Menopause (from the Greek words for "month" and "cessation") marks the end of the menstrual flow. The word is sometimes used interchangeably with the broader term *climacteric* (from the Greek words meaning "rung of the ladder" and "critical time"). The climacteric refers to the few years before and after the actual cessation of bleeding and encompasses all the physical and emotional symptoms a woman may experience around the time her periods stop. Other expressions for the menopause are *change of life, critical time, the change, the dangerous age,* and *the dodging time.* The menopause is the last phase of the menstrual cycle. As with every other aspect of menstruation, the same old taboos appear among both primitives and psychoanalysts regarding the menopause.

Menstruation stops when the ovaries cease functioning. One authority has suggested that women stop bleeding when the ovaries have exhausted their egg supply,[1] an unlikely explanation because a newborn girl comes equipped with over half a million eggs. Another doctor thinks that a reduction in the graafian follicles (egg sacs) causes the ovaries to stop functioning.[2] It is known, however, that the cessation in ovarian activity means a sharp reduction in the supply of estrogen, the female sex hormone, and it is the loss of estrogen that causes many of the more noticeable symptoms and side effects of the climacteric.

The average American woman stops menstruating around the age of 50, although menopause can occur normally at any time between the ages of 40 and 60. A century ago, age at menopause could not have been a subject for scientific investigation; average life expectancy was low, and the majority of European and American women did not live to experience menopause. This fact did not prevent widespread speculation about what race or class of women would menstruate the longest. The results and prejudices are similar to those involved in speculations about age at menarche. One doctor thought that "Red Indian" women menstruate beyond the age of 50 but that for "the teeming millions of Chinese" the end of the cycle comes before the fortieth year.[3] Today, the American woman, with an average life expectancy of 80, is likely to outlive her ovaries by about thirty years.

Premature menopause (menopause before the age of 40) is experienced by about 8 percent of all women. Perhaps the earliest case on record is the age of 9. One nineteenth-century gynecologist reported the case of a "Hungarian Jewess, fat from her youth," who had her first menstruation at the age of 9, was married at 15½, and went through the menopause at the age of 17.[4]

Explanations for age at menopause reflect the assumptions of the male "experts" who offer them. One nineteenth-century physician said that bad news could bring on an early menopause. He related the unfortunate story of Elizabeth C., who stopped menstruating at the age of 30 when, one day as she was nursing her baby, her husband dropped dead at her feet. The mother's milk "turned to water," and her periods never returned.[5]

In the same century, a Dr. Andrew Currier explained that "irregular and unwomanly occupations" could cause an early menopause. Those workers most in danger were fishwives, metalworkers, day laborers, cooks, and laundresses. "Surely this is not woman's work," wrote the doctor, "or we would not see such pitiful spectacles of decrepit and wrinkled and worn-out creatures at a period when the blush should still be on their cheeks." Cooks, he thought, had an early menopause from overeating; laundresses, from being exposed to high temperatures. Other causes for premature menopause, said the same doctor, were alcohol, poverty, opium, typhoid, and "excessive sexual indulgence."[6] Dr. Currier's speculations express the moral and class biases of a comfortable Victorian paterfamilias. To this day, there is no proven correlation between a woman's menopausal age and her socioeconomic class. Premature menopause is almost always the result of a hormonal imbalance, whether natural or surgically induced.

So, too, those women who remain fertile into their nineties owe that pleasure or pain to the levels of estrogen being produced in their bodies rather than to sexual restraint or working conditions. The oldest age at menopause on record is 104. If we take the title of hormone advocate

Robert A. Wilson's book at face value, then 104 is not a very remarkable age at all; women can be, he claims, *Feminine Forever.*[7]

The most common physical symptom of the climacteric is irregular menstrual flow. Another is hot flashes: sensations of warmth in the upper chest and face, often followed by perspiration and chills. Doctors differ on how many women have significant menopausal symptoms. One says 25 percent; Wilson, the author of *Feminine Forever,* says 88 percent.

The Victorian gynecoloist Edward Tilt decreed that a major difficulty of the climacteric was a gradual "loss of feminine grace." At change of life, women begin to look "masculine," their bones either stick out or are sunken in fat, their skin gets flabby, and "tweezers are sometimes required to remove stray hairs from the face."[8] In *Feminine Forever,* Wilson gives much the same portrait. Especially grim is Wilson's description of postmenopausal breasts (he calls breasts "psychological organs," so important are they to a woman's sense of self-esteem):

> After menopause, when estrogen and progesterone sink to a low level, the breasts begin to shrivel and sag. Once the supply of these two nourishing hormones is cut off, the breasts become pendulous, wrinkled, and flabby. Often the skin of the breasts coarsens and is covered with scales. The breasts lose their erotic sensitivity and sometimes do not respond to pain stimuli. Only timely estrogen replacement therapy can prevent this premature decline of a woman's symbol of femininity.

Breast flab is not all women have to look forward to. Among other blessings of the climacteric Wilson lists a "stiff and unyielding" vagina, aching joints, palpitating organs, frequent urination, itching skin, loss of memory, the inability to concentrate, and dryness of the mouth, nose, and eyes.[9] Another doctor observes that menopausal women are often allergic to detergents and to certain kinds of floor polishes.[10]

Some researchers have associated the menopause with bone decalcification, high cholesterol, high blood pressure, and heart disease. But the disease that women fear most, one that has been associated with the menopause since Galen, is cancer.

Popular books and magazine articles almost always warn the menopausal woman that irregular bleeding, particularly any marked increase in the flow, may be a sign of cancer. We are conditioned to think that irregularity means malignancy. Although it is indeed prudent for any person, regardless of age or sex, to be aware of the danger signals of cancer, the dwelling on cancer during the menopause can compound a woman's negative attitude toward aging. Among the 100 women whom Bernice

Neugarten interviewed about menopausal attitudes, only 4 saw the end of their periods as a problem of the menopause, but many mentioned the fear of cancer.[11]

Most of us know women who have developed cancer of the breast, cervix, or uterus at a time in their lives that coincided with the menopause. The average age for the menopause for American women is 49; the peak age for cancer of the cervix is 48.[12] The highest incidence of cancer of the ovary, a difficult disease to detect, occurs between the ages of 55 and 65. Wilson sees the uterus as a "possible breeding ground for cancer," but one that can be controlled through estrogen and hysterectomy. Wilson looks forward to the day when hysterectomy will be accepted as a "general preventive route." "If your uterus has been removed," Wilson writes, "estrogen therapy will provide all its benefits without the annoyance of menstrual bleeding. You are a lucky woman indeed."[13]

A lucky (i.e., wealthy) woman living in London in the 1850s could, if she had the courage to talk about intimate problems with a male doctor, make an appointment with Edward Tilt. Tilt had a wide range of solutions to the problem of menopause, among them mineral water, morphine, syrup of iron and potassium, exercise, traveling, bandaging of limbs, sedatives, and abdominal belts. His preferred method of treatment, however, was bleeding (general venesection). Tilt reasoned that although many women grew stronger during the menopause because their bodies used up the nutrition in the unexpelled blood, many others suffered from the body's failure to dispose of it. Severe headaches were a sign that the woman was storing up the excess blood in her head; if her arm were bled, the unneeded blood would leave the body and her well-being would be restored. Tilt also liked applying leeches—to the anus in the case of hemorrhoids but behind the ears or at the nape of the neck for menopausal disorders. Bleeding was a widely recommended procedure in the nineteenth century for many ailments; it was particularly useful for the menopause, Tilt argued, because it was an "imitation of nature." Tilt's bleeding of twelve ounces of blood from the arm of a 51-year-old patient is alleged to have reduced her dizziness, flushes, and perspiration.

A woman consulting the American gynecologist Andrew Currier in the 1890s would have been told that leeches were still an effective remedy for congested genitals but that venesection was old-fashioned and ineffectual. In his book *The Menopause,* Currier attacked those physicians (such as Tilt) who frightened women with their negative attitudes toward the menopause and who were, in Currier's words, "bleeders, pukers, and purgers." The great cure, according to Currier, was not bleeding but surgery. Riding on the wave of progress evoked by Robert Battey's invention of "female castration" in 1872, Currier proclaimed its merits in the treatment of the menopause. He advocated "artificial menopause": the removal of any organ that directly affects the menstrual process. Be thorough, he advised his colleagues. If you remove the fallopian tubes, then you might as well remove the ovaries, too, because without the tubes the ovarian function is gone. Remove the whole ovary instead of just part of one, and remove the ovaries in the case of any new growth, benign or malignant. Of course, one always stumbled across the rare patient for whom surgery offered no salvation: "This would include some who had long been subject to vicious habits, to the use of alcohol, chloral, opium, etc."[15]

Currier's method is still highly favored among American doctors. Apparently, 63 percent of American women between the ages of 50 and 64 have had "artificial menopause." The methods may vary, but the end result is the same as it was almost a century ago: the literal castration of the female.

Although surgery is the preferred American technique for destroying the function of a woman's ovaries and her uterus, another is called *radiation menopause*. This controversial treatment can be achieved through X-ray of the pelvic area or through circulating radium in the uterus through a tube. With the latter method, there is said to be a greater risk of uterine cancer. With both methods, there are some unpleasant side effects, including uncontrollable bleeding and loss of sexual desire.

Besides surgery and radiation, other modern proposals for cheating nature have been monkey gland transplants and injections of the cells of an unborn lamb. One doctor has ironically suggested "grafting 'young' ovaries into menopausal women" as a way to eliminate the process of aging.[16] But the most widely acclaimed "cure" for the menopause, the one that made headlines in 1966, is estrogen-replacement therapy.

The two female hormones that affect the menstrual cycle are estrogen and progesterone, which are produced by certain cells of the ovaries and possibly by the adrenal glands. The decrease in estrogen levels brings on the menopause, although some researchers say that 40 percent of all women maintain moderate hormonal activity even after the menopause.

Estrogen was first isolated in 1923 by Allen and Doisey. It is the general name for three collective hormones (estradiol, estrone, and estriol) that are converted into usable substances in the liver. To make his first drop of estrogen in the 1920s, Doisey used up the ovaries of 80,000 sows. Another source of natural estrogen is Australian clover, which has been said to make grazing sheep sterile. But the most common source of natural estrogen is the urine of pregnant mares.

Today, most estrogen is produced synthetically and is administered primarily in pill form. There are also some local preparations, prescribed for women who cannot take estrogen orally. These creams help to restore the vaginal tissue; their primary deficiency is that they are too easily absorbed. Another form of estrogen, not currently in wide use but destined to be if the present trend continues, is a hormone pellet implanted under the buttocks. One English doctor who recommends this treatment says that the implantation method is superior to all others: It is weaker than a daily dosage; the hormones are not apt to lose their effectiveness in the liver; there is no way of affecting the stomach or intestines; there is little risk of embolism; and there is the psychological advantage of not having to think about taking medicine. This very optimistic physician has had excellent results with the more than 1,000 women he has treated. Like Wilson, he sees estrogen therapy as a revolutionary discovery that will retard the aging process.[17]

Others have been less optimistic, less willing to proclaim estrogen as the elixir of youth. The drug has had many reported side effects, including a high incidence of heart disease and blood clotting. Synthetic estrogens, particularly the substance known as *diethylstilbestrol* (DES), have been linked with cancer. Other synthetic estrogens have been connected with liver disturbances and shifts in blood-sugar levels.

Defenders of estrogen therapy have answered these charges. Huggins, for example, won a Nobel Prize for discovering that oral contraceptives (which contain estrogen and progesterone) are more likely to reduce cancer than cause it. Wilson, in his more than twenty-seven years of prescribing estrogen for menopausal women, had not a single woman develop cancer, although the odds were that 18 of the 304 women would contract the disease. As we write this (1976), convincing evidence is beginning to appear that links excessive estrogen therapy with an increased risk of cancer.

The choice of estrogen therapy must be a highly individual one. We think all women should educate themselves about this issue so that they can make intelligent individual decisions when the choice becomes necessary. All women should visit a gynecologist for an annual checkup and Pap smear; it might be a good idea to make an annual visit to a medical library as well. There is no waiting in line, and the service is free. The reference book called *Biological Abstracts* contains, under the category "Menopause," a summary of the medical findings for that year on that topic. It is not too difficult to learn what is being said about the menopause and by whom.

The more technical essays tend to avoid the kind of rhetoric that characterizes Wilson's book. For the main fault of *Feminine Forever* lies not in the medicine but in the moralizing. Wilson's insistent theme is that women are delightful creatures whose beauty must be preserved. Each man, he argues, marries an Aphrodite or a Helen of Troy. The sensitive doctor is the one who keeps Helen glowing through the dismal years of her middle age. "A woman's physical appeal is her starting capital in the venture of life—the 'ante' which lets her into the game," Wilson writes in defense of his theory.

One gynecologist told us that Wilson's reputation in medical circles has suffered because of his evangelical approach to estrogen therapy for all. The fact is, all women in their climacteric do not require estrogen therapy. The ones who do, get it from their doctors as needed. No competent or honorable gynecologist, face to face with an anxious 49-year-old woman, would dare to promise eternal youth as Wilson does from the safety of the printed page.

In the foreword to *Feminine Forever*, Dr. Greenblatt praises his colleague: "Like a gallant knight he has come to rescue his fair lady not at the time of her bloom and flowering but in her despairing years; at a time of her life when the preservation and prolongation of her femaleness are so paramount." But in emphasizing a woman's breasts and legs rather than her intelligence or skills, the gallant knight reinforces the most destructive stereotypes in our sexist society.

Nor can we be thoroughly convinced, as Wilson is, that estrogen therapy is woman' s salvation. What seems true in one age can be judged folly in another. Edward Tilt had the most knightly of intentions, surely, when he sapped away his menopausal patients' strength by removing the blood from their arms, in imitation of nature. To thumb one's nose at Mother Nature now, during the estrogen craze, would be a disservice to those women who have little need either for hormone replacement or for identification with Aphrodite.

Note: The Afterwords to Chapters 20, 21, and 22 are combined and appear at the end of Part 5: The Menopause.

Chapter 21

Psychology and the Menopausal Menace

Victorian medicine men knew in their hearts that during the menopause, a woman could expect to have mental problems. According to Dr. Edward Tilt, the change-of-life woman was susceptible to certain mental diseases, among them "morbid irrationality," "minor forms of hysteria," melancholia, and the impulses to drink spirits, to steal, and perchance, to murder.[1] Freud, although he did not see the menopause as a disease, nonetheless thought it to be a stage of potential crisis, a time when previously undisturbed women could become neurotic. Often, said Freud, menopausal women "become quarrelsome and obstinate, petty and stingy, show typical sadistic and anal-erotic features which they did not show before."[2]

Freud's occasional perceptions of the menopause, like his comments on the menarche, were fully developed by the analyst Helene Deutsch. Deutsch viewed the menopause as the "third edition" of the infantile stage, the second being the menarche. During both of these traumatic times, she argued, women act out certain unconscious fantasies. The first menstruation is fraught with fears of castration and lost children; the last is filled with fantasies of rape and prostitution. Her theory that the menarche is the moment at which a woman becomes the "servant of the species" justifies her view of the menopause as the stage at which the woman's service to the species ends.[3] The woman becomes biologically useless; she can have no more children. Here is another instance of psychoanalysts converting the complaints of a few women seeking psychiatric help into a universal theory of female sexuality. The medical-psychiatric community considers the menarche, menstruation, and now the menopause "conditions" to be treated, and their theories of treatment spill over into definitions of the normally functioning woman.

Deutsch's influence can be seen in the writings of other analysts and popularizers of psychoanalytic ideas. Eric Erikson, for example, writes that when a woman's womb is "empty" she experiences pain. Her grief for lost children, reiterated at each menstruation, becomes during the menopause "a permanent scar."[4] Joseph Rheingold, in *The Fear of Being a Woman*, relates the menopause to his theory of maternal destructiveness. The menopause is a traumatic event, accompanied by an "isolation by loss," the loss of the childbearing capacity. "Some women make a career of the menopause," claims Rheingold.[5]

How do these dismissed servants of the race behave during their menopausal years? Well, writes one doctor, unless they have the right outlet, menopausal women are apt to become *"mischief makers,* developing a heightened interest in their married sons and daughters and often becoming a great menace as meddlesome mothers-in-law."[6] The menacing mother-in-law is a major stereotype for the menopausal woman; another is the television addict. Morton Hunt, in a book entitled, inappropriately, *Her Infinite Variety,* has a rather one-dimensional idea about the menopausal type. She is foolish and what people call "typically feminine." Her time is spent pursuing astrologists and palm readers, writing letters to advice columnists, watching television, playing bridge, and making "lemming-like migrations to see visiting movie stars."[7]

Philip Wylie's menacing mom, the American Cinderella gone to flab, exhibits "caprices" that Wylie labels "menopausal": "These caprices are of a menopausal nature at best—hot flashes, rage, infantilism, weeping, sentimentality, peculiar appetite."[8] In *The Second Sex,* Simone de Beauvoir also presents a momish portrait of the menopausal woman, although she places her middle-class menace more clearly within a cultural context than Wylie does. Because woman lives in a patriarchal culture where she is denied selfhood, argues de Beauvoir, she will inevitably behave in an infantile manner. Relying on both Deutsch and Wylie as sources, de Beauvoir describes the menopausal woman in rather negative terms. Denied identity by the male society, she retreats to infantile fantasies of what might have been. At the verge of a new independence, the menopausal woman will usually reject it. "She babbles to men in a childish voice and with naive glances of admiration, and she chatters on about when she was a little girl: she chirps instead of talking, she claps her hands, she bursts out laughing." Some women may revive their abandoned dreams of playing the piano or painting pictures; others become willing dupes of religious or spiritualist happiness peddlers. Restless, irritable, tormented by the flesh, she is likely to seek the attention of young men and will, in fact, buy that attention if it does not come freely. Finished and outdated in a culture that has no use for her, the menopausal woman tyrannizes over her sons and daughters, even promoting the daughter's abortion in order to keep the privilege of maternity to herself. Some women, says de Beauvoir, bless the appearance of a war or a famine, for then their knitting will be needed.

Of all menopausal women, says the French philosopher, it is the American who is the worst. She must agree with Wylie that the American mom cannot think or read, knows nothing of science or art. De Beauvoir goes so far as to blame the American woman for the decline of literature: best sellers are written for the American mom market, "to entertain idle women in search of escape."[9]

Fortunately for the future of the race, some writers give more humane and realistic assessments of the "menopausal personality." The analyst Clara Thompson, for one, thinks the menopause is a threat primarily to two distinct types of women: "those who have postponed living until too late and those who have managed to maintain a feeling of importance and value only through the adulation of men."[10] Most of the hazards of the menopause are culturally induced. Thompson reports the fact that among Chinese women there are almost no menopausal problems because older women in China are given power and respect as they reach maturity. The psychoanalyst George Devereux has noted similar circumstances among Mohave women. In that society, the menopause is a sign of achievement; Mohave women are free to work, to flirt, and to be wise during their middle years.[11] In over-emphasizing the plight of the white American woman of the middle class, de Beauvoir neglects this broader cultural view.

Today, a more common theme is the menopause as "rebirth," a time when woman is freed from childbearing and child rearing, freed to a new enjoyment of sex and a renewed dedication to her work. Women writing about themselves have actually sounded this note throughout history, but it seems to have been ignored by the clinicians.

The suffragist Eliza Farnham, writing in the 1860s, saw menopause as a time of "secret joy," of spiritual growth, of "super-exaltation." She attributed the negative attitudes toward menopause to "masculine errors."[12] Anna Garlin Spencer, an American writer of the early twentieth century, found in the change of life a new freedom. Released from the ties of home and childbearing, the woman in her middle years can have a life "as 'straight' as man's, and the 'curves' that had required consideration at their weakest point are no longer a part of her existence."[13]

Clelia Mosher, the author of *Health and the Woman Movement,* claimed that women are taught to dread the menopause. Yet, those women who are "busy and useful," who have "absorbing occupations," have little to worry about.[14]

More recent testimonies indicate that if a woman has a positive attitude toward the menopause, this stage of life need not be a threat. Seven California women, most of them post-menopausal, spoke on video tape of their feelings during the climacteric. Only two had experienced any anxiety in the menopause. One of the women found menopause to be a "liberation," a more "joyful" time than she had had in the preceding twenty years.[15] The 100 women in the Neugarten study were generally happy about their own menopause. One woman said, "I'm so happy about not menstruating any more, I could dance with joy. I was looking forward to it for years."[16]

No longer bound to their rhythms or their families, post-menopausal women are freed from any of the social and biological restrictions that patriarchy imposes on their lives. They have no need for baby-sitters or birth control. They are in the position to establish, perhaps for the first time in their lives, a separate identity. Many women celebrate this new liberty with a divorce. Others, however, discover a renewed sexual life with their long-term mates.

For it is a myth that with the end of the menstrual cycle comes an end to sexual desire. Some, it is true, may use the menopause as an excuse for sexual denial, but only those women who never liked sex in the first place. A thirty-three-year-old woman who went through premature menopause was very much worried that her sexual appeal would diminish. But her doctor sagely remarked: "Men don't marry us for our periods, you know." When she told her husband the bad news that they would soon be unable to have any more children, he answered: "But honey, we weren't seriously thinking about having any more, anyway." Her husband's tenderness and understanding, plus the decreasing need for contraceptive devices, made their sexual relationship "more satisfying than ever."[17]

Extremists in the past have predicted either complete frigidity or uncontrollable nymphomania as the sexual response to the menopause. However, a number of recent studies show that there is very little change in sexual attitude for the majority of women during the climacteric. Some of Thompson's patients continued to have a strong sex life into their seventies. The majority of women in Neugarten's study found little or no change in their sexual attitudes as they entered the menopause; of the thirty-five women who did experience a change, they were equally divided on whether sex got better or worse. Neugarten and some other current investigators have concluded that it is *not* physiological change but rather the cultural attitude toward aging which creates depression or negative self-concepts in menopausal women.

As women gain increased control of their own bodies, as they continue to talk to each other about menstruation, the menopause, and other socially tabooed topics, they will help to clear away some of the misconceptions about female sexuality. There is much in print concerning the menopausal menace. Perhaps this is because women, silenced for so long, have had too many "authorities" describe them. But women's stories exist— in letters, in journals, in unpublished manuscripts. In these documents, as in the published works of many, are to be found the women who have been too busy or too committed to flock to movie houses or the arms of adolescent men. As their lives are made public, the menopausal menace shall, like the mom and the mother-in-law, resume her human and un-menacing dimensions.

Note: The Afterwords to Chapters 20, 21, and 22 are combined and appear at the end of Part 5: The Menopause.

Chapter 22

"November of the Body": The Menopause and Literature

Until the last quarter of the nineteenth century, the word *menopause* did not exist in the English language. Andrew Marvell and Sir Thomas Browne, English writers of the seventeenth century, had used the word *climacter* to indicate a critical stage in a man's life, but not in a woman's. The sexual decline of a woman's body, generally called *change of life,* was not a significant theme in British or American literature until the twentieth century.

The absence of women's voices from the centuries-old record of the human experience must surely be responsible for this void in literature. On the other hand, there are countless references to old age in European literature, from the Greeks to the moderns. The process of aging was a concern of Euripides, Shakespeare, Donne, Hugo, Tolstoy, Baudelaire, T. S. Eliot. Even Simone de Beauvoir, in *The Coming of Age,* although she provides a thorough analysis of the theme of old age in literature, gives no specific attention to woman's change of life. We shall try to fill in the record here.

One of the earliest and most introspective writers on the fear of reproductive decay was Elizabeth Barrett Browning. In a letter written to Robert Browning during their courtship, Elizabeth Barrett warned her fiance that marrying her would be like emptying his "water gourds into the sand." The sand suggests dryness or absence of fluid, the sterility of the womb. Her famed *Sonnets from the Portuguese,* written shortly before the elopement, show similar fears of barrenness. Elizabeth Barrett was then thirty-nine years old, too old, she feared, for a fruitful marriage. She describes herself in images of dust, ashes, decay. In Sonnet 18 she remarks that her youth is gone:

> My days of youth went yesterday,;
> My hair no longer bounds to my foot's glee,
> Nor plant I it from rose or myrtle-tree,
> As girls do, any more:

In Sonnet 4 she compares her body to a dilapidated house: "Look up and see the casement broken in,/ The bats and owlets builders in the roof!" Elizabeth Barrett is communicating, in these premarital sonnets, a dread of her approaching change of life; but, in fact, she was not sterile. She bore one son and suffered four miscarriages during her marriage, the last being her most serious illness since leaving England for the healthier climate of Italy.[1]

The desire for a child is strong in the menopause of Joanna Burden, Joe Christmas's mistress in Faulkner's *Light in August:* "It was as if she knew somehow that time was short, that autumn was almost upon her, without knowing yet the exact significance of autumn." Like Anne Sexton's "November of the body," Joanna Burden's autumn signifies the ending of fertility, the last chance for bearing a child. Miss Burden tells Joe Christmas that she is pregnant. But her body has lied. In his shame and disgust, Christmas strikes her, calling her an old woman. "You haven't got any baby," he said. "You never had one. There is not anything the matter with you except being old. You just got old and it happened to you and now you are not any good any more." The unnamed *it* is, of course, the menopause.

Some menopausal women in literature who want a child meet a happier fate than Joanna Burden did. The Old Testament, for example, records the story of Sarah, the barren wife of Abraham, who, though old, "conceived, and bare Abraham a son [Isaac] in his old age, at the set time of which God had spoken to him" (Genesis 21:2).

There is a parallel legend in the New Testament in the Book of Luke. Zacharias and Elisabeth, both "now well stricken in years," have no child (1:7). But an angel comes to Zacharias telling him that the barren wife will bear a son, to be named John. When the angel comes to Mary to announce the blessedness of her womb, he informs Mary that Elisabeth, her cousin, has also conceived a son: "And this is the sixth month with her, who was called barren. For with God nothing shall be impossible" (1:36-37). Shortly afterward, Mary visits her cousin: "When Elisabeth heard the salutation of Mary, the babe leaped in her womb" (1:41).

In both of these stories from the Bible, it is the Lord, not the mothers, who are primarily responsible for the conceptions. In both, a son is born, not a daughter. The birth of a son is the wish granted to an Irish peasant woman in Jack London's story "Samuel." But in London's story, the menopausal pregnancy is seen by the people as the work of the devil rather than the work of God.

Margaret Henan, the central character of "Samuel," is the mother of six sons and six daughters. But the sons named Samuel, in honor of Margaret's brother, do not survive. After the third Samuel's death by drowning, Margaret bears, at the age of forty-seven, still another Samuel, whom she must take to another town to christen, so frightened are the people at this point of Margaret's name choosing. One woman tells the narrator: "She was forty-seven, I'm tellun' ye, and she had a child ot forty-seven. Thunk on ut! Ot forty-seven! Ut was fair scand'lous." The baby is born an "eediot." Disturbed by his fourth Samuel's braying, the father kills the child and then himself. Without the father, Margaret is unable to conceive a fifth Samuel.

This story, supposedly a legend of McGill Island, is told from the point of view of a stranger to the island. As a detached observer, he is able to admire Margaret's strength and self-determination. For the natives, however, Margaret is a threat, a witchlike woman who is in touch with the devil and whose moribund fertility brings destruction.

In *Hamlet,* the sexual corruption and lack of judgment that make something rotten in the state of Denmark seem to emanate from a middle-aged woman. Gertrude has a characteristic observable in other change-of-life women in literature, what her son calls "an increase of appetite." Hamlet, furious that his mother has remarried immediately after the death of his father, generalizes that fury: "Frailty, thy name is woman!" (Act 1, Scene 2). In the confrontation scene in Gertrude's bedroom (Act 3, Scene 4), Hamlet condemns his mother for not acting her age:

> You cannot call it love, for at your age
> The heyday in the blood is tame, it's humble
> And waits upon the judgment.

Here again, Hamlet makes a general statement about female nature from his own philosophical presupposition, then goes on to say that with such mutiny in a "matron's bones," we can hardly expect virtue from youth. Gertrude's menopausal passion is responsible for the dissolution of the family and the collapse of the state.

The majority of mutinous matrons in literature confine their destructiveness to the smaller unit. They suffer and complain, threatening their sons and daughters and husbands and, of course, themselves. For example, Alma, the doting white mother of Lillian Smith's novel *Strange Fruit,* finds it difficult to control either her children or herself during the menopause. *"Change of life makes you like that.* She must not permit herself to go to pieces over something trivial." F. Scott Fitzgerald, so often in search of a simple explanation for his wife Zelda's misbehavior, found a perfect one in the menopause; Fitzgerald even asked Zelda's doctor to discuss the mother's menopausal imbalance with Scottie, their daughter.

In John O'Hara's last novel, *The Ewings,* Ada's son and daughter-in-law speculate about the effects of the menopause on Ada's behavior. Edna has heard a lot of talk about menopause that she passes on to her husband: "You stop menstruating, and have these hot flashes, and I *have* heard that you lose all sexual desire, but on the other hand, I've heard that when it's over your sexual desire is as great as ever." Some women, Edna continues, get depressed or even "suicidal."

Kate Brown, the heroine of Doris Lessing's novel *The Summer Before the Dark,* has, like Ada Ewing, some offspring terribly concerned about their mother's menopause. Kate's children start treating her in a humorous and indulgent manner, assuming that she's going through the change of life. They treat the mother like "an invalid" and her stray cats like "medicine." One day, Kate overhears the children talking about the cat: "Just the thing for the menopause," they say.

In the case of Gertrude in *Hamlet,* the menace is the woman herself. In the domestic situations described by Lessing and O'Hara, however, the real menace seems to be the children, who attempt to define, as indeed Hamlet did with Gertrude, their mothers' behavior.

A number of fictional characters experience the menopause alone, without husbands or children. For Mrs. Stone of Tennessee Williams's *The Roman Spring of Mrs. Stone* and Mrs. Eliot of Angus Wilson's *The Middle Age of Mrs. Eliot,* the menopause coincides with widowhood. Mrs. Stone experiences three critical events in the same year: the abandonment of her career, the death of her husband, and "that interval of a woman's life when the ovarian cycle is cut off." At first, Mrs. Stone is depressed and "unfocused"; at the end of what Williams calls the "moon of pause," however, she temporarily discovers a new life and new energy. Although Angus Wilson is less graphic about Meg Eliot's menopause, he nonetheless gives his forty-three-year-old heroine certain characteristics usually associated with that stage: a lack of purpose, a tendency toward headaches and crying spells, a feeling of barrenness, like an old virgin afraid of turning sour. The widow is on the brink of psychic disintegration until, aided by her brother, she works her way back into the world.

For some women, the problems and anxieties of the climacteric are insurmountable. Hamlet's mother's wantonness leads to her destruction and to the deaths of her son, her lover, and quite a few others. Mrs. Stone, who becomes after the "moon of pause" a woman of passion, is eventually discarded by her young Italian lover. In the last scene of the novel, she throws her keys to a sinister gigolo who has been following her for months, thus openly inviting him to rob and perhaps murder her. Joanna Burden, rejected by Joe Christmas because he finds her old and useless, plans a suicide pact with him. Christmas, however, runs from the burning house after Miss Burden shoots herself. He is eventually lynched.

At times, the menopause is associated with death by cancer. When she meets an acquaintance she doesn't want to see again, Mrs. Stone invents the story that she had had her uterus removed but that the cancer has spread. Telling the lie gives Karen Stone a feeling of liberation, of having arrived at the "void." Her lie becomes the truth, of course, at the end of the novel. The cancer is a moral one, the final loss of dignity; the "void" is sexual abandon and ultimately death.

Molly Bloom, the aging wife in Joyce's *Ulysses,* is menstruating near the end of the novel. She notices that her periods have become irregular: "Is there anything the matter with my insides or have I something growing in me getting that thing like that every week when was it last Whit Monday yes its only about three weeks I ought to go to the doctor." "That thing" is her period, come again after only three weeks. She worries that something is the matter with her "insides," that there might be "something growing" in her. The worry is probably the fear of cancer.

But the most unusual connection between the menopause and cancer appears in Thomas Mann's novel *The Black Swan.* In that story a middle-aged mother, a woman of feeling, goes on a journey with her daughter, a woman of reason. The mother falls in love with the young guide who takes them on a tour of a damp cave. In her sexual excitement, the mother, Rosalie, begins to bleed. She rejoices that the cycle has reasserted itself, calling her new blood "my visitation—this Easter of my womanhood." Instead, the blood signals cancer of the uterus.

Women who threaten themselves or their families during the menopause often do so in response to the fear that they may lose their sexual desirability. A character in Betty Smith's *A Tree Grows in Brooklyn* regrets that she has had so few lovers now that the menopause is approaching and "soon all her woman-ness will be lost." In a poem called "Two" from *Pro Femina,* Carolyn Kizer taunts those women who invest everything in their looks: "You can wait for the menopause, and catch up on your reading." But nowhere is the disappearance of a woman's sex appeal at the menopause more brutally stated than in Henry Miller's *Tropic of Cancer*. "If she were only ten years younger!" complains Carl to Henry.

> If she were only ten years younger I might overlook the streak of grey hair ... and even the brittle arms. But she's too old. You see, with a cunt like that every year counts now .... She said she was turning forty. That means fifty or sixty. It's like fucking your own mother ... you can't do it ... it's impossible.

In this passage, Miller captures, in livelier language to be sure, the brittle, saggy, unyielding female who Robert Wilson in *Feminine Forever* warns us we will someday become if we don't take estrogen.

However, not all women in literature turn brittle or lose their sexual drive at the menopause, nor even their appeal to men. Molly Bloom, in her middle age, is still an Andalusian flower. After menopause Mrs. Stone, no longer subject to the "red tides," finds that, with the danger of pregnancy gone, she is capable of "desire and its possible gratification." She feels no physical deterioration following the menopause. "On the contrary, now that her body was rising out of the tangled woods of the climacteric, she felt a great resurgence of physical well-being." Unfortunately, the new energy leads her to the wrong man, a younger version of Henry Miller's friend Carl, a man who makes his living servicing women. It is the lover's rejection of her that causes Mrs. Stone's degeneration.

Some of the women in fiction who pull through the change with renewed vigor do so without relating sexually to a man. Meg Eliot of Angus Wilson's novel recovers after being nursed by her homosexual brother. She recovers and eventually leaves him to become the personal secretary of a woman member of parliament. The heroine of May Sarton's novel *Mrs. Stevens Hears the Mermaids Singing* experiences nothing that Ms. Sarton calls the menopause. But at the age of forty-five, Mrs. Stevens finds a new Muse, Dorothea, and from this relationship Mrs. Stevens creates new art. Ada Ewing, the main character of O'Hara's *The Ewings*, discovers sexual rebirth and a new life at the age of fifty-two. She masturbates for the first time and enjoys it. She also has an affair with a younger woman but eventually leaves town and goes to the West Coast to live with a woman her own age, leaving behind the son and daughter-in-law who had been so concerned that she would be suicidal or depressed during the menopause.

But the two best-known symbols in literature for menopausal renewal have been with us longer than Ada Ewing or Molly Bloom. One is Penelope, the character from the *Odyssey* on whom Molly is modeled. Penelope, who waits faithfully for her husband while he fights wars and seduces goddesses, grows old in his absence. When she and Odysseus are reunited, Penelope describes her suffering:

> Think what difficulty the gods gave: they denied us life together in our prime and flowering years, kept us from crossing into age together.

In the reunion, nonetheless, the gods are kind. For Athena makes both husband and wife younger, more attractive, more desirable than either had been during the separation. Both they and Ithaca are restored.

Chaucer's Wife of Bath is a more realistic and less monogamous menopausal model than Penelope. In the course of her very active life, the sensuous Wife wears out five husbands, thus reversing the stereotype of the aging *male* who runs through a series of young mates. "The Wife of Bath's Tale" also has menopausal implications. In that story, a young knight is forced to marry the old hag who saves his life by telling him what women want: mastery over men. On their wedding night, the hero is miserable; he is unable to kiss his wife because she is so "foule," so "lothly and so old," so ill-bred. After a long lecture, the aged wife asks him to choose between a wife who is "foule and old" but humble and a wife who is "yong and fair" but apt to entertain visitors. The knight, in keeping with the spirit of the story, turns the choice over to his wife. Now that she has mastery, she changes into a beautiful and young but faithful wife.

In the world of epics and folktales, menopausal women such as Penelope and the old hag are magically transformed into young women. In real life, there are no such options. Estrogen, the magical substance of our own scientific age, has some of the power of Athena's potion. But estrogen will not take away the wrinkles already there nor straighten bent backs.

The twentieth-century Penelope, Molly Bloom, had neither magic nor synthetic hormones to halt the aging process. Molly's solution was to keep on living, to affirm the power of her womanhood. In her soliloquy, the dominant word is *yes*.

> I love flowers I'd love to have the whole place swimming in roses . . . yes he said I was a flower of the mountain yes so we are flowers all a womans body yes that was one true thing he said in his life and the sun shines for you today yes that was why I like him because he saw he understood or felt what a woman is . . . and first I put my arms around him yes and drew him down to me so he could feel my breasts

all perfume yes and his heart was going like mad and yes I said yes I will Yes!

Molly's monologue occurs while she is menstruating. Although worried about her irregularity and afraid that she should see a doctor, Molly still affirms the flowering and bleeding of her body, aware as she does so of the inevitable wilting. Like the Wife of Bath, she has mastery over herself.

Afterword to Part 5: The Menopause

The menopause remains, particularly in literature, the most neglected phase of the menstrual cycle. Novelists, poets, and anthropologists are far more curious about puberty rites than about midlife passage; in most cultures the November of the body goes by quietly, without ceremony.[2] Although significant research has been done in the psychological and medical investigation of the menopause, the general concerns are what they were in 1976, with women still being prey to the uncertainties of hormone replacement therapy (HRT) and to promises of eternal youth.

Recent medical studies tend to address the three physiological symptoms of menopause which relate to estrogen fluctuation—hot flashes, vaginal dryness, and changes in menstrual flow. Many of these studies raise the issue of estrogen and cancer. A 1982 investigation by R. Don Gambrell, Jr., applauded estrogen for preventing bone loss and heart disease but concluded that "unopposed estrogen therapy increases the risk of endrometrial cancer," a risk which Gambrell claimed to be, however, "greatly overestimated."[3] In the same year Barbara Hulka found the risk of breast cancer to be greater for short-term rather than long-term use, and four times greater with injectable rather than oral products.[4] Recently the same Dr. Gambrell was quoted as saying that a combined estrogen/progestin treatment actually decreases the risk of breast cancer.[5]

These investigations by Gambrell, Hulka, Carr, Jenson, and others represent the efforts of medical researchers over the past decade to document the advantages and disadvantages of hormone replacement.[6] Estimates from 1986 indicate that four million women in America are taking some form of estrogen replacement therapy.[7] Yet as we write, the medical community has still to produce conclusions definitive enough to dispel our earlier skepticism, voiced one year before the FDA warned about possible cancer risk for women using estrogen replacement.

One of the most sensitive of the recent articles on drugs and the menopause was written by Kathleen I. Mac Pherson, an associate professor in the School of Nursing at the University of Maine. Mac Pherson is so concerned about distortions surrounding the menopause that she attacks the medical, political, and economic establishments for having transformed a natural process into a disease. Mac Pherson, an activist nurse, deplores the intervention of drug companies (Searle, Upjohn, and Ayerst laboratories) in the promotion of Robert Wilson's "Feminine Forever" theory. Ayerst Laboratories actually funded a so-called Information Center on the Mature Woman—without telling the public where the money was coming from. Until 1976 and the cancer warnings, Ayerst's slogan was "Keep Her on Premarin."[8]

Better news about estrogen comes from Penny Wise Budoff, M.D., who in 1983 published a medical best seller called *No More Hot Flashes and Other Good News*. Budoff, who has been administering a combined dosage of estrogen and progesterone to her patients since the mid-1970s, claims that since both estrogen and progesterone are depleted during the menopause, then both should be replaced to maintain hormonal balance. Hormone replacement therapy (HRT) spreads other good menopausal news—no more vaginal dryness, no more postmenopausal blues, no greater risk of breast cancer. Budoff, whose therapy has received wide medical approval, nonetheless cautions that certain women should not use HRT, especially women with suspected breast cancer or blood clotting. She also insists that research into hormonal matters continue and that such research be taken seriously by the medical profession. For as we know from past experience, the bad news too often follows, delayed sometimes for years as people in laboratories document the effects of diethylstilbestrol, clonidine, tampons, the "pill," the IUD, nicotine, estinyl, aerobics, and aspirin on the female body.[9]

One innovative form of estrogen replacement is the skin patch, developed by Ciba Pharmaceutical Company and approved in the fall of 1986 by the Federal Food and Drug Admimistration. The patch is placed on the abdomen and should be changed two times a week. According to reports, it delivers low dosages of estrogen directly into the bloodstream and offers fewer complications than estrogen pills, which must be metabolized by the liver. However, doctors testing the patch caution that women using this method of estrogen replacement, like those women taking estrogen orally, must combine estrogen with progestin and have "regular checkups and endometrial biopsies."[10]

The Boston Women's Health Collective has been, almost from the inception of the new women's movement, articulating the doubts and concerns of women at large. In their updated *New Our Bodies, Ourselves,* they are fairly negative about hormone therapy, offering in its place certain nonmedical approaches to the problems surrounding the menopause. Among these are vitamins (especially C, D, and E), diet, herbal teas, meditation, acupuncture, sex, and exercise.[11]

Sex and exercise are getting considerable attention as remedies for the midlife crisis. In a special "Over-40" issue of *Harper's Bazaar,* Dr. Morton Walker claims that "sex—either intercourse or masturbation—can provide relief by keeping vaginal tissues toned and moist and releasing endorphins, the body's pleasure chemicals."[12] An editorial in the *Journal of the American Medical Association* tells where to send for a battery-operated machine which will improve vaginal muscle tone during the menopause.[13]

For midlife exercise without batteries, one might consult Jane Fonda. Her *Women Coming of Age,* offers a sensible approach to the process of aging, from the point of view of a woman who has thought about it and is going there.[14] Like *The New Our Bodies, Ourselves, Women Coming of Age* is skeptical of estrogen replacement therapy. Fonda urges that women in serious need of estrogen combine it with progestin and that women keep informed on medical findings about hormone replacement. Fonda's program emphasizes the Prime Time Workout, an exercise plan designed for midlife problem areas—the back, the joints, the muscles.

Such basic diet-exercise ideas are becoming more and more common in popular magazines, an example being Carol Kahn's "The Total Anti-Aging Plan," whose title is an unfortunate rejecting of a life process rather than an intelligent accepting of it. Still, the content of Kahn's program helps to neutralize the Cosmetic Answer promoted in these same supermarket publications—face lifts, tummy tucks, mega-moisturizers, wrinkle-concealer wands.[15]

Reduction in estrogen levels has also been linked with another unidentified symptom of midlife, namely "menopausal depression." It is telling that Penny Wise Budoff, who speaks so confidently of HRT as a treatment for hot flashes and bone deterioration, is far less emphatic when she discusses "postmenopausal blues." Budoff does not recommend hormones as a cure-all for midlife depression. She does believe such treatment useful in cases where women in generally good mental health throughout their lives develop signs of depression in the mid-forties. She also feels that HRT is a safer remedy than the tranquilizers and antidepressants so frequently prescribed at the menopause.[16] On the other hand, in a survey of recent British findings, Madeline Osborn concludes that there is *no* clearly proven association between estrogen and menopausal depression. "The result of treatment trials with oestrogen have on the whole been disappointing. It seems wisest to treat the depressed menopausal patients with methods that are appropriate to depression at *any other time of life.*"[17]

Researchers appear to be turning more and more toward cultural explanations for menopausal depression. Investigations by Malkah Notman, Paula Weideger, Kathleen Mac Pherson, Arne Holte, and others suggest that the negative symptoms associated with the menopause have less to do with hormonal change than with other coinciding midlife crises—children leaving, the death of a parent, economic problems, divorce, job dissatisfaction, sexual dissatisfaction, and so forth.[18] Psychiatrist Maggie Scarf in fact suggests that "a special form of female depression—precipitated by the hormone changes accompanying ovarian-reproductive-system decline—actually doesn't exist at all."[19]

The symbolic importance of the menopause might in fact bear greater weight than the occasional physiological or psychological disturbances. Throughout our menstrual lives we may have felt depressed, been unable to sleep, or noticed wrinkles under the eyes. But the actual changing of the cycle, the expectation that soon there will be no blood, brings into focus other common signs of aging, labeled "menopause," that we had simply been ignoring.

In our search for literature about the menopause, we have unearthed very little fiction, new or old, to add to our survey. The program *"Golden Girls"* keeps the topic alive on television, but novels, from what we have seen, depict middle-aged women without their menopausal fears.[20]

In her work on black women writers, however, Mary Jane has discovered two crucial references to the menopause in the novels of Zora Neale Hurston. In *Their Eyes Were Watching God* (1937) the heroine, Janie Crawford, returns home to Eatonville, her homecoming ironically coinciding with her menopause. She then, like Demeter and other midlife fertility figures, plants seeds, as if to continue the life cycle despite the fact that Janie herself had never borne fruit. In Hurston's last novel, *Seraph on the Suwanee* (1948), the menopause is more directly and far less favorably treated. Arvey Meserve, the menopausal wife, is dependent and terrified as she goes through the change of life. Identifying herself completely within the closed sphere of wife and mother, Arvey faces the early autumn of her womb with self-hatred.[21]

One is more likely to encounter the menopausal hag in works from independent women's presses. One such publication, *Broomstick,* is directed specifically to women over forty. The lead story in the September-October 1986 issue is a fantasy called "The Change," about full moons, werewolves, and Hilde, a menopausal woman. Hilde's "change" is not typical. She becomes a werewolf: "It started happening after my 'change.' I suddenly felt more powerful. At first I only felt hot flashes. But one night I was outside, and the moon was full. I looked down and saw the fur on my arms and hands. I had changed."[22]

In poetry, dreams, and folklore the moon, usually the empty moon, is associated with the "change." When the moon in her continuous cycle vanishes from view, we have Mother Nature's closest parallel to the menopause.

Nisa, the !Kung woman in Marjorie Shostak's anthrobiography, describes her midlife change as the moon leaving: "One month I felt a little pain and then I menstruated. The next month, I felt even more uncomfortable. After than, the moon left me and I didn't see any more periods. But the discomfort remains. Because, when the moon doesn't come to you, it causes your insides to hurt."[23]

Distance from the moon is the theme of a brittle poem by Virgina Terris called "At 59":

> The moon comes up.
> I don't rush to meet it.
> It goes down.
> I don't care.
> The moon isn't my sister.
>
> I have joined the old women
> who no longer
> cringe at her rising.
>
> I laugh at the traps
> she sets others.
> My bones point to the stars.
> That's how I travel.

Terris, finished with the moon change, stands outside of the menstrual process, free to laugh at her trapped sisters, at the moon herself. The aloofness expressed in "At 59" shows a positive response to the empty-moon syndrome, with its promises of weeping and depression.[24]

In a special issue on aging published in late 1976, the feminist journal *Women* explored in depth the midlife passage of women. The essays, fiction, and poetry touched on many aspects of menopausal and post-menopausal life. A number of poems published in this issue deal with menopausal attitudes; most of them offer positive solutions to the problems of "change-of-life."[25] In Mary Winfrey's "at menopause" the poet compares her body to a fruitless grapevine. Although the grapes are gone, the vine continues to grow strong and to give shelter: "people shelter beneath me like birds my roots send/ more roots into the kind earth, never has the earth been kinder." Like May Sarton's tree in "She Shall Be Called Woman "(quoted in Chapter 18), so Winfrey's strong, sinewy grapevine celebrates the endurance and vitality of the female body.

The aging issue of *Women* has a number of imaginative responses to the menopause, including one brutal poem in which a woman sees herself as a half-chewed bone that someday will lie clean in the desert sun, "Having to nourish no one!" Harriet Murphy's sense of having been eaten alive by others is indeed disturbing, especially if we interpret the resolution of the poem to signify death. However, the clean, discarded bone could also be a symbol of the menopause, when nature is no longer making its insistent demands on woman's body. Like the empty moon, so the sun-bleached bone is freed from responsibility.

The harshness in the above poem reflects the enormous anger which many women discovered in themselves during the 1970s, as they began to question the roles they had long been accustomed to playing—housewife, daughter, mother. In "Midpoint," the lead poem in the aging issue, Kathy Kozachenko uses the menopause as the cycle in which the anger ascends, erupts, subsides.

> She stored up the anger
> for twenty-five years,
> then she put it on the table
> like a casserole for dinner.
>
> "I have stolen back
> my life," she said.
> "I have taken possession
> of the rain and the sun
> and the grasses," she said.
>
> "You are talking
> like a madwoman,"
> he said.
>
> "My hands are rocks,
> my teeth are bullets,"
> she said.

"You are my wife"
he said.

"My throat is an eagle.
My breasts,
are two
white hurricanes," she said.

"Stop!" he said.
"Stop or I shall call
a doctor."

"My hair
is a hornet's nest,
my lips
are thin snakes
waiting for their victim."

He cooked his own dinners,
after that.

The doctors diagnosed it
common change-of-life.

She, too, diagnosed
it change of life.
And on leaving the hospital
she said to her woman-friend
"My cheeks
are the wings
of a young virgin dove.
Kiss them."

The first metaphor of the poem emerges from the woman's domestic life; she serves her anger "like a casserole." The images become progressively more violent as she identifies herself with rocks, bullets, hurricanes, the destructive Medusa from Greek myth: "my lips/are thin snakes/waiting for their victim." Her madness is diagnosed "change-of-life," a cliche which Kozachenko uses ironically, in that indeed life has changed both for husband and for wife. He now cooks his own dinners. She has been transformed from eagle to dove, from "crazy" housewife to a woman-identified woman.

"Midpoint" represents an extreme response to the midlife crisis and particularly to the unhappy marriage which triggers her anger. Most menopausal women don't end up in hospitals. Yet the heightened discourse between male and female in Kozachenko's poem gives breath to feelings shared by many women in the mid-1970s and right now—feelings too dangerous to articulate. Break-ups and break-downs have long been associated with the end of the menstrual cycle. What Kozachenko, Terris, and other recent poets reveal is that the change of life can be an affirmation of our uniquely female experience and an opportunity for new directions.

PART SIX

Sideshow

Chapter 23

The Menstrual Hall of Fame

On a fancy Long Island beach, a young woman goes for a midnight swim. She is bitten in half by a shark. All that rolls ashore is her head on her shoulders. Later, it's suggested that she had her period, a thing attractive to sharks.

This grisly incident is the trigger for the plot in Peter Benchley's 1974 novel, *Jaws*. A similar real-life event happened in the summer of 1967, in Glacier National Park, Montana. Two young women campers were mauled to death by a grizzly bear. It was later said that one of them had been menstruating and that the smell of blood had enticed the bear.

Probably no famous queens or female leaders have been cut off in midcareer by sharks or grizzly bears, but menstruation has sometimes changed the course of history. If Queen Elizabeth I had menstruated regularly, she might have married, might have had a child and changed the future of the British monarchy. If the seventeenth-century American reformer Anne Hutchinson had not been undergoing menopause at a critical time, she might have given birth to a child rather than the premature deformity that confirmed her enemies' belief that she was a witch. The biblical Salome allegedly suffered from menstrual cramps. Was her request for John the Baptist's head a desire for revenge against the non-menstruators of the human race, a desire to see a man bleed?

Joan of Arc, it is said, never menstruated at all; she was twenty when she was burned at the stake. The eccentric French historian Jules Michelet writes of Joan that "in her the life of the spirit dominated, absorbed the lower life, and held in check its *vulgar infirmities*. . . . She grew up to be robust and handsome; *but the physical curse of women never affected her.*" Although Michelet seems to regard the possibility of Joan's menstruating with disgust, he was fascinated with his own wife's monthly bleedings and recorded them meticulously: date and time of day they began, color and character of the discharge, his feelings (but rarely hers) about the flow. His observations may still be read today in his *Journal.*[1]

For Joan of Arc, lack of periods may have been useful in battle. For Queen Mary I of England (1516-1558) and her younger half sister, Elizabeth I (1533-1603), their childlessness (probably due to syphilis inherited from their father, Henry VIII) created great dynastic problems. Queen Mary suffered all her life from "ischomenia" (now called *amenorrhea,* or lack of periods). Without success, she tried all the medical remedies known to her era: bleeding; manus Christi (literally, "the hand of Christ," an exotic mixture of powdered pearls, gold leaf, sugar, and rose water, to be eaten in the morning with the yolk of an egg), and "aqua composita" (a compound of Gascoigne wine, infusion of ginger, galingale, which is another kind of ginger, camomile, cinnamon, nutmeg, grains, cloves, and anise seed). Mary's barrenness, left uncured by these remedies, was a source of great unhappiness to her and a cause of the rift between her and her husband, King Philip II of Spain. Her nickname in history, bestowed because of her fierce persecutions of Protestants, is curiously ironic: Bloody Mary.

The Roman Catholic Mary desperately wanted a child so that the throne would not pass to her Protestant half sister, Elizabeth. But Elizabeth, it turned out, was also childless (she was succeeded by James I, a cousin whose wife bore the necessary son). Elizabeth, known as the Virgin Queen, never married; it is frequently said that she did not want to share her throne with a man. But her periods were infrequent, and it may be that she assumed she was sterile and hence felt no need to legitimize her relationships with the male flatterers who always surrounded her. Or she may have indeed preferred chastity to the possibility of dying in childbirth, which was not uncommon in her era.

Elizabeth became queen in 1558; by the following year, there were many rumors that she was sterile and that her frequent bleedings were intended to remedy her lack of periods. Her laundresses noticed that she had very few monthly periods, and this fact became widely known. In addition to bleedings, Elizabeth also followed the directions of Lord Cecil, her chief adviser: Use only foods and scents "vouched for"; avoid irritant skin poisons by checking carefully anything touching her bare body; keep doors closed where her laundresses and wardrobe women did their work. Elizabeth's regimen was, apparently, no more successful than Mary's.

In seventeenth-century America, it was not uncommon for a woman who behaved improperly—a shrew, a gossip, a religious questioner—to be considered a witch. This was the case of Anne Hutchinson (1591-1643) of Massachusetts, who preached the doctrine of salvation through grace and argued that women should have a voice in church affairs. Because she was successful in medicine (healing herbs) and midwifery, she acquired a ready following for her theological opinions. Mistress Hutchinson was placed on trial for these opinions in 1637.

During this trial, she was pregnant and seriously ill, but she was not allowed to sit down until it was obvious that she could no longer stand; her archenemy, Governor John Winthrop, records unfeelingly that "her countenance discovered some bodily infirmity."[2] Because of her ill health, she was finally broken and unable to carry on her defense; as a result, she was excommunicated and banished from the colony.

Menopausal pregnancy seems to have been the cause of Anne Hutchinson's medical troubles. She suffered from hot flashes and other symptoms. During her menopause, she aborted New England's first hydatidiform (watery) mole. Dr. John Clarke, a physician and preacher, described this "monstrous birth" with grotesque precision. It was "twenty-seven lumps of man's seed without any alteration or mixture of anything from the woman . . . every one of them greatly confused." The lumps were knit together by strings, which Clarke believed were the beginnings of veins and nerves and which were snarled together. The lumps contained "partly wind and partly water"; six of them were as large as a man's fist, and one as large as two fists. "The globes were round things included in the lumps, about the smallness of a small Indian bean, and like the pearl in a man's eye. The two lumps which differed from the rest were like liver or congealed blood, and had no small globes in them as the rest had."[3] This was taken as a further sign of her being a witch and did not help her case.

Anne Hutchinson's troubles were probably increased by the psychological stresses of the trial. Queen Marie Antoinette (1755-1793), anticipating the guillotine, developed traumatic menstrual bleeding several days before her execution. On that final day, she had wanted to wear a white dress, the color of royal mourning, but found her chemise stained with blood. The gendarme refused to let her out of his sight to change her clothes, so she crouched in the narrow space between the bed and the wall, with the kitchen maid standing between her and the gendarme, to hide her nakedness. She was ashamed to leave her soiled linen for the prying eyes of those who would examine her cell after she was gone, so she stuffed her chemise into a crevice in the wall behind the stove. Her bleeding served as one of her final punishments.

Emma Goldman, the feminist-anarchist (1869–1940), was known as "Red Emma the Witch"—but for her politics, not her periods. Her periods were, however, irregular and painful. Like Marie Antoinette, she bled as a result of psychological stress. When her family was being smuggled from Konigsberg in 1881 to escape the pogroms, young Emma's period came early, "due to the excitement of our departure," she writes in her autobiography, *Living My Life*. The family had to plunge through icy water, and Emma says "the sudden chill froze my blood; then I felt a stinging sensation in my spine, abdomen, and legs, as if I were being pierced with hot irons."[4] When they reached their destination, Emma was given hot tea, packed in hot bricks, and covered with a large feather bed. She was an invalid for weeks; her spine remained weak for years afterward.

As an adult, Emma found her periods were still painful and consulted a doctor who suggested an operation that would free her from menstrual pain, allow her to have full sexual pleasure, and enable her to have children. But consulting her political ideals, Emma finally decided to "find an outlet for my mother-need in the love of *all* children." The operation did not take place. Emma devoted her life to writing and political action.

Other women writers have suffered from menstruation. The British poet Elizabeth Barrett Browning (1806–1861) took opium for her cramps and may have become addicted. Olive Schreiner (1855–1920), the South African-British novelist, suffered greatly from premenstrual tension that prevented her from working. She lamented that her friend Eleanor Marx (Karl's daughter) was the only person with whom she could discuss her trouble. The French novelist George Sand (1804–1876) once mistook menstrual pains for a serious fever and later said apologetically to her husband, "I was afraid that I might be threatened with a serious illness, but realize now that this indisposition coincided with the bad time of the month for me."[5] It also coincided with her first adultery.

For the British novelist Virginia Woolf (1882-1941), however, menstruation unleashed the flow of imagination. In her diary entry for February 18, 1928, she records that

> I had thought to write the quickest most brilliant pages in Orlando yesterday—not a drop came, all, forsooth, for the usual physical reasons, which delivered themselves today. It is the oddest feeling: as if a finger stopped the flow of the ideas in the brain; it is unsealed and the blood rushes all over the place.[6]

Menstruation, then, is not always an impediment to women. Although it may be an embarrassment or a source of pain, it may also be a liberation, as with Virginia Woolf and with Lizzie Borden, that legendary New England murderess (1860–1927). When her period coincided with an epileptic attack, she took an ax to her parents and left them both bloody, both dead.

Lizzie had always been noted for "peculiar spells" that had all the symptoms of what is now called *epilepsy of the temporal lobe,* or *psychomotor epilepsy.* Popular opinion in Fall River, Massachusetts, held that "poor Lizzie was always sort of crazy."

Her epileptic seizures came only during her menstrual period, and then only three or four times a year. The spells were brief, no more than an hour long, and ceased when Lizzie reached menopause. In the previous year, Lizzie had committed a daylight robbery of her own house during a menstrual-epileptic seizure. She had her period on August 4, 1892, the morning of the murders; this is a matter of court record.

Murder during an epileptic seizure is rare, and one cannot say that Lizzie killed her parents (actually, her father and stepmother) *because* of her epilepsy; but all evidence indicates that she killed the stepmother, at least, *during* a seizure. She had wanted to kill her stepmother earlier; the day before, she had tried to buy prussic acid (a form of cyanide) for the purpose, but the druggist refused to sell it to her. So she was forced to use an ax. Contrary to the folk rhyme, she gave her father only twenty whacks with the ax and her stepmother only ten.

At her inquest and trial, Lizzie benefited from the confusion of blood. Was the blood on her skirt menstrual or matricidal-patricidal? Menstruation was a delicate subject, especially when discussed in front of the all-male juries of that time. At the inquest, Lizzie was asked how a bloodstain could get on her skirt. She answered, "I have fleas" (still another euphemism for menstruation). The kind of spot she had could hardly be from her period, however. A female jury, Victoria Lincoln notes, would not have acquitted Lizzie, for women knew that

> over their heavy napkins, women wore ruffled drawers to the knee and short white petticoats under the underskirt. . . . A widish smear caused by a heavy period was quite possible; a small, clear-edged spot, so placed, would have been wildly improbable even if it had come from the inside, not the outside, of the garment.[7]

After she was acquitted of the murders—although everyone assumed she had committed them—Lizzie Borden was ostracized in Fall River, where she remained until her death. She is still, as far as we know, the only menstrual murderess.

Afterword

We may have been the first, but alas were not the last, to chronicle the cramps and craziness that may have changed the world. The books that followed *The Curse* were eager to continue the "hall of fame" genre, notably Norris and Sullivan's *PMS: Premenstrual Syndrome*. Now, with the experience of age and twelve more years of menstruating, we wonder why we were so eager to celebrate the Lizzie Bordens and other menstrual madwomen, instead of the millions of the rest of us who manage families and nations, corporations and classrooms, who face the empty page, the washing machine, the assembly line, the unsown field, and the unsewn hem while we are premenstrually "tense," or bleeding through our tampons, or doubled over with cramps. These should be the real members of a menstrual hall of fame, along with the hundreds of women all over the world who are doing scientific, medical, sociological, and psychological research into menstruation and its meaning in the quality of women's lives. You will find evidence of their work throughout this edition. Please consider the whole book a menstrual hall of fame.

Chapter 24

Moving the Menses, or Vicarious Menstruation

A woman does not have to bleed from the womb alone. The extremely rare phenomenon *vicarious menstruation* is a monthly bleeding from a mucous membrane other than the uterus. Most of the cases (70 percent) are *supplementary;* that is, bleeding occurs along with the regular menstrual flow. The other 30 percent are *substitutive;* that is, bleeding occurs some place other than the uterus, sometimes even after menopause.[1]

The most common place is the nose, the site of 30 percent of vicarious menstruation.[2] Most women's nasal mucosa become red and swollen before their periods. This swelling, aptly named *rhinorrhea,* is a part of the premenstrual syndrome. If unusual hormonal changes occur, the period may come in two places at once.[3]

Fortunately, the blood lost through vicarious menstruation is usually scanty. Vicarious menstruation has not been studied extensively. Physicians still cite a 1920 report by O. H. Roth, who examined 225 cases of vicarous menstruation reported between 1870 and 1920.[4] Roth found that 30 percent of the cases of bleeding occurred in the nose; 18 percent, in uterine ulcers; 8 percent each, in the skin and in the lungs; 5 percent, in the breasts; and the rest, in the stomach, mouth pharynx, bladder, ears, eyes, larynx, and vagina. (It should be recalled that the menstrual fluid, although it passes through the vagina, does not originate there. The uterus, not the vagina, bleeds.)

Vicarious menstruation does have its human-interest side. In 1882, J. T. Gordon reported the case of Mrs. H., who was forty-one years old and weighed 254 pounds. She had profuse bleeding from her thumb; the bleeding had occurred simultaneously with her period for more than three years. The bleeding lasted three to five days; a bandage around it had to be changed frequently. When the spot was not bleeding, it could be recognized "only by a slight blueness of the skin over an area not larger than a half pea." Mrs. H. reported no pain from her thumb while it was bleeding and added that "it rather feels good."[5]

It is tempting to regard the female *stigmatics*, those saints whose bodies bleed in different spots in imitation of Christ's wounds, as vicarious menstruators. However, the stigmata of three of the best known (Catherine de Ricci, Marie de Moerl, and Louise Lateau) appeared every Thursday noon through Friday afternoon, not monthly.

Why do the vicarious menstruate where they do? Psychoanalyst Helene Deutsch claims that the choice of organ for vicarious menstruation is determined by the patient's psyche. There is little evidence to prove or disprove her, but there are medical reasons for the phenomenon.

Most common is sensitivity of some tissues to a high level of estrogen in the blood, with the mucous membranes of the nose being most likely to be affected by it. The other possible source of vicarious menstruation is surgical error. Bits of the lining of the womb may be mistakenly implanted in the incision during cesarean sections, removal of fibroid tumors, or in episiotomy during childbirth. The lining of the womb will menstruate wherever it is.

The unfortunate victims of medical mistakes or hormonal sensitivity can be helped. Vitamins K, C, and P will strengthen capillary walls. As the last resort, medical texts recommend "castration" (presumably hysterectomy). But for most women, who suffer nothing more serious than a nosebleed, vicarious menstruation is a minor annoyance.

Afterword

Vicarious menstruation is treated vicariously elsewhere in this book. In the Afterword to "Woman Unclean" we observe this phenomenon in John Pielmeier's 1984 play *Agnes of God*. Agnes bleeds from her hands, in imitation of Christ's wounds (*stigmata*) but also in imitation of menstrual blood, which is a sign of Agnes's human sexuality.

Director Brian de Palma makes excellent use of displaced or vicarious menstruation in a number of his films. In *The Fury* (1979) the teen-aged heroine is capable of making people bleed from their hands and their nostrils, a gift clearly connected with the displacement of menstrual blood.

And in de Palma's *Body Double* (1984) a menstruating actress bleeds from her breasts. But the film which would surely win the Academy Award for Vicarious Menstruation is *Carrie* (1976), also directed by Brian de Palma and based on the 1974 novel by Stephen King (which we discuss in Chapter 17). The opening scene occurs in a gym. When ignorant Carrie starts to bleed, her classmates throw tampons at her. This is Carrie's menarche, her first *real* menstruation. The menstrual theme is repeated throughout the film, climaxing at the moment when a bucket of pig's blood is dumped on Carrie from above the stage. The camera shows a blood-drenched Carrie, who is bleeding everywhere—from her hair, her lips, her arms, her shoulders, her feet. Brian has moved Carrie's menses from the shower to the stage, from her vagina to her entire body, so that she visually resembles a saturated tampon. Much of this scene is photographed with a red filter. Even the camera, it seems, is menstruating vicariously.[7].

Chapter 25

Escaping the Monthlies

"No woman would menstruate if she did not have to," Germaine Greer has said.[1] And it is a rare woman, indeed, who hasn't at some time wished she didn't menstruate; many a female has cursed the curse. But there is very little she can do about it except wait for pregnancy or menopause.

Medical texts list many causes for amenorrhea. Most are exotic, if not impossible to attain. Turner's syndrome, for instance, is characterized by a lack of periods. But women born with this syndrome also have low-set ears, a webbed neck, and a low intellect, and are unlikely to be more than 4 feet 8 inches in height. There is also the Stein-Leventhal syndrome, characterized by loss of menstruation and fertility, ovaries that are "oysterlike" in appearance, and abnormal growth of facial hair.

For most women, menstruation is virtually inescapable, although there have been attempts to thwart it. In 1934, a Los Angeles physician named George Starr White published a peculiar book entitled *The Emancipation of Women, or Regulating the Duration of the Menses*. White felt that women's periods are "unnatural," that the normal state is a natural mucous flow, like that of animals. Moreover, the more "naturally" a woman lived, the shorter the duration of her menses was, according to White.

Finally, he discovered a process called *Naturizing*, invented by his family physician to stop the menstrual flow for circus performers. It consists of the doctor's inserting a tampon under the uterus while pressing on a woman's abdomen. The next day, the doctor removes the tampon and replaces it. With this method, the flow usually does not last more than two or three days, regardless of previous bleeding. After four or five months, the average case becomes a "one-day woman"; after a year, she may be in the "one-hour class."[2]

White claims that the treatment was successful in fifteen case histories he provides and that it has added benefits. It eliminates pimples and rough skin, and the daughters and granddaughters and great-granddaughters of women treated this way have no blood in their menstrual flow, which lasts only a few hours.

The success of White's method seems unlikely; the inheritance of acquired characteristics, impossible. Nevertheless, White was attempting to fulfill a need that standard medical science has still not answered. What, indeed, does a circus performer do if she has a heavy flow?

There are several things she can do that will not work. In Katherine Anne Porter's *Old Mortality,* the girls suck on salt and lemon in order to stop their periods before going to a ball. Instead, they just make themselves sick. *Warren's Household Physician* (1901), a handbook commonly used around the turn of the century, strongly advises girls against dipping their feet in cold water to stop their periods. According to Warren, "The most lovely and innocent girls have done this for the purpose of attending a party; and, in some instances, the stoppage induced has ended in death within a few hours."[3]

In both of these instances, the girls want to halt their periods because of social events, not because their professional fulfillment might be impaired. Frivolous rather than serious reasons are given. Perhaps it is the same failure to take women seriously that has kept medicine from finding a way to end menstruation, short of menopause. Nevertheless, there are several ways, none of them conducive to good health, in which menstruation can be ended.

One is pathological dieting, the refusal to eat called *anorexia nervosa,* which is fundamentally an emotional disturbance. The woman with this disease is usually bright, articulate, self-disciplined, but with a horror of fat. She rarely eats more than token meals, may make herself vomit, and exercises compulsively. She will cease menstruating, but she may also starve to death if she is not given medical and psychological treatment.

Other illnesses may also cause missed periods. One is tuberculosis. White warns his readers against folklore: "The idea that the eradication of blood from the menstrual period will cause tuberculosis, is rank superstition and based on no finding of fact."[4] Instead, the reverse is true; tuberculosis in advanced stages will cause the eradication of the menses. But as in the case of anorexia nervosa, loss of periods is a sign of loss of good health.

Another illness that will end menstruation is heroin addiction. Addiction to opiates commonly causes infertility, lack of ovulation, and loss of menstruation, probably through the action of drugs on the hypothalamus, a part of the brain. In one study, 67 percent of women heroin addicts entering a methadone maintenance program menstruated infrequently, if at all. After they had been on methadone for two months, all but one resumed their regular periods. Poor nutrition is probably a factor in the missed periods (as it is with anorexia nervosa) because the women placed on methadone were also given better, supervised diets. Women addicts who withdraw without methadone take longer to regain their cycles.[5]

Menstruation can be eliminated through good health, claim the followers of Dr. Shelton's School of Hygiene. The Sheltonians see menstruation itself as the illness, as did the nineteenth-century gynecologist Dr. A. F. A. King. King's "cure" for the menstrual disease was continual pregnancies; Shelton's is proper care of the abdominal organs. As the common toad bloodlessly sheds its skin, as the bird bloodlessly sheds its feathers, so a truly healthy woman can shed her membranes without bleeding.[6] One woman has written to us that she has followed Shelton's prescription of diet and exercise and that she no longer menstruates.

Menstruation may also be ended by the atomic bomb. One of the effects of radiation sickness, as it appeared after the bombing of Hiroshima, was the cessation of menstruation. John Hersey writes in *Hiroshima*: "And, as if nature were protecting man against his own ingenuity, the reproductive processes were affected for a time; men became sterile, women had miscarriages, menstruation stopped."[7]

There remains the possibility of hysterectomy, the surgical method of ending menstruation. In a complete hysterectomy, the uterus is removed (the removal of the ovaries is called an *oophorectomy*.) With no uterus, there is no lining of the uterus; hence, no menstruation. Although many American doctors, as we have noted, are eager to perform hysterectomies (perhaps they should be called *remunerectomies*, so profitable are they for the practitioners), the operation is a serious and expensive one and does not increase woman's control over her own body. She may also begin aging prematurely. It is not a practical solution to the bother of menstruation.

Undoubtedly the least unsafe suppressor of menstruation is the hormone. Hormones have been given to paraplegic and severely handicapped women and to women in plaster casts in order to stop their monthly bleeding until they are in better condition. The birth control pill and similar products can stop menstruation indefinitely if taken continually; prostitutes, as we have seen, use them for this purpose. But long-range side effects are unknown.

It is apparent that most "cures" for menstruation are worse than the curse. No one would prefer tuberculosis, heroin addiction, or the deadly embrace of an atomic bomb. But *menstrual extraction* may open a new era in women's history: an age of real control over our bodies, over the menstrual process.

Menstrual extraction was developed by women for women. A group of feminists in Los Angeles, at the Self-Help Clinic of the Feminist Women's Health Center, were troubled by menstruation and decided to end it. Lorraine Rothman, Carol Downer, and other women developed the technique, a very simple one.

In menstrual extraction, a woman or one of her friends may end her period almost as soon as it starts. When her bleeding begins, or when her period is due if she is late, she or her friend inserts into her uterus a tube (called a cannula) about one-tenth of an inch in diameter; this tube is attached to a collection bottle and to a syringe, about 6 inches long, that literally pumps out the period. The built-up lining of the womb, which is sloughed off naturally over several days of menstruation, is pumped away in minutes. Enthusiasts claim a "sixty-second period."

Menstrual extraction is not a backroom procedure. In November 1973, the feminists of Los Angeles presented a "Menstrual Extraction Review" for the American Public Health Association conference. The Self-Help Clinic performed a menstrual extraction for the women in the audience (the males, ten in an audience of over seventy people, were asked to leave and did so reluctantly). The response from the women was wildly enthusiastic, and the historic event was recorded on video tape.[8]

Two of the most unusual practitioners of menstrual extraction are Lolly and Jeanne Hirsch, a mother-and-daughter team who also publish *The Monthly Extract: An Irregular Periodical.* Traveling mostly on the East Coast, they appear before women's groups, showing women how to examine their genitals and demonstrating menstrual extraction on each other.

For the Hirsches and for the rest of us, menstrual extraction is revolutionary. It is cheap, quick, simple. It eliminates belts, pads, pins, plugs, and pains except for possible cramping during extraction. It gives a woman complete control of her body, for if she is pregnant, the process serves as a *mini-abortion* (another term used for the procedure). And there's the rub—or one of them.

Today, menstrual extraction is embroiled in controversy. There are those who question its safety: Will it cause infection, which might lead to pain, fever, and possibly hospitalization and a D and C? It is true that the female organs are more prone to infection during menstruation than at any other time in a woman's cycle, but physicians disagree about the likelihood of uterine infections. Does menstrual extraction always work? No one can be certain.

There are legal questions: Is it abortion? If it is, the state and the medical profession would like to control it. Similarly, is it practicing medicine without a license? Again, the medical profession steps in.

Currently, there are no certain answers to these questions. The health establishment has involved itself directly in the process. Calling it *menstrual regulation,* doctors used it experimentally on the raped women of Bangladesh. Nor is the profit motive far behind. As early as 1971, Upjohn considered manufacturing a do-it-yourself extraction kit—in time for Christmas gift giving.

Menstrual extraction has become a political as well as a health issue. The safety factor is ignored when profit and population control are possible; men, especially one Harvey Karman of Los Angeles, have claimed that they invented the procedure and should control it. When Ellen Frankfort first described the extraction process in the *Village Voice* in 1971, she received dozens of letters of protest from doctors about its supposed dangers. But, says Frankfort, the doctors were

> more upset at the independence that period extraction in particular and self-help in general gave women rather than at the dangers of either. Few argued or even considered that the device could be made safer; none remembered that the first camera or radio or airplane was not perfect and that only in time could a new invention be judged.[9]

Menstrual extraction is by far the most exciting discovery of the women's health movement. At the same time, the extraction controversy bears watching because it illustrates contemporary menstrual politics at work; will we be able to keep our newfound control over our own bodies, or will we once again have to submit to men's definitions of our needs?

Afterword

Today menstrual extraction is still considered an extralegal procedure, to be performed among women in advanced self-help groups. In no way has it become a mainstream alternative to the pains and pleasures of the more traditional ways of handling the monthly cycle. Some of the techniques of menstrual extraction have been incorporated into the vacuum-aspiration abortion techniques, performed in very early pregnancies, helping to make these the safest and least disruptive of all abortions. But the political realities of abortion itself continue to inhibit the further dissemination of menstrual extraction information among women and the study of both the immediate and long-term effects of repeated artificial evacuation of the contents of the uterus.

Lorraine Rothman of the Los Angeles Federation of Feminist Women's Health Centers told us that no one can do studies on menstrual extraction and determine its safety as long as it exists outside the law. She noted that extraction is rarely used in states or municipalities where abortion is readily available but that the "ultimate control" for women would be to be able to use the techniques for whatever reason they choose—be it relief of cramps or termination of pregnancy.[10]

Beryl Benderly, on the other hand, in *Thinking About Abortion* confronts menstrual extraction strictly as an "end run" around abortion, noting that it exposes women who are not pregnant to the risks of "surgery." If performed on a woman whose period is late, without testing for pregnancy, menstrual extraction obscures the real reason for the period's delay, possibly preventing the woman from getting the medical attention she needs.[11]

Whether women want to use menstrual extraction as an alternative to abortion or as a way of escaping the mess of menstruation, it is important to remember its orgins in the self-help movement, which has worked to give women knowledge, power, and ultimately control over their bodies. A single menstrual extraction is always performed by at least three women in the company of a group who meet regularly for the purpose, who are experienced with the techniques, and who are familiar with the physiological changes brought about by each others' menstrual cycles. Laura Punnett calls it "a form of woman-controlled medical research" and reminds us not to confuse it with "menstrual regulation," a procedure performed by physicians and used around the world as a form of population control.[12]

PART SEVEN

Men

Chapter 26

Saignade:
Simulated Menstruation
in the Male

Not content to surround menstruation with images of filth and fear, man has tried for at least a few aeons to learn how to do it himself. From time to time, men have participated either physically or intellectually in the *couvade,* the imagined motherhood of the male (from *couver,* to hatch). In certain societies, men imitate their wives as they give birth, suffer the pains, and receive all the attention when it's over.

Analogies to couvade abound in Western literature and myth. In Hemingway's story "Indian Camp," the Indian husband is so upset by his wife's pain in giving birth that he slits his own throat. In the medieval French romance, *Aucassin et Nicolette,* Aucassin gives birth, but he is beaten for so doing. Even some of the Greek gods are born without mothers: Athena from Zeus's forehead; Dionysus from his thigh; Aphrodite from Cronus's testicles thrown into the sea. All these seem to represent a male refusal to allow the birth-giving function to be solely female; the men want to share in and to define the act themselves.

Mary Ellmann points out the subtle couvade in Malamud's *The Fixer:*

> The heroism is that of a spiritual pregnancy. Yakov Bok, we are steadily told, does not seek out or demand his ordeal, he receives it. . . . The virtues of Bok are those of the pregnant woman: endurance, patience, the gradual growth and focusing of purpose. The end of the book is the incipient delivery: Bok is on his way to some kind of birth.[1]

The Fixer also contains, in effect, the imagined menstruation of the male. There is no term for that. Perhaps *saignade* would be analogous to couvade (from *saigner,* to bleed).

Many primitive societies impose on their young men a puberty rite that causes them to bleed from the genitals. The boys are therefore able to mark their initiation into adulthood with a dramatic physical sign that can be equated with the menarche of the girls. More advanced civilizations have abandoned such rites, but they incorporate in their literature allusions to the male's desire to imitate, control, or assimilate the female functions within his own body, to compensate for the lack of a womb and a vagina.

Classic interpretations of male puberty rites such as *circumcision* (the cutting of the foreskin from the penis) and *subincision* (slitting the underside of the penis along the urethra, producing a permanent disfigurement of the form and function of the penis) do not include envy. They rely on the psychoanalytic interpretation that circumcision is a symbolic castration of sons by fathers and on the anthropological view that circumcision was a rite of initiation into adult society. Read, the first anthropologist to study these rites in depth, went a little farther. He believed that the male mutilations expressed a rigid sexual solidarity among the men and the essential opposition of the community of male interests to the "sphere of women."[2] Read's views satisfied most students of this field until some began to probe more deeply into the causes of this supposed antagonism between men and women.

Bruno Bettelheim, in 1954, was the first to look beyond castration anxiety and male superiority as causes of the bloody initiation rites and to offer instead "the premise that one sex feels envy in regard to the sexual organs and functions of the other."[3] He was not talking about penis envy, which originates, according to Freud, when a little girl, seeing a boy's penis for the first time, immediately assumes that it must be better for masturbation than her own minuscule clitoris and wants one for herself. Her quest for a penis will never be completely satisfied, but she will find contentment if she will accept her mother role and the child in the womb as the next-best thing to a penis. There are today many reasons to question this theory, especially in the light of long-established anthropological evidence of couvade. But Freud's work is so important to the understanding of the human psyche that even his most tenuous theories have been swept along to respectability in the tidal wave of his influence. Bettelheim's premise, on the other hand, is that men envy women their ability to bear children. Joseph Campbell, the mythologist, explains:

> The fear of woman and the mystery of her motherhood have been for the male no less impressive imprinting forces than the fears and mysteries of the world of nature itself. And there may be found in the mythologies and ritual traditions of our entire species innumerable

instances of the unrelenting efforts of the male to relate himself effectively—in the way, so to say, of an antagonistic cooperation—to these two alien yet intimately constraining forces: woman and the world.[4]

By "the world," Campbell means such things as the change of seasons, the rhythms of the moon and the tides, processes that even the most primitive human link in the great chain of being could recognize as being analogous to the lives of women: the twenty-eight-day lunar cycle, on which he believed the menstrual cycle was dependent; the growth, ripening, and fall of fruit from the trees, so like the bursting fecundity of women. To maintain a dominance over mysterious, bleeding woman, man had to assimilate woman's functions within himself: to bleed from the genitals, to give birth, and to assume a ritual maternity in order to fool the goddesses of nature into accepting him as the dominant sex.

The most widespread male puberty rite among all the preliterate peoples of the earth is circumcision. So important is the cutting of the foreskin that it is still widely practiced today on infant boys as a hygiene measure. Elizabeth Gould Davis theorizes that the practice originated in the mythical days when a "mountain of foreskins" was showered on the Great Goddess in tribute and at the insistence of the ruling women.[5] Yet, women were not even mentioned when circumcision became the sign of the covenant between the Hebrew patriarchal God and his chosen people.

Bettelheim, by linking circumcision rites with ancient fertility rites, rather than with simple rites of passage, advances the convincing hypothesis that genital mutilation is a direct attempt by the male to overcome the problem of woman's ascendancy in procreation. He stresses the importance in primitive societies of bestowing the severed foreskin on one's mother, sister, or another female who will then wear it, honor it, cook it, and eat it. In return, the male expects to receive symbolically that female's power of maternity. For example, certain rituals of circumcision emphasize that by shedding genital blood the boy will assume the powers of menstruation and childbearing possessed by the mythical women of the Creation stories. In Australian myth, circumcision is said to originate with a semihuman bird, *Jurijurilia;* the bird throws a boomerang that, on its return, circumcises the bird and cuts the vulvas of its wives, causing the first menstruation.

The extreme secrecy of boys' puberty rites, Bettelheim believes, is closer than any other tribal phenomenon to the secrecy among the women surrounding the act of childbirth. He suggests that the men exclude women from any knowledge of their secret rites in retaliation for women's refusal to share the mysteries of childbirth. Men of one Australian tribe go to such lengths to enforce a ritual solidarity that they attempt to convince their women that they do not defecate. Boys' rectums are stopped up temporarily as part of the puberty rite, but the women are led to believe that the blockage is permanent. If a man becomes incapacitated through illness, his wife is told by the others that the illness is responsible for the rupture of the seal of puberty. The image of men constantly hiding their feces from the women suggests vividly the image of women hiding their menstrual rags from the eyes of men, both believing they are preserving the integrity of their own sex and its secrets.

We give prolonged attention to Bettelheim's theories here because they seem in accord with the belief that fear of woman's procreative powers is one of the most profound of human imprints. Although classic anthropological explanations for the origin of circumcision claim that it is a hygienic practice, a preparation for sex life, a test of endurance, a tribal mark, a sacrifice to the goddess of fertility, or a sanctification of the generative faculties, such explanations tend to overlook that in causing himself to bleed from his genitals, man is *pretending to menstruate.* He is thereby recreating in himself the role that biology has assigned exclusively to women. *What actually happens* at adolescent circumcision is at least as important as the ceremony's sociological implications.

The rites of subincision, practiced almost exclusively in Australia, intensify this belief. It follows circumcision in the sequence of the initiation rites. Unlike circumcision, which can occur only once, subincision frequently takes place two or three times, as a further assimilation of female power in the maturing male. In an extreme case, the tribesmen of the Wogeo Islands of New Guinea periodically incise the penis and allow blood to flow to rid themselves of the impurities of sexual intercourse, of which women are naturally cleansed by menstruation.[6]

Ashley Montagu is one who believes that subincision is simulated menstruation, based on the bloodletting common to both and the "feminization" of the appearance of the penis that results.[7] Men who have been subincised are forced to urinate in a squatting position, like women. Even more convincingly, Gesa Roheim notes that the subincised penis is called *vagina* in the sacred songs; blood squirting from the penis is described by words that mean "women" or "milk." And during the ritual in one tribe, the subject runs backward in a creek, flicking up his penis to show the wound; the words for vagina and creek are used interchangeably. Some tribes use parallel names for menstrual blood and blood from the subincision wound.[8]

More evidence of the womb envy in boys' initiation rites is revealed when boys' rites are compared with girls'. A girl's initiation normally follows the first appearance of her menstrual blood. The flowing of the blood is the significant event; what happens at the rites merely commemorates nature's decision. The timing of the first menstruation is beyond the control of the girls or their elders; the aerial spirits or supernatural snakes that bring on the menarche do not invade several pubescent vaginas at once. Consequently, most of the societies studied tend to conduct separate initiation rites for each girl who reaches her menarche (although in some places girls who have already been initiated may take part in a new girl's ceremony).

Because there is no spontaneous biological event that heralds adulthood in a boy, boys of an appropriate age are usually initiated in groups. In these group rites, the all-important fertility aspect of the ceremony gets submerged in the appearances of induction into the tribe. Perhaps this is one reason why the imitative character of such rites has so long been overlooked; it has been too easy to make the obvious connection between puberty rites in primitive societies and the initiation rites of fraternal organizations of all types, which have been popular for centuries throughout the Western world. Yet, even in those fraternal rites, there must be a suggestion of men imitating women, of men getting together to share trivial or ritual secrets with one another because they are perpetually excluded from the greatest secret of all.

A dramatic example of the male attempt to control menstruation by assimilating it to himself is given by the French historian Jules Michelet (1798-1874). He avidly recorded the details of the menstruation of his young wife, Athénais Mialaret, whom he married when he was fifty-one and she was twenty-three.

Michelet was fascinated with blood and with woman. He defines historical characters by the quality of their blood: for example, the thin blood of Robespierre is opposed to the carmine and generous blood of the people. Woman is the incarnation of nature; like nature, she is ruled by rhythms. Woman represents grace and emotion; man, law and intellect. Michelet is interested in woman as spectacle, in watching, not to possess her, but to uncover her.

Hence, although Michelet reports that his wife was frigid and rarely allowed sexual consummation, he adored watching her, especially when she was menstruating. He studied her intestinal life in order to shed light on the vaginal. Apparently, she complied with his study, even with his whims; on one occasion, he sat below her while she added a few drops to the sea.

Michelet wanted to serve as his wife's "*homme femme-de-chambre,*" serving all the functions of a maid and friend. He had much opportunity, for she was frequently ill. He wanted to be her mentor; supervising her studies of insects, he taught her also to watch. He liked to think of the sexes being assimilated to one another. He wrote a fantasy about a couple who constantly impregnated each other; he said his wife impregnated him with her perfume.

Beginning in 1857 and lasting through 1860, Michelet's *Journal* contains much about sex and especially about menstruation. From Michelet, one can chart his wife's menstrual cycles. In 1857, *les règles* arrived June 30, then July 30; he remarks that the second period was five days late. As in this case, he usually anticipates a twenty-five-day cycle, although his wife's ranges from twenty-five to thirty days. He becomes upset at deviations from the cycle, but sometimes, he makes obvious counting mistakes. Usually, he also gives the time of day that her period arrived; sometimes, he describes the color.

He does not, however, criticize superstitions surrounding her periods. Apparently, she was not to bathe during them, for he says at one point that she took a bath too soon afterward. He sees nothing odd in her washing her own chemise so that the laundress will not know of her menstruation, although it sounds to a modern reader like an avoidance taboo. Probably, some superstition is behind his surprise that she has a bloody nose during her period.[9]

Why is Michelet so fascinated by menstruation? As a historian, Michelet wants to record and, by recording, have a sense of mastery. He wants to subsume his wife in himself, assimilating both male and female. Menstruation in Michelet's journals can be read as a symbol of his desire to consume woman, especially those of her processes most closely connected with the rhythms of nature. In this, he is clearly not alone.

Note: The Afterwords to Chapters 26 and 27 appear at the end of Part 7: Men.

Chapter 27

Cycles and Rhythm in Men

When Shakespeare has his Julius Caesar proclaim, "I am constant as the northern star," the Bard may have been making use of the usual stereotypes: women are flighty, men firm; females are emotional, males are reasonable; women have cycles, men don't.[1] Julius Caesar (or Shakespeare) was wrong. Although most men do not bleed from their genitals every month as women do, men's behavior does follow distinct cycles. Even epilepsy (Julius Caesar's "falling sickness") may be cyclical. And unlike women's periodic bleedings, "raging hormonal imbalances" in men may be all the more dangerous because they are less predictable.

Both sexes are subject to *circadian*, or twenty-four-hour, cycles: a flux in hormones, moods, strengths, and weaknesses. Those lucky persons whose body times are synchronized with their work hours will find that their temperatures rise in the morning, giving them a greater push to get up and go; their temperatures will drop in the evening. Circadian rhythms are difficult to alter: night-shift workers are more likely to have nervous disorders or ulcers. The phenomenon of jet lag, which strikes the traveler who flies overnight to Peking, is widespread; often mental efficiency will be affected by it.

Most males are conditioned to see themselves as overcoming such rhythms, such external forces: their "manhood" may be dependent on such a self-image. But a chink in the armor appeared in the 1974 perjury case of California Lieutenant Governor Ed Reinecke. One of Reinecke's defenses was that because of jet lag after a trip from California to Washington, D.C., he may not have known what he was saying.

Monthly rhythms are, perhaps inevitably, more difficult for men to face because we are all taught that only females suffer from periodic craziness. But as early as 1897, it was noted that both sexes bleed periodically with lung hemorrhages, hemorrhoids, and hyperemia of the liver. A research study in 1933 observed monthly epilepsy attacks in the "stronger sex."[2]

The male menstrual (the word means "monthly") cycle does not confine itself to diseases. Dr. Rex Hersey of the University of Pennsylvania studied factory workers in 1929 and 1930. He chose to observe "average" and "well-adjusted" workers and managers, those who seemed "normal" in overt respects.[3] For a year, he interviewed each man four times a day, made regular physical examinations, and interviewed the men's families. He arrived, finally, at charts for each individual, showing that emotional variations were predictable not only in twenty-four hour (circadian) cycles but also in a near-monthly rhythm, a cycle of four to six weeks.

One twenty-two-year-old man showed a four-and-a-half week cycle, with variations no greater than those in a woman's menstrual cycle. During low periods, he was apathetic at home and at work; he temporarily abandoned his artwork. Another man with a five- to six-week cycle had manic periods during which he felt outgoing and confident, with great vigor and energy. During his low periods, he found work a burden, needed more sleep, and preferred to sit quietly. In his manic periods, he slept less and even weighed less.

One happy sixty-year-old in the study claimed that he never changed (the "I am as constant as the northern star" syndrome). He, it turned out, had a nine-week cycle. His mood decline was so gradual that he did not realize he was criticizing his superiors, refusing to make jokes with his colleagues, and in general, withdrawing. Yet, if he had accepted (as women must because of their bleeding) the role of cycles in his life, he would have had a much better understanding of himself.

"Flighty women" are usually the butts of jokes about "women drivers." But men drivers, it has been shown, have higher accident rates. Even the Auto Safety Committee of the conservative American Medical Association concluded that women are better drivers because "they're less emotional than men."

Men drivers do, indeed, have their ups and downs, monthly ones. Estelle Ramey relates this incident in her *Ms.* article on men's cycles: The Omi Railway Company of Japan directs a private transportation system in Kyoto and Osaka, operating more than 700 buses and taxis in dense traffic areas. The directors of the company became concerned in 1969 over the high losses resulting from accidents. The company's efficiency experts began a study of each man working for the company, trying to discover his lunar cycle of mood and efficiency. Then, they adjusted schedules and routes to coincide with the best time of the month for each worker. Since then, traffic has increased, but the Omi accident rate has dropped an amazing one-third.

If monthly cycles in normal men can be damaging, what of the abnormal? Adolescent boys have been known to have monthly psychotic episodes, which may be the male equivalent of premenstrual tension. Monthly oscillations are common in manic-depressive psychosis, catatonic fits, epilepsy, and its close cousin, migraine.

Periodic illnesses may be the effects of sudden excitement in certain regions of the brain, especially the hypothalamus (which regulates many basic body functions, such as temperature). Periodic illnesses may come from changes in the number of certain blood cells or from local swelling of tissues and skin, concurrent fever, and edema (an abnormal accumulation of fluid, also characteristic of the premenstrual syndrome in women). Periodic edema may be inherited through a dominant gene.

One's ethnic group may determine one's periodic illness. Peritonitis (inflammation of the membrane that lines the abdomen) is periodic mainly within Mediterranean ethnic groups: Jews, Armenians, Arabs. Periodic edema, however, appears to be limited to Northern European types, limited, that is, to most of the men who run things in the United States and who try to keep our ship of state on an even keel.[4]

When Dr. Edgar Berman said that women are unfit for leadership because of "raging hormonal imbalances," he neglected the role hormones play in men. In Denmark, for instance, a sixteen-year study charted the fluctuating amounts of male sex hormones in men's urine.[5] The discovery: the ebb and flow of hormones followed a pronounced thirty-day rhythm. The male hormonal balance was constantly changing.

In *The Menstrual Cycle,* Katharina Dalton argues that there is no evidence for male cycles because no cyclical patterns have been found in such aspects as school infractions, eye pain in glaucoma, blood pressure, and lower pain threshhold. But Dalton inadvertently describes another form of men's cycles, one that we might call, for lack of any other name, the *vicarious cycle.*[6]

Just as males sometimes feel sympathetic labor pains (couvade) when their wives are giving birth, men also show symptoms when the women around them menstruate. In one case, a salesman's selling ability changed mysteriously for one week in every four. For three weeks he averaged

$200 a week in commissions; every fourth week, his earnings fell to around $50. During the weeks his earnings were low, he became more depressed and started to work later. When he checked his wife's menstrual record, he found that his "low week" coincided with her premenstrual symptoms: irritability and fatigue.

Another man had chronic bronchitis, with periodic intensifications correlating with his wife's periods. After she had an ovarian cyst removed, his periodic attacks disappeared. In a British study of industrial workers, some men had monthly spells of lateness. These, it turned out, occurred when his wife or mother had overslept or was slower than usual preparing sandwiches or breakfast because of her menstrual cycles. In these instances, the sharing of household duties clearly would have benefited both sexes.[7]

Even children may react vicariously to their mother's periods. Dalton, studying children brought to a doctor's office with colds, found that 50 percent were brought by the mother while she was in the four days before or during menstruation. In one case, three-year-old Keith had colds every month, coinciding with his mother's menstruations. Dalton, in effect, sees the mother as the cause of the child's illess. It is possible, however, that mothers at "that time of the month" are simply more concerned about their offspring's well-being, more likely to fuss over them, more likely to take them to the doctor.[8]

It is undeniable that there are male cycles. Scientific evidence points to biological, circadian, monthly, and emotional rhythms. But there is also an imaginative and appealing cyclic theory that has had its own ups and downs in popularity over the years.

Occasionally, newspapers and magazines carry ads about *biorhythms,* claiming that the formula to be sold will teach the reader to chart his own cycle and plan his activities to his advantage. These formulas go back to the eccentric Wilhelm Fliess, who in 1857 published *The Rhythm of Life: Foundations of an Exact Biology.*

According to Fliess, everyone is bisexual. The "male component" of this bisexuality (consisting of such traditionally male qualities as strength, endurance, and courage) is keyed to a cycle of twenty-three days. The "female component" (not menstrual bleeding, but a cycle of sensitivity, intuition, love, and other feelings) has a period of twenty-eight days. Fliess believed that both cycles are present in every cell and counter each other throughout life. Moreover, they are shown in the ups and downs of each person's physical and mental vitality. And, finally, they may be used eventually to determine the date of one's death. In the 1930s, a teacher at

Innsbruck added a third dimension to Fliess's theory: a thirty-three-day creativity cycle of mental acuteness and power.

Fliess's rather bizarre theory would have been forgotten except for Freud, who was a friend and a passionate devotee of Fliess. Fliess linked his twenty-three- and twenty-eight-day cycles with the changes in the mucosal lining of the nose. He spoke of the "genital cells" in the interior of the nose and related nasal irritation to neurotic symptoms and sexual abnormalities. His treatment: diagnosing ills by inspecting the nose and applying cocaine to its interior. Fliess even operated twice on Freud's nose.

The main objection to Fliess's theories is this: There is no proof that they correspond with reality in any way. Like remarks about hormonal imbalances, they may represent a wish fulfillment, a desire to create order through pigeon-holing men and women into biological models.

Although Dr. Berman envisioned hazardous possibilities if "a menopausal President" had presided over the Cuban missile crisis in 1962, many American presidents have survived hormonal and/or cyclical disabilities. Thomas Jefferson had periodic migraines; Abraham Lincoln had periodic depressions. At least one writer suggested that Richard Nixon's "raging hormonal imbalances" may have caused the Watergate morass. Even John F. Kennedy, who did preside over the Cuban missile crisis, had a serious hormonal disorder, Addison's disease (adrenal insufficiency). Moreover, a man old enough to be eligible for the presidency is liable to be in worse physical health than his female counterpart. Not only does she live longer, but her menopause is likely to be more manageable than his, if only because it has been more fully observed and understood.

More has been written about the male menopause than about any other aspect of the male cycle. For women, their menopause is more immediately obvious: an end to monthly bleeding. Psychologically, of course, it is complicated by other factors: society's devaluing older women, in part because they are no longer youthfully beautiful; the woman's losing her children to adulthood.

For a man, the *menopause* or *male climacteric* (the words are used interchangeably) is more insidious. The men are likely to be at the height of their careers, but at the same time, there is a decrease, usually gradual, in the secretion of testosterone, the male hormone. There are also the usual fears of death and aging.

What are the symptoms of the male menopause? Loss of sexual potential is one, almost certainly traceable to the decline in testosterone production. By the time a man reaches age sixty-five, he may require medical assistance to continue a full sex life. Not only does the menopausal male lose sexual potency, but he is also characterized by indecisiveness, irritability, vasomotor troubles (the contraction and dilation of blood vessels), general ineptness, insecurity, and uncertainty. The sexual changes of the male climacteric are perhaps the most worrisome to him because they most closely involve his "manhood."

In our years in colleges and universities, we have observed a particular syndrome that seems characteristic of the male menopause in academia. At about the time a man becomes a full professor with tenure (in his early or middle forties, say), he usually begins attending academic conventions more frequently and without his wife. At the conventions, he seeks out young women to tell them "My wife doesn't understand me"; or if he's trying to be more hip, he explains about his "open marriage." He mentions that he's in a position to hire new faculty and that he wants to interview the young woman for the job—in his room or for lunch or for dinner, but at some point, in his room.

When he returns home, he often becomes the mentor of his female students, who are flattered by his attention. He may seek out new young women each semester, or he may shed his old wife for a new one, marrying a student twenty years his junior. For a while at least, he has come to terms with his own aging. Not seeing across from him the woman who aged along with him, he is not reminded of his own bodily changes. At the height of his career, his increase in power serves as a partial substitute for a decrease in potency. Hence, the male academic successfully weathers his crisis.

Successful men in all professions have played this familiar role for themselves and the women in their lives. We don't know what happens to those less successful ones who have to suffer the same physical diminutions without the protecting emoluments of money and status—or what happens to the women they leave behind. Perhaps because men, who run the scientific establishment, would prefer to deny the existence of male cycles, there has been little research done on the subject. Men, because of their socially conditioned role, find it more comfortable to believe they are as constant as the northern star. But it would benefit us all to know more about the forces controlling us. As the old saw goes, time and tide wait for no man; but if we understand the time and the tide, perhaps we can be waiting for them.

Afterword to Part 7: Men

Throughout this book we have seen numerous examples of the male desire to define menstruation, to become intimately involved in this exclusively female experience. Stephen King imagines Sue's blood coursing down her thighs, whereas Lawrence Sanders imagines Zoe's menstrual cramps and her ensuing violence. Few men, however, have actually emulated menstruation to the point of physically mutilating their bodies. Imaginary participation in the menstrual process (what we call *saignade*) seems perfectly adequate for most of them.

The Wogeo of New Guinea are rare exceptions. Like the societies studied by Bruno Bettelheim (see chapter 26), the Wogeo people of New Guinea practice subincision—the splitting of the penis to resemble the female organs. In *The Island of Menstruating Men,* a remarkable book which escaped our notice in 1976, Ian Hogbin describes the ritual. At dawn the male catches a crab or crayfish and keeps one sharp claw. After fasting all day he goes to the beach and gets an erection, "either by thinking about desirable women or by masturbation." Then he "pushes back the foreskin and hacks at the glans, first on the left side, then on the right." The ceremony over, the male goes into seclusion for several days, and he abstains from intercourse until the next new moon. The male induces menstruation frequently but not every month, Hogbin observes, for this would curtail the growth of the population.[10]

Whereas Bettelheim examines subincision in light of the male's desire to emulate women's procreative powers, Hogbin explains male menstruation as a "periodic disinfection." Menstruation *naturally* frees women from contamination; men can purify their bodies only through an artificial blood-letting, in imitation of the menstrual process.[11] The practice of subincision is hardly universal, being limited to certain tribesmen in Australia and New Zealand. Hogbin did his anthropological work many years ago, in 1934 and then briefly in 1948.[12] With the continued modernization of these cultures, the rituals performed in imitation of women's menstrual privilege are likely to disappear completely.

If males everywhere wanted to menstruate, however, subincision would become a sacrament. If all men wanted to menstruate, then the Wogeo of New Guinea would be the world's model surgeons, the world's greatest philosophers. If men wanted to menstruate, then the crab and the crayfish would become objects of veneration. And here, in America, generation after generation of insurance salesmen and truck drivers and male novelists would practice subincision, at periodic intervals, on our beaches—then retire to their clubs for two or three days of solitude.

There is great satisfaction in knowing that in some exceptional cultures men grant enormous privilege to menstruation, a biological function which they have almost universally feared and devalued.

Conclusion:

Lifting the Curse

The long silence has been broken. Menstruation is ceasing to be a subject for whispered confidences, muttered during the seclusion of slumber parties and coffee klatches. Not only are women beginning to talk to each other frankly and casually about their common bond; contemporary feminist artists are forcing us literally to look at our bleedings. Today, menstruation appears as theme or subject in the graphic arts, in painting and sculpture, in feminist comic strips, and in menstrual shows of all kinds.

Despite the menstrual taboos of the primitives, visual representations of the period are actually very old. Menstruation, pregnancy, and birth appear in prehistoric rock drawings of North America,[1] and there is some evidence that ancient peoples may have used the menstrual cycle for telling time. According to Bart Jordan, various "menstrual notations" helped the ancients keep track of weeks and months. The notations include arrow strokes, rosettes, and square-framed symbols. Examples of these notations have been found in the Old World and, from eras thousands of years later, in native American sites.[2]

The menstrual notation symbol frequently used to denote two fortnights bears some resemblance to two frogs sitting back to back with a moon between them. The frogs have what Jordan calls "womb-like body lines." Out of this figure, according to Jordan, developed the prototypical female fertility figure: the steatopygous Venus, with her exaggerated breasts, hips, and thighs. Jordan sees this new design as evidence of the sophistication of ancient artists and mathematicians; for us, it is a sign of the hold menstruation had on the primitive mind. It was not enough to record menstrual data, as if recording meant control of the mysterious process; the period also had to be domesticated into art, the menstrual symbol transformed into woman in her most acceptable role.

At least one modern artist has tried to return to folklore and found menstruation. Faith Wilding, who has exhibited her work in California, was raised in Paraguay and became interested in what she calls "female mythology," especially its "very primitive sources."[3] Her constructions use such symbols as eggs, rocks, shells, and blood; some use the form of the Venus of Willendorf, the best-known steatopygous Venus. Wilding particularly uses the triangle as a symbol of the vagina.

She rejects the idea of female "mystery," but instead tries to make "the blood rituals of women" (menstruation, pregnancy and birth, lactation, and menopause) into rites invested with magic. As feminist art historian Arlene Raven suggests, Wilding is concerned with "transubstantiation—to the body and blood of the spirit." In one Wilding construction, grass skirts cover but do not conceal a triangular form, open in the center, with a suggestion of blood hanging from it.

Wilding's forms are a return to the past, perhaps to an Amazon nation. But it is Judy Chicago, also a Californian, who is most responsible for the breaking of the menstrual taboo in modern art. No folklore could be as striking as Chicago's handmade lithograph *Red Flag* (1971). Chicago's intent was frankly political. She wrote us:

> I wanted to validate overt female subject matter in the art community and chose to do so by making "Red Flag" as a handmade litho, which is a high art process, usually confined to much more neutralized subject matter. By using such overt content in this form, I was attempting to introduce a new level of permission for women artists. It really worked.

Red Flag is at first shocking, a red flag designed to enrage puritanical souls. The picture, in tones of pink and gray and black, shows one nude female leg, softly shadowed. The other leg is obscured by a hand that is removing a reddened tampon by pulling on the string. Although the average woman may perform this ritual thousands of times in her lifetime, she probably has never seen it pictured. She probably has never watched another woman remove a tampon. Thus does an act most of us would class simply as personal acquire the dimensions of a taboo.

Judy Chicago's later theories have become a focus for much controversy, centering on her insistence that round, pulsating, womblike forms (such as the froglike figures Bart Jordan discovered) are an intrinsically female imagery. What is undeniable is that Chicago has made an enormous contribution to freeing women artists from the menstrual taboo, not only in *Red Flag* but in her classes at Fresno State, the California Institute of the Arts, and the Feminist Studio Workshop, in which she encourages students to express their feelings about womanhood through art.

At Cal Arts, she, Faith Wilding, and about twenty other women artists constructed *Womanhouse*. Convincing an elderly woman to donate an old, ramshackle house to them, they transformed it into a grand symbol of female culture. In the kitchen, there are aprons in the shape of breasts and lips; fried eggs are transformed to breasts. In the nursery, there are androgynous toys, built larger than usual to give adults the feeling of smallness children have. In the closet, there are hundreds of shoes, including spike heels decorated with real spikes. In one bedroom, a woman sits, endlessly applying makeup to her face.

Another bathroom became Judy Chicago's *Menstruation Bathroom*. The room is covered with a gauze veil and is white, clean, and deodorized. On a shelf are Modess and Tampax boxes; the wastebasket overflows with used napkins. On the floor, a saturated tampon lurks. Judy Chicago has written, "However we feel about our own menstruation is how we feel about seeing its image in front of us."

Chicago reports to us that men are especially fascinated with *Menstruation Bathroom*. She ties their interest to what happens to boys in adolescence: They identify with their mothers but

> are forced by social pressure, to make an identification with men. . . . This is symbolized for many men by that moment in school when the girls are taken into the other room and shown a film on menstruation—the secret, so to speak, puberty ritual that separated the boys from the girls. Seeing the bathroom was a connection to the mother, to the female, to that which has been forbidden to them.

Although Chicago is interested in men's responses to her *Menstruation Bathroom*, she and other contemporary feminist artists are more concerned with liberating women's creative potential from the cultural censorships imposed on purely female experiences. Judith Jurasek, for example, titles her sculptural weaving *The Subject Is Taboo*. Her piece, which hangs from the ceiling, is large and in the colors of menstrual fluid: bright blood red to black and dark maroon. A furry covering sits over dark blood-red pods or drops of stuffed vinyl, along with long black and red yarn fringes. The overall shape is a modified mound, narrow at the top, wide at the base. It symbolizes both the placenta of birth and the blood of menstruation, two aspects of uniquely female life. Its womblike form is the kind of female imagery Judy Chicago discusses.

Mary Beth Edelson's *Blood Mysteries* invites women to participate in the artwork. The figure of a powerfully built nude woman, with a circle around her abdomen and flowing hair surrounding her head, is drawn on a wall above a real wooden box that is divided into four compartments: Menstruation Stories, Blood Power Stories, Menopause Stories, and Birth Stories. Women viewing the piece were asked to contribute their experiences on the topics and place their stories in the box. Women generally expressed pleasure with the chance to share their experiences; much hostility came from men.

One of the Blood Power Stories contributed is about the takeovers of the Whitney Museum in New York by women artists. The protestors had been objecting to the Whitney's evident sexism in giving scant attention to the work of women artists, and protests have been annual events since 1970. What is rarely mentioned in media reports is the women's symbolic actions: strewing raw eggs around the galleries and festooning the Whitney with tampons.

But the center for menstrual shows in America is hardly New York; it is California, especially the Los Angeles area. Isabel Welsh, a political science student at the University of California, has created a traveling theater piece, *Menstrual Blood;* two writer-artists in Laguna Beach have produced the hilariously raunchy *Tits & Clits;* Womanspace, a gallery and all-around meeting center for L.A. women, has sponsored "Menstruation Weekends."

Welsh's menstrual show (the first event of the "Menstruation Weekend") is a thirty-minute tape collage of women talking about their menstruation experiences, mixed with readings on the subject from Doris Lessing, Mary McCarthy, and Colette and short quotations about menstrual pollution in so-called primitive societies. Simultaneously, technicolor slides are flashed on three screens of Welsh using Kotex, Tampax, Tassaway,

> spray deodorants, douches, etc.—lots of blood—and very graphic— the piece is broken in the middle with a woman in a white jacket who reads a brief, dry medical statement on the physiology of menstruation. After the tape and slides are finished, there is a "ritual" ending, the symbolic tasting of menstrual blood.

Welsh sees her piece as presenting a "positive ritual" for a "confused secular society." She uses her material to help others get at their true feelings about "body images"; like Chicago, Edelson, and the other feminist artists, she seeks to have all women liberated from menstrual taboos.

Less serious than Welsh but perhaps in its way more striking is "The Menses Is the Message!"—one of the stories in *Tits & Clits*, an adult comic book.[4] Mary Multipary, the heroine of the story, feels a general depression, then realizes it's "merely premenstrual tension." Because all is explained, she feels cheerful again. Mary then suffers through all the tabooed torments we've been exploring in this book. There are no directions on how to insert two tampons at one time; the tampons leak too easily and must be changed constantly, especially with an IUD; carnivorous hemophile dogs chase bloody Mary down the street.

Finding herself broke and still menstruating, Mary tries to wash her used sanitary napkins in the laundry. Unfortunately, she becomes absorbed in a Wonder Woman comic—pondering the question, "Does Wonder Woman work during her period?"—and her napkins disintegrate in the washer.

But then lucky Mary finds a "Berkeley book by Alicia Grapevine, a sister" (obviously a reference to Alicia Bay Laurel's *Living on the Earth*), that tells her to cut a rubber sponge to size. Mary carves her sponge into a phallus and exults in how good it feels. She decides to wear it all the time for "that nice feeling of being loved." Delighted with her discovery, Mary decides to have a party for her women friends, and they all cut sponges for menstrual use. Mary says, "The men would say we're having a 'poke-her' game; Mary's friend is more outspoken when she tries on the sponge: "The hell with the old man! This is fun!" In the final panels, Mary and her friends do a sisterly cheer and dance: "No more cotton! No more hooks! No more boxboy's knowing looks!"

Tits & Clits may provoke outrage or applause, but like Judy Chicago's *Red Flag* and Isabel Welsh's ritual blood tasting, it is a great breakthrough toward ending menstrual taboos. Furthermore, its jaunty drawing style and dialogue suggest possibilities for releasing more and more of the embarrassed laughter that fills the air when women furtively share their common experiences.

When we became involved with this book, we felt—like Judy Chicago, like Isabel Welsh, like all the feminist artists—that we needed a ritual of female culture to inspire us. There were no precedents, so we created our own: a "Bleed-In."

We chose Friday, July 13, 1973, for our "Bleed-In" because Friday, the number thirteen, and the full moon (it shone on us that night) are all ancient female symbols. By chance, thirteen women attended the party, held at Mary Jane's house in Baltimore.

For the occasion, Mary Jane had decorated the bathroom with the signs and symbols of menstruation. Large paper flowers were hanging from the mirror and the door. Stained pads (tomato sauce) were lying at random on the floor. Near the red wastebasket lay a pair of white pants with a red "Friday" stitched on the front and a telltale stain on the crotch, meant to recall the high school myth that a girl who wore red on Friday "had the rag on." Red yarn dangled from the rim of the toilet, and Erica Jong's poem "Gardener" was pasted on the door. On the wall was a piece of paper, titled "Menstrual Graffiti," on which women wrote such witticisms as "We all need someone to bleed on"; "Woman's place is in the bathroom"; and "Vampire to schoolteacher: See you next period."

In the living room, we all sat in a circle (a female, womb-like form). By chance, the two women who were menstruating were sitting a half-circle apart, so everyone was encircled by them. We told anecdotes of our first periods and discovered three of us were wearing white when "it came"; two were at camp. All had feelings of helplessness and embarrassment; some had never shared those experiences before, despite years of consciousness-raising groups. We toasted our stories with the drink of the evening: a Bloody Mary.

Later in the evening, we viewed the educational films from Modess and Kotex and the video tape of eight older women discussing menopause. Watching the movies together removed the last traces of self-consciousness by giving an ordinary focus to this extraordinary event. By the end of the evening, it became clear—to the three of us, especially—that our "Bleed-In" had given a new meaning to our idea of sisterhood. We had brought together in the city of Baltimore thirteen American women to share menstrual experiences and gain self-awareness. But we had also brought those thirteen women together with their sisters in ancient Cambodia, prehistoric New Guinea, contemporary Israel.[5] Beneath the hilarity and irreverence of the evening was a solemn celebration of women's mysteries, an attempt to honor what is generally defiled, to raise to consciousness what has been repressed in fear for millennia. That we had so much fun at our rites is a positive sign that we succeeded. We believe that this generation of women will ultimately exorcise the curse over us all as we pass "Eve's blessing" on to our daughters.

Afterword

If the Bleed-In were held today, it would probably be called a Brood-In, as thirteen women who have finished childbearing and are eagerly looking forward to the menopause sit around a bowling alley and complain about their PMS. They read aloud from *The Third Deadly Sin* between strikes and promise to testify for the PMS defense at each other's trials. They toast each other with Virgin Marys, since alcohol is fattening and exacerbates their PMS symptoms.

Or—thirteen women somewhere between puberty and the first child sit around the conference room of a 250-person law firm, of which they are all junior associates. They promise that they will never reveal, to each other or to the other members of the firm (all male), that menstrual periods exist, by any absence from work, "irrational" behavior, or tears. They take (decaffeinated) herbal tea together and repair to their aerobics class.[5]

If neither scenario was in our crystal ball ten years ago, the seeds for such images were—if only because the women in the bowling alley have always represented one half of the prevailing attitude towards menstruation and women's capacities (menstruation is a drag), while the young lawyers represent the other half (menstruation can't prevent me from doing my job like a man).

The first edition of *The Curse* painstakingly explored both attitudes and tried to reveal their roots and flaws. Celebrating a "Bleed-In" was our effort to introduce a third side, creating a female triangle of choice, while this edition continues those efforts by presenting some of the other kinds of choices women now have, choices of treatment, therapies, and physical regimens to bring even the most unpleasant menstrual symptoms under women's control. But what, we wonder, would be reported if another book on menstruation were to leak its way onto the literary scene in 2001? Would revisionism still be the norm? Would we all be living in menstrual huts of the mind or body, still wondering if the latest technological advance in "menstrual protection" would kill us? Would "menstrual protection" itself have reverted to its primeval meaning, of protecting the society from menstruation's evil influence? Or would we have seen a decade of light and understanding, of the essential mystery of women's bodily rhythms revered and celebrated?

If the work of two of the people we told you about in the first edition were to be the millenium's harbinger, there would be no doubt of a change for the better. Judy Chicago continues to raise "red flags" but with her stunning installations, *The Dinner Party* and *The Birth Project,* raises them in far vaster skies. In both of these she has moved from menstrual images per se and into a total confrontation with the realities of women's bodies and the minds that live in them. *The Dinner Party* is a massive, triangular table setting celebrating thirty-nine women of myth, legend, and history, thirteen to a side, using the "womanly arts" of ceramics and needlework to illustrate their actual contributions and symbolic importance. Most of the designs, especially on the dinner plates, emanate from vulval representations, made fantastic by their reach into art. A deliberate play on the Last Supper of the New Testament, which also had thirteen guests, *The Dinner Party* simultaneously represents women's accomplishments and their struggles. The women are honored guests at the "party," but in a sense they are also trapped on the plates, "eaten alive" and erased from history.[6]

The Birth Project contains huge wall hangings of needlework graphically depicting the realities and agonies of childbirth, often confronting the viewer at eye level with a child emerging from the womb. These images are not "menstrual," but they do bring women face to face with images of their anatomy, which has universally been called their destiny. Vital to an understanding of Chicago's intention is the realization that she has employed hundreds of needlewomen and ceramic painters in both projects. In this way does the process itself become the art, and the installations ironic as well as literal depictions of "women's work."

Meanwhile, Bart Jordan, whom we came to know during the writing of this edition, has gone farther back into the recesses of human history than almost anyone writing or thinking today, to prove that at least thirty thousand years ago, and perhaps 300 thousand years ago, human beings on this planet were measuring the movement of the stars and planets with a sophisticated system that emanated from, and mathematically depended upon, the human menstrual cycle.[7]

Drawing on his knowledge of Ice Age art, and prehistoric musical notation, complemented by knowledge of some twenty languages, Greek, Mesopotamian, and Hebraic myth, and a relentless curiosity, he has performed leaps of the imagination to arrive at diagrams and symbols based on the 364-day year of 13 moon cycles, the 280-day human gestation period, and the 584-day transit of the planet Venus around the sun—only to find, time and again, that the diagrams already existed on the carved tusks, stone earth goddesses (such as the Venus of Lespuges), and other manifestations of what had been believed to be the artistic expressions of a primitive and preliterate people.

Jordan's work is too complicated to reproduce here. It has been published, imperfectly, in various places. We have seen his drawings and examined the evidence of the archeological finds, only to agree with the staggering fact he is trying to introduce into current scientific thinking.

It is this. The Ice Age "art" that is commonly displayed, and the even earlier "art" known to paleontologists and other specialists, is really Ice Age "science." The ancients, the Cro-Magnon ancestors of our human race, were not scratching pretty designs onto their reindeer tusks or fashioning grotesque models of the female form to give vent to their need to make art. They were, in fact, recording their scientific observations on the way the moon and planets and their own earth went through the phases of the year and using the menstrual clock of the women of the society as the observable data from which to draw.

Crucial to Jordan's calculations is the difference between the lunar and menstrual calendars. The real lunar calendar, he says, counting the nights when the moon is "dark," is 29.5 days. But the calculations evident in the carved tusks and obese goddesses reflect a calendrical notation of 28 days, and its multiple, 280, the human gestation period. Menstrual averaging was not unknown to our Cro-Magnon ancestors, Jordan believes, and it was this sophistication that enabled them to create symbols in their art (such as the early Greek meander) that were actually representations of the movement of time as measured by the female body clock and its numerical connection to the travels of Venus around the sun.

Today this kind of primordial evidence of harmony with the universe strikes a richer chord with us as we look at the infinitesimal moment in human history that is the last two thousand years. Going from the ridiculous to the sublime, as it were, how can we not celebrate our rhythms, knowing that they have marked the rhythms of the earth and skies for millennia? A greater leap of faith and transcendence is possible for women now if they will "embrace the blood," see beyond its messy interference with daily life, and take pride in the mark of the universe it has placed upon them.

Notes

Preface

1. Alice Dan, Effie A. Graham, and Carol P. Beecher, *The Menstrual Cycle* (New York: Springer, 1980), vol.1, *A Synthesis of Interdisciplinary Research,* pp. 1-2.

2. Penny Wise Budoff, *No More Menstrual Cramps and Other Good News* (New York: G. P. Putnam's Sons, 1980), and idem., *No More Hot Flashes and Other Good News* (New York: G. P. Putnam's Sons, 1983).

3. Sharon Golub, ed., *Lifting the Curse of Menstruation* (Binghamton, N.Y.: Haworth Press, 1983).

4. Paula Weideger, *Menstruation and Menopause: The Physiology and Psychology, the Myth and the Reality* (New York: Knopf, 1976); Penelope Shuttle and Peter Redgrove, *The Wise Wound: Eve's Curse and Everywoman* (New York: Richard Marek, 1978).

Chapter 1. Women in the Closet: Taboos of Exclusion

1. Franz Steiner, *Taboo* (Baltimore: Penguin, 1956), p. 21.

2. Sigmund Freud, *Totem and Taboo* (New York: Dodd, Mead, 1919), p. 128.

3. M. J. Meggitt, "Male-Female Relationships in the Highlands of Australian New Guinea," *American Anthropologist* 66 (1964).

4. Theodor Reik, *Pagan Rites in Judaism* (New York: Farrar, Straus, 1964), pp. 87-88.

5. George D. Thomson, *Studies in Ancient Greek Society* (London: Lawrence, 1949), p. 205.

6. Mary Chadwick, *The Psychological Effects of Menstruation* (New York: Nervous & Mental Disease, 1932), p. 6.

7. Bruno Bettelheim, *Symbolic Wounds: Puberty Rites and the Envious Male* (New York: Collier, 1962), p. 137.

8. Elizabeth Davis, *The First Sex* (Baltimore: Penguin, 1972), p. 92.

9. William N. Stephens, *A Cross-cultural Study of Menstrual Taboos* (Provincetown, Mass.: Genetic Psych. Monographs, 1961), pp. 399-400.

10. Alfred Ernest Crawley, *The Mystic Rose: A Study of Primitive Marriage* (New York, 1902), p. 90.

11. Meggitt, "Male-Female Relationships in the Highlands of Australian New Guinea."

12. Hutton Webster, *Taboo, A Sociological Study* (Stanford: Stanford University Press, 1942), p. 87.

13. Pliny, *Natural History*, trans. H. Rackham (Cambridge: Harvard University Press, 1961), book 7, p. 549.

14. E. Novak, "The Superstition and Folklore of Menstruation," *Johns Hopkins Hospital Bulletin* 27 (1916).

15. Margaret Mead, *Male and Female* (New York: Morrow, 1949), p. 222.

16. Crawley, *The Mystic Rose: A Study of Primitive Marriage*, p. 149.

17. Sir James George Frazer, *The Golden Bough*, 1 vol. abr. ed. (New York: Macmillan, 1953), p. 206.

18. L. Deslange, *Le Plateau Central Nigerian* (Paris, 1904), p. 227.

19. Webster, *Taboo, A Sociological Study*, p. 83.

20. Webster, *Taboo, A Sociological Study*, p. 87.

21. H. R. Hays, *The Dangerous Sex: The Myth of Feminine Evil* (New York: Putnam, 1965), p. 279.

22. Webster, *Taboo, A Sociological Study*, pp. 83-85.

23. Simone de Beauvoir, *The Second Sex* (New York: Knopf, 1952), p. 138.

24. Cited in C. Frederic Fluhmann, *Menstrual Disorders: Pathology, Diagnosis and Treatment* (Philadelphia and London: Saunders, 1939). Schick's experiment is described more fully in Fritz Vosselmann, *La Menstruation: Lègendes, Coutumes et Superstitions* (Lyon, 1935).

25. William Freeman and Joseph M. Looney, with the technical assistance of Rose R. Small, "Studies on the Phytotoxic Index II. Menstrual Toxin ('menotoxin')," *Journal of Pharmacology and Experimental Therapeutics* 52 (1934).

26. Cited in Earl T. Engle, ed., *Menstruation and Its Disorders* (Springfield, Ill.: Thomas, 1950), pp. 187-205 and pp. 207-231.

27. Webster, *Taboo, A Sociological Study*, p. 86.

28. N. N. Bhattacharyya, *Indian Puberty Rites* (Calcutta, 1968), p. 19.

29. Frazer, *The Golden Bough*, p. 145.

30. Mead, *Male and Female*, p. 182.

31. Frazer, *The Golden Bough*, Third edition, unabridged (New York, 1935), vol. 10, p. 27.

32. Reik, *Pagan Rites in Judaism*, p. 81.

33. Crawley, *The Mystic Rose: A Study of Primitive Marriage*, p. 198.

34. Hays, *The Dangerous Sex: The Myth of Feminine Evil*, pp. 67-68.

35. Robert Snowden and Barbara Christian, eds., *Patterns and Perceptions of Menstruation: A World Health Organization International Collaborative Study* (New York: St. Martin's Press, 1983).

36. Margarita Artschwager Kay, "Meaning of Menstruation to Mexican American Women," in *Culture, Society and Menstruation*, Virginia L. Olesen and Nancy Fugate Woods, eds. (Washington, D.C.: Hemisphere, 1986).

37. D. L. Lawrence, "Reconsidering the Menstrual Taboo: A Portugese Case," *Anthropological Quarterly* 55, no. 2 (1982): 84-89.

38. Marjorie Shostak, *Nisa: The Life and Words of a !Kung Woman* (Cambridge, Mass.: Harvard University Press, 1981, rpt. New York: Random House, Vintage Books, 1983).

39. Shostak, *Nisa: The Life and Words of a !Kung Woman*, p. 68.

40. Shostak, *Nisa: The Life and Words of a !Kung Woman*, p. 353.

41. B. B. Harrell, "Lactation and Menstruation in Cultural Perspective," *American Anthropologist* 83,4 (1981): 823.

42. Doreen Asso. *The Real Menstrual Cycle* (New York: John Wiley & Sons, 1983), p. 40.

Chapter 2. "Not Tonight, Dear": Taboos of Sex

1. This idea was first suggested to us by Nancy Scheper-Hughes, "Woman as Witch," *Popular Psychology*, 4 (1973).

2. William N. Stephens, *A Cross-cultural Study of Menstrual Taboos* (Provincetown, Mass.: Genetic Psych. Monographs, 1961), p. 401.

3. J. M. Rodwell, trans., *The Koran* (London: Dent, 1953), p. 363.

4. Isser Yehuda Unterman, "Family Purity: Its Wide Implications," reprinted in *Israel Magazine* 4 (January 1972): 68-74.

5. Cited in Ben Barker-Benfield, "The Spermatic Economy: A Nineteenth Century View of Sexuality," *Feminist Studies* 1 (Summer 1972): 45-74.

6. Soranus, *Gynecology*, trans. Owesei Temkin (Baltimore: Johns Hopkins University Press, 1956), p. 35.

7. William S. Sadler and Lena K. Sadler, *Living a Sane Sex Life* (Chicago: Follett, 1938), p. 243.

8. Isidor Silberman, "A Contribution to the Psychology of Menstruation," *International Journal of Psychoanalysis* 31 (1950): 260.

9. Hutton Webster, *Taboo, A Sociological Study* (Stanford: Stanford University Press, 1942), pp. 82, 130.

10. Chester B. Martin, Jr., and Eugene M. Long, Jr., "Sex during the Menstrual Period," *Medical Aspects of Human Sexuality* 3 (1969): 40.

11. Fritz Vosselmann, *La Menstruation; Lègendes, Coutumes et Superstitions* (Lyon, 1935), p. 79.

12. Fred P. Robbins, "Psychosomatic Aspects of Dysmenorrhea," *American Journal of Obstetrics and Gynecology* 66 (1953): 808-815.

13. Mary Jane Sherfey, "A Theory of Female Sexuality," in *Sisterhood is Powerful*, ed. Robin Morgan (New York: Random House, 1970), p. 221.

14. Mary E. Luschen and David Pierce, in "Effect of the Menstrual Cycle on Mood and Sexual Arousability," *Journal of Sex Research* 8 (February 1972): 41-47, found through studying women's reactions to pictures of sexually attractive males that women are more easily aroused during ovulation than during menstruation.

15. William H. Masters and Virginia E. Johnson, *Human Sexual Inadequacy* (Boston: Little, Brown, 1970), p. 221. This finding has been supported by others in the field.

16. Silberman, "A Contribution to the Psychology of Menstruation," p. 260.

17. T. O. Beidelman, "Pig (Guluwe): An Essay on Ngulu Sexual Symbolism and Ceremony," *Southwestern Journal of Anthropology* 20 (1964): 375.

18. L. M. Terman, *Psychological Factors in Marital Happiness* (New York: McGraw-Hill, 1938), cited in Martin and Long, "Sex during the Menstrual Period," p. 40.

19. William H. Masters and Virginia E. Johnson, *Human Sexual Response* (Boston: Little, Brown, 1966), p. 26.

20. Katharina Dalton, *The Menstrual Cycle* (New York: Pantheon, 1971), p. 26.

21. Unterman, "Family Purity: Its Wide Implications," p. 70.

22. Webster, *Taboo, A Sociological Study*, p. 82.

23. *Tits & Clits*, produced by Lyn Chevli and Joyce Sutton (Laguna Beach, Calif., 1972).

24. Martin and Long, "Sex during the Menstrual Period," p. 43.

25. Cited in Webster, *Taboo, A Sociological Study*, pp. 105, 220n.

26. Karen Paige, "Women Learn to Sing the Menstrual Blues," *Psychology Today*, September 1973, pp. 43-44.

27. Martin and Long, "Sex during the Menstrual Period," pp. 43-46.

28. Paige, "Women Learn to Sing the Menstrual Blues," p. 43.

29. Martin and Long, "Sex during the Menstrual Period," p. 43.

30. Barbara G. Walker, *The Woman's Encyclopedia of Myths and Secrets* (New York: Harper & Row, 1983), pp. 635-45.

31. Quoted by John Langone, "AIDS: Special Report," *Discover* 6, no. 12 (December 1985): 28-53; Barbara Visscher quoted p. 50.

32. Jonathan Leiberson, "The Reality of AIDS," *New York Review of Books* 32 (January 16, 1986): 43-48.

33. John Langone, "AIDS Update: Still No Reason for Hysteria," *Discover* (September 1986): 41.

34. Germaine Greer, *Sex and Destiny: The Politics of Human Fertility* (New York: Harper & Row, 1984), p. 241.

35. Naomi M. Morris and Richard J. Udry, "Menstruation and Marital Sex," *Journal of Biosocial Science* 15 (1983): 173-81.

36. Alice Ross Gold and David B. Adams, "Menstrual Factors Affecting Fluctuations of Female Sexual Activity at Menstruation," *Psychology of Women Quarterly* 5, no. 5 (Supplement, 1981): 670-80.

37. William C. Manson, "Desire and Danger: A Reconsideration of Menstrual Taboos," *Journal of Psychoanalytic Anthropology* 7, no. 3 (Summer 1984): 241-55.

38. Sherri Matteo and Emilie F. Rissman, "Increased Sexual Activity During the Midcycle Portion of the Human Menstrual Cycle," *Hormones & Behavior* 18, no. 3 (September 1984): 249-55.

39. An excellent study of sexual attitudes surrounding menstrual intercourse has recently been called to our attention: F. Edmonde Morin, *La rouge différence ou les rhythmes de la femme* (Paris: Editions de Seuil, 1982). In this book Morin conducts intimate interviews with both sexes and argues that women fear menstrual intercourse because they fear the rejection of their sexuality, whereas men fear menstruation because it signifies "difference," something they cannot fully recognize or control. "Les hommes font l'amour *malgré* les règles, pas *à cause* d'elles," p. 29. (Men make love in spite of menstruation, not because of it; translation ours).

Chapter 3. Putting Her in Her Place: Rites of the Menarche

1. Ruth Benedict, *Patterns of Culture* (Boston: Houghton Mifflin, 1944), pp. 28-29.

2. Sir James George Frazer, *The Golden Bough*, 1 vol. abr. ed. (New York: Macmillan, 1953), pp. 690-691.

3. George Devereaux, "The Psychology of Feminine Genital Bleeding," *International Journal of Psychoanalysis* 31 (1950): 242-243.

4. Frazer, *The Golden Bough*, p. 695.

5. Frazer, *The Golden Bough*, p. 698.

6. N. N. Battacharyya, *Indian Puberty Rites* (Calcutta, 1968), p. 16.

7. Frazer, *The Golden Bough*, p. 693.

8. Deveraux, "The Psychology of Feminine Genital Bleeding," pp. 242-243.

9. Frazer, *The Golden Bough*, p. 696.

10. Frazer, *The Golden Bough*, p. 703.

11. Karen Paige, "Women Learn to Sing the Menstrual Blues," *Psychology Today*, September 1973.

12. Mary Douglas, *Purity and Danger: An Analysis of Concepts of Pollution and Taboo* (New York: Praeger, 1966), p. 116.

13. Charlotte Frisbie, *Kinaaldá: A Study of the Navaho Girl's Puberty Ceremony* (Middletown, Conn.: Wesleyan University Press, 1967), p. 350; and Deveraux, "The Psychology of Feminine Genital Bleeding," p. 242.

14. Bhattacharyya, *Indian Puberty Rites*, p. 6.

15. Frazer, *The Golden Bough*, p. 24.

16. Bhattacharyya, *Indian Puberty Rites*, p. 8.

17. Bhattacharyya, *Indian Puberty Rites*, p. 20.

18. Bruno Bettelheim, *Symbolic Wounds: Puberty Rites and the Envious Male* (New York: Collier, 1962), p. 172.

19. Frazer, *The Golden Bough*, p. 693.

20. Devereaux, "The Psychology of Feminine Genital Bleeding," p. 246.

21. Simone de Beauvoir, *The Second Sex* (New York: Knopf, 1952), p. 141.

22. *The Ante-Nicene Fathers: Translation of the Writing of the Fathers Down to A.D. 352*, vol. 3 (Baltimore, 1885), p. 688.

23. Frazer, *The Golden Bough*, p. 61.

24. Hutton Webster, *Taboo, A Sociological Study* (Stanford: Stanford University Press, 1942), p. 88.

25. Webster, *Taboo, A Sociological Study*, pp. 90-91.

26. Marie Smith, "Menstrual Disorders" (Ph.D. diss., University of Denver, 1971), p. 47.

27. H. R. Hays, *The Dangerous Sex: The Myth of Feminine Evil* (New York: Putnam, 1965), p. 51.

28. Bettelheim, *Symbolic Wounds: Puberty Rites and the Envious Male*, pp. 143-145.

29. C. Beals, "Sex Life in Latin America," in *The Encyclopedia of Sexual Behavior*, eds. A. Ellis and A. Abarbanel, vol. 2 (New York, 1961), pp. 600-601.

30. Bhattacharyya, *Indian Puberty Rites*, p. 29.

31. Frisbie, *Kinaaldá: A Study of the Navaho Girl's Puberty Ceremony*, p. 9.

32. Bhattacharyya, *Indian Puberty Rites*, p. 18.

33. Margaret Mead, *Male and Female* (New York: Morrow, 1949), p. 184.

34. Minda Borun et al., *Women's Liberation: An Anthropological View* (Pittsburgh, 1971), p. 7.

35. Judith K. Brown, "A Cross-cultural Study of Female Initiation Rites," *American Anthropologist* 65 (1963): 947. See the discussion of Brown's cross-cultural theory in Karen Eriksen Paige and Jeffrey M. Paige, *The Politics of Reproductive Ritual* (Berkeley: University of California Press, 1981), pp. 111-118.

36. Blaine Harden, "Africans Keep Rite of Girls' Circumcision," *Washington Post*, July 13, 1985, sec. A.

37. Paige and Paige, *The Politics of Reproductive Ritual*, pp. 88-89.

38. It is easier to try to remove our Western cultural bias when one reads of efforts to reconsider menarcheal rites and menstrual taboos using as an example the Native American Oglala which, like those of the Navaho, emphasize the positive, communal effects of female puberty. Marla N. Powers, in "Menstruation and Reproduction: An Oglala Case," proves that menstruation is not treated as defilement in this society but rather that "myths and rituals related to female puberty in general and to menstruation in particular are aspects of the same phenomenon, which emphasizes the importance of the female reproductive role." In *Women: Sex and Sexuality*, ed. Catharine R. Stimpson and Ethel Spector Person (Chicago: University of Chicago Press, 1980), pp. 117-28.

Chapter 4. *Woman Unclean: Menstrual Taboos in Judaism and Christianity*

1. Bracha Sacks, "Why I Choose Orthodoxy," *Ms.*, July 1974.

2. Sr. Albertus Magnus McGrath, O.P., *What a Modern Catholic Believes about Women* (Chicago, 1972), p. 22.

3. McGrath, *What a Modern Catholic Believes about Women*, p. 22.

4. *Interpreter's Bible*, ed. Nolan B. Harmon (New York: Abingdon, 1953), p. 74.

5. Bede, *History of the English Church and People* (Baltimore: Penguin, n.d.), pp. 76-81.

6. D. M. Prumner, O.P., *Handbook of Moral Theology*, trans. G. W. Sheldon (Cork, 1963), p. 270.

7. McGrath, *What a Modern Catholic Believes about Women*, p. 110.

8. McGrath, *What a Modern Catholic Believes about Women*, p. 11, citing the *Proto-Evangelum of James*, an apochryphal book of the early Christians.

9. *Encyclopedia of Religion and Ethics*, ed. James Hastings (Edinburgh and New York, 1921), p. 574.

10. *Basic Writings of St. Thomas Aquinas*, ed. Anton C. Pegis (New York: Random House, 1948), p. 880.

11. *Malleus maleficarum*, trans. by Rev. Montague Summers (Great Britain: John Rodker, 1928), part 1.

12. *Malleus maleficarum*, part 1.

13. David Turner, *The Prodigal Daughter*, as performed at the John F. Kennedy Center for the Performing Arts, Washington, D.C., November 12, 1973.

14. Readers who saw the movie *Agnes of God*, rather than the play, may be a bit confused. While the film was awash in the color red, in symbols like the bleeding heart on a statue of Mary or the blood itself pouring from Agnes's hands, some key elements of the play were changed in Hollywood. Agnes does not die at the end of the movie, for example, nor does Martha begin to menstruate. Those who fashioned the film from this extremely complex play (key elements of the plot, not relevant to the menstrual theme, have not been discussed here) focused on other aspects of the story in creating a new work of art. The validity of the menstrual message in the play, however, remains its most powerful image.

Chapter 5. Menstruation and Medical Myth

1. Aristotle, *On the Generation of Animals*, trans. A. L. Peck (London: Heinemann, 1943), 2. 4. 185. All other citations from this edition will be given in the text.

2. Pliny, *Natural History*, 7. 13, cited in G. Frederic Fluhmann, *Menstrual Disorders: Pathology, Diagnosis and Treatment* (Philadelphia and London: Saunders, 1939), p. 20.

3. Cited in Una Stannard, "Adam's Rib, or the Woman Within," *Transactions* 1 (1970): 27.

4. Fritz Vosselmann, *La Menstruation, Lègendes, Coutumes et Superstitions* (Lyon, 1935), p. 16.

5. Fluhmann, *Menstrual Disorders: Pathology, Diagnosis and Treatment*, p. 19.

6. Soranus, *Gynecology*, trans. Owsei Temkin (Baltimore: Johns Hopkins University Press, 1956), p. 23.

7. Vosselmann, *La Menstruation, Lègendes, Coutumes, et Superstitions*, pp. 16-17.

8. Fluhmann, *Menstrual Disorders: Pathology, Diagnosis and Treatment*, pp. 19-20.

9. John Freind, *Emmenologis*, trans. Thomas Dale (London, 1752), pp. 19, 67.

10. William Stephenson, *American Journal of Obstetrics* 15 (1882): 287-294.

11. G. Stanley Hall, *Adolescence*, vol. 1 (New York: Appleton, 1904), p. 487.

12. J. M. Tanner, "Growing Up," *Scientific American* 229 (1973): 43.

13. Soranus, *Gynecology*, p. 17.

14. Albertus Magnus, *Le Grand et let Petit Albert* (Paris, 1970), p. 70.

15. Hermann Heinrich Ploss, Max Bartels, and Paul Bartels, *Woman: An Historical Gynaecological and Anthropological Compendium*, ed. Eric John Dingwall (St. Louis: Mosby, 1936), p. 564.

16. Fluhmann, *Menstrual Disorders: Pathology, Diagnosis and Treatment*, p. 18.

17. August Bebel, *Woman and Socialism*, trans. Meta Stern (New York, 1910), p. 50. Bebel's work was originally published in 1883.

18. Pye Henry Chavasse, *Woman as a Wife and Mother* (Philadelphia, 1871), pp. 90-91.

19. Ploss, Bartels, and Bartels, *Woman: An Historical Gynaecological and Anthropological Compendium*, p. 573.

20. Fluhmann, *Menstrual Disorders: Pathology, Diagnosis and Treatment*, p. 34.

21. Quoted in C. L. Henton, "A Comparative Study of the Onset of Menarch among Negro and White Children," *Journal of Psychology* 46 (1958): 65.

22. Chavasse, *Woman as a Wife and Mother*, p. 89.

23. Ira Warren et al., *New Warren's Household Physician* (Boston, 1901), p. 381. This is a reissue of an earlier text.

24. The pro-blonde study is cited in Fluhmann, *Menstrual Disorders: Pathology, Diagnosis and Treatment*, p. 32; the redhead and brunette studies are reported in Ploss, Bartels, and Bartels, *Woman: An Historical Gynaecological and Anthropological Compendium*, pp. 573, 589.

25. Ploss, Bartels, and Bartels, *Woman: An Historical Gynaecological and Anthropological Compendium*, p. 567.

26. Ploss, Bartels, and Bartels, *Woman: An Historical Gynaecological and Anthropological Compendium*, p. 581; and Hall, *Adolescence*, pp. 478-479.

27. James V. Ricci, *The Genealogy of Gynaecology* (Philadelphia: Blakiston, 1950), pp. 367-368.

28. Ploss, Bartels, and Bartels, *Woman: An Historical Gynaecological and Anthropological Compendium*, p. 586.

29. Cited in Chavasse, *Woman as a Wife and Mother*, pp. 90-91.

30. Cited in Marie Smith, "Menstrual Disorders" (Ph.D. diss., University of Denver, 1971), p. 9.

31. Sharon Golub, "Menarche: The Beginning of Menstrual Life," in *Lifting the Curse of Menstruation*, ed. Sharon Golub (New York: Haworth Press, 198), pp. 24-25. See also Vern L. Bullogh, "Age at Menarche: A Misunderstanding," *Science*, July 17, 1981, p. 213; "Why Girls Are Maturing Earlier," *USA Today*, August 1980, p. 109; D. D. Logan, "The

Menarcheal Experience in 23 Foreign Countries," *Adolescence,* 15, no. 58 (1980): 247-56.

32. Martha K. McClintock, "Menstrual Synchrony and Suppression," *Nature* 229, no. 22 (January 1971): 244-45.

33. John Leo, "The Hidden Power of Body Odors," *Time,* December 1, 1986, p. 67.

34. Stephen Budiansky, "Siren Song of the Pheromones," *U.S. News and World Report,* December 1, 1986, p. 64.

Chapter 6. Modern Menstrual Politics

1. U.S., Congress, Senate, *Congressional Record,* March 22, 1972, p. S4531.

2. Historical data on the women's rights movement of the nineteenth and early twentieth centuries come from Eleanor Flexner, *Century of Struggle: The Woman's Rights Movement in the United States* (Cambridge: Harvard University Press, 1959).

3. Edward H. Clarke, *Sex in Education* (1873), p. 45.

4. *Sex and Education: A Reply to Dr. E. H. Clarke's "Sex in Education,"* ed. Julia Ward Howe (Boston, 1874; New York: Arno, 1972).

5. Azel Ames, Jr., *Sex in Industry* (Boston, 1875), p. 43.

6. Clelia Duel Mosher, *Health and the Woman Movement* (New York: Woman's Press, 1916), revised and expanded to *Woman's Physical Freedom* (New York: Woman's Press, 1923), p. 20.

7. Mosher, *Health and the Woman Movement,* p. 30.

8. Mary Putnam-Jacobi, *The Question of Rest for Women during Menstruation* (New York, 1877), p. 15.

9. Grace Naismith, *Private and Personal* (New York: McKay, 1966), p. 147.

10. Naismith, *Private and Personal,* p. 174.

11. The most thorough study of this subject we have found is "Two Contributions to the Experimental Study of the Menstrual Cycle," by the Great Britain Industrial Health Research Board, 1928.

12. Cited in David R. Zimmerman, "Medicine Today," in *Ladies' Home Journal,* March 1974, p. 20. Three studies we have found useful in exploring the effects of athletics on the menstrual cycle are Theresa W. Anderson, "Swimming and Exercise during Menstruation," *Journal of Health, Physical Education and Recreation* (October 1965); Marjorie Phillips et al., "Sports Activity for Girls," *Journal of Health, Physical Education and Recreation* (December 1959); Grace Thwing, "Swimming during the Menstrual Period," *Journal of Health and Physical Education* (March 1943).

13. Maury Levy, "Mother Freedom," *Philadelphia,* January 1974, p. 100 ff.

14. Research & Forecasts, Inc., *The Tampax Report* (New York, 1981), passim.

15. Susan Brownmiller, *Femininity* (New York: Linden Press/Simon & Schuster, 1984), p. 195. Brownmiller's comment is taken from Simone de Beauvoir's remark in *The Second Sex:* "It is not easy to play the idol, the fairy, the faraway princess, when one feels a bloody cloth between one's legs."

16. Albert W. Diddle, "Athletic Activity and Menstruation," *Southern Medical Journal* 76, no. 5 (May 1983): 620.

17. P. S. Wood's "Sex Differences in Sports" in the *New York Times Magazine,* May 1980, contains a useful summary of research in this relatively new field.

18. Rose E. Frisch, "Fatness, Menarche and Female Fertility," *Directives in Biology and Medicine* 28, no. 4 (1985): 611-33.

19. Wood, "Sex Differences in Sports."

20. Mona Shangold, M.D., "Menstrual Irregularity in Athletes: Basic Principles, Evaluation and Treatment," *Canadian Journal of Applied Sport Sciences* 7, no. 2 (1982): 68.

21. Diddle, "Athletic Activity and Menstruation," 622.

22. Nadine Brozan, "Training Linked to Disruption of Female Reproductive Cycle," *New York Times,* April 17, 1978, sec. C1.

23. Cited in Brownmiller, *Femininity,* p. 195.

24. Ellen Goodman, "Heckler Wasn't Twice as Good," *Washington Post,* October, 1985. For more information on menstruation and active women, we suggest the reader consult Jacqueline L. Puhl and C. Harmon Brown, eds., *The Menstrual Cycle and Physical Activity,* the proceedings on a 1984 seminar at the Olympic Training Center, Colorado Springs, Colorado, under the sponsorship of the U.S. Olympic Committee Sports Medicine Council, in cooperation with Tampax, Inc. (Champaign, Ill. Human Kinetics Publishers, Inc., 1984). Particularly useful to us were "The Menstrual Cycle and Athletic Performance" by Jeanne Brooks-Gunn, Janine Fargiulo, and Michelle P. Warren, and "Etiology of Athletic Amenorrhea" by Charlotte Feicht Sanborn. A description of current research on menstruation in the workplace can be found in Sioban D. Harlow's "Function and Dysfunction: A Historical Critique of the Literature on Menstruation and Work" in *Culture, Society and Menstruation,* ed. Virginia L. Oleson and Nancy Fugate Woods (Washington, D.C.: Hemisphere, 1986).

Chapter 7. The Menstrual Process

1. We wish to thank Sharon Golub for suggesting our approach to this Afterword and for providing us with a recommended list of books.

Chapter 8. The First Pollution: Psychoanalysis and the Menarche

1. Otto Fenichel, *The Psychoanalytic Theory of Neuroses* (New York: Norton, 1945), p. 11.

2. Sigmund Freud, *The Complete Psychological Works*, trans. James Strachey, vol. 1 (London: Hogarth, 1961), p. 390. All subsequent references to Freud are to this edition.

3. Mary Chadwick, *The Psychological Effects of Menstruation* (New York: Nervous & Mental Diseases, 1932), p. 33.

4. Helene Deutsch, *The Psychology of Women*, 2 vols. (New York: Grune, 1944), vol. 2, pp. 460-470. Further citations from Deutsch are from this edition.

5. Erik Erikson, *Identity: Youth and Crisis* (New York: Norton, 1968), p. 278.

6. Melanie Klein, *Papers on Psycho-Analysis*, 2d ed. (London, 1918), p. 560.

7. Klein, *Papers on Psycho-Analysis*, pp. 307-309.

8. Norman O. Brown, *Love's Body* (New York: Random House, 1966), p. 63.

9. Vivian Gornick and Barbara K. Moran, eds., *Woman in Sexist Society* (New York: Basic Books, 1971), p. 18.

10. Chadwick, *The Psychological Effects of Menstruation*, pp. 28-35.

11. Karen Horney, *Feminine Psychology* (New York: Norton, 1967), pp. 78-79.

12. Clara M. Thompson, *Interpersonal Psychoanalysis: The Selected Papers of Clara M. Thompson*, ed. Maurice R. Green (New York: Basic Books, 1964), p. 305. Subsequent references are to this edition.

13. Natalie Shainess, "A Re-evaluation of Some Aspects of Femininity Through a Study of Menstruation: A Preliminary Report," *Comprehensive Psychiatry* 2 (1961):24.

14. Fenichel, *The Psychoanalytic Theory of Neuroses*, pp. 411, 240.

15. Karen Horney, "The Problems of Feminine Masochism" (1933), in *Feminine Psychology*, pp. 232-233.

16. Horney, "The Problems of Feminine Masochism," pp. 234-241.

17. Thompson, *Interpersonal Psychoanalysis: The Selected Papers of Clara M. Thompson*, pp. 234-235.

18. Judith Kestenberg, "Menarche," in *Adolescents: A Psychoanalytic Approach to Problems and Therapy*, ed. Sandor Lorand and Henry Scheer (New York: Harper & Row, 1964), p. 34.

19. The ideas presented in this Afterword are part of a forthcoming book by Mary Jane Lupton on feminism and psychoanalysis, and should be so acknowledged.

20. Claude Dagmar Daly, "The Role of Menstruation in Human Phylogenesis and Ontogenesis," *International Journal of Psychoanalysis* 24 (1943): 151-70.

21. Luce Irigary, *This Sex Which Is Not One,* trans. Catherine Porter (Ithaca: Cornell University Press, 1985), p. 168. Originally published in 1977 by Editions de Minuit.

22. Luce Irigaray, *Speculum of the Other Woman,* trans. Gillian C. Gill (Ithaca: Cornell University Press, 1985), p. 29. Originally published in French in 1974 by Les Editions de Minuit.

23. Irigary, *This Sex Which Is Not One,* p. 168.

Chapter 9. The Storm Before the Calm: The Premenstrual Syndrome

1. Karen Horney, "Premenstrual Tension," in *Feminine Psychology,* (New York: Norton, 1967), pp. 99-106; and Robert Frank, "The Hormonal Causes of Premenstrual Tension," *Archives of Neurology and Psychiatry* 26 (1931): 1053.

2. Katharina Dalton, *The Menstrual Cycle* (New York: Pantheon, 1971).

3. Judith Bardwick and Melville Ivey, *Psychology of Women* (New York: Harper & Row, 1971), pp. 30-33.

4. Karen Paige, "Women Learn to Sing the Menstrual Blues," *Psychology Today,* September 1973, pp. 41-46.

5. Horney, "Premenstrual Tension," in *Feminine Psychology,* pp. 99-106.

6. Therese Benedek, *Psychosexual Functions in Women* (New York: Ronald, 1952).

7. Mary Brown Parlee, "The Premenstrual Syndrome," *Psychological Bulletin* 80 (1973): 454-465.

8. K. Jean and R. John Lennane, "Alleged Psychogenic Disorders in Women—Possible Sexual Prejudice," *New England Journal of Medicine* 288, no. 6 (February 8, 1973): 288-292. Cited in Parlee, "The Premenstrual Syndrome."

9. Other explanations locate the source of premenstrual discomfort in the pituitary gland, in the overproduction of desoxycorticosterone (DOC), or in the effects of monoamine oxidase upon the central nervous system. These theories are contained in "A Symposium on Premenstrual Tension," ed. Joseph H. Morton, in *International Record of Medicine* 166 (1953). This symposium contains the following essays: S. Charles Freed, "History and Causation of Premenstrual Tension," pp. 465-468; S. Leon Israel, "The Clinical Pattern and Etiology of Premenstrual Tension," pp. 469-474; Edward L. Suarez-Murias, "The Psychophysiologic Syndrome Premenstrual Tension with Emphasis on the Psychiatric Aspect," pp. 475-486; Harvey E. Billig, Jr., "The Role of Premenstrual Tension in Industry," pp. 487-491; Howard L. Oleck, "Legal Aspects of Premenstrual Tension," pp. 492-501; J. P. Greenhill, "The Treatment of Premenstrual Tension by

Electrolytes," pp. 502-504; Joseph H. Morton, "Treatment of Premenstrual Tension," pp. 505-510.

10. Quoted in Paige, "Women Learn to Sing the Menstrual Blues," p. 44, from a speech made by Berman in July 1970.

11. I. L. McKinnon, P. C. B. McKinnon, and A. D. Thompson, "Lethal Hazards of the Luteal Stage of the Menstrual Cycle," *British Medical Journal* 1 (1959): 1015-1017.

12. Katharina Dalton, "Menstruation and Crime," *British Medical Journal* 2 (1961): 1752.

13. Erna Wright, *Painless Menstrual Periods* (New York: Hart, 1968).

14. R. E. Whitehead, "Notes from the Department of Commerce: Women Pilots," *Journal of Aviation Medicine* 5 (1934): 47-49.

15. C. M. Tonks, "Attempted Suicide and the Menstrual Cycle," *Journal of Psychosomatic Research* 11 (1968): 319-323.

16. Richard D. Wetzel, James N. McClure, and Theodore Reich, "Premenstrual Symptoms in Self-Referrals to a Suicide Prevention Service," *British Journal of Psychiatry* 119 (1971): 525-526.

17. Ayres L. Ribero, "Menstruation and Crime," *British Medical Journal* 640 (1962).

18. A. Alvarez, *The Savage God: A Study of Suicide* (New York: Random House, 1972).

19. Emile Durkheim, *Suicide*, trans. John A. Spaulding and George Simpson (New York: Free Press, 1951), p. 341.

20. Edward B. Allen and George W. Henry, "The Relation of Menstruation to Personality Disorders," *American Journal of Psychiatry* 13 (1933): 239-276.

21. E. Y. Williams and L. R. Weekes, "Premenstrual Tension Associated with Psychotic Episodes," *Journal of Nervous and Mental Diseases* 116 (1952): 321-329.

22. Oleck, "Legal Aspects of Premenstrual Tension," pp. 492-501.

23. Irwin N. Peer, "Medical, Psychiatric and Legal Aspects of Premenstrual Tension," *American Journal of Psychiatry* 115 (1958): 211-219.

24. Aleta Wallach and Larry Rubin, "The Premenstrual Syndrome and Criminal Responsibility," *UCLA Law Review* 19 (1971): 210-312.

25. In the fall of 1973, Susan Lee of the Baltimore Women's Law Center directed a discussion of PMS and the law. According to Ms. Lee, the participants, most of them lawyers or law students, agreed that the issue should be studied more extensively before any move is made to gain its acceptance by the legal community. There was concern that the recognition of PMS as a defense might damage women, owing to the enormous confusion surrounding the syndrome.

26. Nancy Milford, in a review of Juliet Mitchell's *Woman's Estate*, *Partisan Review* (Winter 1973): 147-151.

27. Parlee, "The Premenstrual Syndrome," pp. 454-465.

28. Rudolf H. Moos, *Menstrual Distress Questionnaire: Preliminary Manual* (Department of Psychiatry, Stanford University School of Medicine, 1969). For a critique of the methods of the questionnaire, consult Parlee, "The Premenstrual Syndrome," pp. 454-465.

29. Michelle Harrison, *Self-help for PMS* (New York: Random House, 1982).

30. Judith Green, "Recent Trends in the Treatment of Premenstrual Syndrome: A Critical Review," in *Behavior and the Menstrual Cycle,* ed. Richard C. Friedman (New York and Basel: Marcel-Dekker, 1982).

31. Guy Abraham, "Premenstrual Tension," in *Current Problems in Obstetrics and Gynecology* (Chicago: Yearbook Medical Publishers, 1981), pp. 1-39, passim.

32. See also Ronald V. Norris, M.D. with Colleen Sullivan, *PMS: Premenstrual Syndrome* (New York: Rawson Associates, 1983), pp. 252-53 and passim.

33. Gwyneth A. Sampson, "Premenstrual Syndrome: A Double-Blind Controlled Trial of Progesterone and Placebo," *British Journal of Psychiatry* 135 (1979): 209-15, cited in Penny Wise Budoff, *No More Menstrual Cramps and Other Good News* (New York: G. P. Putnam's Sons, 1980), p. 59. Dalton's work is described in her now-classic *Once a Month* (New York: Hunter House, 1979).

34. Budoff, *No More Menstrual Cramps and Other Good News,* p. 54.

35. Statement on suitable treatment from Judith M. Abplanalp, Ph.D., "Premenstrual Syndrome: A Selective Review," in *Lifting the Curse of Menstruation: A Feminist Appraisal of the Influence of Menstruation on Women's Lives,* ed. Sharon Golub (New York: The Haworth Press, 1983), p. 119. On safety of therapy see Andrea Boroff Eagan, "The Selling of Premenstrual Syndrome," *Ms. Magazine,* October 1983.

36. Mary Brown Parlee, "The Psychology of the Menstrual Cycle: Biological and Physiological Perspectives," in Friedman, *Behavior and the Menstrual Cycle,* p. 80.

37. Norris and Sullivan, *PMS: Premenstrual Syndrome,* p. 47.

38. Rudolph H. Moos, *Premenstrual Symptoms: A Manual and Overview of Research with the Menstrual Distress Questionnaire* (Palo Alto, Calif.: Social Ecology Laboratory, Department of Psychiatry and Behavioral Sciences, Stanford University School of Medicine and Veterans Administration Medical Centers, 1985).

39. Parlee, "The Psychology of the Menstrual Cycle," p. 84.

40. Norris and Sullivan, *PMS: Premenstrual Syndrome,* pp. 269ff.

41. Norris and Sullivan, *PMS: Premenstrual Syndrome,* p. 273.

42. Norris and Sullivan, *PMS: Premenstrual Syndrome,* p. 274. The insanity question is also discussed in Elissa Benedek, M.D., "Premenstrual

Syndrome: A New Defense?" in *The Psychiatric Implications of Menstruation,* ed. Judith Gold, M.D. (Washington, D.C.: American Psychiatric Press, 1985), and in Sharon Golub, "The Effects of Premenstrual Anxiety and Depression on Cognitive Function," *Journal of Personal and Social Psychology* 99 (1976): 99-104.

43. Sandy Rovner, "New PMS Theories Discount Hormones," *Washington Post,* February 19, 1986, Health, 17.

44. Randi Daimon Koeske, "Theoretical Perspectives on Menstrual Cycle Research: The Relevance of Attributional Approaches for the Perception and Explanation of Premenstrual Emotionality," in Gold, *The Psychiatric Implications of Menstruation,* p. 13.

45. See also S. Laws, V. Hey, and A. Eagan, *Seeing Red: The Politics of Premenstrual Tension* (Dover, N.H.: Hutchinson, 1985).

46. Eric Eckholm, "Premenstrual Problems Seem to Beset Baboons," *New York Times,* June 4, 1985, sec. C. The study was done by Glenn Hausfater and Barbara Skoblik and published as "Perimenstrual Behavior Changes among Female Yellow Baboons: Some Similarities to Premenstrual Syndrome (PMS) in Women" in *American Journal of Primatology* 9, no. 3 (1985): 165-72.

47. More valuable insights on the unreliability and inconclusiveness of research into PMS can be found in Anne Fausto-Sterling's *Myths of Gender: Biological Theories About Women and Men* (New York: Basic Books, 1986). She makes an especially cogent argument for more basic research on the female reproductive cycle itself, noting the difficulty of defining a "symptom" or a "syndrome" when we don't know for sure what is "normal."

Chapter 10. "What Every Girl Should Know"

1. *A Notebook of Intimate Problems* (New York, 1934), pp. 13-14, 97.

2. William S. Sadler, *A Doctor Talks to Teenagers* (St. Louis: Mosby, 1948), pp. 270-272.

3. Judy Blume, *Are You There God? It's Me, Margaret* (New York: Bradbury, 1970), pp. 94-97.

4. Boston Women's Health Collective, *Our Bodies, Ourselves: A Book By and For Women* (New York: Simon and Schuster, 1973), p. 15.

5. "Battle of the Badge: Philadelphia's Proposed Womanhood Badge," *Newsweek,* July 23, 1973.

6. Susan Okie, "Teaching Young Women About Toxic Shock," *Washington Post,* July 31, 1985, Health, p. 9.

7. Byllye Y. Avery, "Breaking the Silence about Menstruation: Thoughts from a Mother/Health Activist," *Sage: A Scholarly Journal on Black Women* 1, no. 2 (Fall 1984): 30.

8. Carin Reuben, "Menstruation: The Shame of It All," *Psychology Today,* July 1980.

9. Susan Marie Stoltzman, "Menstrual Attitudes, Beliefs and Symptom Experiences of Adolescent Females, Their Peers, and Their Mothers," in *Culture, Society and Menstruation,* ed. Virginia L. Olesen and Nancy Fugate Woods (Washington, D.C.: Hemisphere, 1986).

10. Lynda Madaras with Area Madaras, *What's Happening to My Body?* (New York: Newmarket Press, 1983).

Chapter 11. The Monthly Euphemism

1. Unless otherwise attributed, all expressions come from our own observations and those of friends (especially Jean Paris of Johns Hopkins University) or from two sources: Hermann Heinrich Ploss, Max Bartels, and Paul Bartels, *Woman: An Historical Gynaecological and Anthropological Compendium,* ed. Eric John Dingwall (St. Louis: Mosby, 1936), p. 588; and Natalie F. Joffe, "The Vernacular of Menstruation," *Word* 4 (1948): 181-186. Joffe's is the most complete discussion and the only study to focus directly on menstrual language. Later discussions of expressions add nothing to her listings.

2. Penelope Shuttle and Peter Redgrove, *The Wise Wound: Eve's Curse and Everywoman* (New York: Richard Marek, 1978), p. 54.

3. Jules Zanger, "Speaking the Unspeakable: Hawthorne's 'The Birthmark,'" *Modern Philology* 80, no. 4 (May 1983): 369, 370.

4. At an academic conference in September 1986 Mary Jane was being introduced by a woman who was glad not to have to mention *The Curse* because she did not want to have to say the word *menstruation* in public. Such silence is not always the case, however. During a lecture at the Johns Hopkins University in October 1986, feminist Jacqueline Rose, co-editor of *Feminine Sexuality: Jacques Lacan and the ecole Freudienne* (New York: W. W. Norton, 1985), openly mentioned menstruation in her discussion of the fiction of George Eliot.

Chapter 12. Red Humor: The Menstrual Joke

1. Unless a book source is given, joke examples come from friends or personal memories or from two joke books: Anonymous, *Still More from Sex to Sexty* (Fort Worth, 1968), and Anonymous, *Cupid Sex to Sexty* (Fort Worth, 1973).

2. Sigmund Freud, *Jokes and Their Relation to the Unconscious,* trans. James Strachey (New York: Norton, 1961), p. 97.

3. G. Legman, *The Rationale of the Dirty Joke* (New York: Grove, 1968), p. 684.

4. Marilyn Coffey, *Marcella* (New York: Charterhouse Books, 1973), p. 92.

5. See Blanche Knott, *Truly Tasteless Jokes* (New York: Ballantine Books, 1982); Blanche Knott, *Truly Tasteless Jokes Two* (New York: Ballantine Books, 1983); and Julius Alvin, *Gross Jokes* (New York: Zebra Books, 1983). Knott and Alvin are both pseudonyms.

6. Alvin, *Gross Jokes,* p. 107.

7. Knott, *Truly Tasteless Jokes,* p. 74.

8. Knott, *Truly Tasteless Jokes,* p. 60.

9. Knott, *Truly Tasteless Jokes,* pp. 58, 77.

10. Knott, *Truly Tasteless Jokes,* p. 70.

11. Knott, *Truly Tasteless Jokes,* p. 62.

12. Knott, *Truly Tasteless Jokes,* p. 62.

13. Knott, *Truly Tasteless Jokes,* p. 58.

14. Knott, *Truly Tasteless Jokes,* p. 75.

15. Knott, *Truly Tasteless Jokes,* p. 58.

16. Gloria Steinem, "If Men Could Menstruate," in *Pulling Our Own Strings,* eds. Gloria Kaufman and Mary Kay Blakely (Bloomington: Indiana University Press, 1980), pp. 25-26. Reprinted in Steinem's *Outrageous Acts and Everyday Rebellions* (New York: Holt, Rinehart & Winston, 1983), pp. 337-40.

17. Kaufman and Blakely, *Pulling Our Own Strings.* Cited materials are from the following: Claire Bretecher, "The First Tampon," pp. 18-21; E. M. Bromer, "Periodical Bea," p. 21; Unsigned, "Mosquitoes & Menses," p. 29; Marilyn French, "Splat," pp. 23-24; Hadley V. Baxendale, M.D., Ph.D, "A Person Who Menstruates is Unfit to Be a Mother," p. 24.

18. Dale Spender and Lynne Spender, *Scribbling Sisters* (Sydney, Australia: Hale & Iremonger, 1984), pp. 148-49.

Chapter 13. Periodic Parade: Menstruation in Advertising

1. Alice Munro, *Lives of Girls and Women* (New York: McGraw-Hill, 1972).

2. Debbie Rewalt, "Trends in Advertising of Feminine Hygiene Products," unpublished paper supplied to us by James Brooks of Campana Corporation.

3. *Supermarket,* October 1972, p. 60.

4. *Supermarket,* October 1972, p. 60.

5. "Dear Abby," *Centre Daily Times,* (State College, Penn.), July 24, 1984, sec. B.

6. Tampax's copy using the word *period* was originally accepted by censors at ABC and NBC, but CBS rejected it as too slangy: they preferred

the term *menstrual cycle*. See Maurine Christopher, "Tampax unveils new candor in 'period' ad," *Advertising Age*, March 11, 1985, p. 62.

7. Miller is quoted in *Savvy*, June 1985.

Chapter 14. Rags to Riches: The Menstrual Products Industry

1. William N. Stephens, *A Cross-Cultured Study of Menstrual Taboos* (Provincetown, Mass.: Genetic Psych. Monographs, 1961), p. 399.

2. H. Frederick Kilander, *Sex Education in the Schools* (London: Collier-Macmillan, 1970), pp. 267-270.

3. Eric Trimmer, *Femina* (New York: Stein & Day, 1966), p. 24.

4. Joseph A. Page, "What the FDA Won't Tell You about FDS," *The Washington Monthly* 5 (March 1973): 19-25.

5. Alicia Bay Laurel, *Living on the Earth* (Berkeley, 1970).

6. Information on testing and research cited below is available from the following manufacturers: Campana Corp., Batavia, Ill. 60410; Kimberly-Clark Corp., N. Lake St., Neenah, Wisc. 54956; Personal Products Co., 501 George St., New Brunswick, N.J.; Tampax, Inc., 5 Dakota Dr., Lake Success, N.Y. 11040; Tassaway, Inc., 155 So. Robertson Blvd., Beverly Hills, Calif. 90211.

7. Christine Russell, "Flu Believed to Trigger Some Toxic Shock Cases," *Washington Post*, March 7, 1986, sec. A.

8. James K. Todd, quoted in Peter Radetsky, "The Rise and (maybe not the) Fall of Toxic Shock Syndrome," *Science 85* 6, no. 1 (January/February 1985): 76.

9. Case numbers: personal communication with CDC researcher Suzanne Giventa, November 25, 1985. New study: "U.S. Study Aims at Assessing Number of Toxic Shock Cases," *New York Times*, December 2, 1985, sec. B.

10. U.S. Senate Committee on Labor and Human Resources, Subcommittee on Health and Scientific Research, *Toxic Shock Syndrome*, (Washington, D.C.: U.S. Government Printing Office, 1980).

11. "Mayo Study Claims Tampons Don't Contain Toxic Elements," *Baltimore Sun*, March 16, 1982.

12. Lawrence K. Altaman, "Clues to Toxic Shock Syndrome Found," *New York Times*, June 6, 1985, sec. A.

13. "Judge Wants Tampon Off Market," *Centre Daily Times* (State College, Penn.), March 22, 1985, sec. A.

14. Nan Robertson, "Toxic Shock," *New York Times Magazine*, September 19, 1982, pp. 30-117.

15. Jane C. Brody, "Personal Health," *New York Times*, July 31, 1985, sec. C.

16. "A Plea from the Boston Women's Health Book Collective," *National Women's Studies Association Newsletter* 2, no. 2 (Spring 1984): 6.

17. "Are Tampons Safer Now?" *Consumer Reports,* May 1986, pp. 332-34.

18. Linda K. Fuller, Ph.D., "Personal Hygiene Products: A Case Study in Forced Compliance," paper presented to the International Communications Association, Chicago, May 1986.

19. "Sea Sponges," FDA "Talk Paper," U.S. Food and Drug Administration, December 12, 1980.

20. Daniel Colburn, M.D., "Tampon Related Injuries," paper presented April 8, 1983, at conference on Menstruation: The Physiology and Pathology of the Menstrual Flow and the Effects of Hygiene Products, sponsored by the University of Medicine and Dentistry of New Jersey–Rutgers Medical School, Department of Obstetrics and Gynecology, in cooperation with the UMDNJ–Office of Continuing Education, Atlantic City, New Jersey, April 8-9, 1983.

21. Personal communication from Susan Keithler, public relations manager for Personal Products Company, September 30, 1985.

22. Radetsky, "The Rise and (maybe not the) Fall of Toxic Shock Syndrome," 78.

23. Nadine Broznan, "Gynecologists as perplexed as patients," *New York Times,* September 24, 1980, sec. C.

24. Information about toxic shock syndrome comes at us almost daily, from the pages of newspapers and women's magazines, from *Time, Newsweek,* and *USA Today.* Because these publications invariably digest their information from major articles in medical journals, we recommend that persons who want the actual record of research consult a medical library. One such source, which we have used, is Charlotte Kenton, compiler, "Literature Search: Toxic Shock Syndrome," *National Library of Medicine* 82-84 (1983), 255 citations. Such searches can be as up-to-date as possible and an invaluable aid to the serious medical researcher.

Chapter 15. Menstruation Goes Public

1. Aaron Latham, "Tom Seaver in the Locker Room," *New York,* April 15, 1974, p. 39.

2. Blair Sabol, "Shooting from the Hip," *Village Voice,* July 4, 1974, p. 40.

3. Jill Johnston, "Living Heavily Ever After," *Village Voice,* January 24, 1974, p. 28.

4. "All in the Family," *New York Times,* February 24, 1974.

5. Interview with Jackie Gleason, *New York Times,* August 5, 1973.

6. "The Bloods" appears in *The Berkeley Music Collective Songbook*, and has been recorded by The Berkeley Women's Music Collective on Olivia Records. Both are available from Debbie Lempke, 2838 Mcgee Ave., Berkeley, Calif. 94703.

7. Judith Krantz, *Princess Daisy* (New York: Bantam, 1981), p. 328.

8. "Santa Barbara," aired on NBC, February 4, 1985.

9. These groups are listed in *The Feminist Dictionary*, ed. Cheris Kramarae (Boston: Pandora Press, 1985), under "Periodicals." We wish to thank Paula Treichler for this information.

10. Carol Erdman, "Song for Sisters in the Moon Hut," in *Womanspirit*, date unknown. Over the years friends have been sending us song titles, television references, and sections from women's rituals, but they haven't always included documentation.

11. Penelope Shuttle and Peter Redgrove, *The Wise Wound: Eve's Curse and Everywoman* (New York: Richard Marek, 1978), p. 272.

12. Walter Evans, "Monster Movies: A Sexual Theory," *Journal of Popular Film* 2, no. 4 (Fall 1983): 357.

13. See the discussion of menstrual symbols in Chapter 18, "The Miracle of Blood."

Chapter 16. The Bleeding Tower: Menstrual Themes in Fairy Tales

1. *Grimm's Household Tales, with the Authors' Notes*, trans. Margaret Hunt (Detroit: Singing Tree, 1968); *The Juniper Tree and Other Tales from Grimm*, ed. Lore Segal and Maurice Sendak (New York: Farrar, Straus, 1973).

2. Wolfgang Lederer, *The Fear of Women* (New York: Grune, 1968), p. 200.

3. Lederer, *The Fear of Women*, p. 200.

4. Arland Ussher and Carl Von Metzradt, *Enter These Enchanted Woods: An Interpretation of Grimm's Fairy Tales* (Dublin, 1966), pp. 9-10.

5. Thirteen is an unlucky number because of its association with women: There are thirteen "moons" in a calendar year and thirteen menstrual periods.

6. Bruno Bettleheim, *The Uses of Enchantment: The Meaning and Importance of Fairy Tales* (New York: Vintage, 1976), p. 235.

7. Bettleheim, *The Uses of Enchantment*, p. 168.

8. Barbara G. Walker, *The Woman's Encyclopedia of Myths and Secrets* (New York: Harper & Row, 1983), pp. 544-55.

9. Jack Zipes, *The Trials and Tribulations of Little Red Riding Hood: Versions of the Tale in Sociocultural Context* (South Hadley, Mass.: Bergin & Gravey, 1983), p. 13.

Chapter 17. Absent Literature: The Menarche

1. Works cited in this chapter were used in the following editions: Edmond de Goncourt, *Chérie* (Paris: Charpentier, 1884); Emile Zola, *La Joie de Vivre* ("Zest for Life"), trans. Jean Stewart (London: Elek, 1955); Collette Audry, *Aux Yeux de Souvenir* (1947), quoted in Simone de Beauvoir, *The Second Sex* (New York: Knopf, 1952), p. 295; Emma Goldman, *Living My Life*, vol. 1 (New York: Dover, 1970), p. 21; *A Young Girl's Diary*, preface by Sigmund Freud, trans. Eden and Cedar Paul (New York: Thomas Seltzer, 1923); Mary McCarthy, *Memories of a Catholic Girlhood* (New York: Harcourt Brace Jovanovich, 1957), pp. 131-134; Anne Frank, *The Diary of a Young Girl* (New York: Pocket Books, 1953), p. 115; Thyde Monnier, *Moi* (1949), quoted in de Beauvoir, *The Second Sex*, p. 292; Radclyffe Hall, *The Well of Loneliness* (London: Hammond, 1956), p. 83; Christopher Morley, *Kitty Foyle* (Philadelphia: Lippincott, 1939), p. 37; Betty Smith, *A Tree Grows in Brooklyn* (New York: Harper, 1943), pp. 194-195; Rumer Godden, *Greengage Summer* (New York: Viking, 1958), p. 167; Jay Kennedy, *Prince Bart* (New York: Farrar, Straus and Young, 1953), p. 287; Ella Leffland, *Mrs. Munck* (New York: Pocket Books, 1970), p. 21; Joyce Carol Oates, *them* (Greenwich: Fawcett, 1969), p. 157; Margaret Embry, *Shadi* (New York: Holiday House, 1971), p. 12; Toni Morrison, *The Bluest Eye* (New York: Pocket Books, 1970), pp. 25-28; Penelope Street, "The Magic Apple," in *Best American Short Stories of 1972*, ed. Martha Foley (Boston: Houghton Mifflin, 1973), p. 309; Peter Marks, *Hangups* (New York: Random House, 1973), pp. 141-142; Julia Whedon, *Girl of the Golden West* (New York: Charterhouse, 1973), p. 105; Sandra Hochman, *Walking Papers* (New York: Ballantine, 1971), p. 60; Lois Gould, *Such Good Friends* (New York: Dell, 1970), p. 107; Alix Kates Schulman, *Memoirs of an Ex-Prom Queen* (New York: Knopf, 1972), p. 41; Judy Blume, *Are You There God? It's Me, Margaret* (New York: Dell, 1970), passim.

2. Stephen King, "On Becoming a Brand Name," in *Fear Itself*, ed. Tim Underwood and Chuck Miller (New York: New American Library, 1984), p. 21.

3. Stephen King, *Carrie* (New York: Signet, 1974), p. 233. See the Afterword to Chapter 15, "Menstruation Goes Public," for a discussion of Brian de Palma's film.

4. Alberto Moravia, *Time of Desecration* (New York: Farrar, Straus & Giroux, 1980), pp. 58, 350.

5. Merrill Joan Gerber, *Now Molly Knows* (New York: Arbor House, 1971), pp. 113-114.

6. Maxine Kumin, "The Facts of Life," in *Why Can't We Live Together Like Civilized Human Beings?* (New York: Viking Press, 1982),

pp. 17-19. See our discussion of the menstruation-death motif in Scott Spenser's *Endless Love* in the Afterword to Chapter 19.

7. Rosa Guy, *A Measure of Time* (New York: Bantam, 1984), p. 152.

8. Maxine Hong Kingston, *The Woman Warrior* (New York: Knopf, 1976), p. 5.

9. Dena Taylor to Mary Jane Lupton, January 27, 1975.

10. Penelope Scambly Schott, "When you phoned home from California to tell me it had started," in *I'm on My Way Running,* eds. Lyn Reese, Jean Wilkinson, and Phyllis Sheon Koppelman (New York: Avon Books, 1983), pp. 39-40.

Chapter 18. The Miracle of Blood: Menstrual Imagery in Myth and Poetry

1. Claude Dagmar Daly, "The Menstruation Complex in Literature," *Psychoanalytic Quarterly* 42 (1935): 307-340.

2. Clark Griffith, *The Long Shadow: Emily Dickinson's Tragic Poetry* (Princeton: Princeton University Press, 1964).

3. Quoted material in this chapter comes from the following sources: Victoria Woodhull is quoted in Page Smith, *Daughters of the Promised Land: Women in American History* (Boston: Little, Brown, 1970); Emily Dickinson, *The Complete Poetry of Emily Dickinson*, ed. Thomas Johnson (Boston: Little, Brown, 1960); Tiamat myth in Padraic Column, *Orpheus: Myths of the World* (New York: Macmillan, 1930); *Collected Poems of Edna St. Vincent Millay,* ed. Norma Millay (New York: Harper, 1956); Nadine MacDonald from *Currents: Concerns and Composition,* ed. Thomas E. Sanders (Beverly Hills: Glencoe, 1971), quoted with permission of editor and Glencoe Press; Persephone myths in Ovid, *Metamorphoses,* trans. Frank Justus Miller, vol. 1, book V, a bilingual edition first published in 1916 (Cambridge: Harvard University Press, 1966) and in Thomas Bulfinch, *The Age of Fable* (New York: Heritage, 1942); Baudelaire, *Flowers of Evil: A Selection,* ed. Martheil and Jackson Mathews, a bilingual text (New York: New Directions, 1955); Sylvia Plath, *The Colossus* (New York: Knopf, 1962), *Ariel* (New York: Harper & Row, 1968), *Crossing the Water* (New York: Harper & Row, 1971), *Winter Trees* (New York: Harper & Row, 1972); Anne Sexton, *To Bedlam and Part Way Back* (Boston: Houghton Mifflin, 1960), *Live or Die* (Boston: Houghton Mifflin, 1966), *Transformations* (Boston: Houghton Mifflin, 1972); *The Collected Poems of W. B. Yeats* (New York: Macmillan, 1956); Adrienne Rich, *The Will to Change* (New York: Norton, 1971); Muriel Rukeyser, in *No More Masks!* ed. Ellen Bass and Florence Howe (New York: 1973).

4. Sigmund Freud, *The Interpretation of Dreams,* trans. A. A. Brill (New York: Random House, 1950), pp. 208-209, 236-237.

5. Winifred Richmond, *The Adolescent Girl: A Book for Parents and Teachers* (New York: Macmillan, 1925), p. 21; and Hutton Webster, *Rest Days: A Study in Early Law and Morality* (New York: Macmillan, 1916), p. 128.

6. Richmond, *The Adolescent Girl: A Book for Parents and Teachers*, p. 5.

7. C. G. Seligmann, *Reports on the Cambridge Anthropological Expedition to Torres Straits*, cited in Webster, *Rest Days: A Study in Early Law and Morality*, p. 128.

8. Fritz Vosselmann, *La Menstruation: Légendes, Coutumes et Superstitions* (Lyon, 1935), pp. 23-24.

9. Penelope Shuttle and Peter Redgrove, *The Wise Wound: Eve's Curse and Everywoman* (New York: Richard Marek, 1978), p. 17.

10. See in particular Bart Jordan's essay "Early Calendrical Art Recreated: A Partial Catalogue," *New England Antiquities Research Association Journal* (NEARA) 19, nos. 1, 2 (Summer/Fall 1984): 1-13.

11. Charles Rycroft, *The Innocence of Dreams* (London: Hogarth Press, 1979), p. 115. For the shift in psychoanalysts' portrayal of the menarche, see Sharon Golub and Joan Catalano, "Recollections of Menarche and Women's Subsequent Experiences with Menstruation," in *Women & Health* 8, no. 1 (Spring 1983): pp. 49-61.

12. The poems cited in this update are from the following editions: Erica Jong, "Inventing My Life," *Ordinary Miracles* (New York: New American Library, 1983), pp. 114-116; Marge Piercy, "The Watch," *Stone, Paper, Knife* (New York: Knopf, 1983), p. 21; Safiya Henderson, "Portrait of a Woman Artist," in *Confirmation: An Anthology of African American Women,* ed. Amiri Baraka and Amina Baraka (New York: Morrow Quill, 1983), p. 131; Audre Lorde, "NEED: A Chorale of Black Women's Voices," in *Confirmation,* pp. 191-97; Ellen Bass, "Tampons," in *For Earthly Survival,* ed. Felicia Rice (Santa Cruz: Moving Parts Press, 1980), pp. 218-31.

Chapter 19. Menstrual Madness in Drama and Fiction

1. Quoted material in this chapter comes from the following sources: August Strindberg, *Miss Julie*, trans. Elizabeth Sprigge (New York: Doubleday, 1965); Alison Lurie, *Love and Friendship* (New York: Macmillan, 1962); Clare Booth Luce, "A Doll's House," *Life*, October 16, 1970; John Fowles, *The French Lieutenant's Woman* (Boston: Little, Brown, 1969); William Faulkner, *The Sound and the Fury* (New York: Random House, 1966) and *Light in August* (New York: Random House, 1967); Miguel de Cervantes, *Don Quixote*, trans. J. M. Cohen (Baltimore: Penguin, 1950); Dan Wakefield, *Going All the Way* (New York: Delacorte, 1970); Alix Kates Schulman, *Memoirs of an Ex-Prom Queen* (New York: Knopf,

1972); Brian Moore, *I Am Mary Dunne* (New York: Viking, 1968); Doris Lessing, *The Golden Notebook* (New York: Simon & Schuster, 1962); and Erica Jong, *Fear of Flying* (New York: Holt, 1973).

2. Rachel M. Brownstein, *Becoming a Heroine: Reading About Women in Novels* (New York: Penguin, 1984), p. 27.

3. The material cited in this Afterword is from the following sources, unless otherwise indicated: Gwen Davis, *Ladies in Waiting* (New York: Macmillan, 1979); Jenny Bates, *Gilded Spring* (New York: Berkley, 1983); Emily Toth, *Daughters of New Orleans* (New York: Bantam, 1983), pp. 392, 291; Toni Cade Bambara, *The Salt Eaters* (New York: Vintage Books, 1981), p. 26; Alice Walker, *The Color Purple* (New York: Harcourt Brace Jovanovich, 1982), p. 161; Tabitha King, *Small World* (New York: Macmillan, 1981), pp. 193-94, 221; Erica Jong, *Parachutes and Kisses* (New York: New American Library, 1984), pp. 283-87; Scott Spencer, *Endless Love* (New York: Knopf, 1979), pp. 298, 316, 227; Lawrence Sanders, *The Third Deadly Sin* (New York: Berkley, 1982), pp. 1, 11, 247.

4. Mary Jane Lupton and Emily Toth, "Out, Damned Spot!" *Ms. Magazine,* January 1974, pp. 97-99. We were also somewhat amused to find menstruation treated with dark red humor in Steven King's latest epic, *IT* (New York: Viking, 1986). Patty, who wants to get pregnant, imagines that the Stayfree napkin box is talking to her: "*Hello, Patty! We are your children. We are the only children you will ever have, and we are hungry. Nurse us. Nurse us on blood*" (p. 50, emphasis King's).

5. Ronald V. Norris and Colleen Sullivan, *PMS: Premenstrual Syndrome* (New York: Rawson, 1983), p. 5.

Chapter 20. From Leeches to Estrogen: The Menopause and Medical Options

1. Charles Richard Gilbert, *Better Health for Women* (Garden City, N.Y.: Doubleday, 1964), p. 72.

2. Peter Curzen, "Eliminating the Menopause," *Practitioner* 208 (1972): 387.

3. G. Courtenay Beale, *Woman's Change of Life* (New York: Self-Science Institute, 1934), p. 46.

4. Cited by Andrew Currier, *The Menopause* (New York, 1897), p. 99.

5. Edward John Tilt, *The Change of Life in Health and Disease*, 2d ed. (London, 1857), p. 29.

6. Currier, *The Menopause*, pp. 153-154, 233-236.

7. Robert A. Wilson, *Feminine Forever* (New York: M. Evans, 1966). Wilson's book literally opened up the subject of menopause in popular magazines.

8. Tilt, *The Change of Life in Health and Disease*, p. 66.

9. Wilson, *Feminine Forever*, pp. 42, 84.

10. Kenneth Hutchin, *How Not to Kill Your Wife* (New York: Hawthorn, 1965), p. 188.

11. Bernice Neugarten, "A New Look at Menopause," *The Female Experience* (Del Mar, Calif., 1973), pp. 39-44.

12. William E. Easterling, "Managing the Menopause," *American Family Physician* 73 (1973): 137-142. Recent research has been conducted to establish a possible connection between menopause and cancer; none of it, however, is conclusive. See Kadhim Mohammed Al-Issa, "Maturation Index in Post-menopausal Risk and other Risk Factors to Recurrence of Carcinoma of the Breast," *Am. L. Epidemiol.* 96 (1972): 173-182; Gilliam Frere, "Mean Age at Menopause and Menarche in South Africa," *S. Afr. J. Med. Sci.* 36 (1971): 21-24. For a less recent but more comprehensive assessment of the menopause-cancer relationship, see Sherwin S. Kaufman, *The Ageless Woman: Menopause, Hormones, and the Quest for Youth* (Englewood Cliffs, N.J.: Prentice-Hall, 1967).

13. Wilson, *Feminine Forever*, pp. 130-139.

14. Tile, *The Change of Life in Health and Disease*, pp. 52-91.

15. Currier, *The Menopause*, p. 249.

16. Curzen, "Eliminating the Menopause," p. 387.

17. M. E. Schleyer-Saonders, "Une Nouvelle Conception du Climactera," *Gynecol. Prac.*, 22 (1971): 493-500.

Chapter 21. Psychology and the Menopausal Menance

1. See the chapter "Disease of the Cerebro-Vascular System," in Edward John Tilt, *The Change of Life in Health and Disease*, 2d ed. (London, 1857).

2. Sigmund Freud, *Complete Psychological Works*, trans. James Strachey (London: Hogarth, 1961), vol. 3, vol. 23, p. 226; quoted by Isidor Silberman, "A Contribution to the Psychology of Menstruation," *International Journal of Psycho-Analysis* 31 (1950): 266.

3. Helene Deutsch, *Psychology of Women*, 2 vols. (New York: Grune, 1944). See especially vol. 2, pp. 460-470, on the climacteric.

4. Erik Erikson, *Identity: Youth and Crisis* (New York: Norton, 1968), p. 278.

5. Joseph C. Rheingold, *The Fear of Being a Woman: A Theory of Maternal Destructiveness* (New York: Grune, 1964), pp. 492-501.

6. William S. Sadler and Lena K. Sadler, *Living a Sane Sex Life* (Chicago: Follett, 1938), p. 296.

7. Morton M. Hunt, *Her Infinite Variety: The American Woman as Lover, Mate and Rival* (New York: Harper, 1962), pp. 189-190.

8. Philip Wylie, *Generation of Vipers* (New York: Holt, 1955, originally published in 1942), pp. 196-199.

9. Simone de Beauvoir, "From Maturity to Old Age," *The Second Sex* (New York: Knopf, 1968), pp. 541-561. Originally published in France by Librairie Gallimard, 1949. Earlier in the book, de Beauvoir claims for the menopausal woman a new health and vigor (p. 28). Generally, however, her attitude is negative.

10. Clara M. Thompson, *Interpersonal Psychoanalysis: The Selected Papers of Clara M. Thompson*, ed. Maurice R. Green (New York: Basic Books, 1964), p. 339.

11. George Devereaux, "The Psychology of Feminine Genital Bleeding: An Analysis of Mohave Indian Puberty and Menstrual Rites," *International Journal of Psycho-Analysis* 31 (1950): 168.

12. Quoted by Carroll Smith-Rosenberg, "Puberty to Menopause: The Cycle of Femininity in Nineteenth-Century America," *Feminist Studies* 1 (1973): 58-72. Smith-Rosenberg quotes from a number of sources, including the diary of Elizabeth Drinker.

13. Ann Garlin Spencer, *Woman's Shares in Social Culture* (Philadelphia: Lippincott, 1925).

14. Clelia Mosher, *Health and the Woman Movement* (New York: Woman's Press, 1916), pp. 46-49.

15. Video tape, "Well-kept Secrets Revealed: Women's Experience with Changes of Life," produced by Feminist Women's Workshop, California Institute of the Arts, distributed by Vision Quest, Inc.

16. Bernice Neugarten, "A New Look at Menopause," *The Female Experience* (Del Mar, Calif., 1973), pp. 39-44.

17. "Menopause at 33," *Good Housekeeping*, October 1973, p. 16 ff.

Chapter 22. "November of the Body": The Menopause and Literature

1. Quoted material in this chapter comes from the following sources: Mary Jane Lupton, *Elizabeth Barrett Browning* (Baltimore: Feminist Press, 1972); William Faulkner, *Light in August* (New York: Random House, 1967); Jack London, "Samuel," reprinted from *Moon Face* in Anne Fremantle's *Mothers: A Catholic Treasury of Great Stories* (New York: Ungar, 1951); Lillian Smith, *Strange Fruit* (New York: Harcourt, Brace, 1944); Nancy Milford, *Zelda* (New York: Harper & Row, 1970); John O'Hara, *The Ewings* (New York: Random House, 1972); Doris Lessing, *The Summer Before the Dark* (New York: Simon & Schuster, 1973); Tennessee Williams, *The Roman Spring of Mrs. Stone* (New York: New Directions, 1969); Angus Wilson, *The Middle Age of Mrs. Eliot* (New York: Harper & Row, 1959); James Joyce, *Ulysses* (New York: Modern Library, 1940); Thomas Mann, *The Black Swan* (New York: Knopf, 1954); Betty Smith,

A Tree Grows in Brooklyn (New York: Harper, 1947); *No More Masks!* ed. Florence Howe and Ellen Bass (Garden City, N.Y.: Doubleday, 1973); Henry Miller, *Tropic of Cancer* (New York: Grove, 1970); May Sarton, *Mrs. Stevens Hears the Mermaids Singing* (New York: Norton, 1965); Homer, *The Odyssey*, trans. Robert Fitzgerald (Garden City, N.Y.: Doubleday, 1961); Geoffrey Chaucer, *The Canterbury Tales: A Selection*, ed. Donald R. Howard and James M. Dean (New York: New American Library, 1969).

2. Emily Toth has noticed that the menopause actually occurs in mid-August rather than in November. We also wish to thank Professor Alan D. Latta of the University of Toronto for informing us of several errors in our discussion of Thomas Mann's *The Black Swan* in the 1976 edition, in particular the following: the outing is in a castle and not a cave; Ken is a tutor and not a guide; Rosalie's period had "already reasserted itself" before the outing.

3. R. Don Gambrell, "The Menopause: Benefits and Risks of Estrogen-progestogen Replacement Therapy," *Fertility and Sterility* 37, no. 4 (1982): 457-74.

4. Barbara S. Hulka et al., "Breast Cancer and Estrogen Replacement Therapy," *American Journal of Obstetrics and Gynecology* 143, no. 6 (1982): 638-44.

5. R. Don Gambrell, quoted by Jane E. Brody, "Personal Health," *New York Times*, April 17, 1985.

6. See also B. R. Carr, et al., "Estrogen Treatment of Post-Menopausal Women," *Advanced Internal Medicine* 2, no. 8 (1983): 491-508; Jean Cooper, "Menopause Diagnosis and Treatment," *British Medical Journal* 289 (October 6, 1984): 889-90; J. Jenson et al., "Cigarette Smoking, Serum Estrogen, and Bone Loss During Hormone-Replacement Therapy Early After Menopause," *New England Journal of Medicine* 313 (October 17, 1985): 973-75; M. J. Tikkanen et al., "Post-Menopausal Hormone Replacement Therapy: Effects of Progestogens on Serum Lipids and Lipoproteins," *Maturitas* 8, no. 1 (March 1986): 7-17.

7. Carol Lawson, "Estrogen Provided in New Skin Patch," *New York Times*, September 17, 1986, sec. C.

8. Kathleen I. Mac Pherson, "Menopause as Disease: The Social Construction of a Metaphor," *Advances in Nursing Science* 3 (1981): 95-113.

9. Penny Wise Budoff, *No More Hot Flashes and Other Good News* (New York: G. P. Putnam's Sons), 1983.

10. Lawson, "Estrogen Provided in New Skin Patch."

11. Boston Women's Health Collective, *The New Our Bodies, Our Selves* (New York: Simon & Schuster, 1984).

12. Morton Walker, "Hot Flash! Super Sex During Menopause," *Harper's Bazaar*, August 1985, p. 92. For a less optimistic view of menopausal

sexuality see James P. and Eva Curtis Semmens, "Sexual Function and the Menopause," *Clinical Obstetrics and Gynecology* 27, no. 3 (September 1984): 717-32.

13. "Editorials," *Journal of the American Medical Association* 254, no. 24 (1984): 3411-12. Write Vagitone Gyn-Tek Inc., P.O. Box 29017, Portland, Oregon.

14. Jane Fonda with Mignon McCarthy, *Women Coming of Age* (New York: Simon & Schuster, 1984).

15. Carol Kahn, "The Total Anti-Aging Plan," *McCall's*, August 1985, pp. 69-73, 136-38.

16. Budoff, *No More Hot Flashes and Other Good News*, p. 47.

17. Madeline Osborn, "Depression at the Menopause," *British Journal of Hospital Medicine* 32, no. 3 (1984): 129. Emphasis ours.

18. Malkah T. Notman, "Psychaitric Disorders of Menopause," *Psychiatric Annals* 14, no. 6 (1984): 448-53; Paula Weideger, *Menstruation and Menopause* (New York: Knopf, 1976); Arne Holte, in an interview with Sally Squires, "Mcnopause: Beyond the Myths," *Washington Post,* October 24, 1984, sec. D.

19. Maggie Scarf, *Unfinished Business: Pressure Points in the Lives of Women* (Garden City, N.Y.: Doubleday, 1980), p. 398.

20. Since its inception "Golden Girls" has been extremely frank about the menopause and about menopausal sexuality. In one episode, aired October 5, 1986, on NBC, Blanche first feels sexy when she thinks she's pregnant, then becomes depressed when she realizes that her irregularity is a sign of menopause.

21. Mary Jane Lupton, "Zora Neale Hurston and the Survival of the Female, *Southern Literary Journal* 15, no. 1 (Fall 1982): 46-54. See also Elaine Morgan, *The Descent of Woman* (New York: Stein & Day, 1972), p. 235, for a discussion on menopause and memory among humans.

22. Julianne Fleenor, "The Change," *Broomstick* 8, no. 5 (September-October 1986): 3-8.

23. Marjorie Shostak, *Nisa: The Life and Words of a !Kung Woman* (New York: Random House/Vintage Books, 1983), p. 326.

24. Virginia Terris, "At 59," *Xanadu* 5 (1979): 43.

25. The poems cited here are from the aging issue published by *Women* (formerly *Women: a Journal of Liberation*) 4, no. 4 (1976):   Mary Winfrey, "at menopause," p. 25; Harriet Murphy, "The Woman," p. 37; Kathy Kozachenko, "Midpoint," p. 1.

Chapter 23. The Menstrual Hall of Fame

1. Jules Michelet, *Joan of Arc* (Ann Arbor: University of Michigan Press, 1957), p. 9.

2. Eleanor Flexner, *Century of Struggle: The Woman's Rights Movement in the United States* (New York: Atheneum, 1968), p. 11.

3. Emery Battis, *Saints and Sectaries* (Chapel Hill, N.C.: University of North Carolina Press, 1962), passim.

4. Emma Goldman, *Living My Life*, vol. 1 (New York: Peter Smith, 1970), pp. 57-61.

5. André Maurois, *Lélia: The Life of George Sand*, trans. Gerard Hopkins (New York: Harper, 1953), p. 94.

6. Virginia Woolf, *A Writer's Diary*, ed. Leonard Woolf (New York: Harcourt, Brace, 1954).

7. Victoria Lincoln, *A Private Disgrace: Lizzie Borden by Daylight* (New York: Putnam, 1967).

Chapter 24. Moving the Menses, or Vicarious Menstruation

1. S. L. Israel, *Diagnosis and Treatment of Menstrual Disorders and Sterility*, 4th ed. (New York: Harper & Row, 1967), p. 213.

2. J. M. Dunn, "Vicarious Menstruation," *American Journal of Obstetrics and Gynecology* 114 (1972): 568.

3. C. Frederic Fluhmann, *The Management of Menstrual Disorders* (Philadelphia: Saunders, 1956), p. 132.

4. Fluhmann, *The Management of Menstrual Disorders*, pp. 288-289; Dunn, "Vicarious Menstruation," pp. 568-569.

5. J. T. Gordon, "An Unusual Case of Vicarious Menstruation," *American Journal of Obstetrics* 15 (1882): 343-344.

6. Marie Allen Smith, "Menstrual Disorders: Incidence and Relationship to Attitudes, Manifest Needs, and Scholastic Achievement in College Freshmen Women" (Ed. D. diss., University of Denver, 1970), p. 21.

7. The discussion of de Palma and vicarious menstruation is based on materials from the Afterword to Chapter 15, "Menstruation Goes Public."

Chapter 25. Escaping the Monthlies

1. Germaine Greer, *The Female Eunuch* (New York: McGraw-Hill, 1971), p. 42.

2. George Starr White, *The Emancipation of Women, or Regulating the Duration of the Menses* (Los Angeles: Privately printed, 1934), p. 27 and passim.

3. Ira Warren et al., *New Warren's Household Physician* (Boston, 1901), p. 395.

4. White, *The Emancipation of Women*, p. 31.

5. The methadone study was done by R. C. Wallach, G. Blinick, and E. Jerez, in "Pregnancy and Menstrual Function in Narcotics Addicts Treated with Methadone: the Methadone Maintenance Treatment Program," *American Journal of Obstetrics and Gynecology* 105 (1969): 1226. The study of those withdrawing without methadone was by Sheldon Stoffer, in "A Gynecologic Study of Drug Addicts," *American Journal of Obstetrics and Gynecology* 101 (1968): 779-783.

6. Dr. Shelton's views are published by the American Natural Hygiene Society, 1920 Irving Park Road, Chicago, Ill. 60613.

7. John Hersey, "Hiroshima," *New Yorker*, August 31, 1946, p. 50.

8. The tape, about ninety minutes long, is available from the Los Angeles Women's Health Center, 746 South Crenshaw, Los Angeles, Calif. 90005, for $100.

9. Ellen Frankfort, *Vaginal Politics* (New York: Quadrangle, 1973), pp. 193-201.

10. Telephone conversation with Lorraine Rothman of the Federation of Feminist Women's Health Centers, 6525 Sunset Blvd., Hollywood, Calif. 90028, July 22, 1985.

11. Beryl Benderly, *Thinking About Abortion* (Garden City, N.Y.: Dial Press, Doubleday, 1984).

12. Laura Punnett, "Menstrual Extraction: Politics," *Quest*, 4, no. 3 (Summer 1978): 48-60, reproduced in *Self Help Resource Guide 7*, (Washington, D.C., National Women's Health Network, 1980), pp. 29-25. Other general information about menstrual extraction comes from this source.

Chapter 26. Saignade: Simulated Menstruation in the Male

1. Mary Ellmann, *Thinking About Women* (New York: Harcourt, Brace, 1970), pp. 17-19.

2. Cited in M. J. Meggitt, "Male-Female Relationships in the Highlands of Australian New Guinea," *American Anthropologist* 66 (1964).

3. Bruno Bettelheim, *Symbolic Wounds: Puberty Rites and the Envious Male* (New York: Collier, 1962), p. 19.

4. Joseph Campbell, *The Masks of God* (New York: Viking, 1959), pp. 59-60.

5. Elizabeth Gould Davis, *The First Sex* (Baltimore: Penguin, 1972), pp. 101-104.

6. Bettelheim, *Symbolic Wounds: Puberty Rites and the Envious Male*, p. 106.

7. M. F. Ashley-Montagu, "The Origin of Subincision in Australia," *Oceania* 8 (1937): 204.

8. Gesa Róheim, "The Symbolism of Subincision," *American Imago* 6 (1949): 321-325.

9. Jules Michelet, *Journal* (Paris, 1962), passim.

Chapter 27. Cycles and Rhythm in Men

1. Dr. Estelle Ramey, the most important writer about male cycles, translated the characteristic remark "that's just like a woman" into modern scientific terms: "This female manifests the characteristic cerebral defects of the XX chromosonal behavior determinants. She is largely restricted to decision making via limbic system-hypothalamic neuronal pathways with little evidence of neocortical influences. Therefore, she is more accurately classified as *Homo emotionalis* or *Homo gonadis.*" See Ramey's "Sex Hormones and Executive Ability," in "Successful Women in the Sciences: An Analysis," *Annals of the New York Academy of Sciences* 208 (1973): 237-245; and her "Men's Cycles (They Have Them Too, You Know)," *Ms.* (Spring 1972): 8, 11-12, 14. This article is one of the best summaries of research on the subject.

2. Schmey, "Zur Theorie den Menstruation u. 2. Behandlung einiger Mens. Störungen," *Therapeut. Monatshefte* (1897), 93, cited in G. Stanley Hall, *Adolescence* (New York: Appleton, 1904), p. 489.

3. Hersey's work is discussed in Gay Luce, *Biological Rhythms in Psychiatry and Medicine* (New York: Dover, 1970), pp. 110-111.

4. Luce, *Biological Rhythms in Psychiatry and Medicine*, p. 111.

5. Luce, *Biological Rhythms in Psychiatry and Medicine*, p. 111.

6. Katharine Dalton, *The Menstrual Cycle* (New York: Pantheon, 1969), pp. 134-136.

7. Dalton, *The Menstrual Cycle*, pp. 105-107.

8. Dalton, *The Menstrual Cycle*, pp. 109-111.

9. Fliess's work is discussed in Luce, *Biological Rhythms in Psychiatry and Medicine*, p. 8.

10. Ian Hogbin, *The Island of Menstruating Men* (Scranton, Penn.: Chandler, 1970), pp. 88-89.

11. Hogbin, *The Island of Menstruating Men*, p. 88.

12. Hogbin, *The Island of Menstruating Men*, p. 7.

Conclusion: Lifting the Curse

1. K. F. Wellmann, "Menstruation, Pregnancy, and Birth in Prehistoric Rock Drawings of North America," *Deutsch. Med. Wochenschrift* 97 (1972): 1670-1671.

2. Bart Jordan, "Deciphering the Distant Past," *Publick Occurrences*, May 17, 1974, pp. 12-13.

3. Arlene Raven, "Faith Wilding: Chambers," *Womanspace* 3 (1973): 18-19.

4. "The Menses Is the Message," *Tits & Clits* (Laguna Beach, Calif., 1972).

5. An interesting attack on the Baltimore Bleed-In takes place in Janet Sayers's *Biological Politics* (London: Tavistock, 1982), pp. 119-20. The author takes issue with the idea that "women of all nations and of all social classes have essentially identical interests, that this identity is given by their shared biology." She quotes the description of the Bleed-In from this book and our celebration of sisterhood with women everywhere and says, "But surely this claim is absurd? Although the goal of sisterhood is certainly laudable it cannot be achieved in this way. Women ... have differing and often conflicting interests, differences that cannot simply be wished away by glorifying and wallowing in our shared biology."

6. Meg Cox, "Judy Chicago: Making Art with a Feminist Message," *Wall Street Journal,* January 8, 1982.

7. While Bart Jordan's work is entirely original, additional evidence that menstrual calendars were the basis of time measurement in the early Chinese, Mayan, Gaelic, Roman, Aryan, Babylonian, Chaldean, Greek, Egyptian, and pre-Christian European societies is presented in Barbara Walker's *The Woman's Encyclopedia of Myths and Spirits* (New York: Harper & Row, 1983), pp. 645-49. Walker even notes that the Romans' word for calculation of time is *mensuration,* or knowledge of the menses, and that the Gaelic words for *menstruation* and *calendar* are the same.

Index